W9-BXF-185

BOWLING, BEATNIKS, AND BELL-BOTTOMS

Pop Culture of 20th- and 21st-Century America

FEB 2 0 2013

BOWLING, BEATNIKS, AND BELL-BOTTOMS

Pop Culture of 20th- and 21st-Century America

VOLUME 2: 1920s–1930s

Cynthia Johnson, Editor
Lawrence W. Baker, Project Editor

U·X·L
A part of Gale, Cengage Learning

Montante Family Library
D'Youville College

GALE
CENGAGE Learning·

Detroit • New York • San Francisco • New Haven, Conn • Waterville, Maine • London

GALE
CENGAGE Learning·

Bowling, Beatniks, and Bell-Bottoms: Pop Culture of 20th- and 21st-Century America, 2nd ed.

Cynthia Johnson, Editor

Project Editor: Lawrence W. Baker

Rights Acquisition and Management: Robyn Young

Composition: Evi Abou-El-Seoud

Manufacturing: Wendy Blurton

Imaging: John Watkins

Product Design: Kristine Julien

© 2012 Gale, Cengage Learning

ALL RIGHTS RESERVED. No part of this work covered by the copyright herein may be reproduced, transmitted, stored, or used in any form or by any means graphic, electronic, or mechanical, including but not limited to photocopying, recording, scanning, digitizing, taping, Web distribution, information networks, or information storage and retrieval systems, except as permitted under Section 107 or 108 of the 1976 United States Copyright Act, without the prior written permission of the publisher.

For product information and technology assistance, contact us at
Gale Customer Support, 1-800-877-4253.
For permission to use material from this text or product, submit all requests online at **www.cengage.com/permissions.**
Further permissions questions can be emailed to
permissionrequest@cengage.com

Front cover photographs: (Left to right) The Game of Life, © CameraShots-Concept/Alamy; Radio City Music Hall, © Sam Dao/Alamy; Slinky, © Garry Gay/Workbook Stock/Getty Images; Hollywood sign, © Gavin Hellier/Alamy. Back cover photographs: (Top to bottom) Nickelodeon, © Lewis Hine/Historical/Corbis; Bobbysoxers, © Bettmann/Corbis; Man bowling, © H. Armstrong Roberts/ClassicStock/Alamy.

While every effort has been made to ensure the reliability of the information presented in this publication, Gale, a part of Cengage Learning, does not guarantee the accuracy of the data contained herein. Gale accepts no payment for listing; and inclusion in the publication of any organization, agency, institution, publication, service, or individual does not imply endorsement of the editors or publisher. Errors brought to the attention of the publisher and verified to the satisfaction of the publisher will be corrected in future editions.

LIBRARY OF CONGRESS CATALOGING-IN-PUBLICATION DATA

Bowling, beatniks, and bell-bottoms : pop culture of 20th- and 21st-century America / Cynthia Johnson, editor ; Lawrence W. Baker, project editor. —2nd ed.
   v. cm. —
   Contents: v. 1. 1900s-1910s — v. 2. 1920s-1930s — v. 3. 1940s-1950s — v. 4. 1960s-1970s — v. 5. 1980s-1990s — v. 6. 2000-2009.
   ISBN-13: 978-1-4144-1165-1 (set : alk. paper)
   ISBN-10: 1-4144-1165-0 (set : alk. paper)
   ISBN-13: 978-1-4144-1166-8 (v. 1 : alk. paper)
   ISBN-10: 1-4144-1166-9 (v. 1 : alk. paper)
   [etc.]
   1. United States—Civilization—20th century—Miscellanea—Juvenile literature. 2. United States—Civilization—21st century—Miscellanea—Juvenile literature. 3. Popular culture—United States—History—20th century—Miscellanea—Juvenile literature. 4. Popular culture—United States—History—21st century—Miscellanea—Juvenile literature. I. Johnson, Cynthia, 1969- II. Baker, Lawrence W.
   E169.1.B7825 2012
   306.097309'04—dc23   2012002579

Gale
27500 Drake Rd.
Farmington Hills, MI, 48331-3535

978-1-4144-1165-1 (set)   1-4144-1165-0 (set)
978-1-4144-1166-8 (vol. 1)   1-4144-1166-9 (vol. 1)
978-1-4144-1167-5 (vol. 2)   1-4144-1167-7 (vol. 2)
978-1-4144-1168-2 (vol. 3)   1-4144-1168-5 (vol. 3)
978-1-4144-1169-9 (vol. 4)   1-4144-1169-3 (vol. 4)
978-1-4144-1170-5 (vol. 5)   1-4144-1170-7 (vol. 5)
978-1-4144-1171-2 (vol. 6)   1-4144-1171-5 (vol. 6)

This title is also available as an e-book.
ISBN-13: 978-1-4144-1181-1   ISBN-10: 1-4144-1181-2
Contact your Gale, a part of Cengage Learning sales representative for ordering information

Printed in China
1 2 3 4 5 6 7 16 15 14 13 12

E
169.1
.B7825
2012
vol. 2

Contents

BOWLING, BEATNIKS, AND BELL-BOTTOMS, 2nd edition

Print Culture

Sports and Games

The Way We Lived

Film and Theater

Food and Drink

Music

Print Culture

Music

Print Culture

Sports and Games

TV and Radio

The Way We Lived

VOLUME 5
1980s

Commerce

Fashion

Entries by Alphabetical Order

Entries by Topic Category

TV and Radio

First-edition Contributors

Timothy Berg. Visiting assistant professor, Western Michigan University. Ph.D., History, Purdue University, 1999.

Charles Coletta, Ph.D. Instructor, Department of Popular Culture, Bowling Green State University. Contributing writer, *St. James Encyclopedia of Popular Culture* (2000).

Rob Edelman. Instructor, State University of New York at Albany. Author, *Baseball on the Web* (1997) and *The Great Baseball Films* (1994). Co-author, *Matthau: A Life* (2002); *Meet the Mertzes* (1999); and *Angela Lansbury: A Life on Stage and Screen* (1996). Contributing editor, *Leonard Maltin's Movie & Video Guide, Leonard Maltin's Movie Encyclopedia,* and *Leonard Maltin's Family Viewing Guide.* Contributing writer, *International Dictionary of Films and Filmmakers* (2000); *St. James Encyclopedia of Popular Culture* (2000); *Women Film-makers & Their Films* (1998); *The Political Companion to American Film* (1994); and *Total Baseball* (1989). Film commentator, WAMC (Northeast) Public Radio.

Tina Gianoulis. Freelance writer. Contributing writer, *World War I Reference Library* (2001–2); *Constitutional Amendments: From Freedom of Speech to Flag Burning* (2001); *International Dictionary of Films and Filmmakers* (2000); *St. James Encyclopedia of Popular Culture* (2000); and mystories.com, a daytime drama Web site (1997–98).

Sheldon Goldfarb. Archivist, Alma Mater Society of the University of British Columbia. Ph.D., English, University of British Columbia. Author, *William Makepeace Thackeray: An Annotated Bibliography, 1976–1987* (1989). Editor, *Catherine,* by William Makepeace Thackeray (1999).

Jill Gregg Clever, A.A., B.A., M.L.I.S. Graduate of Michigan State University, Thomas Edison State College, and Wayne State University. Business-technology specialist, Toledo–Lucas County Public Library.

Justin Gustainis. Professor of communication, State University of New York at Plattsburgh. Author, *American Rhetoric and the Vietnam War* (1993).

Audrey Kupferberg. Film consultant and archivist. Instructor, State University of New York at Albany. Co-author, *Matthau: A Life* (2002); *Meet the Mertzes* (1999); and *Angela Lansbury: A Life on Stage and Screen* (1996). Contributing editor, *Leonard Maltin's Family Viewing Guide.* Contributing writer, *St. James Encyclopedia of Popular Culture* (2000); *Women Filmmakers & Their Films* (1998); and *The American Film Institute Catalog of Feature Films.*

Edward Moran. Writer of American culture, music, and literature. Associate editor, *World Musicians* (1999); *World Authors* (1996); and *Random House Dictionary of the English Language* (1987; 1991). Contributing writer, *St. James Encyclopedia of Popular Culture* (2000). Editor, *Rhythm,* a magazine of world music and global culture (2001).

Sara Pendergast. President, Full Circle Editorial. Vice president, Group 3 Editorial. Co-editor, *St. James Encyclopedia of Popular Culture* (2000). Co-author, *World War I Reference Library* (2001), among other publications.

Tom Pendergast. Editorial director, Full Circle Editorial. Ph.D., American studies, Purdue University. Author, *Creating the Modern Man: American Magazines and Consumer Culture* (2000). Co-editor, *St. James Encyclopedia of Popular Culture* (2000).

Karl Rahder. M.A., University of Chicago Committee on International Relations. Author, several articles on international history and politics.

Chris Routledge. Freelance writer and editor. Ph.D., American literature, University of Newcastle upon Tyne (UK). Author, "The Chevalier and the Priest: Deductive Method in Poe, Chesterton, and Borges," in *Clues: A Journal of Detection* (2001). Editor, *Mystery in Children's Literature: From the Rational to the Supernatural* (2001).

Robert E. Schnakenberg. Senior writer, History Book Club. Author, *The Encyclopedia Shatnerica* (1998).

Steven Schneider. Ph.D. candidate, philosophy, Harvard University; Ph.D. candidate, cinema studies, New York University. Author, *An Auteur on Elm Street: The Cinema of Wes Craven* (forthcoming). Co-editor, *Horror International* (forthcoming) and *Dark Thoughts: Philosophic Reflections on Cinematic Horror* (forthcoming). Contributing writer, *British Horror Cinema* (2002); *Car Crash Culture* (2001); and numerous film journals.

Robert C. Sickels. Assistant professor of American film and popular culture, Whitman College. Ph.D., English, University of Nevada. Author, "A Politically Correct Ethan Edwards: Clint Eastwood's The Outlaw Josey Wales" in *Journal of Popular Film & Television* (forthcoming); "'70s Disco Daze: Paul Thomas Anderson's Boogie Nights and the Last Golden Age of Irresponsibility" in *Journal of Popular Culture* (forthcoming). Contributor, *St. James Encyclopedia of Popular Culture* (2000).

Reader's Guide

Popular culture—as we know it—was born in America, though historians disagree as to exactly when. Was it in 1893, when magazine publishers used new technologies to cut the costs of their magazines to a dime and sell hundreds of thousands of copies? Or was it in 1905, when the invention of the nickelodeon brought low-cost films to people all across the nation? Or was it back in 1886, when Richard Sears and Alvah Roebuck sent out their first catalog, which allowed people from all over to choose from among hundreds and then thousands of the same goods?

No matter the exact date, by the turn of the twentieth century, American magazine publishers, retailers, moviemakers, and other entertainers were bringing their goods before larger numbers of Americans than ever before. These magazines, movies, advertisements, shopping experiences, sports teams, and more were what we know as "popular culture," because they could be enjoyed firsthand by masses of Americans.

The story of America as revealed by its popular culture is complex and fascinating. Readers of *Bowling, Beatniks, and Bell-Bottoms: Pop Culture of 20th- and 21st-Century America* will discover, for example, that the comedic forms first developed by vaudeville comedians at the turn of the twentieth century lived on in film, radio, and finally television. They will learn that black musicians created the musical forms that are most distinctly American: blues and jazz. And they will realize that popular culture reacted to things like war and economic depressions in ways that were surprising and unexpected. The study of popular culture has a great deal to teach the student who is interested in how people use entertainment and consumption to make sense of their lives and shape their experience.

Bowling, Beatniks, and Bell-Bottoms gathers together essays that reflect the variety, diversity, and excitement of American popular culture of the twentieth and twenty-first centuries. This collection focuses more on events, fads, programs, performances, and products than on biographies of people, which are well documented in other sources. Even so, brief biographies of notables are sprinkled throughout. With approximately 850 essays on individual topics and dozens of overviews of pop culture trends, *Bowling, Beatniks, and Bell-Bottoms* covers a great deal of American popular culture, though not nearly enough. There are hundreds more people, bands, TV programs, films, and products that were worthy of mention but were left out due to space consideration. Our advisory board of media specialists, however, helped assure that the most prominent and studied subjects were included.

Have you ever wondered how the Slinky was invented, what Velveeta cheese is made of, or what people danced to before rock and roll? Those answers are in *Bowling, Beatniks, and Bell-Bottoms,* along with many others. It is our hope that this collection will bring both information and pleasure to all students of American culture.

Organization

Bowling, Beatniks, and Bell-Bottoms is arranged chronologically by decade over six volumes (two decades per volume for the twentieth century, and one volume covering the first decade of the twenty-first century). The approximately 850 entries are grouped into nine topic sections: Commerce, Fashion, Film and Theater, Food and Drink, Music, Print Culture, Sports and Games, TV and Radio, and The Way We Lived (though not all topics appear in every decade). Many subjects can easily appear in several different decades, so those essays are placed in either the decade in which the product was invented or the fad initiated, or in the decade in which the subject was most prominent or popular. In addition, several of the essays could have appeared under different topics (such as a book that was made into a movie), so those essays appear under the topic where it was best known. Users should make frequent use of the index or the two additional tables of contents (arranged alphabetically by entry name and by topic category) to locate an entry.

Essays range in length from 150 to 1000 words, with the majority averaging less than 500 words. Every essay aims to describe the topic and analyze the topic's contribution to popular culture. Each essay lists additional sources on the topic, including books, magazine or journal articles, and Web sites. Whenever possible, references to books are geared to younger readers. The editor and writers have personally visited every Web site mentioned and believe that these sites contain content that will assist the reader in understanding the subject. Due to the nature of the World Wide Web, it is possible that not all Web links will still function at the time of publication.

Bowling, Beatniks, and Bell-Bottoms also provides these features:

- A timeline that highlights key historic and pop culture events of the twentieth and twenty-first centuries
- A general overview of each decade
- A multipaged "At a Glance" box that breaks down "What We Said," "What We Read," "What We Watched," "What We Listened To," and "Who We Knew"
- An overview of each topic section in each decade
- Approximately 450 photos and illustrations
- Extensive use of cross references (pointing to decade, topic, and volume)

Acknowledgments

A thank-you encore goes to the advisors of this publication (their professional affiliation at the time of the publication of the first edition is noted): Catherine Bond, Department Chair, Library and Media Services, Conestoga High School, Berwyn, Pennsylvania; Cathy Chauvette, Assistant Regional Branch Manager, Fairfax County Public Library, Fairfax County, Virginia; Nancy Schlosser Garabed, Library Media Specialist, Council Rock High School, Newtown, Pennsylvania; Ann West LaPrise, Junior High/Elementary Media Specialist, Huron School District, New Boston, Michigan; and Nina Levine, Library Media Specialist, Blue Mountain Middle School, Cortlandt Manor, New York. Their input during the preparation of the first edition remains valuable.

The contributions of the writers from the first edition are noted on the contributors page (which reprints their background at the time of the first edition). For this second edition, much gratitude is given to writers David Larkins, Annette Petrusso, Maureen Reed, Patrick Walsh, and Greg Wilson.

Much appreciation goes to copyeditor Maxwell Valentine, proofreader Rebecca Valentine, indexer Theresa Murray, and typesetter

PreMediaGlobal. Additional thanks to Scott Rosen at the Bill Smith Group for permissions and imaging selection and Barry Puckett for image processing assistance.

Comments and Suggestions

We welcome your comments on *Bowling, Beatniks, and Bell-Bottoms.* Please send correspondence to: Editors, *Bowling, Beatniks, and Bell-Bottoms,* U•X•L, 27500 Drake Rd., Farmington Hills, MI 48331-3535; call toll-free: 800-877-4253; fax to 248-414-5043; or send e-mail via www.cengage.com.

Cynthia Johnson, Editor

Timeline

1900 On January 29, Ban Johnson forms the American League to compete against baseball's National League.

1900 In February, Eastman Kodak introduces the Brownie Camera.

1900 In March, the Good Roads Campaign tries to build support for better roads. At the time, there are only ten miles of paved roads in the nation.

1900 On March 31, the first ad for an automobile appears in the *Saturday Evening Post.*

1900 On April 23, Buffalo Bill Cody's *Wild West Show* opens at Madison Square Garden in New York City.

1900 On November 6, Republican William McKinley is reelected U.S. president, with New York governor Theodore Roosevelt as his vice president.

1900 On November 12, *Floradora,* one of the most popular theatrical musicals of the decade, premieres in New York. It runs for more than five hundred performances.

1901 On February 25, U.S. Steel is formed out of ten companies and becomes the world's largest industrial corporation.

1901 On March 13, steel tycoon Andrew Carnegie donates $2.2 million to fund a New York public library system.

1901 On September 6, President William McKinley is shot by an assassin in Buffalo, New York, and dies eight days later from complications from gangrene due to improperly dressed wounds. Theodore Roosevelt becomes president.

1901 On October 16, President Theodore Roosevelt starts a national controversy when he dines with black leader Booker T. Washington in the White House.

1902 The Teddy Bear is introduced, named after President Theodore Roosevelt.

1902 On January 1, in the first Rose Bowl football game, the University of Michigan defeats Stanford 49–0.

1902 On March 18, Italian opera singer Enrico Caruso produces his first phonographic recording.

1902 On April 16, Tally's Electric Theater, the first theater solely devoted to presenting motion pictures, opens in Los Angeles, California.

1902 On December 21, Guglielmo Marconi transmits the first wireless signals across the Atlantic Ocean.

1903 *Redbook* magazine is founded.

1903 The Portage Lakers of Houghton, Michigan—the first professional hockey team from the United States—win the International Hockey League championship.

1903 On January 22, the United States signs a 99-year lease on what will become the Panama Canal Zone, where it will build a canal that connects the Caribbean Sea to the Pacific Ocean.

1903 In February, the *Ladies' Home Journal* becomes the first American magazine to reach one million paid subscriptions.

1903 On May 23, two men make the first transcontinental automobile trip from San Francisco to New York in sixty-four days. Upon returning home, one driver is ticketed for exceeding the speed limit of six miles per hour.

1903 On August 14, Jim Jeffries defeats James J. "Gentleman Jim" Corbett to retain the world heavyweight boxing title.

1903 On September 12, Scott Joplin's ragtime opera *A Guest of Honor* begins a midwest tour.

1903 In October, the Boston Pilgrims defeat the Pittsburgh Pirates in the first World Series to pit an American League team against a National League team.

1903 On December 1, Edwin S. Porter's film *The Great Train Robbery* is considered the first Western and the first American film with a plot.

1903 On December 17, Wilbur and Orville Wright make the first sustained flight at Kitty Hawk, North Carolina.

1904 The Ford Motor Company sells fourteen hundred of its Model A cars.

1904 On April 20, the World's Fair opens in St. Louis, Missouri.

1904 On May 5, Cy Young pitches baseball's first perfect game.

1904 On November 8, Theodore Roosevelt is reelected president.

1905 The German navy launches the first submarine.

1905 African American leader W. E. B. Du Bois helps found the Niagara Movement, an organization to advance African American issues.

1905 On May 5, the *Chicago Defender,* the first major black newspaper, begins publication.

1905 In June, the era of the nickelodeon begins when Harry Davis's Pittsburgh, Pennsylvania, movie theater offers continuous movie showings. By the end of the decade, more than eight thousand nickel-admission movie theaters are in operation.

1905 On June 18, the Twentieth Century Limited begins train service between Chicago, Illinois, and New York City and boasts a travel time of only eighteen hours.

1906 Kellogg's Corn Flakes breakfast cereal is introduced.

1906 In February, Upton Sinclair publishes *The Jungle,* a novel depicting the horrible conditions in the meat-packing industry. The work prompts the passage of the Meat Inspection Act.

1906 On April 14, President Theodore Roosevelt coins the term "muckraking" when he criticizes journalists who expose abuses and corruption and miss the larger social picture.

1906 On April 18, a major earthquake and fire destroy much of San Francisco, California.

1906 On May 3, the First Annual Advertising Show in New York City heralds the beginning of an important American industry.

1906 On November 21, the first voice radio transmission travels eleven miles from Plymouth to Brant Rock, Massachusetts.

1907 Work begins on the Panama Canal.

1907 On January 23, in what newspapers call the "trial of the century," millionaire Harry K. Thaw is tried for the murder of world-famous architect Stanford White over the honor of Thaw's wife, showgirl Evelyn Nesbit.

1907 On June 10, French motion picture pioneers Auguste and Louis Lumière announce they have developed a method for producing color film.

1907 On July 8, Florenz Ziegfeld's musical revue, the *Ziegfeld Follies,* opens in New York.

1907 On December 3, actress Mary Pickford makes her stage debut in *The Warrens of Virginia.*

1908 The world's first skyscraper, the forty-seven-story Singer Building, is completed in New York City.

1908 The General Motors Corporation is formed and soon becomes the biggest competitor of the Ford Motor Company.

1908 In March, the Original Independent Show, organized in New York, includes works by American painters Edward Hopper, George Bellows, and Rockwell Kent.

1908 On September 6, Israel Zangwill's play *The Melting Pot* opens in New York City; the title becomes an internationally recognized description of the United States.

1908 On October 1, the Ford Motor Company unveils its Model T with a price tag of $825. It soon becomes the best-selling automobile of its time.

1908 On November 3, former U.S. secretary of war William Howard Taft is elected president.

1908 On December 26, Jack Johnson defeats Tommy Burns to become the first black world heavyweight boxing champion. His victory is considered an outrage by white racists.

1909 The fifty-story Metropolitan Life Insurance Tower in New York City becomes the world's tallest building.

1909 The Ford Motor Company manufactures nineteen thousand Model T cars.

1909 On March 16, the Federal Bureau of Investigation is created as a federal law enforcement agency.

1909 On March 23, former president Theodore Roosevelt leaves for a safari in Africa. He is paid $50,000 by *Scribner's Magazine* for his account of the trip.

1909 On April 6, U.S. Navy commander Robert Peary reaches the North Pole.

1909 On May 3, the first wireless press message is sent from New York City to Chicago, Illinois.

1909 On July 12, the U.S. Congress asks the states to authorize a national income tax.

1910 Western novelist Zane Grey's book *Heritage of the Desert* becomes a huge commercial success, starting his career of bringing the American West to the reading world.

1910 Levi Strauss and Company begins making casual play clothes for children.

1910 The Boy Scouts of America are founded in Chicago, Illinois.

1910 On February 28, Russian ballerina Anna Pavlova makes her American debut at the Metropolitan Opera House in New York City.

1910 On March 28, the first one-man show by artist Pablo Picasso opens at photographer and editor Alfred Stieglitz's 291 Gallery in New York City.

1910 In November, the National Association for the Advancement of Colored People (NAACP) publishes the first issue of the *Crisis* magazine, edited by W. E. B. Du Bois.

1910 On November 3, the Chicago Grand Opera opens with a production of *Aida,* by Giuseppe Verdi.

1911 Irving Berlin composes "Alexander's Ragtime Band," the song that popularized ragtime music.

1911 Air conditioning is invented.

1911 *Photoplay,* the first movie fan magazine, is published.

1911 On March 25, in New York City, 146 female workers are killed in the Triangle Shirtwaist Factory fire, alerting Americans to the dangers women face in industrial labor.

1911 On May 23, President William Howard Taft dedicates the New York Public Library.

1911 On May 30, the first Indianapolis 500 auto race is won by Ray Harroun with an average speed of 74.59 mph.

1911 On August 8, *Pathe's Weekly,* the first regular newsreel to be produced in the United States, is released to motion picture theaters.

1911 On December 19, the Association of American Painters and Sculptors is founded.

1912 New Mexico and Arizona become the forty-seventh and forty-eighth states.

1912 The Little Theater in Chicago, Illinois, and the Toy Theater in Boston, Massachusetts, the first influential little theaters in the United States, are founded.

1912 Dancers Irene and Vernon Castle start a craze for ballroom dancing.

1912 On April 15, the *Titanic* sinks on its maiden voyage from Ireland to the United States, killing 1,517.

1912 In August, photographer and editor Alfred Stieglitz devotes an entire issue of his periodical *Camera Work* to the modern art movement.

1912 On August 5, former president Theodore Roosevelt is nominated as the presidential candidate of the newly formed Progressive Party.

1912 On October 31, *The Musketeers of Pig Alley,* a film by D. W. Griffith that points out the social evils of poverty and crime on the streets of New York, is released.

1912 On November 5, New Jersey governor Woodrow Wilson is elected president.

1912 On December 10, the Famous Players Film Company registers for copyright of the five-reel feature film *The Count of Monte Cristo,* directed by Edwin S. Porter.

1913 The 792-foot-high Woolworth Building in New York City becomes the world's tallest building, a record it holds until 1930.

1913 The first crossword puzzle is published.

1913 The Jesse Lasky Feature Play Co., which later would become Paramount Pictures, is established in Hollywood, California.

1913 The Panama Canal is completed, and officially opens on August 15, 1914.

1913 On February 17, the International Exhibition of Modern Art, known as the Armory Show, opens in New York City. It is the first opportunity for many Americans to view modern art.

1913 On February 25, the Sixteenth Amendment to the Constitution is approved, authorizing a federal income tax.

1913 On March 24, the million dollar, eighteen-hundred-seat Palace Theatre opens in New York City.

1913 On May 31, the Seventeenth Amendment to the Constitution is approved, providing for the direct election of U.S. senators by citizens, rather than by state legislatures.

1914 On February 13, the American Society of Composers, Authors, and Publishers (ASCAP), an organization that seeks royalty payments for public performances of music, is founded in New York City.

1914 In March, comedian Charles Chaplin begins to evolve the legendary character of the Little Tramp in the film *Mabel's Strange Predicament.*

1914 On July 3, the first telephone line connects New York City and San Francisco, California.

1914 On August 3, World War I starts in Europe when Germany invades Belgium. Soon all of Europe is drawn into the conflict, though the United States remains neutral.

1914 On September 5, a German submarine scores its first kill, sinking the British cruiser *Pathfinder,* as World War I intensifies.

1914 In September, in the World War I Battle of the Marne, Germany's advance into France is halted.

1914 On November 3, the first American exhibition of African sculpture opens at the 291 Gallery in New York City.

1914 On December 3, the Isadorables, six European dancers trained by American dancer Isadora Duncan, perform at Carnegie Hall in New York City after escaping with Duncan from her war-torn Europe.

1915 The first taxicab appears on the streets of New York City.

1915 The first professional football league is formed in Ohio and is called simply the Ohio League.

1915 Modern dancers Ruth St. Denis and Ted Shawn found the Denishawn School of Dancing in Los Angeles, California.

1915 Five hundred U.S. correspondents cover World War I in Europe.

1915 On March 10, the Russian Symphony Orchestra plays the American debut performance of the symphony *Prometheus* by Aleksandr Scriabin at Carnegie Hall in New York City. Color images are projected onto a screen as part of the show.

1915 On December 10, the Ford Motor Company manufactures its one millionth Model T automobile.

1916 The Boeing Aircraft Company produces its first biplane.

1916 Newspaper publisher William Randolph Hearst inaugurates the *City Life* arts section as a supplement to his Sunday newspapers.

1916 In November, inventor and radio pioneer Lee De Forest begins to transmit daily music broadcasts from his home in New York City.

1916 On November 7, Woodrow Wilson is reelected president after campaigning on the pledge to keep the United States out of the war in Europe.

1917 The Russian Revolution brings communism to Russia, setting the stage for nearly a century of intermittent conflict with the United States.

1917 Showman George M. Cohan composes the song that was a musical call-to-arms during World War I: "Over There."

1917 Motion picture pioneer Cecil B. DeMille directs *The Little American,* a patriotic melodrama starring Mary Pickford.

1917 On April 6, the United States declares war on Germany after German submarines continue to attack U.S. merchant ships.

1917 On May 28, Benny Leonard wins the lightweight boxing championship, which he holds until his retirement in 1924 while building a record of 209–5; he makes a comeback in 1931.

1917 On August 19, the managers of the New York Giants and Cincinnati Reds are arrested for playing baseball on Sunday.

1917 On October 27, sixteen-year-old Russian-born violinist Jascha Heifetz makes his debut American performance at Carnegie Hall in New York City.

1918 The annual O. Henry Awards for short fiction are inaugurated in honor of short story writer O. Henry (a pseudonym for William Sydney Porter).

1918 On January 8, President Woodrow Wilson delivers his "Fourteen Points" address before Congress, outlining his plans for the shape of the postwar world.

1918 In March, *The Little Review* begins to serialize the novel *Ulysses,* by James Joyce, which features stream of consciousness techniques and a kind of private language.

1918 On November 11, Germany signs an armistice with the Allies, ending the fighting in World War I.

1918 In December, the Theatre Guild is founded in New York City.

1919 *Maid of Harlem,* an all-black-cast musical starring "Fats" Waller, Mamie Smith, Johnny Dunn, and Perry Bradford, draws enthusiastic crowds at the Lincoln Theatre in New York City.

1919 On January 29, Prohibition begins with the adoption of the Eighteenth Amendment to the Constitution, which bans the manufacture, sale, and transportation of intoxicating liquors.

1919 On February 5, United Artists, an independent film distribution company, is founded by Charles Chaplin, Douglas Fairbanks, D. W. Griffith, and Mary Pickford.

1919 On June 28, the Treaty of Versailles is signed by the Allied powers, officially ending World War I. Germany is forced to pay costly reparations for the damage it caused during the war.

1919 On July 4, Jack Dempsey defeats Jess Willard to win the world heavyweight boxing championship.

1919 On October 31, the Provincetown Players stage *The Dreamy Kid,* by Eugene O'Neill, with an all-black cast.

1919 On December 22, Attorney General A. Mitchell Palmer authorizes government raids on communists, anarchists, and other political radicals. These "Palmer raids" are part of a nationwide "red scare."

1920 Sinclair Lewis publishes the novel *Main Street.*

1920 Douglas Fairbanks stars in the film *The Mark of Zorro.*

1920 On January 5, the Radio Corporation of America (RCA) is founded and becomes a leading radio broadcaster.

1920 On February 12, the National Negro Baseball League is founded.

1920 On August 20, the first radio news bulletins are broadcast by station 8MK in Detroit, Michigan.

1920 On August 26, the Nineteenth Amendment to the Constitution gives women the right to vote.

1920 On September 28, eight Chicago White Sox players are charged with throwing the 1919 World Series in what becomes known as the "Black Sox Scandal." They are eventually banned from the game for life.

1920 On September 29, New York Yankee Babe Ruth breaks his own single-season home run record with 54 home runs.

1920 On November 1, Eugene O'Neill's play *The Emperor Jones* opens in New York City.

1920 On November 6, U.S. senator Warren G. Harding of Ohio is elected president.

1921 The Ford Motor Company announces a plan to produce one million automobiles a year.

1921 The Phillips Gallery in Washington, D.C., becomes the first American museum of modern art.

1921 In this year, 13 percent of Americans own telephones.

1921 On March 10, the first White Castle hamburger chain opens in Wichita, Kansas.

1921 On April 11, radio station KDKA in Pittsburgh, Pennsylvania, broadcasts the first sports event on radio, a boxing match between Johnny Ray and Johnny Dundee. Later that year, the World Series is broadcast.

1921 On May 23, *Shuffle Along* is the first black Broadway musical written and directed by African Americans.

1921 On July 29, Adolf Hitler is elected dictator of the Nazi Party in Munich, Germany.

1921 On September 8, the first Miss America pageant is held in Washington, D.C.

1921 On November 2, Margaret Sanger founds the American Birth Control League in New York City, raising the anger of many religious groups, especially Catholic groups.

1922 Robert Flaherty releases the documentary film *Nanook of the North*.

1922 Irish author James Joyce publishes *Ulysses,* which is banned in some countries for its alleged obscenity.

1922 F. Scott Fitzgerald publishes *Tales of the Jazz Age.*

1922 The American Professional Football Association changes its name to the National Football League (NFL).

1922 *Reader's Digest* magazine is founded.

1922 Al Jolson pens the popular song "Toot Toot Tootsie."

1922 On May 5, Coco Chanel introduces Chanel No. 5, which becomes the world's best-known perfume.

1922 On August 28, the first advertisement is aired on radio station WEAF in New York City.

1922 On December 30, the Union of Soviet Socialist Republics (USSR) is established with Russia at its head.

1923 Cecil B. DeMille directs the epic film *The Ten Commandments.*

1923 Charles Kettering develops a method for bringing colored paint to mass-produced cars.

1923 Bessie Smith's "Down Hearted Blues" is one of the first blues songs to be recorded.

1923 *Time* magazine begins publication.

1923 On April 6, trumpet player Louis Armstrong records his first solo on "Chimes Blues" with King Oliver's Creole Jazz Band.

1923 On August 3, President Warren G. Harding dies and Vice President Calvin Coolidge takes office.

1924 John Ford directs the Western film *The Iron Horse.*

1924 The Metro-Goldwyn-Mayer (MGM) film studio is formed in Hollywood, California.

1924 Evangelist Aimee Semple McPherson begins broadcasting from the first religious radio station, KFSG in Los Angeles, California.

1924 The stock market begins a boom that will last until 1929.

1924 On January 1, there are 2.5 million radios in American homes, up from 2,000 in 1920.

1924 On February 12, the tomb of King Tutankhamen, or King Tut, is opened in Egypt after having been sealed for four thousand years.

1924 On February 24, George Gershwin's *Rhapsody in Blue* is performed by an orchestra in New York City.

1924 On March 10, J. Edgar Hoover is appointed director of the Federal Bureau of Investigation.

1924 In June, the Chrysler Corporation is founded and competes with General Motors and Ford.

1924 On November 4, incumbent Calvin Coolidge is elected president.

1925 In one of the most famous years in American literature, F. Scott Fitzgerald publishes *The Great Gatsby,* Ernest Hemingway publishes *In Our Time,* and Theodore Dreiser publishes *An American Tragedy.*

1925 Lon Chaney stars in the film *The Phantom of the Opera.*

1925 The *WSM Barn Dance* radio program begins broadcasting from Nashville, Tennessee; the name is later changed to *Grand Ole Opry* and it becomes the leading country music program.

1925 The *New Yorker* magazine begins publication and features the prices paid for bootleg liquor.

1925 In February, the Boeing aircraft company builds a plane capable of flying over the Rocky Mountains with a full load of mail.

1925 On May 8, the Brotherhood of Sleeping Car Porters, founded by A. Philip Randolph, is one of the first black labor unions.

1925 In July, in the Scopes "Monkey" trial, a Tennessee teacher is tried and found guilty of teaching evolution in a trial that attracts national attention.

1925 On August 8, forty thousand Ku Klux Klan members march in Washington, D.C., to broaden support for their racist organization.

1926 Latin idol Rudolph Valentino stars in the film *The Son of the Sheik.*

1926 Ernest Hemingway publishes *The Sun Also Rises.*

1926 The Book-of-the-Month Club is launched to offer quality books to subscribers.

1926 On March 7, the first transatlantic radio-telephone conversation links New York City and London, England.

1926 On March 17, *The Girl Friend,* a musical with songs by Richard Rodgers and Lorenz Hart, opens on Broadway.

1926 On April 18, dancer Martha Graham makes her first professional appearance in New York City.

1927 Al Jolson stars in the film *The Jazz Singer,* the first film to have sound. Clara Bow—the "It" girl—stars in *It.*

1927 On January 1, the Rose Bowl football game is broadcast coast-to-coast on the radio.

1927 On April 7, television is first introduced in America, but investors are skeptical.

1927 On May 21, Charles Lindbergh completes his nonstop flight from New York City to Paris, France, and is given a hero's welcome.

1927 On May 25, the Ford Motor Company announces that production of the Model T will be stopped in favor of the modern Model A.

1927 On September 22, the heavyweight championship fight between Jack Dempsey and Gene Tunney becomes the first sports gate to top $2 million.

1927 On December 4, Duke Ellington's orchestra begins a long run at the Cotton Club nightclub in Harlem, New York.

1927 On December 27, the Jerome Kern and Oscar Hammerstein musical *Show Boat* opens on Broadway in New York City.

1928 On April 15, the New York Rangers become the first American team to win the National Hockey League Stanley Cup.

1928 On May 11, WGY in Schenectady, New York, offers the first scheduled television service, though the high price of televisions keeps most people from owning them.

1928 On July 30, the Eastman Kodak company introduces color motion pictures.

1928 On November 6, former U.S. secretary of commerce Herbert Hoover is elected president.

1928 On December 13, George Gershwin's *An American in Paris* opens at Carnegie Hall in New York City.

1928 On December 26, swimmer Johnny Weissmuller retires from competition after setting sixty-seven world records.

1929 Mickey Mouse makes his first appearance in *Steamboat Willie,* an animated film made by Walt Disney.

1929 Commercial airlines carry 180,000 passengers during the year.

1929 Ernest Hemingway publishes *A Farewell to Arms,* a novel set during World War I.

1929 Nick Lucas's "Tiptoe through the Tulips with Me" and Louis Armstrong's "Ain't Misbehavin'" are two of the year's most popular songs.

1929 On February 14, in the Saint Valentine's Day Massacre, gunmen working for Chicago, Illinois, mobster Al Capone gun down seven members of a rival gang.

1929 On October 29, the stock market collapses on a day known as "Black Tuesday," marking the start of what will become the Great Depression.

1930 Grant Wood paints *American Gothic.*

1930 The Continental Baking company introduces Wonder Bread to the nation, the first commercially produced sliced bread.

1930 Unemployment reaches four million as the economy worsens.

1930 On January 14, jazz greats Benny Goodman, Glenn Miller, Jimmy Dorsey, and Jack Teagarden play George and Ira Gershwin's songs, including "I've Got a Crush on You," in the musical *Strike Up the Band* at the Mansfield Theater in New York City.

1930 On March 6, General Foods introduces the nation's first frozen foods.

1930 On May 3, Ogden Nash, a poet who will become famous for his funny, light verse, publishes "Spring Comes to Murray Hill" in the *New Yorker* magazine and soon begins work at the magazine.

1930 On September 8, the comic strip *Blondie* begins.

1930 On October 14, *Girl Crazy,* starring Ethel Merman, opens at New York's Guild Theater. The musical features songs by George Gershwin, Walter Donaldson, and Ira Gershwin, including "I Got Rhythm" and "Embraceable You."

1931 The horror films *Dracula* and *Frankenstein* are both released.

1931 Nevada legalizes gambling in order to bring revenue to the state.

1931 On March 3, "The Star Spangled Banner" becomes the national anthem by congressional vote.

1931 On April 30, the Empire State Building, the tallest building in the world, opens in New York City.

1931 On June 3, brother-and-sister dancers Fred and Adele Astaire perform for the last time together on the first revolving stage.

1931 On July 27, *Earl Carroll's Vanities,* featuring naked chorus girls, opens at the three-thousand-seat Earl Carroll Theater in New York City.

1931 On October 12, the comic strip *Dick Tracy* begins.

1932 Edwin Herbert Land, a Harvard College dropout, invents Polaroid film.

1932 On May 2, *The Jack Benny Show* premieres as a variety show on radio and runs for twenty-three years and then another ten years on television.

1932 On July 30, the Summer Olympic Games open in Los Angeles, California, and feature record-breaking performances by Americans Babe Didrikson and Eddie Tolan.

1932 On July 31, in German parliamentary elections, the Nazi Party receives the most seats but is unable to form a government.

1932 On November 7, the radio adventure *Buck Rogers in the Twenty-Fifth Century* premieres on CBS and runs until 1947.

1932 On November 8, New York governor Franklin D. Roosevelt is elected president, promising to take steps to improve the economy. In his first one hundred days in office, Roosevelt introduces much legislation to use the government to aid those harmed by the Great Depression.

1932 On December 27, Radio City Music Hall opens at the Rockefeller Center in New York City.

1933 President Franklin D. Roosevelt presents the nation with his first radio address, known as a "fireside chat."

1933 Walt Disney releases the feature film *The Three Little Pigs.*

1933 On January 3, *The Lone Ranger* radio drama premieres on WXYZ radio in Detroit, Michigan.

1933 On January 30, Nazi leader Adolf Hitler becomes chancellor of Germany. Hitler soon seizes all power and sets out to attack his party's political enemies.

1933 On May 27, fan dancer Sally Rand attracts thousands with her performance at the Chicago World's Fair that celebrated the Century of Progress.

1933 On September 30, *Ah, Wilderness,* acclaimed American playwright Eugene O'Neill's only comedy, opens at the Guild Theater in New York City.

1933 On December 5, the Twenty-first Amendment to the Constitution puts an end to Prohibition.

1934 The first pipeless organ is patented by Laurens Hammond. The Hammond organ starts a trend toward more electrically amplified instruments.

1934 Dashiell Hammett publishes *The Thin Man,* one of the first hard-boiled detective novels.

1934 The Apollo Theater opens in Harlem, New York, as a showcase for black performers.

1934 German director Fritz Lang flees Nazi Germany to make movies in the United States.

1934 On May 5, bank robbers and murderers Bonnie Parker and Clyde Barrow are killed by lawmen in Louisiana.

1934 On July 1, the Motion Picture Producers and Distributors of America (MPPDA) association creates the Hay's Office to enforce codes that limit the amount and types of sexuality and other immoral behavior in films.

1934 On July 22, "Public Enemy No. 1" John Dillinger is shot and killed outside a Chicago, Illinois, theater by FBI agents and local police.

1934 On August 13, Al Capp's *Li'l Abner* comic strip debuts in eight newspapers.

1934 On August 19, Adolf Hitler is declared president of Germany, though he prefers the title Führer (leader).

1935 One out of four American households receives government relief as the Depression deepens.

1935 Twenty million Monopoly board games are sold in one week.

1935 The first Howard Johnson roadside restaurant opens in Boston, Massachusetts.

1935 The Works Progress Administration Federal Arts Projects, some of President Franklin D. Roosevelt's many New Deal programs, give work to artists painting post offices and other federal buildings.

1935 In April, *Your Hit Parade* is first heard on radio and offers a selection of hit songs.

1935 On April 16, the radio comedy-drama *Fibber McGee and Molly* debuts on NBC and runs until 1952.

1935 On May 24, the first nighttime major league baseball game is played in Cincinnati, Ohio.

1935 On October 10, *Porgy and Bess,* known as the "most American opera of the decade," opens in New York City at the Alvin Theater. The music George Gershwin wrote for the opera combined blues, jazz, and southern folk.

1936 American Airlines introduces transcontinental airline service.

1936 Ten African American athletes, including Jesse Owens, win gold medals in the Summer Olympics held in Berlin, Germany, embarrassing Nazi leader Adolf Hitler, who had declared the inferiority of black athletes.

1936 Dust storms in the Plains states force thousands to flee the region, many to California.

1936 Popular public-speaking teacher Dale Carnegie publishes his book *How to Win Friends and Influence People.*

1936 To increase feelings of nationalism, the Department of the Interior hires folksinger Woody Guthrie to travel throughout the U.S. Southwest performing his patriotic songs such as "Those Oklahoma Hills."

1936 In the Soviet Union, the Communist Party begins its Great Purge, executing anyone who resists the party's social and economic policies. By 1938, it is estimated that ten million people have been killed.

1936 Throughout Europe, countries scramble to form alliances with other countries for what seems to be a likely war. Germany and Italy join together to support the military government of Francisco Franco in Spain, while Great Britain and France sign nonaggression pacts with the Soviet Union.

1936 On July 18, the Spanish Civil War begins when Spanish military officers rise up against the Republican government of Spain.

1936 In October, the New York Yankees win the first of four World Series in a row.

1936 On November 3, Franklin D. Roosevelt is reelected as president of the United States.

1936 On November 23, the first issue of *Life* magazine is published.

1937 Dr. Seuss becomes a popular children's book author with the publication of *And to Think That I Saw It on Mulberry Street.*

1937 The Hormel company introduces Spam, a canned meat.

1937 A poll shows that the average American listens to the radio for 4.5 hours a day.

1937 *Porky's Hare Hunt,* a short animated cartoon by Warner Bros., introduces audiences to the Bugs Bunny character and the talents of Mel Blanc, the voice of both Bugs Bunny and Porky Pig.

1937 The first soap opera, *Guiding Light,* is broadcast. It continues as a radio program until 1956 and moves to television.

1937 British writer J. R. R. Tolkien publishes *The Hobbit.*

1937 On June 22, black boxer Joe Louis knocks out Jim Braddock to win the world heavyweight boxing championship.

1937 On December 21, *Snow White and the Seven Dwarfs,* the first feature-length animated film, is presented by Walt Disney.

1938 Glenn Miller forms his own big band and begins to tour extensively.

1938 On January 17, the first jazz performance at Carnegie Hall in New York City is performed by Benny Goodman and His Orchestra, with Duke Ellington, Count Basie, and others.

1938 In June, the character Superman is introduced in *Action Comics #1.* By 1939, he appears in his own comic book series.

1938 On August 17, Henry Armstrong becomes the first boxer to hold three boxing titles at one time when he defeats Lou Ambers at New York City's Madison Square Garden.

1938 On October 31, Orson Welles's radio broadcast of H. G. Wells's science fiction novel *The War of the Worlds* is believed by many listeners to be a serious announcement of a Martian invasion, resulting in panic spreading throughout the country.

1938 On November 11, singer Kate Smith's performance of "God Bless America" is broadcast over the radio on Armistice Day.

1939 Singer Frank Sinatra joins the Tommy Dorsey band, where he will soon find great success.

1939 Federal spending on the military begins to revive the economy.

1939 Pocket Books, the nation's first modern paperback book company, is founded.

1939 The National Collegiate Athletic Association (NCAA) holds it first Final Four championship basketball series, which is won by the University of Oregon.

1939 *Gone with the Wind,* David O. Selznick's epic film about the Civil War, stars Vivien Leigh and Clark Gable.

1939 *The Wizard of Oz* whisks movie audiences into a fantasyland of magic and wonder. The film stars Judy Garland and includes such popular songs as "Somewhere Over the Rainbow," "Follow the Yellow Brick Road," and "We're Off to See the Wizard."

1939 On May 2, baseball great Lou "The Iron Man" Gehrig ends his consecutive game streak at 2,130 when he removes himself from the lineup.

1939 On September 1, German troops invade Poland, causing Great Britain and France to declare war on Germany and starting World War II. Days later, the Soviet Union invades Poland as well, and soon Germany and the Soviet Union divide Poland.

1940 The radio program *Superman* debuts, introducing the phrases "Up, up, and away!" and "This looks like a job for Superman!"

1940 On February 22, German troops begin construction of a concentration camp in Auschwitz, Poland.

1940 The first issue of the comic book *Batman* is published.

1940 On May 10, German forces invade Belgium and Holland, and later march into France.

1940 On June 10, Italy declares war on Britain and France.

1940 On June 14, the German army enters Paris, France.

1940 On August 24, Germany begins bombing London, England.

1940 On November 5, President Franklin D. Roosevelt is reelected for his third term.

1940 On November 13, the Disney film *Fantasia* opens in New York City.

1941 "Rosie the Riveter" becomes the symbol for the many women who are employed in various defense industries.

1941 *Citizen Kane,* which many consider the greatest movie of all time, is released, directed by and starring Orson Welles.

1941 On January 15, A. Philip Randolph leads the March on Washington to call for an end to racial discrimination in defense-industry employment. President Franklin D. Roosevelt eventually signs an executive order barring such discrimination.

1941 On March 17, the National Gallery of Art opens in Washington, D.C.

1941 On July 1, CBS and NBC begin offering about fifteen hours of commercial television programming each week—but few consumers have enough money to purchase television sets.

1941 On October 19, German troops lay siege to the Russian city of Moscow.

1941 On December 7, Japanese planes launch a surprise attack on the U.S. naval and air bases in Pearl Harbor, Hawaii, and declare war against the United States.

1941 On December 11, the United States declares war on Germany and Italy in response to those countries' declarations of war.

1942 On January 1, the annual Rose Bowl football game is played in Durham, North Carolina, rather than the usual Pasadena, California, location, to avoid the chance of a Japanese bombing attack.

1942 Humphrey Bogart and Ingrid Bergman star in *Casablanca,* set in war-torn Europe.

1942 On February 19, President Franklin D. Roosevelt signs an executive order placing all Japanese Americans on the West Coast in internment camps for the rest of the war.

1942 On May 5, sugar rationing starts in the United States, followed by the rationing of other products.

1942 In June, American troops defeat the Japanese at the Battle of Midway.

1942 On December 25, the comedy team of Abbott and Costello is voted the leading box-office attraction of 1942.

1943 Gary Cooper and Ingrid Bergman star in *For Whom the Bell Tolls,* the film version of the novel by Ernest Hemingway.

1943 On January 25, the Pentagon, the world's largest office complex and the home to the U.S. military, is completed in Arlington, Virginia.

1943 On March 14, composer Aaron Copland's *Fanfare for the Common Man* premieres in Cincinnati, Ohio.

1943 On March 30, the musical *Oklahoma!* opens on Broadway in New York City.

1943 During the summer, race riots break out in Detroit, Michigan, and Harlem, New York.

1943 On September 8, Italy surrenders to the Allies.

1943 On November 9, artist Jackson Pollock has his first solo show in New York City.

1943 On December 30, *Esquire* magazine loses its second-class mailing privileges after it is charged with being "lewd" and "lascivious" by the U.S. Post Office.

1944 *Seventeen* magazine debuts.

1944 *Double Indemnity,* directed by Billy Wilder, becomes one of the first of a new genre of movies known as *film noir.*

1944 On March 4, American planes bomb Berlin, Germany.

1944 On June 6, on "D-Day," Allied forces land in Normandy, France, and begin the liberation of western Europe.

1944 On June 22, the Serviceman's Readjustment Act, signed by President Franklin D. Roosevelt, provides funding for a variety of programs for returning soldiers, including education programs under the G.I. Bill.

1944 On August 25, Allied troops liberate Paris, France.

1944 On November 7, Franklin D. Roosevelt is reelected for an unprecedented fourth term as president.

1945 Chicago publisher John H. Johnson launches *Ebony* magazine.

1945 The radio program *The Adventures of Ozzie and Harriet* debuts.

1945 On January 27, the Soviet Red Army liberates Auschwitz, Poland, revealing the seriousness of German efforts to exterminate Jews.

1945 On April 12, President Franklin D. Roosevelt dies of a cerebral hemorrhage and Vice President Harry S. Truman takes over as president.

1945 On April 21, Soviet troops reach the outskirts of Berlin, the capital of Germany.

1945 On April 30, German leader Adolf Hitler commits suicide in Berlin, Germany, as Allied troops approach the city.

1945 On May 5, American poet Ezra Pound is arrested in Italy on charges of treason.

1945 On May 8, Germany surrenders to the Allies, bringing an end to World War II in Europe.

1945 On August 6, the United States drops the first atomic bomb on the Japanese city of Hiroshima, killing more than fifty thousand people.

1945 On August 9, the United States drops a second atomic bomb on Nagasaki, Japan.

1945 On September 2, Japan offers its unconditional surrender onboard the U.S.S. *Missouri* in Tokyo Bay, bringing an end to World War II.

1946 The Baby Boom begins as the birthrate rises 20 percent over the previous year.

1946 *It's a Wonderful Life,* starring Jimmy Stewart and directed by Frank Capra, becomes one of the most popular Christmas movies of all time.

1946 On January 10, the first General Assembly of the United Nations meets in London, England.

1946 On June 19, Joe Louis retains his title by knocking out Billy Conn in the first heavyweight boxing match ever shown on television.

1946 On December 11, country singer Hank Williams cuts his first single, "Calling You."

1947 On January 29, Arthur Miller's play *All My Sons* opens in New York City.

1947 On March 12, President Harry S. Truman announces his "containment" policy aimed at stopping the spread of communism. It will later become known as the Truman Doctrine.

1947 On March 21, Congress approves the Twenty-second Amendment, which limits the president to two four-year terms in office. The amendment is ratified in 1951.

1947 On April 10, Jackie Robinson breaks the "color barrier" when he signs a contract to play for professional baseball's Brooklyn Dodgers. He is later named Rookie of the Year by the *Sporting News.*

1947 Beginning September 30, the World Series is televised for the first time as fans watch the New York Yankees defeat the Brooklyn Dodgers in seven games.

1947 On October 13, the Hollywood Ten, a group of film directors and writers, appears before the House Un-American Activities Committee (HUAC).

1947 On December 3, Tennessee Williams's *A Streetcar Named Desire* opens on Broadway in New York City.

1948 The Baskin-Robbins ice cream chain opens.

1948 On April 3, Congress approves $6 billion in Marshall Plan aid for rebuilding European countries.

1948 On May 14, the state of Israel is established.

1948 On May 29, the play *Oklahoma!* closes after a record 2,246 performances.

1948 On June 25, heavyweight boxing champion Joe Louis knocks out Joe Walcott for his twenty-fifth title defense; following the fight, he announces his retirement from boxing.

1948 On September 13, Margaret Chase Smith of Maine becomes the first woman elected to the U.S. Senate.

1948 On November 2, incumbent Harry S. Truman is elected president.

1949 Builder Abraham Levitt and his sons begin construction on a Long Island, New York, suburb called Levittown, which will become a symbol for the postwar housing boom.

1949 On February 10, Arthur Miller's *Death of a Salesman* opens on Broadway in New York City.

1949 On April 4, the North Atlantic Treaty Organization (NATO) is formed by the United States and twelve other mainly European countries to provide for mutual defense.

1949 On September 23, American, British, and Canadian officials reveal that the Soviet Union has successfully detonated an atomic bomb.

1949 On October 1, the Communist People's Republic of China is proclaimed.

1950 The first Xerox copy machine is produced.

1950 Miss Clairol hair coloring is introduced, making it easy for women to dye their hair at home.

1950 Desegregation continues when Charles Cooper becomes the first black player in the National Basketball Association and Althea Gibson becomes the first black woman to compete in a national tennis tournament.

1950 In March, the Boston Institute of Contemporary Art and New York's Metropolitan Museum and Whitney Museum release a joint statement on modern art opposing "any attempt to make art or opinion about art conform to a single point of view."

1950 On May 8, President Harry S. Truman sends the first U.S. military mission to Vietnam.

1950 On June 30, U.S. combat troops enter the Korean War.

1950 On October 2, *Peanuts,* the comic strip written and drawn by Charles Schulz, debuts in seven U.S. newspapers.

1951 *The Caine Mutiny,* a war novel by Herman Wouk, is published and soon becomes one of the longest lasting best-sellers of all time, holding its place on the *New York Times* list for forty-eight weeks.

1951 On April 5, Julius and Ethel Rosenberg receive death sentences for allegedly giving secret information to the Soviet Union.

1951 On June 25, CBS offers the first color television broadcast.

1951 On August 5, the soap operas *Search for Tomorrow* and *Love of Life* premiere on CBS.

1951 On October 15, the sitcom *I Love Lucy* premieres on CBS.

1951 On November 18, the news program *See It Now,* hosted by Edward R. Murrow, premieres on CBS.

1952 *Gunsmoke* debuts as a radio drama. In 1955, the Western drama moves to TV where it lasts until 1975. The show, which starred James Arness as Marshal Matt Dillon, becomes the longest running prime-time TV show with continuing characters.

1952 In January, *American Bandstand,* a popular teen-oriented music program, debuts as a local show in Philadelphia, Pennsylvania. Dick Clark, its most famous host, joins the show in 1956.

1952 On January 14, *The Today Show* debuts on NBC.

1952 In September, *The Old Man and the Sea,* a short novel by Ernest Hemingway, is printed in *Life* magazine and is the Book-of-the-Month Club's co-main selection.

1953 On October 5, the New York Yankees become the first team in history to win five consecutive World Series when they defeat the Brooklyn Dodgers.

1952 In November, *Bwana Devil,* the first 3-D movie, is released.

1952 On November 4, World War II general Dwight D. Eisenhower is elected president.

1953 *Playboy* becomes the first mass-market men's magazine and rockets to popularity when it publishes nude pictures of rising movie star Marilyn Monroe.

1953 IBM introduces its first computer, the 701.

1953 On January 1, Hank Williams, the father of contemporary country music, dies at age twenty-nine from a heart disease resulting from excessive drinking.

1953 On April 3, the first national edition of *TV Guide* is published.

1953 On July 27, the Korean War ends.

1953 On September 13, Nikita Khrushchev is named first secretary of the Soviet Union's Communist Party.

1953 In November, an eleven-day photoengravers strike leaves New York City without a daily newspaper for the first time since 1778.

1954 U.S. senator Joseph McCarthy of Wisconsin leads hearings into the presence of communists in the U.S. Army; his actions are later condemned by the Senate.

1954 *Sports Illustrated* becomes the first glossy weekly magazine about sports.

1954 Swanson Foods introduces the first TV dinners.

1954 On April 4, legendary conductor Arturo Toscanini makes his final appearance conducting the NBC Symphony Orchestra. The concert is broadcast on the radio live from New York City's Carnegie Hall.

1954 On April 4, Walt Disney signs a contract with ABC to produce twenty-six television films each year.

1954 On May 14, the Soviet Union joins with seven Eastern European countries to form the Warsaw Pact, a union of nations pledged to mutual defense.

1954 On May 17, with its *Brown v. Board of Education* decision, the U.S. Supreme Court ends segregation in public schools.

1954 In July, the Newport Jazz Festival debuts in Newport, Rhode Island.

1954 On July 19, "That's All Right, Mama" and "Blue Moon of Kentucky," the first professional records made by Elvis Presley, are released on Sun Records.

1954 On September 27, *The Tonight Show* debuts on NBC.

1954 In October and November, Hungary tries to leave the Warsaw Pact but is attacked and reclaimed by the Soviet Union.

1955 Velcro is invented.

1955 *The $64,000 Question* debuts and soon becomes the most popular game show of the 1950s.

1955 In January, Marian Anderson becomes the first black singer to appear at the Metropolitan Opera.

1955 On January 19, President Dwight D. Eisenhower holds the first televised presidential news conference.

1955 In March, *The Blackboard Jungle,* the first feature film to include a rock and roll song on its soundtrack—"Rock Around the Clock," by Bill Haley and The Comets—opens. The song becomes the country's number-one single in July.

1955 On April 12, large-scale vaccinations for polio are administered throughout the United States.

1955 On July 17, the Disneyland amusement park opens in Anaheim, California.

1955 On September 30, actor James Dean dies after his Porsche roadster slams into another car on a California highway.

1955 On October 13, poet Allen Ginsberg gives the first public reading of *Howl,* his controversial poem-in-progress.

1955 On December 5, Rosa Parks refuses to give up her seat to a white man on a bus in Montgomery, Alabama, sparking a bus boycott that will become a key moment in the Civil Rights Movement.

1956 On June 20, Loew's Inc. releases MGM's pre-1949 film library—excluding *Gone with the Wind* (1939)—for television broadcast.

1956 On November 6, President Dwight D. Eisenhower is reelected.

1956 On November 30, videotape is first used commercially on television, during the broadcast of CBS's *Douglas Edwards with the News.*

1957 On September 26, the landmark musical *West Side Story,* a modern-day adaptation of *Romeo and Juliet* by William Shakespeare, opens on Broadway at the Winter Garden Theatre in New York City.

1957 On October 5, the Soviet Union launches the satellite *Sputnik,* the first man-made satellite in space.

1958 On October 2, Leonard Bernstein begins his first season as director of the New York Philharmonic.

1958 On October 16, sponsors drop the NBC quiz show *Twenty-One* after a grand jury investigation determines that contestants were provided with pre-show answers.

1959 On January 2, revolutionary leader Fidel Castro assumes power in Cuba.

1959 On January 3, Alaska becomes the forty-ninth state.

1959 On February 3, rock and roll legends Buddy Holly, Ritchie Valens, and J. P. Richardson (known as "The Big Bopper") die in a plane crash outside Clear Lake, Iowa.

1959 On August 21, Hawaii becomes the fiftieth state.

1959 On October 21, the Solomon R. Guggenheim Museum, designed by architect Frank Lloyd Wright, opens in New York City.

1960 Designer Pierre Cardin introduces his first fashion designs for men.

1960 On January 3, the Moscow State Symphony begins a seven-week tour at New York City's Carnegie Hall, becoming the first Soviet orchestra to perform in the United States.

1960 On February 11, Jack Paar, host of *The Tonight Show,* walks off the show when an NBC censor deletes a joke from his performance without his knowledge.

1960 On February 20, black students in Greensboro, North Carolina, stage sit-ins at local lunch counters to protest discrimination.

1960 In April, the New York state legislature authorizes the City of New York to purchase Carnegie Hall, which was scheduled for demolition.

1960 On April 1, Lucille Ball and Desi Arnaz appear for the last time as Lucy and Ricky Ricardo on *The Lucy-Desi Comedy Hour.*

1960 On May 5, the Soviet Union announces the capture of American pilot Francis Gary Powers, whose U-2 spy plane was shot down over the Soviet Union.

1960 On September 26, U.S. senator John F. Kennedy of Massachusetts and Vice President Richard M. Nixon appear in the first televised presidential debate.

1960 On October 13, jazz trumpeter Louis Armstrong begins a goodwill tour of Africa, partially sponsored by the U.S. State Department.

1960 On November 8, U.S. senator John F. Kennedy of Massachusetts is elected president.

1961 On January 20, Robert Frost reads his poem "The Gift Outright" at the inauguration of President John F. Kennedy.

1961 On January 27, soprano Leontyne Price first performs at New York's Metropolitan Opera.

1961 In April, folk singer Bob Dylan makes his debut at Gerde's Folk City in New York City's Greenwich Village.

1961 On April 12, Soviet cosmonaut Yuri Gagarin becomes the first man to orbit the Earth.

1961 During the summer, Freedom Rides across the South are aimed at desegregating interstate bus travel.

1961 On August 15–17, East Germany constructs the Berlin Wall, separating communist East Berlin from democratic West Berlin.

1961 On October 1, Roger Maris sets a new single-season home run record with 61 homers.

1962 On February 10, Jim Beatty becomes the first person to run a mile in less than four minutes with a time of 3:58.9.

1962 On May 30, jazz clarinetist Benny Goodman begins a six-week, U.S. State Department–arranged tour of Russia.

1962 On July 10, the *Telstar* satellite is launched and soon brings live television pictures to American television viewers.

1962 On August 5, actress Marilyn Monroe dies from an overdose of barbiturates.

1962 On September 25, Philharmonic Hall, the first completed building of New York's Lincoln Center for the Performing Arts, is inaugurated by Leonard Bernstein and the New York Philharmonic.

1962 On September 29, *My Fair Lady* closes on Broadway after 2,717 performances, making it the longest-running show in history.

1962 In October, the United States and the Soviet Union clash over the presence of Soviet missiles in Cuba.

1962 On October 1, James Meredith becomes the first black person to enroll at the University of Mississippi as federal troops battle thousands of protesters.

1963 On January 8, *Mona Lisa,* by Leonardo da Vinci, is shown at Washington's National Gallery, the first time the painting ever has appeared outside the Louvre in Paris, France.

1963 On May 7, the Guthrie Theatre in Minneapolis, Minnesota, the first major regional theater in the Midwest, opens.

1963 On November 22, President John F. Kennedy is assassinated in Dallas, Texas, and Vice President Lyndon B. Johnson assumes the presidency.

1963 On November 24, the murder of alleged presidential assassin Lee Harvey Oswald is broadcast live on television.

1964 Ford introduces its Mustang, a smaller sporty car.

1964 On February 9, the Beatles make their first live appearance on American television, on *The Ed Sullivan Show.*

1964 On February 25, Cassius Clay (who later changes his name to Muhammad Ali) beats Sonny Liston to become the heavyweight boxing champion of the world.

1964 In May, the just-remodeled Museum of Modern Art in New York City reopens with a new gallery, the Steichen Photography Center, named for photographer Edward Steichen.

1964 On July 2, President Lyndon B. Johnson signs the Civil Rights Act of 1964, which bans racial discrimination in public places and in employment.

1964 On August 7, in the Gulf of Tonkin Resolution, Congress gives President Lyndon B. Johnson the power to use military force to protect U.S. interests in Vietnam.

1964 On November 3, incumbent Lyndon B. Johnson is elected president.

1965 In January, Bob Dylan plays an electric guitar on his new single, "Subterranean Homesick Blues."

1965 On February 21, black leader Malcolm X is murdered in Harlem, New York.

1965 On March 8, the first U.S. combat troops are sent to Vietnam.

1965 On April 26, *Symphony No. 4* by Charles Ives is performed in its entirety for the first time by the American Symphony Orchestra, conducted by Leopold Stokowski.

1965 On May 9, piano virtuoso Vladimir Horowitz returns to the Carnegie Hall stage after a twelve-year "retirement."

1965 On June 2, in a letter to President Lyndon B. Johnson, Pulitzer Prize–winning poet Robert Lowell declines an invitation to attend a White House arts festival, citing his "dismay and distrust" of American foreign policy.

1965 In July, Bob Dylan and his electric guitar are booed off the Newport Folk Festival stage.

1965 On September 29, President Lyndon B. Johnson signs into law the Federal Aid to the Arts Bill.

1965 On October 15, demonstrations against the Vietnam War occur in forty U.S. cities.

1965 On December 9, *A Charlie Brown Christmas* becomes the first *Peanuts* special to air on TV.

1966 The National Organization for Women (NOW) is established.

1966 On June 8, the National Football League and the American Football League merge.

1966 On July 12, rioting by blacks breaks out in twenty U.S. cities over racial discrimination.

1966 On August 29, the Beatles play their last live concert.

1966 On December 8, philanthropist, horse breeder, and art collector Paul Mellon donates his collection of British rare books, paintings, drawings, and prints, valued at over $35 million, to Yale University.

1967 On January 15, in the first Super Bowl, the Green Bay Packers defeat the Kansas City Chiefs, 35–10.

1967 On February 18, the National Gallery of Art arranges to purchase Leonardo da Vinci's *Ginevra dei Benci* for between $5 million and $6 million, the highest price paid to date for a single painting.

1967 In June, the Monterey International Pop Festival, an important early rock music event, is held in California.

1967 On June 20, Muhammad Ali is stripped of his boxing titles after being found guilty of tax evasion.

1967 On July 23, federal troops are called in to put a stop to rioting in Detroit, Michigan. Forty-three people are killed in the rioting, which lasts a week.

1967 On November 9, the first issue of *Rolling Stone* magazine is published. On the cover is a portrait of the Beatles' John Lennon.

1967 In December, Universal News, the last of the movie newsreel companies, closes because it is unable to compete with television news.

1968 On January 30, North Vietnam launches the Tet Offensive, escalating the war in Vietnam.

1968 On April 4, civil rights leader Martin Luther King Jr. is murdered in Memphis, Tennessee.

1968 On April 19, *Hair* opens on Broadway, at New York City's Biltmore Theatre.

1968 On June 5, presidential candidate and U.S. senator Robert F. Kennedy of New York is murdered in Los Angeles, California.

1968 On September 16, presidential candidate and former vice president Richard Nixon appears as a guest on TV's *Rowan and Martin's Laugh-In* and delivers one of the show's signature lines: "Sock it to me."

1968 On November 1, the Motion Picture Association of America inaugurates its film ratings system.

1968 On November 5, former vice president Richard Nixon is elected president.

1969 Hot pants make their first appearance.

1969 On July 20, U.S. astronaut Neil Armstrong becomes the first man to walk on the moon when the *Apollo 11* mission succeeds.

1969 On August 15–17, the Woodstock Music and Art Fair is held on a six-hundred-acre hog farm in upstate New York.

1969 On November 15, a quarter million Vietnam War protesters march in Washington, D.C.

1969 On December 6, a fan is murdered during the Altamont Rock Festival in California.

1970 Soviet cosmonauts spend seventeen days in space, setting a new record for space longevity.

1970 Across the nation, protests continue over the ongoing Vietnam War.

1970 Rock stars Jimi Hendrix and Janis Joplin die within three weeks of each other, both as a result of drug overdoses.

1970 In March, three women—Elizabeth Bishop, Lillian Hellman, and Joyce Carol Oates—win National Book Awards.

1970 On May 4, National Guard members shoot antiwar protesters at Kent State University in Ohio, killing four students.

1970 On April 10, the Beatles disband.

1970 On April 30, U.S. and South Vietnamese troops invade Cambodia, which has been sheltering North Vietnamese troops.

1970 On September 6, four airliners bound for New York are hijacked by Palestinian terrorists, but no passengers are harmed.

1970 On September 19, *The Mary Tyler Moore Show* debuts on CBS.

1970 On September 21, *Monday Night Football* debuts on ABC.

1970 On October 2, the Environmental Protection Agency (EPA) is created to regulate environmental issues.

1971 Disney World opens in Orlando, Florida.

1971 Hot pants become a fashion sensation.

1971 On January 2, cigarette advertising is banned from television and radio.

1971 On February 6, British troops are sent to patrol Northern Ireland.

1971 On February 9, the European Economic Community, a precursor to the European Union, is established.

1971 On March 8, Joe Frazier defeats Muhammad Ali to retain the world heavyweight boxing title.

1971 On April 20, the U.S. Supreme Court rules that students can be bused to end racial segregation in schools.

1971 In June, the Twenty-sixth Amendment to the Constitution lowers the legal voting age to eighteen.

1971 On June 13, the *New York Times* publishes the "Pentagon Papers," which reveal Defense Department plans for the Vietnam War.

1971 In September, a prison uprising in Attica, New York, ends with forty-three people killed, including ten hostages.

1971 On October 12, the rock musical *Jesus Christ Superstar* opens on Broadway in New York City.

1971 On October 13, the Pittsburgh Pirates and the Baltimore Orioles play in the first World Series night game.

1971 On December 25, "Christmas bombing" occurs in North Vietnam.

1972 In a sign of the cooling of Cold War tensions, East and West Germany and North and South Korea each enter into negotiations to normalize relations.

1972 *Ms.* magazine begins publication.

1972 *Pong*, the first video game available to play at home, becomes popular, as does the first video game machine, Odyssey, introduced by Magnavox.

1972 On February 14, the musical *Grease* opens on Broadway in New York City.

1972 On February 21, President Richard Nixon begins a seven-day visit to Communist China.

1972 On May 22, President Richard Nixon begins a nine-day visit to the Soviet Union.

1972 On June 17, the Watergate scandal begins with the arrest of five men caught trying to bug the Democratic National Committee headquarters at the Watergate building in Washington, D.C. The investigation soon reveals deep corruption in the Nixon administration.

1972 On July 24, the United Nations asks the United States to end its bombing of North Vietnam.

1972 On August 12, the last American combat troops leave Vietnam.

1972 On November 8, cable TV network HBO premieres in Pennsylvania with 365 subscribers.

1973 Three major American cities—Los Angeles, California; Atlanta, Georgia; and Detroit, Michigan—elect a black mayor for the first time.

1973 Investigations into the Watergate affair capture the public attention and shatter the Nixon administration.

1973 The Sears Tower (now known as the Willis Tower), at the time the world's tallest building, is completed in Chicago, Illinois.

1973 Ralph Lauren designs the costumes for the film *The Great Gatsby,* helping build his reputation.

1973 Fantasy-adventure game Dungeons and Dragons is created by Dave Arneson and Gary Gygax.

1973 The first Internet is set up by the U.S. Department of Defense as a way of connecting all the department's computers.

1973 On January 14, the Miami Dolphins win the Super Bowl and become the first professional football team to finish a season undefeated.

1973 On October 16, the Organization of Petroleum Exporting Countries (OPEC) declares an embargo (ban) on the export of oil to the United States and other Western countries.

1973 On October 23, the House of Representatives begins impeachment proceedings against President Richard Nixon.

1974 The Ramones launch the American punk movement with their performances at the New York City club CBGB.

1974 The streaking fad sweeps the country.

1974 President Richard Nixon tours the Middle East and the Soviet Union.

1974 On January 18, Israel and Egypt sign a peace accord that ends their long armed conflict.

1974 On April 8, Hank Aaron of the Atlanta Braves breaks Babe Ruth's lifetime home run record when he hits his 715th career homer.

1974 In May, screenwriter Dalton Trumbo, who had been blacklisted in the 1950s during the anticommunist crusades of U.S. senator Joseph McCarthy of Wisconsin, receives an Academy Award for the 1957 film *The Brave One*.

1974 On August 8, Richard Nixon announces that he would become the first U.S. president to resign from office, amid evidence of a cover-up of the Watergate affair.

1974 On August 9, Vice President Gerald Ford replaces Richard Nixon as president. Less than a month later, he officially pardons Nixon.

1974 On September 8, motorcycle stunt rider Evel Knievel tries to jump a rocket over the Snake River Canyon in Idaho but falls short.

1974 On October 3, Frank Robinson joins the Cleveland Indians as major league baseball's first black manager.

1974 On October 30, boxer Muhammnad Ali regains his world heavyweight boxing title by defeating George Foreman.

1974 In December, unemployment hits 6.5 percent amid a prolonged economic slump and rises to 8.9 percent by May 1975.

1975 The video cassette recorder (VCR) is invented by Sony Corporation in Japan.

1975 The first personal computer, the Altair 8800, is sold in a kit form.

1975 The cult film *The Rocky Horror Picture Show* is released.

1975 Skateboarding becomes popular, and mood rings and pet rocks are popular fads.

1975 Rock star Bruce Springsteen appears on the cover of both *Time* and *Newsweek* thanks to his popular album *Born to Run*.

1975 The Soviet Union and the United States cooperate in the manned *Apollo-Soyuz* space mission.

1975 On January 5, the all-black musical *The Wiz* opens on Broadway in New York City. It eventually tallies 1,672 performances.

1975 On April 30, Saigon, the capital of South Vietnam, is invaded by the communist North Vietnamese, ending the Vietnam War.

1975 On October 1, the Organization of Petroleum Exporting Countries (OPEC) raises crude oil prices by 10 percent.

1975 On October 11, *Saturday Night Live* debuts on NBC.

1976 The first personal computer, the Apple, is developed by Steve Jobs and Steve Wozniak. The Apple II, introduced a year later, offers color graphics.

1976 Model and actress Farrah Fawcett-Majors sets a trend with her feathered haircut and appears on millions of posters in her tiny red bathing suit.

1976 On July 4, the United States celebrates its bicentennial.

1976 On November 2, former Georgia governor Jimmy Carter is elected president.

1976 On November 6, *Gone with the Wind* is broadcast on TV for the first time.

1977 The film *Saturday Night Fever* helps make disco music popular.

1977 Studio 54 becomes New York City's hottest nightclub featuring disco music.

1977 Egyptian artifacts from the tomb of King Tutankhamen, or King Tut, draw huge audiences across the nation.

1977 Alex Haley's book *Roots* becomes a best-seller after the airing of the TV miniseries based on the book.

1977 On January 21, President Jimmy Carter signs an unconditional pardon for most Vietnam-era draft evaders.

1977 On February 8, *Hustler* magazine publisher Larry Flynt is convicted of obscenity.

1977 In April, the Christian Broadcasting Network (CBN) makes its debut.

1977 On August 16, Elvis Presley, the king of rock and roll, dies at Graceland, his Memphis, Tennessee, mansion.

1978 The Walkman personal cassette player is introduced by Sony.

1978 On July 25, the first human test-tube baby is born in England.

1978 On September 17, U.S. president Jimmy Carter hosts negotiations between Israeli prime minister Menachem Begin and Egyptian president Anwar Sadat at Camp David, Maryland.

1978 On October 13, punk rock musician Sid Vicious of the Sex Pistols is arrested for the stabbing death of his girlfriend.

1978 On November 18, Jim Jones and over nine hundred followers of his People's Temple cult are found dead after a mass suicide in Jonestown, Guyana.

1978 On December 5, the Soviet Union and Afghanistan sign a treaty of friendship, and within a year U.S. support for the Afghan government disappears.

1979 Eleven people are trampled to death at a Who concert in Cincinnati, Ohio.

1979 Jerry Falwell organizes the Moral Majority to lobby politicians regarding the concerns of Christian fundamentalists.

1979 On January 1, the United States and the People's Republic of China establish formal diplomatic relations.

1979 On March 28, a major accident in the nuclear reactor at the Three Mile Island power plant near Harrisburg, Pennsylvania, raises concerns about nuclear power.

1979 On November 4, Iranian militants seize the U.S. embassy in Tehran, Iran, and take fifty-two hostages, whom they will hold for over a year.

1979 On December 27, the Soviet Union invades Afghanistan, beginning more than two decades of war and disruption in that country.

1980 Post-it notes are created by 3M chemist Arthur Fry.

1980 On February 22, the U.S. Olympic ice hockey team wins the gold medal, sparking national celebration.

1980 On April 12, the United States votes to boycott the Summer Olympics in Moscow to protest the Soviet presence in Afghanistan.

1980 On April 21, the Mariel boatlift begins, bringing 125,000 refugees from Cuba to Florida before being halted in September.

1980 In June, the all-news CNN cable TV network debuts.

1980 On August 19, a report issued by the *Los Angeles Times* indicates that 40 to 75 percent of NBA players use cocaine.

1980 On November 4, former California governor Ronald Reagan is elected president.

1980 On November 21, the "Who Shot J.R.?" episode of *Dallas* draws the largest television audience of all time.

1980 On September 4, Iraq begins an eight-year war with Iran.

1980 On October 2, in his last fight, heavyweight boxer Muhammad Ali is defeated by World Boxing Council champion Larry Holmes.

1980 On December 8, former Beatles musician John Lennon is shot and killed in New York City.

1981 Nintendo's *Donkey Kong* is the most popular coin-operated video game.

1981 NASA launches and lands the first reusable spacecraft, the space shuttle.

1981 On January 13, the National Collegiate Athletic Association (NCAA) votes to sponsor women's championships in twelve sports after the 1981–82 season.

1981 On January 20, American hostages held at the U.S. embassy in Tehran, Iran, are released on the day of President Ronald Reagan's inauguration.

1981 On January 23, the United States withdraws support for the Marxist government of Nicaragua and begins to support antigovernment rebels known as Contras.

1981 On March 26, comedian Carol Burnett wins a $1.6 million libel lawsuit against the tabloid *National Enquirer.*

1981 On March 30, President Ronald Reagan and three others are wounded in an assassination attempt in Washington, D.C.

1981 On July 29, Great Britain's Prince Charles marries Lady Diana Spencer in an event televised around the world.

1981 On August 1, the Music Television Network (MTV) starts offering music videos that soon become as important as the actual music.

1981 On September 21, Sandra Day O'Connor is confirmed as the first woman to serve on the U.S. Supreme Court.

1982 The compact disc is introduced.

1982 The popular movie *E.T.: The Extra-Terrestrial* sets box office records.

1982 Michael Jackson's album *Thriller* is the year's most popular recording.

1982 Americans frustrate themselves trying to solve Rubik's Cube, a popular puzzle.

1982 On April 2, Argentina invades the Falkland Islands off its coast, sparking a short war with Great Britain, which claims the islands.

1982 On June 7, Graceland, the late Elvis Presley's Memphis, Tennessee, home, is opened as a tourist attraction.

1982 On July 27, acquired immune deficiency syndrome (AIDS) is officially named.

1982 On September 15, *USA Today* becomes the first national newspaper.

1982 On October 7, *Cats* opens on Broadway in New York City and will become the decade's most popular musical.

1983 First lady Nancy Reagan announces a "War on Drugs."

1983 Sally Ride becomes the first woman astronaut in space when she joins the crew of the space shuttle *Challenger.*

1983 Actor Paul Newman introduces his own line of spaghetti sauces to be sold in grocery stores; he uses the proceeds to benefit charities.

1983 On February 28, the farewell episode of the sitcom *M*A*S*H* is seen by 125 million viewers.

1983 On March 23, President Ronald Reagan proposes a space-based antimissile defense system that is popularly known as "Star Wars."

1983 On April 18, terrorists bomb the U.S. embassy in Beirut, Lebanon, killing sixty-three.

1983 On September 1, the Soviet Union shoots down a Korean Air Lines flight that has strayed into its airspace, killing 269.

1983 On October 25, three thousand U.S. soldiers invade the Caribbean island nation of Grenada to crush a Marxist uprising.

1983 In November, Cabbage Patch Kids dolls, with their soft faces and adoption certificates, become the most popular new doll of the Christmas season.

1984 Trivial Pursuit becomes the nation's most popular board game.

1984 *The Cosby Show* debuts on NBC.

1984 Rap group Run-DMC is the first rap group to have a gold album.

1984 Apple introduces a new personal computer, the Macintosh, with a dramatic advertising campaign.

1984 On November 6, Ronald Reagan is reelected president.

1984 On December 3, a Union Carbide plant in Bhopal, India, leaks poison gas that kills two thousand and injures two hundred thousand.

1985 Nintendo Entertainment System, a home video game system that has brilliant colors, realistic sound effects, and quick action, is introduced to the United States.

1985 On March 16, U.S. journalist Terry Anderson is kidnapped in Lebanon; he will be held until December 4, 1991.

1985 In April, Coca-Cola changes the formula of its popular soft drink and the public reacts with anger and dismay, prompting the company to reissue the old formula as Classic Coke.

1985 On July 13, British rock star Bob Geldof organizes Live Aid, a charity concert and album to aid the victims of African famine.

1985 On October 2, the death of handsome movie star Rock Hudson from AIDS raises awareness about the disease.

1986 Country singer Dolly Parton opens a theme park in Tennessee called Dollywood.

1986 On January 28, the space shuttle *Challenger* explodes upon liftoff, killing the six astronauts and one teacher who were aboard.

1986 On February 26, Robert Penn Warren is named the first poet laureate of the United States.

1986 On April 26, a serious meltdown at the Chernobyl nuclear power plant near Kiev, Ukraine, releases a radioactive cloud into the atmosphere and is considered a major disaster.

1986 On May 1, in South Africa, 1.5 million blacks protest apartheid (the policy of racial segregation). Around the world, foreign governments place sanctions on South Africa.

1986 On June 10, Nancy Lieberman becomes the first woman to play in a men's professional basketball league when she joins the United States Basketball League.

1986 On July 15, the United States sends troops to Bolivia to fight against drug traffickers.

1986 On July 27, Greg LeMond becomes the first American to win France's prestigious Tour de France bicycle race.

1986 In October, it is discovered that members of the Reagan administration have been trading arms for hostages in Iran and illegally channeling funds to Contras in Nicaragua. This Iran-Contra scandal will eventually be investigated by Congress.

1986 On November 22, twenty-one-year-old Mike Tyson becomes the youngest heavyweight boxing champion when he defeats World Boxing Council champ Trevor Berbick.

1987 On March 19, televangelist Jim Bakker resigns after it is revealed that he has been having an adulterous affair with church secretary Jessica Hahn.

1987 On June 25, Soviet leader Mikhail Gorbachev announces *perestroika,* a program of sweeping economic reforms aimed at improving the Soviet economy.

1987 On October 3, Canada and the United States sign a free-trade agreement.

1987 On October 17, the stock market experiences its worst crash in history when it drops 508 points.

1987 On November 11, Vincent van Gogh's painting *Irises* is sold for $53.9 million.

1988 McDonald's opens twenty restaurants in Moscow, Russia.

1988 Singer Sonny Bono is elected mayor of Palm Springs, California.

1988 On February 5, former Panamanian dictator General Manuel Noriega is charged in a U.S. court with accepting bribes from drug traffickers.

1988 On February 14, Ayatollah Khomeini of Iran calls author Salman Rushdie's book *The Satanic Verses* offensive and issues a death sentence on him. The author goes into hiding.

1988 On April 14, Soviet forces withdraw from Afghanistan after ten years of fighting in that country.

1988 On July 3, believing it is under attack, a U.S. warship shoots down an Iran Air passenger liner, killing 290 passengers.

1988 On November 8, Vice President George Herbert Walker Bush is elected president.

1988 On December 21, Pan Am Flight 747 explodes over Lockerbie, Scotland, killing 259 on the flight and 11 on the ground. Middle Eastern terrorists are eventually charged with the crime.

1989 On March 24, the Exxon *Valdez* oil tanker runs aground in Alaska, spilling 240,000 barrels of oil and creating an environmental disaster.

1989 In May, more than one million Chinese demonstrate for democracy in Beijing.

1989 In June, Chinese troops crack down on demonstrators in Tiananmen Square, drawing attention to the repressive government.

1989 On August 9, Colin R. Powell becomes the United States' first black chairman of the Joint Chiefs of Staff.

1989 On August 23, the Soviet states of Lithuania, Latvia, and Estonia demand autonomy from the Soviet Union. Later, across the former Soviet-dominated region, Soviet republics and satellite countries throw off communist control and pursue independence.

1989 On August 24, former baseball star Pete Rose is banned from baseball for life because it is believed that he bet on games in which he was involved.

1989 On October 15, Wayne Gretzky of the Los Angeles Kings becomes the National Hockey League's all-time leading scorer with his 1,850th point.

1989 On October 17, a major earthquake hits the San Francisco, California, area.

1989 On December 16, American troops invade Panama and seize dictator General Manuel Noriega. Noriega will later be convicted in U.S. courts.

1989 On December 22, the Brandenburg Gate in Berlin is officially opened, allowing people from East and West Berlin to mix freely and signaling the end of the Cold War and the reunification of Germany.

1990 The animated sitcom *The Simpsons* debuts on the FOX network.

1990 Ken Burns's documentary *The Civil War* airs on PBS.

1990 British scientist Tim Berners-Lee invents the World Wide Web.

1990 On April 25, the Hubble Space Telescope is deployed in space from the space shuttle *Discovery*.

1990 On July 26, President George Herbert Walker Bush signs the Americans with Disabilities Act, which provides broad protections for those with disabilities.

1990 On August 2, Iraq invades Kuwait, prompting the United States to wage war on Iraq from bases in Saudi Arabia. Much of this conflict, called the Persian Gulf War, is aired live on television and makes CNN famous for its coverage.

1990 On October 3, East and West Germany are reunited.

1991 Mass murderer Jeffrey Dahmer is charged with killing fifteen young men and boys near Milwaukee, Wisconsin.

1991 On March 3, U.S. general Norman Schwarzkopf announces the end of the Persian Gulf War.

1991 In October, confirmation hearings for U.S. Supreme Court justice nominee Clarence Thomas are carried live on television and feature Anita Hill's dramatic accusations of sexual harassment. Despite the charges, Thomas is confirmed.

1991 On November 7, Los Angeles Lakers basketball star Earvin "Magic" Johnson announces that he has contracted the HIV virus.

1991 On December 8, leaders of Russia and several other former Soviet states announce the formation of the Commonwealth of Independent States.

1992 On April 29, riots erupt in Los Angeles, California, following the acquittal of four white police officers in the beating of black motorist Rodney King. The brutal beating had been filmed and shown widely on television.

1992 On May 21, Vice President Dan Quayle criticizes the CBS sitcom *Murphy Brown* for not promoting family values after the main character has a child out of wedlock.

1992 In August, the Mall of America, the nation's largest shopping mall, opens in Bloomington, Minnesota.

1992 On August 24, Hurricane Andrew hits Florida and the Gulf Coast, causing a total of over $15 billion in damage.

1992 On October 24, the Toronto Blue Jays become the first non-U.S. team to win baseball's World Series.

1992 On November 3, Arkansas governor Bill Clinton is elected president, defeating incumbent George Herbert Walker Bush and strong third party candidate H. Ross Perot.

1992 On December 17, the United States, Canada, and Mexico sign the North American Free Trade Agreement (NAFTA).

1993 Jack "Dr. Death" Kevorkian is arrested in Michigan for assisting in the suicide of a terminally ill patient, his nineteenth such action.

1993 On February 26, six people are killed when terrorists plant a bomb in New York City's World Trade Center.

1993 On April 19, more than eighty members of a religious cult called the Branch Davidians are killed in a mass suicide as leaders set fire to their compound in Waco, Texas, following a fifty-one-day siege by federal forces.

1993 In July and August, the Flood of the Century devastates the American Midwest, killing forty-eight.

1994 Tiger Woods becomes the youngest person and the first black to win the U.S. Amateur Golf Championship.

1994 Special prosecutor Ken Starr is appointed to investigate President Bill Clinton's involvement in a financial scandal known as Whitewater. The investigation will ultimately cover several scandals and lead to impeachment proceedings against the president.

1994 In January, ice skater Nancy Kerrigan is attacked by associates of her rival, Tonya Harding, at the U.S. Olympic Trials in Detroit, Michigan.

1994 On May 2, Nelson Mandela is elected president of South Africa. The black activist had been jailed for decades under the old apartheid regime and became the country's first black president.

1994 On August 11, major league baseball players go on strike, forcing the cancellation of the playoffs and World Series.

1994 On November 5, forty-five-year-old boxer George Foreman becomes the oldest heavyweight champion when he defeats Michael Moorer.

1995 On April 19, a car bomb explodes outside the Alfred P. Murrah Federal Office Building in Oklahoma City, Oklahoma, killing 168 people. Following a manhunt, antigovernment zealot Timothy McVeigh is captured, and later he is convicted and executed for the crime.

1995 On September 1, the Rock and Roll Hall of Fame opens in Cleveland, Ohio.

1995 On September 6, Cal Ripken Jr. of the Baltimore Orioles breaks the long-standing record for most consecutive baseball games played with 2,131. The total reaches 2,632 games before Ripken removes himself from the lineup in 1998.

1995 On October 3, former football star O. J. Simpson is found not guilty of the murder of his ex-wife and her friend in what many called the "trial of the century."

1996 Three years after the introduction of H. Ty Warners's Beanie Babies, the first eleven toy styles are retired and quickly become collector's items.

1996 On September 26, American astronaut Shannon Lucid returns to Earth after spending 188 days in space—a record for any astronaut.

1996 On November 5, Bill Clinton is reelected to the presidency.

1997 Researchers in Scotland successfully clone an adult sheep, named Dolly.

1997 The Hale-Bopp comet provides a nightly show as it passes by the Earth.

1997 Actress Ellen DeGeneres becomes the first openly gay lead character in her ABC sitcom *Ellen.*

1997 On January 23, Madeleine Albright becomes the first woman sworn in as U.S. secretary of state.

1997 On March 27, thirty-nine members of the Heavens Gate religious cult are found dead in their California compound.

1997 On April 13, Tiger Woods becomes the youngest person and the first black to win a major golf tournament when he wins the Masters with the lowest score ever.

1997 On June 19, the play *Cats* sets a record for the longest-running Broadway play with its 6,138th performance.

1997 On June 20, four major tobacco companies settle a lawsuit with states that will cost companies nearly $400 billion.

1997 On June 28, boxer Mike Tyson is disqualified when he bites the ear of opponent Evander Holyfield during a heavyweight title fight.

1997 On July 5, the *Pathfinder* spacecraft lands on Mars and sends back images and rock analyses.

1997 On August 31, Britain's Princess Diana is killed in an auto accident in Paris, France.

1998 Mark McGwire of the St. Louis Cardinals sets a single-season home run record with seventy home runs.

1998 The final episode of the popular sitcom *Seinfeld* is watched by an estimated audience of seventy-six million.

1998 On January 22, Unabomber Ted Kaczynski is convicted for a series of mail bombings and sentenced to life in prison.

1998 On March 24, the movie *Titanic* wins eleven Academy Awards, tying the record set by *Ben-Hur* in 1959.

1998 On April 10, a new drug for male impotence known as Viagra hits the market and is a popular sensation.

1998 On August 7, terrorists explode bombs outside the U.S. embassies in Nairobi, Kenya, and Dar es Salaam, Tanzania.

1998 In November, former professional wrestler Jesse "The Body" Ventura is elected governor of Minnesota.

1998 On December 19, the House of Representatives initiates impeachment proceedings against President Bill Clinton, but the U.S. Senate acquits Clinton on two charges in early 1999.

1999 The U.S. women's soccer team wins the World Cup by defeating China.

1999 On March 24, NATO launches a bombing campaign against Serbia to stop its actions in Kosovo.

1999 On March 29, the Dow Jones Industrial Average closes above 10,000 for the first time in history thanks to a booming stock market dominated by high-tech companies.

1999 On April 20, in Littleton, Colorado, two students go on a vicious shooting spree, killing themselves and twelve other students.

1999 On September 24, *IKONOS,* the world's first commercial, high-resolution imaging satellite, is launched into space; it can detect an object on Earth as small as a card table.

2000 The world wakes up on January 1 to find that the so-called "Y2K" computer bug had failed to materialize.

2000 In May, Eminem releases his *Marshall Mathers LP,* which sells 1.76 million copies in its first week, becoming the fastest-selling album by a solo artist of all time.

2000 The fourth Harry Potter book, *Harry Potter and the Goblet of Fire,* is released in July and sets new publishing sales records.

2000 Tiger Woods becomes the youngest golfer to win all four Grand Slam golf tournaments.

2000 The first inhabitants of the International Space Station take up residence in orbit over the Earth.

2000 In November, outgoing First Lady Hillary Rodham Clinton wins a seat in Congress as a senator representing New York state.

2000 On December 12, over a month after Election Day, Texas governor George W. Bush is declared the winner of the presidential race against Vice President Al Gore after contentious vote recounting in Florida is ordered stopped by the Supreme Court. Bush takes Florida by a margin of 527 votes and edges Gore in the Electoral College by only four votes.

2000 On December 28, squeezed by "big box" retailers like Wal-Mart, Montgomery Ward announces it will be closing its doors after 128 years in business.

2001 Wikipedia is launched.

2001 On April 1, a U.S. spy plane collides with a Chinese fighter jet and is forced to land on Chinese soil, causing an international incident.

2001 The first draft of the human genome, a complete sequence of human DNA, is published.

2001 The "dot com bubble" bursts, leading to widespread bankruptcies in the software and Internet industries.

2001 On September 11, nineteen terrorists hijack four planes, flying two into the twin towers of the World Trade Center in New York City and one into the Pentagon in Arlington, Virginia. The fourth plane goes down in a field in Pennsylvania during a fight over the controls and fails to reach its intended target, believed to be the White House.

2001 In October, Afghanistan, accused of harboring terrorist training camps and 9/11 mastermind Osama bin Laden, is invaded by the United States and its allies, initiating the so-called War on Terror.

2002 Europe introduces its first universal currency, the Euro, initially accepted in twelve countries.

2002 The U.S. State Department issues its report on state sponsors of terrorism, singling out seven countries: Cuba, Iran, Iraq, Libya, North Korea, Sudan, and Syria.

2002 The United States begins detaining suspected terrorists without trial at its military base in Guantanamo Bay, Cuba.

2002 Halle Berry wins the Academy Award for best actress, becoming the first African American to win the honor.

2002 Bulgaria, Estonia, Latvia, Lithuania, Romania, Slovakia, and Slovenia, all former Soviet bloc nations, are invited to join the North Atlantic Treaty Organization (NATO).

2003 On February 1, the space shuttle *Columbia* disintegrates during reentry, scattering the craft's debris across the United States and killing all seven astronauts aboard.

2003 SARS, a new respiratory disease, first appears in Hong Kong before spreading around the world.

2003 In the face of mass global protests, the United States invades Iraq on March 19 as part of its continuing war on terror. By April 9, the capital city of Baghdad is taken. The weapons of mass destruction that were reported to be harbored by Iraqi dictator Saddam Hussein and were the publicly stated reason behind the invasion are never found.

2003 On December 13, Saddam Hussein is found hiding in a bolt hole in an Iraqi village.

2004 Online social network Facebook is founded.

2004 On March 11, Madrid, Spain, is the target of the worst terrorist attacks since September 11, 2001; 191 people are killed and 2,050 wounded in a series of coordinated train bombings.

2004 George W. Bush is elected to a second term by a wider margin than in 2000.

2004 On December 26, a tsunami caused by an earthquake measuring 9.3 on the moment magnitude scale in the Indian Ocean kills over three hundred thousand people across eleven countries in Southeast Asia and Sri Lanka.

2005 The video-sharing Web site YouTube is launched.

2005 Prince Charles, the heir to the throne of Great Britain, marries his longtime love, Camilla Parker Bowles.

2005 In June, pop star Michael Jackson is acquitted of child molestation charges.

2005 On July 7, coordinated bombings on three trains and a bus kill fifty-six people in London, England.

2005 On July 26, American cyclist Lance Armstrong wins his record seventh-straight Tour de France.

2005 On August 29, Hurricane Katrina makes landfall on America's Gulf Coast. The resulting destruction, largely centered on New Orleans, Louisiana, after the city's levee system fails, leads to billions of dollars in damage and over eighteen hundred deaths. The federal government is widely criticized for its slow reaction to the disaster, with rapper Kanye West famously declaring on live television, "George Bush doesn't care about black people."

2005 In November, French surgeons perform the world's first face transplant.

2006 The issue of global warming becomes a mainstream subject of discussion with the release of former vice president Al Gore's film *An Inconvenient Truth* and the accompanying book of the same name.

2006 The *Oxford English Dictionary* adds the verb "google" to its pages.

2006 Online social network Twitter is launched.

2006 The United States reaches a population of three hundred million only thirty-two years after hitting the two hundred million mark.

2006 Pluto is downgraded from planetary status, reducing the number of planets in the solar system to eight.

2006 On February 22, the one billionth digital song is downloaded from Apple's iTunes store.

2006 Riding a backlash against the ongoing wars in Iraq and Afghanistan and dissatisfaction with the George W. Bush administration, the Democratic Party wins back majorities in both houses of Congress for the first time in twelve years.

2006 On December 30, Iraqis execute former president Saddam Hussein.

2007 President George W. Bush announces that 21,500 more troops will be sent to Iraq as part of a "surge" to stem the ongoing guerrilla attacks being carried out against U.S. troops and Iraqi civilians by Iraqi dissidents and Arab terrorists.

2007 On the night of February 17, pop star Britney Spears, increasingly under media scrutiny for her erratic behavior, shaves her head and lashes out against paparazzi and reporters who had been tailing her.

2007 Apple introduces the iPhone.

2007 In the wake of Barry Bonds setting a new home run record amongst whispers of his use of performance-enhancing drugs, the Mitchell Report is released, detailing a year-long investigation into the widespread abuse of steroids in major league baseball.

2008 The Iraq troop surge is judged largely a success by July, eighteen months after it was implemented.

2008 On August 17, swimmer Michael Phelps sets a new Olympic record when he wins his eighth gold medal.

2008 With the September 15 collapse of lending firm Lehman Brothers, a major panic sweeps the world financial markets. Along with the collapse of the housing bubble, these are the first clear signals of the onset of the Great Recession, the worst global economic crisis since the Great Depression.

2008 On November 4, U.S. senator Barack Obama of Illinois becomes the first African American elected president of the United States.

2009 Barack Obama's historic inauguration on January 20 draws over one million people to the National Mall in Washington, D.C.

2009 Upon assuming office, President Barack Obama orders the closing of the Guantanamo Bay detention center and passes a $75 billion economic stimulus package.

2009 On April 15 (tax day), protests break out across the country, marking the beginning of the loosely affiliated Tea Party movement. Although lacking a single guiding organization or national leader, the conservative, ostensibly grassroots, movement is united by its concern over certain types of government spending and increasing federal deficit levels.

2009 On June 25, pop star Michael Jackson is found dead of an apparent prescription drug overdose. His passing ignites worldwide mourning and an outpouring of grief from hundreds of millions of fans, despite the singer's legal and personal troubles through the 1990s and the first decade of the 2000s.

2009 On October 31, jobless claims break the 10 percent barrier for the first time since the Great Recession began.

2009 With the situation in Iraq less dire and attacks by the Afghan Taliban on the rise, President Barack Obama announces a surge of thirty thousand more troops in Afghanistan.

BOWLING, BEATNIKS, AND BELL-BOTTOMS

Pop Culture of 20th- and 21st-Century America

1920s
The Roaring Twenties

Popular histories of the 1920s are filled with dramatic stories of this vibrant decade. According to legend, bold bootleggers made fortunes off the thirsty habits of a nation rebelling against the prohibition against alcohol. High-rolling stock market speculators rode an optimistic wave in American business when money seemed to come easily to those who already had it. Women shortened their hair and hemlines to dance the Charleston in smoke-filled speakeasies (illegal bars). These stories of easy money, frivolous excesses, and general naughtiness carried a kernel of truth and gave the decade such nicknames as "The Jazz Age," "The Lawless Decade," and "The Era of Wonderful Nonsense." To be sure, "The Roaring Twenties" was truly one of the more interesting decades in an interesting century.

Business growth in America fueled the optimistic mood of the time. Before World War I (1914–18), American trade with the rest of the world had been limited. During the war, the United States geared up its economy to supply its allies in Europe with solid American steel, agricultural goods, and all sorts of raw materials. With federal funding, the automobile, aircraft, and radio industries developed significantly, making America one of the most technologically advanced countries in the world. Rather than harming American business with a dramatic drop in orders, the end of the war left America in a dominant position in world trade, a position it would nurture for years to come. Presidents Warren G. Harding (1865–1923)

1920s At a Glance

WHAT WE SAID:

Blind date: This type of date was between two people who had never met before and usually had been arranged by mutual friends.

Cat's meow or Bee's knees: Some of the most popular slang expressions of the 1920s, these terms referred to a cute or great person or thing. "She's the cat's meow" means, "She's cute."

"For crying out loud!": A phrase used to express frustration or anger.

Giggle water: Even though Prohibition was vigorously enforced during the decade, alcohol was available. Flappers called it giggle water, while men preferred the more macho name "hooch."

"Go fly a kite!": "Get away from me."

Hick: Even though the word hick had been used for centuries to refer to a rural person, the word became very popular in the 1920s as more people moved to urban areas and rejected rural lifestyles. No hip flapper or sheik would want to be associated with a "hick from the sticks" (a naive person from the country).

"Hot diggity dog!": An expression of happiness or of haste.

It: Sex appeal was flaunted in the 1920s; to have sex appeal was to have "It." Clara Bow had "It"; she was even dubbed the "It Girl." Rudolph Valentino had "It," too.

Lounge lizard: Flappers, young women in the 1920s, had a language all their own. One of many terms they created was lounge lizard, a phrase used to mean a ladies' man. The term has been used in almost every following decade.

Park: As more people bought cars, they thought of more ways to use them. One favorite pastime of young lovers was to park, or to stop their car in a secluded area to kiss each other.

Rumrunner: Smuggler of alcohol into the United States. The demand for alcohol during Prohibition offered an opportunity for rumrunners to earn huge profits.

Speakeasy: Illegal bar. Prohibition did not stop people's thirst for alcohol; it forced the start-up of speakeasies.

Swanky: A term used to describe something that is high class, quality, cool.

Upchuck: Vomit.

WHAT WE READ:

The Man of the Forest: Started as a serial in *Country Gentleman* magazine in 1917, Zane Grey's Western became a best-seller in 1920.

The Age of Innocence **(1920):** Edith Wharton's novel about upper-class New York society provides readers with an insider's view of the confines of that group's strict social rules.

The Sheik **(1920):** Edith M. Hull's romantic novel about a sheik who abducts and later falls in love

and Calvin Coolidge (1872–1933) were pro-business. Herbert Hoover (1874–1964), the secretary of commerce under Coolidge, ran for—and won—the presidency in 1928 as a champion of business, especially business related to the development of aviation and radio.

This frivolity and merriment were not universally available, however. Some citizens, particularly those living in rural America, were largely with an English girl. The story became a movie that made Rudolph Valentino a popular romantic hero.

***The Outline of History* (1920):** H. G. Wells' nonfiction book that traces human history and attempts to show that education is the savior of society, not revolution.

***Main Street* (1921):** Sinclair Lewis's first major novel. *Main Street* satirizes life in the American Middle West, criticizing Americans' frivolous purchasing habits and desires to conform.

***Black Oxen* (1923):** Gertrude Atherton's novel about female sexuality.

***Etiquette* (1923):** Emily Post's nonfiction manual that describes proper behavior for many traditional occasions and social situations.

***When We Were Very Young* (1925):** A. A. Milne's children's book about Winnie-the-Pooh and his friends became a best-seller in the United States.

***Gentlemen Prefer Blondes* (1926):** Anita Loos' comic novel about a young blonde flapper who charms men into giving her expensive gifts.

***The Plutocrat* (1927):** Booth Tarkington's novel about the adventures of a wealthy razor blade "king."

***All Quiet on the Western Front* (1929):** A novel by German writer Erich Maria Remarque that fictionalizes his experiences during World War I.

WHAT WE WATCHED:

***Pollyanna* (1920):** This silent film stars twenty-eight-year-old Mary Pickford as a young orphaned girl who moves to New England to live with her grumpy spinster aunt. Pollyanna finds joy in every activity as she plays her "glad game" and eventually transforms the attitudes of her aunt and the entire community. Based on a novel by Eleanor H. Porter, the film has been remade several times for cinema and television.

***The Mark of Zorro* (1920):** A silent film, starring Douglas Fairbanks as Zorro, about the oppression of the Spanish government in colonial California and how the masked Zorro heroically and humorously protects common people. Zorro has proven to be a favorite movie hero, and his story has been remade into several different movies over the years.

***The Three Musketeers* (1921):** Douglas Fairbanks stars as the young Gascon d'Artagnan, who travels to Paris to become one of the French king's musketeers in this silent film. He is apprenticed by three of the king's best musketeers and soon becomes involved in their effort to save France from the evil Cardinal Richelieu. The film has been remade for cinema and television more than thirty times.

***Orphans of the Storm* (1921):** Lillian and Dorothy Gish star in this silent film directed by D. W. Griffith about two girls (one an orphan) raised as sisters who travel to Paris and become separated as the French Revolution erupts and overthrows the aristocracy.

excluded from enjoying the benefits of the recent economic expansion. Business success was most readily available to urban, upper-middle-class Americans. Even though the economic indexes rose every year during the decade and politicians pronounced the end of poverty, most Americans lived a very different life from the "shebas" and "sheiks" (fashionable young women and men) who spent money without care and drank like

1920s At a Glance (continued)

***The Ten Commandments* (1923):** Starring Richard Dix and Rod LaRoque and directed by Cecil B. DeMille, this silent film tells the ancient story of Moses leading the Jews from Egypt and receiving the tablets and, in a second part, illustrates the benefits of the commandments in a story about two brothers fighting over the love of one woman in modern day San Francisco. DeMille remade this movie again in 1956.

***The Pilgrim* (1923):** A short comedic silent film starring Charlie Chaplin who plays an escaped prisoner who dresses as a preacher and becomes the minister for a small town.

***The Phantom of the Opera* (1925):** Promoted as the "Greatest Horror Film of Modern Cinema," this silent film stars Lon Chaney as the disfigured "phantom" who haunts a Paris opera house and tries to advance the career of his beloved Christine. Gaston Leroux's novel has been retold in eleven different movies and in the theater.

***Ben-Hur* (1925):** With a cast of 125,000 (an unprecedented number), this silent film offered viewers a stunning depiction of the conflict between a Roman officer, Messala (played by Francis X. Bushman), and his former childhood friend, the conquered Israelite, Judah Ben-Hur (played by Ramon Novarro). The film was remade in 1959 with great success.

***The Son of the Sheik* (1926):** Movie star Rudolph Valentino's last film, and some say his best. The silent film depicts the story of the young son of a sheik falling in love with a dancing girl.

***The Jazz Singer* (1927):** Starring Al Jolson, this was the first "talkie" film. Jolson plays a young man who gives up his dream of becoming a Broadway singer to replace his father as cantor at a synagogue after his father's death.

First televised news broadcast (1928): This event featured the Democratic nomination of Al Smith for president and aired on WGY in Schenectady, New York.

***Steamboat Willie* (1929):** Produced by Walt Disney, this was the first animated film with synchronized sound and the first film to feature the now-beloved character, Mickey Mouse.

WHAT WE LISTENED TO:

First radio sports broadcast (1921): The boxing match between Johnny Ray and Johnny Dundee aired over KDKA in Pittsburgh, Pennsylvania.

First World Series broadcast (1921): The fall classic between the New York Yankees and the New York Giants was broadcast on WJZ in Newark, New Jersey.

First radio broadcast of a full-length play (1922): WGY in Schenectady, New York, broadcast *The Wolf,* a two-and-a-half-hour play by Eugene Walter.

First football game broadcast (1922): The game between Princeton and the University of

---

fish. At the beginning of the decade, the census recorded the total population at 105,273,049; by the end of the decade, the number had risen to 122,288,177. Along with the population, big business grew at a dizzying pace, nearly 7 percent each year between 1922 and 1927. Jobs in the increasingly crowded cities abounded. But workers in rural areas suffered; farmers actually lost business, with four million of them quitting

Chicago aired over WEAF in New York using long distance telephone lines from Chicago.

First presidential political convention broadcasts (1924): The conventions that led to the nominations of Republican Calvin Coolidge and Democrat John W. Davis were the first of their kind to air on radio.

WSM Barn Dance: Later renamed the *Grand Ole Opry,* this favorite began broadcasting from Nashville, Tennessee, in 1925.

Sam 'n' Henry: Freeman Gosden and Charles Correll, two white actors, created this "colored comedy" about two black men from Alabama who moved to Chicago in search of their fortunes. It first aired on WGN in Chicago, Illinois, in 1926. *Sam 'n' Henry* was later renamed *Amos 'n' Andy;* in 1929, it became the first comedy series in history to be broadcast nationwide when it aired over the NBC network.

Car radios: Listening to music and other programming in one's automobile became possible in 1927.

Rose Bowl: Coverage of the classic, annual football game—this time between Stanford and Alabama—was the first coast-to-coast broadcast in 1927.

WHO WE KNEW:

Charles Atlas (1894–1972): Dubbed "America's Most Perfectly Developed Man" in a body-building contest held at Madison Square Garden in 1922.

Al Capone (1899–1947): Nicknamed "Scarface Al," he became a wealthy, powerful bootlegger in Chicago after the leader of the Five Points Gang, Johnny Torrio, became permanently disabled in 1925. Although there were other gangs running illegal liquor rackets, Capone led the most successful and became the most notorious criminal of the time.

Coco (Gabrielle) Chanel (1883–1971): A French fashion designer who provided a personal example to women around the world of the "new woman": independent, business-savvy, and free. Her designs and fragrances continue to be fashionable.

Clarence Darrow (1857–1938): A powerful and eloquent defense lawyer who represented John T. Scopes in the highly publicized Scopes "Monkey" Trial of 1925. Although he technically lost the trial about teaching evolution in Tennessee to the prosecution, later rulings about evolution indicate that the eloquent Darrow had swayed public opinion in his favor. He also became known as a defender of civil rights from his representation of the Sweets family in 1925–26 for their efforts to defend themselves against a white mob that tried to drive them off their own property in a white neighborhood in Detroit, Michigan.

Jack Dempsey (1895–1983): A heavyweight boxing champion who symbolized the 1920s pursuit of success by winning the first million-dollar boxing prize and four more throughout the decade.

to move to the city during the 1920s. For the first time in American history, more people lived in urban areas than in rural areas. Technology was transforming the lives of those living in cities, with public utilities providing electricity, natural gas, and running water. Rural areas were left out of these advances, however; only 10 percent of American farms had electricity and only 33 percent had running water by the end of the

1920s At a Glance (continued)

Harry Houdini (1874–1926): A magician well known in the 1920s for his elaborate tricks and his crusade to denounce believers in the occult. In 1926, he successfully completed his most dangerous trick when he escaped after ninety minutes from a submerged coffin. He died later that year from complications of appendicitis.

Hans von Kaltenborn (1878–1965): Became the first radio news commentator in 1922 when his analysis of a coal strike was broadcast. His comments were regularly broadcast nationally on the Columbia Broadcasting System (CBS) in the 1930s.

Charles Lindbergh (1902–1974): An aviator who captivated the world with his solo cross-Atlantic flight in 1927. He flew his *Spirit of St. Louis* monoplane 33.5 hours from New York to Paris.

Maud Wood Park (1871–1955): First president of the League of Women Voters, which was formed in 1920 to educate new voters.

Babe Ruth (1894–1948): A home-run hitter who thrilled crowds in his games with the New York Yankees, making baseball a tremendously profitable venture. When he hit a home run on the opening day of Yankee Stadium in 1923, the place was dubbed "The House That Ruth Built."

David C. Stephenson (1891–1966): Ku Klux Klan leader convicted of second-degree murder in the 1920s. Upon his conviction, evidence of corruption in the Klan was publicized. The group had reformed after World War I to guard against not only blacks but also Jews, Catholics, socialists, and communists. In the 1920s, the group hired a public relations firm to recruit members and by 1925, membership swelled to four million and had elected several members to political positions in Texas, Oklahoma, Indiana, Oregon, and Maine.

Billy Sunday (1862–1935): The most well-known evangelist in the country since 1917. He found his quest for a "totally dry America" difficult as the decade wore on and Americans began questioning the Eighteenth Amendment and its supporters.

Walter Winchell (1897–1972): The most well-known "gossip" columnist and perhaps the first. His columns and radio broadcasts were read or listened to by between twenty-five and fifty million people at the height of his popularity during this decade.

decade. New paved roads between cities left small towns isolated from the advances of the decade and effectively killed many of them.

In addition, as jobs in factories demanded new skills, colleges opened in urban areas. But rural people were cut off from such educational opportunities. To make matters worse, 23 percent of black citizens, most of whom lived in the rural South, were illiterate in 1920. But even with these inequalities, the average person did lead a healthier life, as shown by the dramatic decline in infant deaths and incidences of epidemic disease.

There were several aspects of popular culture that almost everyone could enjoy. Jazz, a musical form created by black musicians, swept the nation and eventually the world. The boom in radio technology and broadcasting—from no radios produced in the United States in 1921 to more than four million in 1929, with more than ten million households owning a radio—brought jazz music into homes across the nation. Although radio broadcasts and recording studios favored white jazz musicians at first, especially "Jazz King" Paul Whiteman (1890–1967) and George Gershwin (1898–1937), African American musicians such as Jelly Roll Morton (1890–1941), Duke Ellington (1899–1974), and Louis Armstrong (1901–1971) soon became truly successful, playing to audiences of all races.

The movie industry, one of the wealthiest components of the economy in the decade, hired writers, composers, designers, and painters for unprecedented sums to create "talkies" that anyone could see and hear on the big screen for a handful of change. Kodak introduced the first color motion pictures in 1928. Movie attendance rose from fifty-seven million weekly in 1927 to ninety-five million weekly by 1929. Broadway musicals soon were made into elaborate movie spectaculars that toured the country.

Magazines and newspapers of the time carried the writings of syndicated columnists. Mass circulation ensured that magazines and newspapers could pay writers decent sums for their work. More and more Americans were reading the same stories and news. Readers thrilled to stories by such writers as Sinclair Lewis (1885–1951), F. Scott Fitzgerald (1896–1940), and Willa Cather (1873–1947), who became some of the most respected American writers of all time. The Western novels of Zane Grey (1875–1939) were top sellers. Raymond Chandler (1888–1959) and Dashiell Hammett (1894–1961) pioneered the American "hard-boiled" (tough-guy) detective story with stories for the *Black Mask* and other pulp magazines.

As F. Scott Fitzgerald wrote in his essay "Echoes of the Jazz Age," "It was an age of miracles." The 1920s produced more enduring figures than any other since, more people who changed their fields and captured the interest and imagination of the nation than in any other time in American history. Along with advances in medicine, science, and social work, the decade nurtured talents in the arts, literature, and sports. Charles A. Lindbergh (1902–1974) flew across the Atlantic in thirty-three and a half hours. Eugene O'Neill (1888–1953) became one of America's greatest playwrights, winning a Pulitzer Prize in 1920,

1922, and 1928. Babe Ruth (1895–1948) won the hearts of baseball fans when he hit his "Ruthian" blasts out of the park and led the New York Yankees to win their first World Series in 1923. The sheer number of advances during the era is a testament to the energy of the 1920s, a time when most Americans thought each day would be better than the last.

The decade of such optimism was halted abruptly by Black Tuesday, the biggest stock market crash in American history, which occurred on October 29, 1929. Less than a month after the crash, unemployment had risen from 700,000 to 3.1 million. News stories remained optimistic about the future and movie theaters played upbeat shows to boost people's spirits, but the country would not recover for nearly another decade as the Great Depression (1929–41) took hold.

1920s

Commerce

At the beginning of the decade, American business was adjusting to its new role in the world economy after the end of World War I (1914–18). During the war, America had supplied the Allied European participants with food, equipment, money, and eventually, troops. The war had created an economic boom in America like no other before it. The war also linked America with other nations through trade; American business grew on the strength of equipment and materials orders from other countries.

The American government provided generous financial support to American businesses during the war, which spurred the growth of technologically advanced manufacturing throughout the country. Those industries most helped were automobile, aircraft, and radio manufacturers. These industries had existed before the war, but federal spending allowed them to grow into massive operations that employed thousands of people. The large number of employees could quickly produce large quantities of products. In the 1920s, massive factories were established around the country. Rural people were transplanted into new urban areas for the relatively lucrative work.

With ready cash on hand, people began buying products like never before. Chain stores popped up in neighborhoods; movie theaters were frequented; and the demand for automobiles seemed endless. Jeeps were one item that caught the interest of Americans. The hardy vehicles once used for the war had a variety of uses at home.

In each year of the decade, the economic indexes grew higher and higher, fueling people's optimism and spending habits. Credit became a popular purchasing method. A variety of new products emerged to entice people to buy more. Two particularly useful items were Tupperware and Saran Wrap. These plastic inventions revolutionized the storage of leftovers in the kitchen.

But not everyone enjoyed the booming economy. Farmers who had prospered during the war struggled in this decade and more than four million had to quit and find other work. Railroad employees felt unfairly treated but had to abandon a strike in 1922 without gaining much. Those living in the South and the Midwest, areas that relied mainly on agriculture, struggled as those living in other areas profited. Residents of the "industrial belt" of the Northeast and the Upper Midwest and the trading and movie mecca of the West Coast benefited much more. The uneven distribution of wealth around the country and the skyrocketing stock market made the stock market crash of 1929 all the more devastating.

Advertising

Advertising performs two important jobs. It informs consumers what products and services are available, and it tries to persuade them to make choices about what to buy. Advertising has been around ever since somebody had something to sell, but in the late 1800s, it became a part of everyday life. At the beginning of the twenty-first century, advertising is everywhere. From **coffee** (see entry under 1990s—The Way We Lived in volume 5) cups to the World Wide Web, from clothing to public garbage cans, advertising appears wherever there is a space to put a logo or a slogan.

Modern advertising began in the 1920s, the decade that saw the rise of the New York City advertising agencies on Madison Avenue. Mass production meant that more people could afford things like cars, radios, and **refrigerators** (see entry under 1910s—The Way We Lived in volume 1). Improved transport also meant that fewer goods and services were supplied locally. In 1920, there were eight million passenger cars on American roads; by the end of the decade, the number was over twenty-three million. Because of such changes in American culture, advertising campaigns became standardized across the United States. An advertisement for a Ford car in California was exactly the same as an ad in Florida and New Hampshire.

Before the 1920s, most advertising was in the form of painted signs, printed cards in **cigarette** (see entry under 1920s—Commerce in volume 2) packets, and small-scale posters or newspaper advertisements. Better printing and photography soon had a dramatic effect. The first annual exhibition of advertising photography was held in New York in 1921. Large poster billboards soon replaced advertisements painted on the sides of buildings. The most famous novel of the period, *The Great Gatsby* (1925) by F. Scott Fitzgerald (1896–1940), even uses a fading advertisement billboard to comment on American society at the time. Soon, glossy photographic ads filled American magazines. The pictures in the ads were often just as beautiful as those accompanying the articles. **Radio** (see entry under 1920s—TV and Radio in volume 2) also played a major role in the growth of advertising. The first radio advertisement was broadcast in 1922. By the 1930s, radio advertising reached almost every American home.

Market research was more or less invented in the 1920s when advertisers began to work out what kinds of people read certain magazines or newspapers. Even as far back as 1923, Claud Hopkins (1866–1922), president of the Lord & Thomas agency in New York, could boast: "The time has come when advertising in some hands has reached the status of a science." In the twenty-first century, film trailers match the style of the main feature; upmarket clothing is advertised in glossy magazines. Computers and the **Internet** (see entry under 1990s—The Way We Lived in volume 5) have made advertising still more personal. Online retailers can keep track of the likes and dislikes of individual consumers and provide advertising just for them.

Despite the increased sophistication of advertising, advertisers do face certain problems. As companies began to advertise and sell their

An early twentieth-century advertisement for Kodak cameras. © BETTMANN/CORBIS.

products all over the world, they learned that they had to choose the names of their products very carefully. Advertisers must avoid using words that might be offensive in a country where the product is sold. For example, there is a soft drink in Italy called Pshitt and a toilet paper in Sweden called Krapp's. Neither of these products would sell well in America. Another downfall of advertising is its high cost. In 1865, American companies spent a total of $50 million on advertising. Less than a century later, in 1956, **General Motors** (see entry under 1900s— The Way We Lived in volume 1) alone spent more than $162 million. In 1997, the chemical company Unilever spent around $2 billion advertising its products worldwide. Do companies get their money's worth from advertising? Many consumers have grown so used to seeing advertising that they no longer pay attention to it. Advertisers have to resort to more creative ways of calling attention to their products.

An example of a new kind of advertising can be found on **television** (see entry under 1940s—TV and Radio in volume 3). Since television became common in the 1950s, it has been crucial to advertisers of all kinds of products. The idea that different groups of people watch different television shows led to advertising aimed at smaller and smaller groups. In the 1990s, TV networks began to use certain shows to deliver groups of consumers to the advertisers. For example, advertising aired during *Dawson's Creek* was aimed at the show's mostly teen audience, whereas ***Ally McBeal*** (see entry under 1990s—TV and Radio in volume 5) provided advertisers with an audience of young professional women. One problem with TV advertising is that viewers avoid commercials by switching channels or leaving the room. Electricity suppliers report surges in demand as viewers make hot drinks and snacks during commercial breaks in popular shows. Advertisers have tried to avoid this by making their commercials unavoidable. Sponsoring a program allows advertisers to force viewers to see their name—as in many branded sporting events—and placing products within an actual program became a common practice in the late 1990s. This product placement was especially important for advertisers, given viewers' penchant for recording programs and, therefore, being able to skip commercials altogether.

In the twenty-first century, advertising provides many of society's most familiar images and is discussed alongside film as a key popular art form of the last century. It has also become more persuasive than ever before. By putting their logo on every piece of clothing they sell, companies like **Nike** (see entry under 1960s—Commerce in volume 4) persuade customers to advertise the company's products at their own expense. Most people claim that advertising does not affect their buying decisions, but the evidence tells a different story.

Chris Routledge

For More Information

Dunn, John. *Advertising.* San Diego: Lucent Books, 1997.

Fox, Stephen. *Mirror Makers: A History of American Advertising and Its Creators.* New York: Morrow, 1984.

Gay, Kathlyn. *Caution! This May Be an Advertisement: A Teen Guide to Advertising.* New York: Franklin Watts, 1992.

Klein, Naomi. *No Logo.* New York: HarperCollins, 2000.

Mierau, Christina. *Accept No Substitutes!: The History of American Advertising.* Minneapolis: Lerner, 2000.

Robinson, Jeffrey. *The Manipulators: A Conspiracy to Make Us Buy.* London: Simon and Schuster, 1998.

Sivulka, Juliann. *Soap, Sex, and Cigarettes: A Cultural History of American Advertising.* 2nd ed. Belmont, CA: Wadsworth, 2011.

Sobieszek, Robert A. *The Art of Persuasion: A History of Advertising Photography.* New York: Harry N. Abrams, 1988.

Tungate, Mark. *Adland: A Global History of Advertising.* Philadelphia: Kogan Page, 2007.

Band-Aid

Like **Kleenex** (see entry under 1920s—Commerce in volume 2) tissues and **Xerox copiers** (see entry under 1960s—Commerce in volume 4), Band-Aid bandages have come to be the common name for the product, in this case an antiseptically sealed adhesive bandage designed for minor cuts and scrapes. The Band-Aid is composed of a pad that is placed over the wound, topped by adhesive "wings" that attach the bandage to the skin. The Band-Aid brand was introduced in 1921 by the Johnson & Johnson Company, which had been making surgical dressings since its incorporation in 1887. The company was founded by Robert Wood Johnson (1893–1968) and his brothers, James and Edward. Their company manufactured first-aid products that supported antiseptic methods then being widely adopted in American medicine.

Earle Dickson (1892–1961), a cotton buyer for Johnson & Johnson, developed the Band-Aid while trying to make a convenient, easy-to-apply bandage for his wife, Josephine, who was prone to many minor cuts and burns in the family kitchen. He placed squares of cotton gauze at intervals on an adhesive strip and covered them with crinoline. When she needed a bandage, his wife just cut as much of the strip as needed to dress a wound. Johnson & Johnson adapted Dickson's idea and began manufacturing the product, eventually rewarding him with a vice presidency within the company.

Made by hand, the first Band-Aids were three inches wide and eighteen inches long. By 1924, they were being machine-made, and have long been sold as individually wrapped bandages in a variety of sizes and shapes. Band-Aid Plastic Strips were introduced in 1951; sheer vinyl versions, in 1958. Sport Strip adhesive bandages made their appearance in 1994. Three years later, Johnson & Johnson unveiled the Band-Aid Antibiotic Adhesive Bandage, the first ever to have specially formulated ointment on the pad. By 2001, more than a hundred billion Band-Aids had been manufactured.

Edward Moran

For More Information

"Band-Aid Brand Adhesive Bandages." http://www.bandaid.com (accessed June 24, 2011).

Foster, Lawrence G. *A Company That Cares: One Hundred Year Illustrated History of Johnson & Johnson.* New Brunswick, NJ: Johnson & Johnson, 1986.

Betty Crocker

One of the most famous U.S. food-product brands, Betty Crocker, is symbolized by the smiling face of a young homemaker. Her picture, together with a trademarked logo of a red spoon, appears on more than two hundred items manufactured by General Mills, ranging from Hamburger Helper to cake mixes, dessert products, and snacks. The Betty Crocker brand name accounts for $1.5 billion in sales annually, nearly one-third of all General Mills sales.

The Betty Crocker name originated in 1921 when Washburn Crosby Company, an earlier name for General Mills, created the image as a way of personalizing its products and services. It was chosen by advertising manager James A. Quint, who selected "Betty" because it was considered a friendly nickname and "Crocker" as a tribute to William Crocker (1876–1950), a retired General Mills

BETTY CROCKER MAKEOVER

The image of Betty Crocker has changed over the years to reflect changing styles. The 1996 portrait was created from seventy-five computer-fed photos of real women. © AP IMAGES.

1936   1955   1965   1968

1972   1980   1986   1996

executive. The Betty Crocker brand first appeared on a food product in 1947, when General Mills introduced her Ginger Cake Mix, now known as Gingerbread Cake and Cookie Mix. By the 1990s, her face and name was appearing on dessert-like products like Betty Crocker Cinnamon Streusel and cereal products like Dutch Apple cereals. The name has also been licensed for a line of small appliances, cooking utensils, and kitchen clocks.

In the nine decades since her creation, the image of Betty Crocker has been altered to suit changing styles, but "Betty" has remained a trusted figure to several generations of families. Although she is not a real person, she has received millions of letters and phone calls and now appears on General Mills Web sites dispensing information about cooking and nutrition to a new generation of computer-savvy consumers. Cooks can even download a "Betty Crocker Kitchen Assistant" application that offers recipes, hints, and interactive help with meal preparation. Betty Crocker is listed as the author of several cookbooks, including *Betty Crocker's Picture Cook Book,* first published in 1950 and reprinted multiple times since then.

Edward Moran

For More Information

General Mills. *BettyCrocker.com.* http://www.bettycrocker.com (accessed June 24, 2011).

Marks, Susan. *Finding Betty Crocker: The Secret Story of America's First Lady of Food.* New York: Simon & Schuster, 2005.

Shapiro, Laura. "Betty Goes Back to the Future." *Newsweek* (October 19, 1998).

Burma-Shave

The advertising campaign for Burma-Shave, a brushless shaving cream, is perhaps the most unique **advertising** (see entry under 1920s—Commerce in volume 2) campaign in history. There was nothing like it before and has been nothing like it since. The campaign began in the mid-1920s and lasted until the early 1960s, although its heyday was the 1930s and 1940s. Burma-Shave's rhyming signs popularized the use of a jingle to sell a product. Its roadside signs were a favorite feature of travel for a generation of Americans.

The Burma-Vita Company came up with the idea of road-sign advertising, but the signs were not like the billboards seen today. Before freeways came into being, driving from one place to another meant using rural roads and driving slower. The Burma-Vita Company paid farmers to place signs on their property. The unique thing about this was how they did it. A rhyming jingle was printed on a series of six signs, about 100 feet apart. Drivers had to read each sign to learn the jingle. One example, taken from *The Verse by the Side of the Road,* was: "Take a tip / For your trip / No wet brush / To soak / Your grip / Burma-Shave." The signs turned the nearly bankrupt Burma-Vita into a company with $3 million in annual sales.

The signs began appearing in Minnesota, where the company was located. By the time the campaign ended, there were signs in forty-five states. There was even a newsletter for the farmers who had signs on their property, called *Burma Shavings.* The jingles used were sometimes humorous, sometimes political, and some even pitched road safety. As the U.S. interstate road system was put into place, fewer people drove on the rural roads where the signs were located. Traffic moved too fast on the

Workers stand in a Burma-Shave warehouse amid the many clever advertising signs that were seen on America's roads for several decades. © B. ANTHONY STEWART AND JACK E. FLETCHER/NATIONAL GEOGRAPHIC SOCIETY/CORBIS.

new interstate highways and freeways for car occupants to be able to read the signs as before. The Philip Morris Company bought Burma-Vita and stopped using the signs in 1963. Company operations ceased in 1967.

Jill Gregg Clever

For More Information

"Burma-Shave in the Fifties." *The Fifties Web.* http://www.fiftiesweb.com/burma.htm (accessed June 24, 2011).

Larson, Michael, and Jill Larson Sundberg. *Sunday Drives: Nostalgic Reminiscing with the Best of Burma-Shave.* New York: iUniverse, 2006.

Rowsone, Frank, Jr. *The Verse by the Side of the Road: The Story of the Burma-Shave Signs and Jingles.* Brattleboro, VT: Stephen Greene Press, 1965.

Starr, Tara, and Edward Hayman. *Signs & Wonders.* New York: Doubleday, 1998.

Vossler, Bill. *Burma-Shave: The Rhymes, the Signs, the Times.* St. Cloud, MN: North Star Press, 1997.

Cigarettes

On his famous voyage in 1492, Christopher Columbus (1451–1506) noticed that the Arawak people of the Caribbean enjoyed smoking the rolled-up leaves of a local plant. Since Columbus took the first tobacco seeds back to Europe, the use of tobacco has spread all over the world. Tobacco has played a visible and distinctive role in societies everywhere. Of all the different forms of tobacco, by far the most popular is the cigarette—the universally recognizable little paper cylinder filled with shredded tobacco, usually with added chemicals.

For centuries considered both glamorous and wicked, cigarette smoking has had a powerful appeal for people (especially adolescents) who wish to appear tough and rugged or cool and sophisticated.

"Dancing cigarettes" a 1950s TV ad from Old Gold Cigarettes. © PICTORIAL PRESS LTD./ ALAMY.

The tobacco companies that portray cigarettes as a mechanism for addressing these emotional insecurities use this sentiment in their advertisements to encourage people to start smoking. The addictive nature of the nicotine found in tobacco ensures that people will keep smoking.

In America, smoking has historically been considered an unhealthy and immoral habit. It is perhaps these very judgments that make cigarettes so attractive to those who wish to rebel. One of the most striking instances of this was in 1929. At the time, smoking was considered "unfeminine" and was socially frowned upon. But when women suffragettes marched in New York's Easter Day parade smoking cigarettes as their "torches of liberty" to show their commitment to equal rights for women, they made smoking fashionable. It did not matter that the idea for the women to smoke in the parade had been the brainchild of Edward Bernays (1891–1995), a tobacco-industry publicity man; the parade had created a link between smoking and women's rights. Within weeks after the parade, more and more women began to smoke.

Cigarette smoking increased in the United States during and after World War I (1914–18). For soldiers in the trenches, cigarettes were a small luxury from home and a way to ease the tensions of battle. In the 1920s, the young generation who had survived the war celebrated with a reckless lifestyle that included cigarettes. In the 1940s, another world war and another generation of dashing soldiers increased the glamour attached to smoking. On the battlefield and in dozens of war movies, lieutenants growled to their exhausted troops, "Smoke 'em if you got 'em." Soldiers and civilians alike lit up.

In the 1950s, the age-old warning that smoking was a "nasty habit" began to get scientific support. Researchers found a link between cigarette smoking and lung cancer. Most manufacturers began to put filters on their cigarettes to absorb some of the dangerous chemicals. In 1964, the surgeon general of the United States made an official statement that cigarettes cause cancer and other respiratory ailments. The next year, the first warnings appeared on cigarette packs, as tobacco companies were forced by law to inform buyers of the danger.

However, the number of smokers continued to increase, not only because smokers felt the habit was "cool." The nicotine in cigarettes causes the brain to release a chemical called dopamine that gives the smoker a feeling of pleasure. Nicotine is a highly addictive drug, and most smokers become addicted quickly, making it very hard for them to quit smoking. The greatest number of Americans smoked during the period between 1974 and 1977. In 1976, antismoking advocates organized a national effort called the "Great American Smokeout" to encourage smokers to quit. The Smokeout became an annual event. Between 1976 and 1997, forty-eight million smokers quit the habit, leaving another forty-eight million still smoking. Of those, thirty-four million say they want to quit, according to Neville Lee in the November 24, 1997, issue of *U.S. News & World Report*. Many aids have been developed to help smokers break their addiction to smoking, from hypnosis and support groups to nicotine chewing-gum and skin patches.

Since the 1970s, the antismoking policy movement has become almost as powerful a social force as smoking ever was. As more is known about the negative health effects of smoking, more and more smokers have quit, and more people have decided not to start smoking in the first place. For many nonsmokers, it is not enough to stop smoking themselves. They also do not wish to be around the smoke created by those who do smoke. Tobacco smoke contains dangerous chemicals like nicotine, carbon dioxide, carbon monoxide, and ammonia. Researchers have discovered that breathing "second-hand" smoke (the smoke that is exhaled by cigarette smokers) can be almost as dangerous as smoking cigarettes oneself.

Antismoking activists have worked to limit where smokers can light up. Once there were smoking sections on airplanes, buses, and movie theaters, and people could freely smoke cigarettes almost anywhere. By the 1990s, smoking was largely forbidden in most public places. A new sort of outcast smokers' culture has grown up in the doorways of office buildings and other public places, where smokers huddle together in all kinds of weather to have their cigarettes.

Cigarettes have always figured prominently in the popular culture media. In films, books, and songs, heroes and heroines light up to express all kinds of emotions, from cool unconcern to intense worry and from angry hatred to passionate love. The desire for a cigarette after sex has become a universal symbol of satisfaction that even shows up in cartoons like *The Simpsons* (see entry under 1980s—TV and Radio in volume 5). In films, from Lauren Bacall's sultry inhale in *To Have and Have Not* (1944), to Leonardo DiCaprio's tough-sensitive cigarette handling in *Romeo and Juliet* (1996), cigarette smoking has meant defiance, romance, and sex appeal. In 1997, singer k. d. lang (1961–) released an album entitled *Drag*, which is a collection of pop songs written over several decades about smoking cigarettes. A nonsmoker herself, lang sees cigarettes as a symbol of all types of self-destructive cravings, whether for love, drugs, or tobacco.

Even cigarette advertisements have become a part of popular culture. Figures like Joe Camel and the **Marlboro Man** (see entry under 1920s—Commerce in volume 2) are as recognizable to the public as characters on television or in films. Tobacco companies realize the value of keeping their products in the public eye. Between 1967 and 1984, as the public was learning about the dangers of smoking, tobacco companies increased their advertising 400 percent. When it was proven the cigarette makers were using advertising strategies such as Joe Camel to directly market to children, medical groups and Congress put pressure on tobacco companies to stop the practice. Joe Camel, for example, was withdrawn from public use in 1997. Some smokers, or their surviving spouses, have successfully sued cigarette makers for millions of dollars in damages. In one case, for example, Mayola Williams, the widow of Jesse Williams, was granted almost $80 million in damages. So far, however, these decisions have been decided case by case and no lawsuit blaming tobacco companies for the unhealthful addiction of all the millions of

Americans—as well as the some 440,000 Americans per year who suffer a tobacco-related death—has been successfully argued in court.

Tina Gianoulis

For More Information

Brandt, Allan M. *The Cigarette Century: The Rise, Fall and Deadly Persistence of the Product That Defined America*. New York: Basic Books, 2006.

"Tobacco Related Mortality." Centers for Disease Control and Prevention. http://www.cdc.gov/tobacco/data_statistics/fact_sheets/health_effects/tobacco_related_mortality/#cigs (accessed June 24, 2011).

DeAngelis, Gina. *Cigarettes*. Philadelphia: Chelsea House, 1999.

Harrald, Chris, and Fletcher Watkins. *The Cigarette Book: The History and Culture of Smoking*. New York: Skyhorse, 2010.

Klein, Richard. "The Dark Beauty of the Cigarette." *Harper's Magazine* (Vol. 287, no. 1722, November 1993): pp. 35–37.

Kluger, Richard. *Ashes to Ashes: America's Hundred-Year Cigarette War, the Public Health, and the Unabashed Triumph of Philip Morris*. New York: Knopf, 1996.

Lee, Neville. "Database: The Great American Smokeout." *U.S. News & World Report* (Vol. 123, no. 20, November 24, 1997): p. 12.

Parker-Pope, Tara. *Cigarettes: Anatomy of an Industry from Seed to Smoke*. New York: New Press, 2000.

Sobel, Robert. *They Satisfy: The Cigarette in American Life*. New York: Doubleday, 1978.

Sullum, Jacob. "Smoke Alarm." *Reason* (Vol. 28, no. 1, May 1996): pp. 40–45.

Department Stores

From its beginnings at the end of the nineteenth century to its decline in the 1970s, the department store was the major center for urban American shoppers. A creative sales idea, the department store offered working people attentive service, an elegant place to shop for almost everything they needed, and the chance to buy on credit. Large department stores, usually named for the families that started them, became central fixtures in the downtown areas of their cities. Eventually, they became the foundations of shopping **malls** (see entry under 1950s—Commerce in volume 3) in the **suburbs** (see entry under 1950s—The Way We Lived in volume 3). In the 1970s, large, no-frills discount stores began to compete with the popularity of department stores. By the twenty-first century, many of the distinguished old department stores had gone out of business.

Before large department stores began to develop, shopping had meant waiting for a traveling peddler to drop by with a cart of goods for sale, or going into a small shop and asking the clerk for items kept on shelves behind the counter. In the late 1800s, the development of a national railroad and a more efficient postal system allowed a wider variety of goods to be shipped. Stores began to expand. To increase sales, shop owners began to display goods openly on shelves in the store where customers could look through them. The shop owners hired sales clerks like those who served in upper class shops. Some successful store owners built multistory buildings for their new department stores. Soon these stores were closely identified with their cities, like Rich's of Atlanta, Georgia; Filene's of Boston, Massachusetts; and Gimbel's of New York City. In 1924, Macy's department store in New York was the largest store in the world—and three years later, it began the **Macy's Thanksgiving Day Parade** (see entry under 1920s—Commerce in volume 2).

Department stores have frequently influenced the culture around them. **Mother's Day** (see entry under 1910s—The Way We Lived in volume 1) had been a minor Catholic holiday until it was turned into a major gift-giving (and therefore, shopping) occasion by the owner of Wanamaker's department store in Philadelphia, Pennsylvania. Of course, the primary gift shopping time in the United States is the Christmas season, and department stores have made it their own, beginning with department store Santas, like the one in the film *Miracle on 34th Street*. In 1939, Robert L. May (1905–1976), an advertising writer for Montgomery Ward, wrote ***Rudolph the Red-Nosed Reindeer*** (see entry under 1940s—Print Culture in volume 2) as part of the company's Christmas sales campaign. During the 1940s, another department store owner, Fred Lazarus, persuaded President Franklin Roosevelt (1882–1945) to change Thanksgiving from the last Thursday in November to the fourth Thursday to allow an extra week of shopping before Christmas.

Tina Gianoulis

For More Information

Bragg, Arthur. "Will the Department Store Survive?" *Sales and Marketing Management* (Vol. 136, April 1986): pp. 60–65.

Cohen, Daniel. "Grand Emporiums Peddle Their Wares in a New Market." *Smithsonian* (Vol. 23, no. 12, March 1993): pp. 22–31.

Katz, Donald R. "The Big Store." *Esquire* (Vol. 108, September 1987): pp. 107–17.

Leach, William R. "Transformations in a Culture of Consumption: Women and Department Stores, 1890–1925." *Journal of American History* (Vol. 71, September 1984): pp. 319–43.

Longstreth, Richard W. *The American Department Store Transformed, 1920–1960.* New Haven, CT: Yale University Press, 2010.
Whitaker, Jan. *Service and Style: How the American Department Store Fashioned the Middle Class.* New York: St. Martin's Press, 2006.
Whitaker, Jan. *The World of Department Stores.* New York: Vendome Press, 2011.

Eddie Bauer

Eddie Bauer is an outdoor-oriented retailer of clothing and accessories. Begun in Seattle, Washington, in 1920 by Eddie Bauer (1899–1986) with a $25 investment, the company that bears his name at first sold only recreational and wilderness gear. Perhaps the most famous product of all was the first quilted down parka, invented by Bauer after a night in 1928 when he nearly froze to death. The down parka has become a staple of winter wear in the United States. Other versions are offered today by companies such as The North Face and Old Navy.

Eddie Bauer equipment has been to Mt. Everest, but since the 1970s, when the company was sold, it has focused on "casual lifestyle" items such as cashmere blazers and home furnishings for its affluent adult customer base. In 2001, the company had over six hundred stores around the globe and was creating enormous revenues while competing with the likes of **Gap** (see entry under 1960s—Commerce in volume 4) and Lands' End. Since then, however, the company has struggled. It has sought bankruptcy protection more than once and has closed many stores, in large part due to the economic downturn beginning in 2008.

Karl Rahder

For More Information
"About Eddie Bauer." *Eddie Bauer.* http://www.eddiebauer.com/custserv/custserv.jsp?sectionId=803 (accessed June 24, 2011).
Spector, Robert. *The Legend of Eddie Bauer.* 2nd ed. Seattle: Documentary Media, 2011.

Kleenex

Kleenex is the rare brand whose name has been appropriated by the public as a generic term for the product itself—in this case, facial tissue. Following World War I (1914–18), the Kimberly-Clark paper company was burdened with a huge surplus of a product called Cellucotton, a thin cotton-based tissue that had been used to dress wounds and line gas masks. The company made a thinner version of its product for women to use to remove makeup. Kimberly-Clark named its product Kleenex and introduced it in 1924.

No sooner was Kleenex introduced in the early 1920s as a makeup remover than consumers found new uses for the soft, disposable tissue. Eager to avoid carrying soiled handkerchiefs, men and women used Kleenex to blow their noses—and then simply threw the soiled Kleenex away. In 1927, advertisements began to promote the product for blowing the nose. In 1928, the popular pop-up box that released one tissue at a time was introduced. It was not long before every disposable facial tissue was commonly known as a Kleenex. Kleenex remains the most popular brand of tissues on the market to this day.

Tom Pendergast

For More Information

"Kleenex Brand Story." *Kleenex Brand Tissues.* http://www.kleenex.com/About. aspx (accessed on June 24, 2011).
"Why Did WWI Change the Way We Blow Our Noses?" *Roy Rosenzweig Center for History and New Media.* http://chnm.gmu.edu/sidelights/why-did-wwi-change-the-way-we-blow-our-noses/ (accessed on June 24, 2011).

La-Z-Boy Loungers

The relaxing comfort of reclining chairs is a familiar part of many American homes. Invented by two cousins, Edward M. Knabusch (1900–1988) and Edwin J. Shoemaker (1907–1998), La-Z-Boy recliners were the first and remain the most popular reclining chairs in America. The cousins built their first chairs out of a garage in Monroe, Michigan. In 1929, they introduced the first upholstered recliner to such success that they decided to incorporate their company and to build a shop in a nearby cornfield. To name their creation, the pair held a contest: La-Z-Boy was the winner.

By the 1950s, La-Z-Boy recliners came with the now easily recognizable automatic footrests. By the 1960s, even sofas were made to recline. By the early twenty-first century, La-Z-Boy had become one of the largest furniture producers and retailers in the United States, with over three hundred stand-alone stores. Their chairs and sofas

La-Z-Boy Inc. cofounder Edwin Shoemaker relaxes in his La-Z-Boy recliner. © AP IMAGES.

reclined, rocked, glided, swiveled, lifted, and massaged. They even had heaters, phones, computer hookups, and compartments to keep drinks cold.

Sara Pendergast

For More Information

La-Z-Boy. http://www.la-z-boy.com/ (accessed Jume 26, 2002).

Rodengen, Jeffrey L., and Richard F. Hubbard. *The Legend of La-Z-Boy.* Fort Lauderdale, FL: Write Stuff Enterprises, 2003.

Macy's Thanksgiving Day Parade

Since 1927, Macy's department store—the self-described largest emporium (retail store) of its type in the world—has sponsored a happy American ritual. Each Thanksgiving morning, Macy's subsidizes an elaborate parade. This procession assembles at West 77th Street and Central Park West in Manhattan and begins promptly at 9 AM. Thousands of New Yorkers and tourists brave the cold late-November winds to watch the parade. It moves down Central Park West to

"Have no fear, Underdog is here!" The famous cartoon animal appears in the 1983 Macy's Thanksgiving Day Parade in New York City. © BETTMANN/CORBIS.

Columbus Circle, and then runs along Broadway to Macy's Herald Square, at West 33rd Street.

The parade consists of large, intricately designed floats, marching bands, entertainers, and helium-filled cartoon-creature balloons that are several stories high. The balloon figures include everything from the generic Toy Soldier and Tom the Turkey to characters popular with children, such as Big Bird from **Sesame Street** (see entry under 1970s—TV and Radio in volume 4), **Barney** (see entry under 1990s—TV and Radio in volume 5), Mickey Mouse from **Disney** (see entry under 1920s—Film and Theater in volume 2), Snoopy from the comic strip **Peanuts** (see entry under 1950s—Print Culture in volume 3), and **Dora the Explorer** (see entry under 2000s—TV and Radio in volume 6). The first cartoon character depicted in the parade's large balloons was **Felix the Cat** (see entry under 1910s—Film and Theater in volume 1).

Not only does the Macy's Thanksgiving Day Parade usher in the Christmas holiday season, but it serves as a reminder of the store's history, and its status as a great American emporium.

Rob Edelman

For More Information

Grippo, Robert M. *Macy's: The Store, the Star, the Story.* Garden City Park, NY: Square One, 2009.

Grippo, Robert M., and Christopher Hoskins. *Macy's Thanksgiving Day Parade.* Mount Pleasant, SC: Arcadia, 2004.

"Macy's Thanksgiving Day Parade." *NYCTourist.com.* http://www.nyctourist.com/macys_news.htm (accessed on June 26, 2011)

Marlboro Man

The Marlboro Man is an American icon (symbol). The cowboy figure used to market Marlboro **cigarettes** (see entry under 1920s—Commerce in volume 2) captures the essence of the ideal American man. The Marlboro Man looks tough and weather-beaten like a man who values a hard day's work. The Marlboro Man wears a cowboy hat, rides a horse, and his clothes are often covered in dust.

The Marlboro Man has displayed the distinctive red Marlboro cigarette pack for almost fifty years—on billboards, in store window

A Marlboro Man billboard above Sunset Boulevard in Los Angeles, 1997. © JOHN CHAPPLE/GETTY IMAGES.

displays, and on the pages of magazines and newspapers. Until the government ban on cigarette commercials in 1971, the Marlboro Man could also be seen on **television** (see entry under 1940s—TV and Radio in volume 3), usually accompanied by the rousing musical theme from the Western film *The Magnificent Seven* (1960).

Marlboro cigarettes were not always sold using the image of this macho figure, however. When Marlboro cigarettes were first introduced in the 1920s, they were marketed to women, with the slogan "Mild as May." This approach was successful until World War II (1939–45), when slow sales caused Marlboro packs to be withdrawn from the market. The cigarettes were revived in the 1950s, as the first medical research linking cigarette smoking with cancer began to reach the public. It was thought that Marlboro cigarettes, with their filter, might offer smokers the illusion of a reduced health risk. However, the filter was regarded as effeminate by many men, who made up the bulk of the tobacco market.

The Leo Burnett Company, a Chicago **advertising** (see entry under 1920s—Commerce in volume 2) agency, was given the task of making Marlboro cigarettes appealing to men. The result was the "tattooed man" campaign. It involved a series of print ads showing a man with a tattoo on his hand holding a Marlboro. The man would be one of several "manly" types, such as a policeman, a firefighter, a construction worker—and a cowboy. The agency studied consumer response, and the cowboy figure proved to be the most popular. First appearing in 1954, the cowboy soon replaced all the other men. The image of the rugged Westerner lighting up amidst the great outdoors became a part of American culture. It also helped make Marlboro the best-selling cigarette in America. Controversy dogged the Marlboro Man, however. More than one of the men who appeared in ads as Marlboro Men later contracted cancer. The widow of one Marlboro Man even sued Philip Morris, the company that produces

Marlboro cigarettes, for wrongful death. Despite all the bad publicity, Marlboro remains one of the most recognized brands in the world.

Justin Gustainis

For More Information

Gilman, Sander and Xun Zhou, eds. *A Global History of Smoking.* London: Reaktion Books, 2004.

Lohof, Bruce A. *American Commonplace.* Bowling Green, OH: Popular Press, 1982.

1920s

Fashion

The 1920s were a turning point in the world of fashion. During the decade, fashion became an increasingly important symbol of a person's social status. Advances in technology made Americans' focus on fashion possible. For the first time in history, Americans could hear the same radio broadcasts and watch the same movies anywhere in the country. By 1925, about fifty million people listened to the radio and heard about the latest clothes, automobiles, and home decor. At the movies, people could see these products. Many Americans started buying what they heard about on the radio and saw at the movies. Moreover, newspapers and magazines like *Vanity Fair* and *Vogue* started printing columns and advertisements about fashion. A culture of fashion had begun.

The 1920s were marked by a new concern for style among Americans. The clothes they wore, the cars they drove, and the decorations in their homes gave them a particular social status, even if they were not born into that social position. The most distinctive looks of the decade were of flappers and sheiks. Flappers were generally young women who bobbed their hair (cut it short). They wore short, loose-fitting dresses and enhanced their faces with makeup. Sheiks were young men who slicked back their hair. They wore fashionable camel-hair jackets and loose, flannel pants, and long raccoon coats. No matter what particular clothes people wore or what negative names given to them for doing so, Americans in the 1920s used fashion to say something about who they were and what social group they belonged to, a habit that has not yet died.

Flappers

Flappers became the ideal for young women in the 1920s. From the clothes they wore to their attitudes, flappers were youthful, chic, and above all, modern. In the 1920s, American society rejected the Victorian attitudes of the pre–World War I (1914–18) generation. Flappers and their happy-go-lucky lifestyle set the tone for American popular culture. They partied, drank, smoked **cigarettes** (see entry under 1920s—Commerce in volume 2), and danced to wild **jazz** (see entry under 1900s—Music in volume 1) music. F. Scott Fitzgerald (1896–1940), whose writings chronicle the "Jazz Age," described flappers as "the generation that corrupted its elders and eventually over-reached itself—through lack of taste." The fun ended with the **Great Depression** (1929–41; see entry under 1930s—The Way We Lived in volume 2). However, many of the freedoms gained by flapper women in the 1920s are taken for granted in the twenty-first century.

Flapper fashion was very distinctive. Women "bobbed" their hair; that is, they cut off their long hair and sported a cheek-length haircut called a

A group of flappers in the Roaring Twenties. © DAZO VINTAGE STOCK PHOTOS/ IMAGES.COM/ALAMY.

bob. Flappers wore simple, straight dresses with knee-length skirts, and they used brightly colored **lipstick** (see entry under 1920s—Fashion in volume 2). Unlike the generation before, flappers rejected the stable, careful life of a wife and mother. Celebrities from starlet **Clara Bow** (1905–1965; see entry under 1920s—Film and Theater in volume 2) to writer Dorothy Parker (1893–1967) adopted the fashions and the reckless attitude of the flapper. Flappers shortened their skirts and became more openly sexual than women had ever been before. The wildest excesses of flapperdom were available only to the very rich, but many American women adopted the clothes, and some of the liberties, of the flapper ideal. They flattened their chests with cloth bindings to make themselves look young and innocent. Flappers have even been blamed for the popularity of skinny models in the late twentieth century.

For all their sense of adventure and freedom, flappers were not seeking equality with men. In fact, the fashion for short skirts and girlish innocence were actually a way of attracting men. Most flappers were married with children, just like their mothers before them, by the 1930s. What did change was women's freedom to go out and enjoy themselves alongside men. After the 1920s, it became much more common for single women to enjoy drinking, dancing, and even active sex lives. Although it is impossible to measure, it is certain that flappers indirectly helped pave the way for women's advances in other aspects of life, including education and careers.

Chris Routledge

For More Information

Blackman, Cally. *The '20s and '30s: Flappers and Vamps.* Milwaukee: Gareth Stephens, 2000.

Gourley, Catherine. *Divas, Flappers, and the New American Woman.* Minneapolis: Twenty-First Century Books, 2008.

Sagert, Kelly Boyer. *Flappers: A Guide to an American Subculture.* Santa Barbara, CA: Greenwood Press, 2010.

Zeitz, Joshua. *Flapper: A Madcap Story of Sex, Style, Celebrity, and the Women Who Made America Modern.* New York: Crown, 2006.

Lipstick

Lipstick has been an essential part of a woman's wardrobe for centuries. Dating back to the time of Cleopatra (69 BCE–30 BCE), the pigmented oil has been used to attract men, boost self-esteem, and complete a woman's face for the world. Lipstick became especially popular in America during the 1920s, when women gained a new political voice in claiming the right to vote. Many liberated suffragettes wore bright red lipstick as a symbol of their newfound voices. While the popularity of lipstick colors changes with the seasons, lipstick remains as one of the most popular accessories in history. In a 2004 survey, for example, 81 percent of American women reporting wearing lipstick.

Sara Pendergast

For More Information

Cohen Ragas, Meg, and Karen Kozlowski. *Read My Lips: A Cultural History of Lipstick.* San Francisco: Chronicle Books, 1998.
Pallingston, Jessica. *Lipstick.* New York: St. Martin's Press, 1999.

Raccoon Coats

Raccoon coats were long worn by nineteenth-century American men who adopted them as a practical emblem of their fur-trapping experiences on the frontier. Early photographs show men wearing smartly tailored versions in the 1890s. Raccoon coats are most closely associated with male college students of the 1920s, however. The ukelele-strumming college students of the 1920s made the garb a fashion craze on campuses from coast to coast. The phenomenon reached its peak in 1928, when George Olsen (1893–1971) and his band (George Olsen and His Music) recorded the lyrics to a peppy dance tune called "Doin' the Raccoon," that described how "rough guys, tough guys, men of dignity / Join the raccoon coat fraternity." The song's opening stanza declared that no respectable frat boy could afford to be caught dead without a raccoon coat as his principal fashion statement: "College men, knowledge men / Do a dance called raccoon; / It's the craze, nowadays, / And it will get you soon. / Buy a coat and try it, / I'll bet you'll be a riot, / It's a wow, learn to do it right now!" The song's remaining stanzas made specific references to how the nation's campuses were (or were not) following the trend, as in: "At Penn, they're made of rabbit, / At Vassar, sex appeal, / At Nebraska, made of airedale, / In Chicago lined with steel!"

Far more refined than their frontier archetypes, the raccoon coats popular in the 1920s were usually full-length dusters reaching to the ground, with exaggerated collars and swank buttons. They became one of the chief emblems of "collegiate style" for "sheiks" who wanted to impress their "shebas." The "Sheik" movies of **Rudolph Valentino** (1895–1926; see entry under 1920s—Film and Theater in volume 2) and the movie *Queen of Sheba* starring **Clara Bow** (1905–1965; see entry under 1920s—Film and Theater in volume 2) inspired these new slang words to refer to someone with sex appeal. "Flaming youth" were redefining mores and morality, aided by new mass media of talking pictures and the record player.

Raccoon coats underwent a short-lived revival in 1957 when adults began seeking vintage 1920s coats in tandem with their children's demand for **Davy Crockett** (see entry under 1950s—TV and Radio in volume 3) coonskin caps. Although not widely available, raccoon coats are still being made, much to the dismay of anti-fur critics like the People for the Ethical Treatment of Animals (PETA).

Edward Moran

For More Information

Allen, Frederick Lewis. *Only Yesterday: An Informal History of the Nineteen-Twenties.* New York: Harper, 1931.
"Doin' the Raccoon." *The Heptune Classical Jazz and Blues Lyrics Page.* http://www.heptune.com/lyrics/doinracc.html (accessed June 26, 2011).

1920s

Film and Theater

The new prosperity that Americans enjoyed in the 1920s meant that more and more people had the time and money to spend on film and theater tickets. The first "talkies" (movies with sound) thrilled audiences. People flocked to see stars like the beautiful Clara Bow (1905–1965) and the popular detective character, Charlie Chan. Soon people were enjoying movie epics around the country. Large Hollywood studios such as MGM and Warner Brothers nurtured the movie industry into one of the largest and most successful industries in the country.

One of the largest movie studios of the twenty-first century, Disney, started in the 1920s and pioneered a new type of film: animation. Disney introduced *Steamboat Willie* in 1928. It was the first animated film to include synchronized sound. *Steamboat Willie* introduced the American public to Mickey Mouse, a character who would become beloved by children around the world.

Though radio and movies took audiences from traveling vaudeville shows, serious theater productions enjoyed serious audience attention. Musicals were especially popular on Broadway. Such hits as *No, No Nanette* (1925), *Show Boat* (1927), and *A Connecticut Yankee* (1927) could be seen in New York and other selected cities.

Josephine Baker (1906–1975)

Josephine Baker, the "Ebony Venus," was a singer, dancer, comedienne, and legend. Born in St. Louis, Missouri, she earned her celebrity as a music-hall star in Paris, France, during the 1920s. She arrived there mid-decade, when she was just nineteen. Baker became a chorus girl and was featured with twenty-five African American dancers in "La Revue Negre," in which she cavorted in a costume of fabric banana skins. The following year, she was a star with the fabled Folies Bergère stage show. Eventually, Baker became the top-salaried performer in Europe.

Legendary performer Josephine Baker strikes a pose in costume in the mid-1920s. © EVERETT COLLECTION INC./ALAMY.

To Parisians, Baker personified the 1920s Jazz Age. She quickly gained the fame that would have eluded her had she remained in the United States. After all, for decades after Baker electrified Paris, African American performers remained locked in demeaning, stereotypical roles. African American women were cast as mammies or maids; African American men, as Pullman porters, comical cowards, and foot-shuffling fools. In Europe, Baker could travel in the same circles as the most distinguished writers, artists, and intellectuals. In 1951, while touring her homeland, she was honored in Harlem, New York's fabled African American community, but was denied service at the Stork Club, a famous—and segregated—midtown-Manhattan nightspot.

Rob Edelman

For More Information

Josephine Baker. http://www.cmgww.com/stars/baker (accessed June 26, 2011).
The Josephine Baker Story (film). HBO, 1991.
Jules-Rosette, Bennetta. *Josephine Baker in Art and Life: The Icon and the Image.* Urbana: University of Illinois Press, 2007.
Ralling, Christopher, director. *Chasing a Rainbow: The Life of Josephine Baker* (video). Channel 4 Television, UK, 1986.
Schroeder, Alan. *Josephine Baker: Entertainer.* New York: Chelsea House, 2006.

Clara Bow (1905–1965)

Clara Bow was a tremendously popular actress of the silent film era. She was the ultimate symbol of the **flappers** (see entry under 1920s—Fashion in volume 2)—the unconventional, independent girls of the 1920s. Bow began her career in motion pictures in 1922. She was said to have "It" (sex appeal). By the 1926 film *Mantrap,* she was one of the top box office stars in Hollywood.

Unfortunately, no other star in early Hollywood was more a product of her time. The 1920s was a time of prosperity in America. However, when the **Great Depression** (1929–41; see entry under 1930s—The Way We Lived in volume 2) began in 1929, her career quickly faded. By 1933, she retired from the screen. She married cowboy actor Rex Bell (1903–1962) in 1931. Bow died in 1965, largely forgotten by the public.

Jill Gregg Clever

For More Information

"Clara Bow." *Filmbug.* http://www.filmbug.com/db/4235 (accessed June 26, 2011).

The Clara Bow Page. http://www.clarabow.net (accessed June 26, 2011).

Morella, Joe, and Edward Z. Epstein. *The "It" Girl: The Incredible Story of Clara Bow.* New York: Delacourt Press, 1976.

Neely, Hugh Munro, and Elaina B. Archer. *Clara Bow: Discovering the "It" Girl.* New York: Kino on Video, 1999.

Stenn, David. *Clara Bow: Runnin' Wild.* New York: Doubleday, 1988.

Charlie Chan

Inspector Charlie Chan of the Honolulu Police Department was the first Asian character to serve as a detective hero in American literature. He became immensely popular and appeared in novels, films, radio serials, and a comic strip.

Charlie Chan was the brainchild of Earl Derr Biggers (1884–1933), who introduced the Chinese-born investigator as a secondary character in *House Without a Key,* a 1925 novel serialized in the **Saturday Evening Post** (see entry under 1900s—Print Culture in volume 1). The response was so positive that the *Post* asked Biggers for another novel, with Chan as the main character. The result was *The Chinese Parrot* (1926), followed by *Behind the Curtain* (1928), *The Black Camel* (1929), *Charlie Chan Carries On* (1930), and *Keeper of the Keys* (1932).

A series of movies also featured Chan, beginning with *Charlie Chan Carries On* (1931), in which he was played by Warner Oland (1880–1938). Later, Sidney Toler (1874–1947) took on the role. Ironically, Charlie Chan has never been portrayed by an Asian actor.

Justin Gustainis

For More Information

Berlin, Howard M. *The Charlie Chan Film Encyclopedia.* Jefferson, NC: McFarland, 1999.

The Charlie Chan Family Home. http://charliechanfamily.tripod.com (accessed June 29, 2011).

Hanke, Ken. *Charlie Chan at the Movies: History, Filmography, and Criticism.* Jefferson, NC: McFarland, 1989.

Huang, Yunte. *Charlie Chan: The Untold Story of the Honorable Detective and His Rendezvous with American History.* New York: W. W. Norton, 2010.

Mitchell, Charles P. *A Guide to Charlie Chan Films.* Westport, CT: Greenwood, 1999.

Schmidt, Kurt. *CharlieChan.net.* http://www.charliechan.net (accessed June 29, 2011).

Disney

The name "Disney" is synonymous with children's entertainment. Disney movies, **television** (see entry under 1940s—TV and Radio in volume 3) shows, and animated characters help create some of the happiest and most magical childhood memories. "Disney" is also the name of the founder of a moving picture empire: Walt Disney (1901–1966), a visionary who in 1923 formed Walt Disney Productions and began producing experimental animated short films. Little did he imagine that this modest beginning would evolve into an entertainment industry giant that would create classic animated short subjects and features, live-action films and television series—and even spawn fantasy-oriented theme parks.

The first Disney series was called *Alice in Cartoonland* and mixed live-action and animation. Among the individual titles in the series were

A parade of Disney characters march down Main Street U.S.A. at Disney World in Orlando, Florida, in 2008.
© PARASOLA.NET/ALAMY.

Alice's Wild West Show (1924), *Alice's Egg Plant* (1925), and *Alice Chops the Suey* (1925). In 1927, Disney and Ub Iwerks (1901–1971), a fellow animator and special-effects wizard, created a series of short films based on a character named Oswald the Rabbit. The following year they conjured up Mickey Mouse, the character who is most closely associated with Disney—and the creation that put Disney on the Hollywood map. *Plane Crazy* (1928) and *The Gallopin' Gaucho* (1928), the first two Mickey Mouse cartoons, were silent. The next, **Steamboat Willie** (1928; see entry under 1920s—Film and Theater in volume 2), was a talkie, with Disney himself providing Mickey's trademark squeaky voice.

Audiences were entranced by the singing, dancing, and talking mouse. Disney followed this success with his *Silly Symphonies* cartoon series, the first of which was *The Skeleton Dance* (1929). What made this series distinctive was that the scenarios and characters' movements were created in conjunction with the sounds of a prerecorded music track. The most famous was *The Three Little Pigs* (1933), which introduced the hit song "Who's Afraid of the Big Bad Wolf?" Meanwhile, Mickey Mouse continued starring in Disney cartoons. He was eventually joined by a host of animated pals, including Pluto (1930), Minnie Mouse (1933), Donald Duck (1934), and Goofy (who first appeared as Dippy Dawg in 1932).

In the early 1930s, Disney worked with the Technicolor corporation to add color to his cartoons. His first colored short, *Flowers and Trees,* won an Academy Award in 1932, and Technicolor signed an exclusive agreement to color Disney's animations.

Disney had long desired to produce a feature-length animated film. At the time, no one had ever chanced such an expensive and risky endeavor. In 1934, he began to realize this dream, all the while aware that he was gambling with the future of his flourishing company. *Snow White and the Seven Dwarfs* (1937), the initial Disney animated feature, was released to great critical and commercial acclaim. The key to its success was that its characters were not artificially or excessively portrayed but rather were presented as distinct personalities who believably expressed emotion. In addition, the film featured original musical numbers. *Snow White* was followed by *Pinocchio* (1940); *Dumbo* (1941); *Bambi* (1942); *Cinderella* (1950); *Alice in Wonderland* (1951); *Lady and the Tramp* (1955); *101 Dalmatians* (1961); and many others. Easily the most ambitious early Disney feature was **Fantasia** (1940; see entry under 1940s—Film and Theater in volume 3), made in conjunction with conductor

Leopold Stokowski (1882–1977). *Fantasia* was a bold attempt to unite classical music and the movements of animated characters.

In 1941, a number of Disney animators went on strike in protest of Disney's authoritarian command of the studio and what by then had evolved into a formulaic (systematic) animation style. Many eventually resigned and established their own animation studio, United Productions of America (UPA). Disney withstood the crisis and soon became heavily involved in the war effort, producing a series of propaganda and training films during World War II (1939–45). Among them were the feature documentary *Victory Through Air Power* (1943), which included live-action and animation, and *Der Fuhrer's Face* (1943), in which Donald Duck lampooned Adolf Hitler (1889–1945).

With the post–World War II era came the production of a short nature documentary, *Seal Island* (1948), whose success prompted a "True-Life Adventure" series of feature-length follow-ups. *The Living Desert* (1953) was the first. The studio also produced its initial live-action feature, *Treasure Island* (1950). Subsequent features ranged from *Rob Roy—The Highland Rogue* (1954) to *20,000 Leagues Under the Sea* (1954), ***Davy Crockett*—King of the Wild Frontier** (1955; see entry under 1950s—TV and Radio in volume 3) to *Old Yeller* (1957) and *Pollyanna* (1960). During the 1960s, the studio produced live-action comedies, beginning with *The Shaggy Dog* (1959) and including *The Absent-Minded Professor* (1961) and *The Parent Trap* (1961). ***Mary Poppins*** (1964; see entry under 1960s—Film and Theater in volume 2) was not the first film to feature animation blended with live action, but it became one of the most beloved.

During the 1950s, television sets were fast becoming staples in American homes, and Disney eagerly entered the TV marketplace. In 1954, he began a weekly anthology series that initially was known as *Disneyland*. This series was broadcast for decades under different titles and on different networks. *Disneyland* was followed by a classic afternoon children's series called ***The Mickey Mouse Club*** (1955–59; see entry under 1950s—TV and Radio in volume 3). In 1955, Disney opened Disneyland, the company's first fantasy theme park, on 160 acres of land in Anaheim, California. That same year, he established his own film distribution company, Buena Vista.

The company suffered artistically in the wake of its founder's death in 1966. In general, Disney movies lost their sparkle. On the upside, Walt Disney World, a second theme park, opened in

Orlando, Florida, in 1971, but the studio's entertainment output was mired in mediocrity. A low point came in 1979 when top animator Don Bluth (1938–) and a number of colleagues left Disney to form their own company, citing the studio's artistic and commercial deterioration.

In 1984, the studio formed Touchstone Pictures, a subsidiary that would produce and release a more adult-oriented product. The first Touchstone film was *Splash* (1984), a romantic comedy about a man who falls for a mermaid. The comedy was a box office smash. Other hits followed, including *Down and Out in Beverly Hills* (1985), *Three Men and a Baby* (1987), *Stakeout* (1987), *Honey, I Shrunk the Kids* (1989), *Pretty Woman* (1990), and *Sister Act* (1992). *Pretty Woman,* which made a star of its leading actress, Julia Roberts (1967–), offered a modern-day twist on the Cinderella story in that it was the tale of a prostitute who is romanced by a millionaire.

Beginning in the mid-1980s, Disney recaptured its status as an animation giant. The production of a series of features—including *The Black Cauldron* (1985), *The Little Mermaid* (1989), *Beauty and the Beast* (1991), *Aladdin* (1992), **The Lion King** (1994; see entry under 1990s—Film and Theater in volume 5), and **Finding Nemo** (2003; see entry under 2000s—Film and Theater in volume 6)—enchanted a new generation of youngsters. Disney expanded its empire to include video distribution; a **cable TV** (see entry under 1970s—TV and Radio in volume 4) station; book publishing; **Broadway** (see entry under 1900s—Film and Theater in volume 1) show production; and the ownership of hotels, real estate, professional sports teams, and the ABC television network, which it purchased in 1996 for $19 billion. By this time, the company had also evolved into a merchandising giant. Decades earlier, it had marketed a line of Mickey Mouse watches that were treasured by coming-of-age **baby boomers** (see entry under 1940s—The Way We Lived in volume 3). In the 1990s, the company opened numerous stores in **malls** (see entry under 1950s—Commerce in volume 3) and storefronts across the globe. On sale were Disney-related **T-shirts** (see entry under 1910s—Fashion in volume 1), pins, figurines, mugs, and stuffed animals—and the latest designs in Mickey Mouse watches.

Across the years, the Disney studio has savored its successes and rode out its rough times. Other motion picture production companies have evolved into mega-giant corporations, and others have produced animated films and children's entertainment. None remains as synonymous with childhood, magic, and Americana as Disney.

Rob Edelman

For More Information

Bailey, Adrian. *Walt Disney's World of Fantasy.* New York: Everest House, 1982.

Gabler, Neal. *Walt Disney: The Biography.* London: Aurum, 2007.

Maltin, Leonard. *Of Mice and Magic: A History of American Animated Cartoons.* Rev. ed. New York: New American Library, 1987.

Official Home Page for All Things Disney. http://disney.go.com/index (accessed June 29, 2011).

Schickel, Richard. *The Disney Version.* 3rd ed. Chicago: Ivan R. Dee, 1997.

Smith, Dave. *Disney A to Z: The Updated Official Encyclopedia.* 3rd ed. New York: Disney, 2006.

Solomon, Charles. *The Disney That Never Was: The Stories and Art from Five Decades of Unproduced Animation.* New York: Hyperion, 1995.

The Jazz Singer

The Jazz Singer (1927) is a landmark motion picture: Its immense popularity as a sound film ushered in the talking motion picture. Prior to the film's release, the actors were in **silent movies** (see entry under

Actor Al Jolson and actress May McAvoy in a scene from the first feature-length "talkie," The Jazz Singer *(1927).*
© MOVIESTORE COLLECTION LTD./ALAMY.

1900s—Film and Theater in volume 1); they performed pantomime-style. When these silent films were shown to audiences, live musical accompaniment provided background sound. With the newly developed ability to synchronize sound with image, movies began to be released with synchronized music and sound effects. The smashing success of *The Jazz Singer*—which included a talking scene with several song numbers and a synchronized musical track—encouraged major film studios to convert their production facilities to sound stages. Theaters converted their projection equipment to accommodate sound. By 1928, it was clear that movies would no longer be silent.

The Jazz Singer, directed by Alan Crosland (1894–1936), was based on a short story, "The Day of Atonement" (1922), by Samson Raphaelson (1896–1983). Al Jolson (1886–1950) starred in the screen adaptation. Jolson was one of the early twentieth century's most popular and influential stage performers and singers. His presence in the film is largely responsible for the film's box office success.

The Jazz Singer is the story of immigrant integration into American culture. Its hero is Jakie Rabinowitz, the son of Jewish immigrant parents and the descendent of a long line of religious leaders, who is expected to succeed his father as cantor of the neighborhood synagogue. But Jakie has ideas of his own. Even as an adolescent, he yearns for success onstage as a **jazz** (see entry under 1900s—Music in volume 1) singer, interpreting American popular songs rather than traditional Jewish religious music. This desire puts Jakie at odds with his stern, unyielding father. The youngster sets out to win success on his own terms.

The Jazz Singer is often referred to as the first sound film, but this is not the case. By the early 1920s, a workable method of recording sound in synch with the image, and then amplifying the sound in theaters, had evolved. However, Warner Bros., the studio that produced *The Jazz Singer,* was the first to undertake sound-film production of feature-length films on a commercial scale. The studio's initial efforts were short, plotless films spotlighting the stage acts of musicians, singers, and dancers. The Fox studios also entered the market, producing its Movietone newsreels. Before the release of *The Jazz Singer, Don Juan* (1926), a silent swashbuckler featuring stage and screen star John Barrymore (1882–1942), had already arrived in movie houses with prerecorded music and sound effects.

The Jazz Singer, which was also remade in 1953 and 1980, capably integrates song numbers and dialog into parts of the scenario. After one musical sequence, Jakie utters a prophetic line: "You ain't heard nothin' yet." Given the rousing public response to *The Jazz Singer* and the new sound film industry that it spawned, this was no small boast.

Audrey Kupferberg

For More Information

Carringer, Robert L., ed. *The Jazz Singer.* Madison: University of Wisconsin Press, 1979.

Dirks, Tim. "The Jazz Singer (1927)." *Filmsite.org.* http://www.filmsite.org/jazz.html (accessed June 30, 2011).

Raphaelson, Samson. *The Jazz Singer.* New York: Brentano's, 1925.

MGM

Of all the movie studios that dotted the landscape of the Los Angeles area during the golden age of motion pictures (a time period lasting from the 1920s through the 1950s), Metro-Goldwyn-Mayer (MGM) was by far the most illustrious. Back then, movie stars were not independent contractors; rather, they signed standard, seven-year contracts with the movie studios that produced the majority of American films. Of all the movie studios, MGM was the biggest and, some say, the best.

Metro-Goldwyn-Mayer, whose trademark was Leo the Roaring Lion, boasted that its roster of contract players included "More Stars Than There Are in the Heavens." During the 1920s, such screen legends as Greta Garbo (1905–1990), John Barrymore (1882–1942), John Gilbert (1899–1936), Joan Crawford (1905–1977), and **Lillian Gish** (1893–1993; see entry under 1910s—Film and Theater in volume 1) signed with the studio. The 1930s brought to the forefront **Clark Gable** (1901–1960; see entry under 1930s—Film and Theater in volume 2), Jean Harlow (1911–1937), Myrna Loy (1905–1993), and Mickey Rooney (1920–). In the 1940s came Gene Kelly (1912–1996), Greer Garson (1904–1996), Lana Turner (1921–1995), Hedy Lamarr (1913–2000), and many others.

The studio was formed in 1924 by movie executive and theater chain owner Marcus Loew (1870–1927). The studio name came from the three previously existing companies that were linked together to become MGM: Metro Pictures Corp.; Louis B. Mayer Pictures, named for its founder, Louis B. Mayer (1885–1957); and Goldwyn

MGM's trademark Leo the Lion opened every film with a roar. © AP IMAGES.

Pictures Corporation, formerly owned by producer Samuel Goldwyn (1882–1974). The MGM studio was a division of Loew's, Inc., one of the largest theater chains in North America. The original powers behind the studio were Mayer, a Russian immigrant who was a fierce businessman, and Irving G. Thalberg (1899–1937), its brilliant young production chief. Thalberg was the motivating force behind many of the studio's most fabled productions, including *Ben-Hur* (1926), *The Crowd* (1928), *Mutiny on the Bounty* (1935), *Romeo and Juliet* (1936), and *The Good Earth* (1937). After Thalberg's death, MGM kept on producing and releasing top Hollywood films: *Mrs. Miniver* (1942), *Woman of the Year* (1942), *National Velvet* (1944), *Meet Me in St. Louis* (1944), *An American in Paris* (1951), *Singin' in the Rain* (1952), *Gigi* (1958), and a remake of *Ben-Hur* (1959).

The demise of MGM actually began in the late 1940s. A court ruling made it a conflict of interest for the same company to produce films and then exhibit those films in its own theaters. That ruling, the rising cost of production, and the increasing popularity of **television** (see entry under 1940s—TV and Radio in volume 3) led to the declining power of MGM and the other major studios. In 1972, MGM was purchased by billionaire financier Kirk Kerkorian (1917–), who sold off its famous back lot (area used for shooting exterior scenes) and auctioned away most of the studio property. Today, the name MGM still may exist as a corporate entity, but its glory days are just a memory.

Audrey Kupferberg

For More Information

Bart, Peter. *Fade Out: The Calamitous Final Days of MGM.* New York: Morrow, 1990.

Bingen, Steven, Stephen X. Sylvester, and Michael Troyan. *MGM: Hollywood's Backlot.* Santa Monica, CA: Santa Monica Press, 2010.

Eames, John Douglas. *The MGM Story.* New York: Crown Publishers, 1976.

Eyman, Scott. *Lion of Hollywood: The Life and Legend of Louis B. Mayer.* New York: Simon & Schuster, 2005.

Hay, Peter. *MGM: When the Lion Roars.* Atlanta: Turner, 1991.

Metro Goldwyn Mayer. http://www.mgm.com (accessed June 30, 2011).

Vieira, Mark. *Hollywood Dreams Made Real: Irving Thalberg and the Rise of M-G-M.* New York: Abrams, 2008.

Steamboat Willie

On September 19, 1928, the cartoon *Steamboat Willie* premiered at the Colony Theater in New York and forever altered the history of animation. The cartoon is noted for both introducing Mickey Mouse to the American public and for being the first animated film to include synchronized sound. The short, which was based on the earlier Buster Keaton (1895–1966) silent film *Steamboat Bill, Jr.,* portrays Mickey as a boat captain who prances about with a cargo of livestock, employing the various animals as musical instruments. He also manages to rescue Minnie Mouse from the villainous Pegleg Pete. The cartoon was an instant success. It is credited with establishing **Disney**'s (see entry under 1920s—Film and Theater in volume 2) dominance in the field of animation.

Walt Disney (1901–1966) was a young animator during the 1920s who had achieved some success with a series of cartoons featuring a

Boat captain Mickey Mouse in the 1928 cartoon Steamboat Willie, *Walt Disney's first talking animated short.*
© AF ARCHIVE/ALAMY.

character named Oswald the Lucky Rabbit. A contractual dispute with Universal Pictures led to Disney losing all rights to Oswald. According to legend, Disney left that meeting and created a new character called Mortimer Mouse while on a train. Lillian, his wife, suggested he rename the mouse "Mickey" because it had a better sound to it. The first Mickey Mouse cartoons to enter production were *Plane Crazy* and *Gallopin' Gaucho.* Before either cartoon could be released, Disney recognized that "talking pictures" were the future of cinema. Disney, along with his brother Roy (1893–1971) and animator Ub Iwerks (1901–1971), led a team of animators, musicians, and technicians in attempting to synchronize sound with the animated action on the screen. Walt Disney himself provided Mickey's squeaky falsetto voice (a high-pitched male voice) and did so for the next twenty years. The great popularity of *Steamboat Willie* led to other talking cartoons and catapulted Mickey Mouse to the ranks of international celebrity.

The Mickey seen in *Steamboat Willie* is not the well-behaved character familiar with modern audiences. The character's original personality was much more mischievous and even hinted at a cruel streak. While transforming the boat's livestock cargo into a makeshift orchestra, Mickey is seen pulling a cat's tail, playing xylophone on a cow's teeth, making piglets squeal, and playing a cow's udder. Disney would soon abandon such gags for more "tasteful" humor.

Steamboat Willie is remembered as the first animated film to successfully blend sight and sound. It cemented Mickey Mouse's position as an American icon.

Charles Coletta

For More Information

Finch, Christopher. *The Art of Walt Disney: From Mickey Mouse to the Magic Kingdoms and Beyond.* Rev. ed. New York: Abrams, 2011.

Heide, Robert, and John Gilman. *Disneyana: Classic Collectibles 1928–1958.* New York: Hyperion, 1994.

Iwerks, Leslie, and John D. Kenworthy. *The Hand Behind the Mouse: An Intimate Biography of the Man Walt Disney Called "the Greatest Animator in the World."* New York: Disney Editions, 2001.

Maltin, Leonard. *Of Mice and Magic: A History of American Animated Cartoons.* Rev. ed. New York: New American Library, 1987.

"Steamboat Willie." *Disney Shorts.* http://www.disneyshorts.org/shorts. aspx?shortID=96 (accessed June 30, 2011).

Thomas, Frank, and Ollie Johnston. *Disney Animation: The Illustration of Life.* New York: Disney Editions, 1981.

Rudolph Valentino (1895–1926)

Rudolph Valentino was one of the premier movie stars of the 1920s. His smoldering good looks and exotic screen roles made him irresistible to female audience members, while many male viewers saw him as little more than an unmanly "powder puff." Nonetheless, for women of the Roaring Twenties, Valentino was a true sex symbol, a figure who represented danger, allure, and forbidden passion. His immense popularity spawned a parade of Valentino imitators—handsome young actors whose dark-featured good looks and aggressive sensuality earned them the title "Latin lovers."

Valentino was born Rodolpho Alfonzo Raffaelo Pierre Filibert Guglielmi di Valentina d'Antonguolla in Castellaneta, Italy. He came to the United States in 1913, where he struggled to make a living. He was eventually hired as a dancer and worked in **vaudeville** (see entry under 1900s—Film and Theater in volume 1) until making his acting debut in a touring play. Valentino then gravitated to Hollywood. He was an extra in

Italian actor Rudolph Valentino smolders in this still from his 1921 film The Sheik.
© MOVIESTORE COLLECTION LTD./ALAMY.

a film titled *Alimony* (1917) and had small roles in several others. While appearing in *The Eyes of Youth* (1919), Valentino impressed screenwriter June Mathis (1892–1927), who recommended him for her upcoming project, *The Four Horsemen of the Apocalypse* (1921). Valentino landed a role in the movie and he won instant stardom as he seductively danced the tango, a Latin American ballroom dance that includes exaggerated pauses and close eye-contact with one's partner. As a result, the tango became a popular **dance** (see entry under 1900s—The Way We Lived in volume 1) craze throughout the United States and Europe.

Several hits followed for Valentino, who reached his high point playing exotic and highly romantic characters in *The Sheik* (1921)—the film that cemented his stardom—and *Blood and Sand* (1922). Meanwhile, his career was taken over by Natasha Rambova (1897–1969), his second wife. Under her guidance, Valentino's screen persona was in danger of becoming increasingly effeminate (more womanly than masculine), but he returned to his previous heroic form in *The Eagle* (1925) and *The Son of the Sheik* (1926).

Valentino became seriously ill with a perforated ulcer while in New York in 1926 and died suddenly on August 23. He was just thirty-one years old. His death resulted in mass hysteria among his female fans, thousands of whom lined the streets outside New York's St. Malachi's Church, the site of his funeral.

Audrey Kupferberg

For More Information

Bothan, Noel. *Valentino: The Love God.* New York: Ace Books, 1977.

Bret, David. *Valentino: A Dream of Desires.* New York: Robson, 2000.

Leider, Emily W. *Dark Lover: The Life and Death of Rudolph Valentino.* New York: Farrar, Straus, and Giroux, 2003.

Tajiri, Vincent. *Valentino.* New York: Bantam Books, 1977.

1920s

Food and Drink

The way people ate and drank in the 1920s reflected the changes in the way people lived and worked. The prosperity of the time came from the emergence of large corporations. Also a factor was the increased productivity of thousands of returning veterans and of women who had grown accustomed to working during the war and opted to remain employed. In families with both parents working, people had more money to spend. The extra money encouraged many to spend quickly and frivolously. The American economy shifted from a focus on thriftiness toward more consumer spending on luxuries and convenience items.

Food and drink became more than just nourishment for the body. They became treats for special occasions and refreshment. For hard-working women, the new convenience items saved precious time in the kitchen. Instead of preparing time-consuming breakfasts of ham and eggs, some people just poured a bowl of Wheaties. Mothers could serve their babies prepackaged Gerber baby food instead of homemade mashed vegetables. Lunch or dinner could be enjoyed at many fast-food restaurants, including White Castle, or be made with some of the new prepackaged food, such as Wonder Bread and Velveeta Cheese. Fizzy, clear 7-Up and frozen popsicles became tasty treats that could be enjoyed anytime.

Fast Food

In many ways, fast food seems the perfect companion to Americans' "on the go" lifestyle. Prior to the rise of fast food in the 1920s, most Americans ate together at home most of the time. As the United States became more modernized and industrial, the pace of life sped up, helped in part by the growing use of automobiles. By the 1920s, more Americans were busier going from home to work and to all kinds of leisure activities than they ever were before. This made it harder to find time for home-cooked meals. The fast-food industry slowly emerged to take advantage of, and to promote, this trend.

The first fast-food restaurant is generally considered to be White Castle, founded in 1921 by Billy Ingram and Walt Anderson. They offered cheap **hamburgers** (see entry under 1950s—Food and Drink in volume 3), sold by the sack, and **French fries** (see entry under 1950s—Food and Drink in volume 3). As they expanded to more locations, they pioneered the use of standardization, which meant that each of their restaurants looked the same, used the same equipment, and served exactly the same food. Although this approach lacked variety, it lowered their costs and gave people something they wanted: predictability. No matter which White Castle customers stopped at, they could be sure of what to expect. White Castle was a big success, especially during the hard times of the **Great Depression** (1929–41; see entry under 1930s—The Way We Lived in volume 2) in the 1930s. White Castle burgers cost only five cents, and they stayed at that price until 1946. White Castle also helped pioneer the use of franchising—selling people the right to open their own White Castle restaurant, with the parent company providing the information, equipment, recipes, and support for success.

This formula was so successful that many other imitators sprang up to take advantage of a growing taste for fast food. In the 1950s, fast food really took off as Americans enjoyed unprecedented prosperity and as American culture became even more mobile and fast paced. The most successful fast-food restaurant during that time and afterward was **McDonald's** (see entry under 1940s—Food and Drink in volume 3), whose first store opened in the late 1940s. Entrepreneur Ray Kroc (1902–1984) joined with the McDonald brothers of San Bernadino, California, to spread the hamburger restaurant across the United States. By 1960, there were more than two hundred McDonald's restaurants.

Kroc did not really do anything new with fast food; in fact, he used many of the same techniques pioneered by the White Castle chain. What he did do was take those techniques to a greater level of success than had ever been seen before. The restaurant's signature sign, the "Golden Arches," forming a big yellow "M," has become the symbol for fast food the world over. Over the years McDonald's added new innovations to its menu and restaurants, including Filet-O-Fish sandwiches, Chicken McNuggets, and outdoor playgrounds for kids.

While McDonald's was becoming the leading fast-food restaurant, it was not without competition. **Burger King** (see entry under 1950s—Food and Drink in volume 3), begun in Miami in 1954, was the closest competitor to McDonald's, offering bigger hamburgers and allowing customers to choose their own toppings. Kentucky Fried Chicken (now KFC) offered southern-style chicken, mashed potatoes, and coleslaw. Taco Bell, begun in 1962, brought Mexican-style food to the world of fast food. Arby's, started in 1964, offered higher-quality roast-beef sandwiches. Wendy's, begun in Columbus, Ohio, in 1972 by Dave Thomas (1932–2002), pioneered the use of drive-through windows. Despite their variations in food and style, all these chains stayed close to the original fast food recipe for success: cheap, uniform food, served quickly and available almost everywhere.

By the 1990s, these restaurants were almost everywhere, mostly in the United States, but also in other countries, notably Japan. But by the 1990s, it was becoming increasingly clear that fast food was bringing other things to American culture besides quick, cheap hamburgers. Critics complained, with good evidence, that fast food was full of fat, cholesterol, salt, sugar, and harmful chemicals used as preservatives, contributing to rising levels of obesity and heart disease. Indeed, American consumption of beef was rising, in no small part due to fast food. Fast-food restaurants were also blamed for contributing to suburban sprawl—an ugly mishmash of restaurants and stores lining American roads, each in its own building, contributing to greater dependence on the car. Furthermore, fast food seemed to be part of a larger trend toward uniformity in American life. Regional differences were disappearing as much of America looked the same no matter where you were. Some recent responses to these concerns are the rising popularity of **farmers' markets** (see entry under 2000s—Food and Drink in volume 6) and the "locavore" movement, which prizes locally sustainably produced foods.

Restaurants are not the only suppliers of fast food in America, of course. The invention of the **TV dinner** (see entry under

1950s—Food and Drink in volume 3) in 1953 brought fast food to the American home. Since that time, American grocery stores have expanded their offerings of convenience foods to allow consumers to purchase a variety of meals that can be prepared quickly at home, often in microwave ovens. By the twenty-first century, fast food had become one of the principle staples of the American diet, for better and for worse.

Timothy Berg

For More Information

Hogan, David. *Selling 'em by the Sack: White Castle and the Creation of American Food.* New York: New York University Press, 1997.

Kroc, Ray, and Robert Anderson. *Grinding It Out: The Making of McDonald's.* Chicago: Contemporary Books, 1977.

Luxenberg, Stan. *Roadside Empires: How the Chains Franchised America.* New York: Viking, 1985.

Schlosser, Eric. *Fast Food Nation: The Dark Side of the American Meal.* Boston: Houghton Mifflin, 2001.

Schlosser, Eric, and Charles Wilson. *Chew on This: Everything You Don't Want to Know about Fast Food.* Boston: Houghton Mifflin, 2006.

Gerber Baby Food

The world's largest producer of baby-food products, Gerber Products, Inc., had a modest beginning in the summer of 1927 when Daniel Frank Gerber (1898–1974) and Dorothy Gerber asked the Fremont Canning Company to relieve them of the chore of hand-straining food for their infant daughter, Sally. The Gerbers had already been making use of Fremont's services to produce a line of canned fruits and vegetables. The success of that venture led the Gerbers to manufacture a line of baby food as well. The first flavors, introduced in late 1928, were strained peas, prunes, carrots, spinach, and beef vegetable soup. To promote the new products, the Gerbers placed advertisements using a picture of a baby's face, later called the "Gerber baby," in magazines ranging from physicians' journals to periodicals for homemakers. The model for the Gerber baby was Ann Turner Cook, who grew up to be a mystery novelist and English teacher; her portrait was sketched in charcoal by Dorothy Hope Smith Barlow. Gerber adopted it as its official trademark in 1931.

Gerber's famous baby, seen in its logo, is actually Ann Turner Cook, rendered in a charcoal portrait in 1928. © AP IMAGES.

Gerber®

By the early twenty-first century, Gerber was making 190 food products for distribution to 80 countries, including its Tender Harvest line of organic baby foods, introduced in 1997. The product mix includes puréed fruits and vegetables as well as cereals and teething biscuits. Its Consumer Relations Department responds to 800,000 consumer questions a year. The department was set up in 1938, with Dorothy Gerber personally responding to each letter. In 1960, the company expanded its line of products to market baby-care items such as bottles, teethers, and breast-feeding accessories. Its line of Wellness products includes lotions, baby powders, shampoos, and vitamins. The Gerber Life Insurance Company, a subsidiary, was established in 1967. It is one of the largest providers of insurance to juveniles, with more than three million policies in force, for a value of $37 billion.

Since 2007, Gerber has been part of the global food giant Nestlé. Gerber is headquartered in Fremont, Michigan.

Edward Moran

For More Information

Gerber. http://www.gerber.com (accessed July 6, 2011).

Gerber, Dan. *Babies Are Our Business: The Story of Commercially Prepared Baby Foods.* New York: Random House, 1964.

Gerber Products Company. *The Story of an Idea and Its Role in the Growth of the Baby Foods Industry.* Fremont, MI: Gerber Products Company, 1953.

7-Up

The lemon-lime soft drink 7-Up has been a fixture of America's **refrigerators** (see entry under 1910s—The Way We Lived in volume 1) for many years. At various times, it has been the number three–selling soft drink in the world, outpaced by only **Coca-Cola** (see entry under 1900s—Food and Drink in volume 1) and Pepsi. Its offbeat ad campaigns, emphasizing the differences between the refreshing flavor of 7-Up and the heavy cola taste of its rivals, have helped shape the brand's quirky image and inspired numerous imitators.

7-Up was first formulated in 1929 in St. Louis, Missouri. The Howdy Corporation originally marketed it under the name the "Bib-Label Lithiated Lemon-Lime Soda," although it soon changed its name to 7-Up Lithiated Lemon Soda. "Lithiated" means it was treated with lithium. There are various explanations for the name 7-Up. Some claimed that there are (or were) seven ingredients in 7-Up. Others contend that the original 7-Up bottle was seven ounces, or that the drink was named after a popular card game of the 1930s. No one knows for sure. In any case, the company became The Seven-Up Co. in 1936.

By the late 1940s, 7-Up had become the third best-selling soft drink in the world. It enjoyed its greatest period of popularity in the 1970s, however, when an ad campaign dubbed it "the Uncola." **Television** (see entry under 1940s—TV and Radio in volume 3) commercials and print ads featuring the catchy tagline helped cement 7-Up's image in the public mind as a refreshing alternative to Coke and Pepsi.

Inevitably, 7-Up's popularity began to slip, as new drinks, like the Coca-Cola Company's lemon-lime Sprite, caught the public's fancy. By 1996, 7-Up had fallen to the eighth best-selling soft drink with about 2.4 percent of the market. Sprite was fourth at 5.8 percent.

In 1997, the makers of 7-Up announced the first major changes to the soft drink's formula. The new taste was designed to produce a "better blend of lemon and lime flavors," according to a company spokesman, and to help 7-Up compete with Sprite. Despite the change, however, 7-Up sales continued to stagnate. Sales did not begin to rise again until the turn of the twenty-first century, when a hip new ad campaign featuring comedian Orlando Jones (1968–) and the tagline "Make 7-Up Yours" breathed new life into an old brand.

Robert E. Schnakenberg

For More Information

Dietz, Lawrence. *Soda Pop: The History, Advertising, Art, and Memorabilia of Soft Drinks in America.* New York: Simon & Schuster, 1973.

Rodengen, Jeffrey L. *The Legend of Dr. Pepper/7-Up.* Fort Lauderdale, FL: Write Stuff Books, 1995.

7-UP. http://www.7up.com (accessed June 30, 2011).

Velveeta Cheese

The brand name of a processed cheese product first marketed in 1928 by the Kraft Foods Corporation, Velveeta cheese became one of the shining examples of American society's love for processed foods. To make Velveeta, a blend of Colby and cheddar cheeses, emulsifiers, and salt is heated, inserted into aluminum foil packaging where it hardens, and sold in half-pound, one-pound, and two-pound bricks.

Critics have long scorned Velveeta as a chemical concoction that symbolizes the low standard of the American sense of taste, one that favors convenience and artificiality over "authentic" natural food. Velveeta has especially come to symbolize the lowbrow cooking style associated with the 1950s, with its emphasis on cheap, easy-to-prepare meals using mass-produced ingredients. It is often used as a substitute for "real" cheese in casseroles, macaroni dishes, omelettes, grilled sandwiches, and on cheeseburgers. Velveeta is heavily promoted by Kraft, whose Web site features its own "clean plate" recipes that make use of the product. In addition to the original, Kraft also markets low-fat, Mexican-style, Pepperjack, and Spicy Buffalo Velveeta.

Edward Moran

For More Information

Velveeta Clean Plate Club. http://www.velveeta.com (accessed June 30, 2011).

Wheaties

For decades, Wheaties has been an all-time-favorite breakfast food. It is marketed as the "Breakfast of Champions," one of the most celebrated of all advertising slogans. Since the 1930s, it has been linked to athletics and accomplishment. It seems that whenever an athlete with a likable personality wins a gold medal at the **Olympics** (see entry under 1900s— Sports and Games in volume 1) or tosses touchdowns in the Super Bowl, he or she is featured on Wheaties packaging. In fact, the line "He didn't

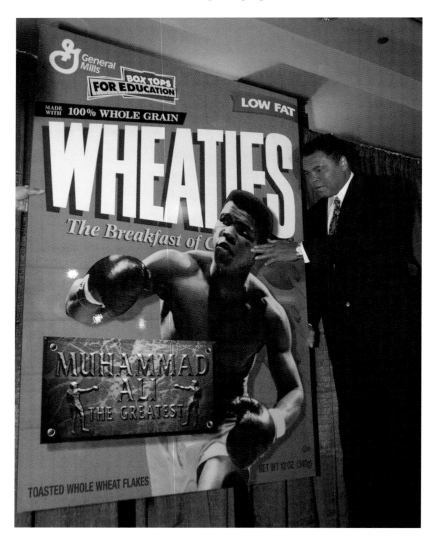

For Wheaties' 75th anniversary in 1999, the "Breakfast of Champions" featured another champion, boxer Muhammad Ali, on the box cover. © PETER MORGAN/REUTERS/CORBIS.

eat his Wheaties today" has long been used to describe youngsters who fall short on the ball field.

The cereal's beginnings date to 1921, when a Minnesota health care professional accidentally spilled some bran gruel on a hot stove, transforming the mixture into a crispy flake. He brought the flake to the Washburn Crosby Company, the precursor of General Mills, which currently produces and markets Wheaties. The Washburn Crosby Company saw the potential of transforming the flake into a mass-market breakfast food. Before the final product debuted in 1924, thirty-six variations of the flake were tested. It was named "Wheaties" in a national contest. Among the almost-successful entries: Nutties and Gold Medal Wheat Flakes.

Wheaties is famed for printing the photos of top athletes on its packaging, a marketing ploy meant to appeal to children. The implication is that, if you eat your Wheaties, you too may grow up to be big and strong enough to become a professional athlete. In 1934, Lou Gehrig (1903–1941), the legendary New York Yankees first baseman, became the first athlete featured on a Wheaties box. Over the years, a variety of athletes have graced the cover of the Wheaties box: baseball star Jimmie Foxx (1907–1967), sports heroine **Babe Didrikson** (1914–1956; see entry under 1930s—Sports and Games in volume 2), Baltimore Orioles iron-man Cal Ripken Jr. (1960–), Olympic gymnast Mary Lou Retton (1968–), golf star **Tiger Woods** (1975–; see entry under 1990s—Sports and Games in volume 5), football great Peyton Manning (1976–), and cycling champion **Lance Armstrong** (1971–; see entry under 2000s—Sports and Games in volume 6). Basketball legend **Michael Jordan** (1963–; see entry under 1990s—Sports and Games in volume 5) has been the Wheaties cover box a record seventeen times, first appearing in 1988. The older and most popular Wheaties boxes are highly valued by memorabilia buffs and collectors.

Rob Edelman

For More Information

General Mills. *Wheaties Home Page.* http://www.wheaties.com (accessed June 30, 2011).

Wonder Bread

• •

Wonder Bread has been a favorite of Americans since its introduction in 1921. The vitamin-enriched soft white bread is easily identified by its white plastic wrapper decorated with pictures of red, yellow, and blue balloons. Legend has it that Wonder Bread outsold all other brands during the first week of its sales by the Taggart Baking Company in Indianapolis, Indiana. Purchased by Continental Baking Company in 1925, Wonder Bread soon became a national brand.

Wonder Bread's bakers have incorporated technology to make the product new and better while at the same time maintaining an image of its wholesome goodness. Wonder Bread was among the first breads sold in plastic wrappers in the 1920s. In the 1930s, Wonder Bread was among the first breads to be sold pre-sliced. During World War II (1939–45), Wonder Bread joined a government effort to enrich breads with essential nutrients. This effort has been called the "quiet miracle" because it brought affordable nutrition to a great number of people and nearly eliminated some diseases, such as beriberi and pellagra. (Beriberi is caused by lack of thiamine, or vitamin B in the diet; pellagra, by a lack of niacin, a B complex vitamin.) In the 1940s, Wonder Bread employed a baking process that ensured each slice would be free of air holes.

Advertising has helped make Wonder Bread popular. Wonder Bread was one of the first products to be promoted on the radio in the 1920s. It also sponsored the first regular color television show, ***The Howdy Doody Show*** (see entry under 1940s—TV and Radio in volume 3) in the 1940s. With catchy tunes, popular characters, and ad campaigns such as "Helps build strong bodies eight ways" (later "twelve ways"), Wonder Bread remains a favorite food of children.

Sara Pendergast

For More Information

Wonderbread.com. http://www.wonderbread.com (accessed June 30, 2011).

1920s

Music

Jazz was the music of the 1920s. It was the best display of black musical talent the world had ever seen. Originating with musicians in New Orleans, Louisiana, the sound soon spread across the country. Jazz grew out of ragtime and Dixieland music and sprang as well from the improvisations of the many musicians of French, Spanish, and African heritage who lived in Louisiana. Although the greatest jazz musicians were black, including Louis Armstrong (1901–1971), Jelly Roll Morton (1890–1941), and Duke Ellington (1899–1974), white musicians were the first to record jazz for profit. White musicians such as Bix Beiderbecke (1903–1931), George Gershwin (1898–1937), and Paul Whiteman (1890–1967; dubbed "The Jazz King") popularized jazz with white audiences by performing it in theaters and cabarets. They paved the way for black musicians to cross racial boundaries and to perform in locations generally attended by whites. Soon black musicians were welcomed and profited from exposure to white audiences and recording contracts with record companies previously closed to them.

The jazz of New Orleans spawned variations in different parts of the country, especially Chicago, Illinois, where jazz musicians played in speakeasies (illegal bars) and dance halls. The Jazz Age encouraged vigorous dances, of which the Charleston was by far the most popular. As jazz evolved throughout the decade, other musical genres took shape, including blues and swing, which would become more popular in the next decade.

Blues

Blues music emerged in the early twentieth century in the United States as one of the most distinctive and original of American musical forms. It is an African American creation and one of the great contributions to American popular culture. Blues music is often thought of as being sad music, expressing the hardships endured by many African Americans. Although it can certainly be sad, the blues is also a way to deal with hardship and celebrate good times. Blues music comes in a wide variety of styles, from acoustic rural blues to urban electric blues. Because of this variety, and because it is about basic human emotions (love and heartbreak, happy times and sad), blues music speaks to people of all races and backgrounds. It has also been a very influential musical form. Without

Blues singing great Ma Rainey and her Gerogia Jazz Band perform in 1923. © FRANK DRIGGS COLLECTION/HULTON ARCHIVES/ GETTY IMAGES.

blues, there would be no **rock and roll** (see entry under 1950s—Music in volume 3). Much of contemporary music in the late twentieth and early twenty-first centuries owes a great debt to blues music.

The origins of blues music go back at least to the 1800s and the time of slavery, but as a popular form, the blues developed in the 1920s. Among the earliest blues recordings were those by black female singers in the 1920s. Among the most significant were Bessie Smith (1894?–1937), Ma Rainey (1886–1939), and Mamie Smith (1883–1946). Their styles were earthier than many of their contemporaries, and they sang songs about love, loss, and heartbreak. Mamie Smith's "Crazy Blues," recorded in 1920, is thought to be the first blues recording. The greatest of these early female blues singers were Rainey and Bessie Smith. Bessie Smith's version of "St. Louis Blues" (written by W. C. Handy, 1873–1958) and Rainey's version of "See See Rider" are among the classics of blues music.

In the 1930s and early 1940s, rural acoustic blues became the dominant sound. Rural acoustic blues was often called "delta" blues because of its origin in the Mississippi delta region. The music was dominated by male singers who accompanied themselves on acoustic guitars that could be carried easily from place to place, allowing them to play for the many poor African American farming communities in the area. Among the most important innovators in the delta blues style were Tommy Johnson (1896–1956), Bukka White (1909–1977), Charley Patton (1891–1934), Son House (1902–1988), and **Robert Johnson** (1911–1938; see entry under 1930s—Music in volume 2). All these musicians made important recordings during the 1930s that have proved highly influential.

With the migration of large numbers of African Americans to northern cities during and after World War II (1939–45), blues music evolved into new forms that reflected the quicker pace of life in these new environments. Two distinct styles emerged, urban blues and electric, or Chicago, blues. Urban blues was a more upscale blues style that featured smooth-voiced singers and horn sections that had more in common with **jazz** (see entry under 1900s—Music in volume 1) than it did with rural Mississippi delta blues. Urban blues was represented by the music of artists such as Dinah Washington (1924–1963), Eddie Vinson (1917–1988), Jimmy Witherspoon (1923–1997), and Charles Brown (1922–1999).

More influential was the electric, or Chicago, blues style, a more direct descendant of the Mississippi delta blues. Most important in its development was McKinley Morganfield, better known as Muddy Waters (1915–1983). Waters began in the rural acoustic style, but when he moved to Chicago in the 1940s, he found that his acoustic guitar could not be heard over the loud crowd noise in the local bars where he played. To overcome that problem, he switched to an electric guitar and amplifier to play his delta blues. Waters soon added more instruments to his sound, including piano, harmonica, drums, bass, and occasionally a second guitar. This arrangement became the classic Chicago blues sound. With these electric instruments, Muddy Waters and his band transformed the blues into a hard-edged, driving sound. A strong beat, a pounding piano, electric lead guitar solos, and over-amplified harmonicas characterized his music. Among Waters' greatest songs are "Hoochie Coochie Man," "Mannish Boy," and "I'm Ready." Waters' innovations were highly influential, spawning hundreds of imitators. His innovations were so influential in fact that the Chicago blues style he helped pioneer still dominates the blues sound. Other great Chicago blues artists include Howlin' Wolf (1910–1976), Sonny Boy Williamson (1914–1948), John Lee Hooker (1920–2001), Willie Dixon (1915–1992), and Koko Taylor (1935–2009).

In the 1960s, blues music experienced a wider popularity than ever before. Innovators like Waters continued to perform and record, but they were now joined by younger artists such as Buddy Guy (1936–), Junior Wells (1934–1998), **B. B. King** (1925–; see entry under 1950s—Music in volume 3), and Magic Sam (1937–1969). Some white musicians were also attracted to blues music. Blues music had helped give rise to rock and roll in the 1950s. In the 1960s, rock musicians such as the **Rolling Stones** (see entry under 1960s—Music in volume 4) and Eric Clapton (1945–) brought blues songs and styles more directly into their music. Blues music also influenced the development of hard rock in the 1970s, heard in such bands as **Led Zeppelin** (see entry under 1970s—Music in volume 4).

The sound of blues music has remained largely the same since the 1960s, and it continues to be popular. In the 1980s, white blues musician Stevie Ray Vaughn (1954–1990) helped introduce a new generation of young people to the blues. In the twenty-first century, blues music remains an immensely important cultural form. Blues music has its own rich tradition and an influential legacy that has reached well beyond its original core audience.

Timothy Berg

For More Information

Awmiller, Craig. *This House on Fire: The Story of the Blues.* New York: Franklin Watts, 1996.

Cohn, Lawrence. *Nothing But the Blues: The Music and the Musicians.* New York: Abbeville Press, 1993.

Davis, Francis. *The History of the Blues.* New York: Hyperion, 1995.

Elmer, Howard. *Blues: Its Birth and Growth.* New York: Rosen, 1999.

Gioia, Ted. *Delta Blues: The Life and Times of the Mississippi Masters Who Revolutionized American Music.* New York: W. W. Norton, 2008.

Jones, LeRoi. *Blues People.* New York: Morrow Quill Paperbacks, 1963.

Palmer, Robert. *Deep Blues.* New York: Viking Press, 1981.

Russell, Tony. *The Blues: From Robert Johnson to Robert Cray.* New York: Schirmer Books, 1997.

Russell, Tony, and Chris Smith. *The Penguin Guide to Blues Recordings.* New York: Penguin, 2006.

Thomas, Roger. *Jazz and Blues.* Des Plaines, IL: Heinemann Library, 1988.

Grand Ole Opry

The longest-running **radio** (see entry under 1920s—TV and Radio in volume 2) show in broadcasting history, the *Grand Ole Opry* has long been the symbolic heart of **country music** (see entry under 1940s—Music in volume 3). For a long time, it represented the pinnacle of success in country music; musicians who were invited to play on the *Grand Ole Opry* radio show knew they were on their way to becoming stars. The *Opry* was important to country musicians, but it played an even more important role in American cultural life by bringing country music to a national audience.

In 1925, George D. Hay (1895–1968) began a show called the *WSM Barn Dance* in Nashville, Tennessee. The show featured local folk musicians. In 1927, Hay changed the name of the show to the *Grand Ole Opry.* The *Opry* was to be serious music for ordinary country people, just like opera was for the rich. Every Saturday night, Hay began the show by saying, "Let her go, boys," and off they went. As the show grew in popularity during the 1930s, 1940s, and 1950s, it featured some of the biggest names in country music, including Roy Acuff (1903–1992), Bill Monroe (1911–1996), Eddy Arnold (1918–2008), Hank Williams (1923–1953), George Jones (1931–), Johnny Cash (1932–2003), Patsy Cline (1932–1963), Loretta Lynn (1934–), and many, many others. Performers were paid very little, but they played for national exposure and the honor of being on the *Opry.*

The *Opry* truly made country music into a national phenomenon. Because the *Opry's* radio signal could reach far from Nashville, even as far north as Canada, country music, which before the *Opry* was largely a musical style from the southern United States, now reached people well beyond the south. As a result, country music became popular across the United States. Although the influence of the *Grand Ole Opry* diminished over the years as performers found concerts and regular radio a better way to attract fans, the show still stands as one of the most powerful forces in the history of American popular music.

Timothy Berg

For More Information

Escott, Colin. *The Grand Ole Opry: The Making of an American Icon.* New York: Center Street, 2006.

Hagan, Chet. *Grand Ole Opry.* New York: Henry Holt, 1989.

The Official Website of the Grand Ole Opry. http://www.opry.com (accessed June 30, 2011).

Stambler, Irwin, and Grelun Landon. *Country Music: The Encyclopedia.* New York: St. Martin's Press, 1997.

Wolfe, Charles K. *A Good-Natured Riot: The Birth of the Grand Ole Opry.* Nashville: Country Music Foundation and Vanderbilt University Press, 1999.

Jimmie Rodgers (1897–1933)

Jimmie Rodgers, known as the "Blue Yodeler" and the "Singing Brakeman," is sometimes called the father of **country music** (see entry under 1940s—Music in volume 3). Although his entire music career spanned only nine years, Rodgers became one of the most beloved performers in America, yodeling his soulful and uplifting **blues** (see entry under 1920s—Music in volume 2) to a country mired in economic depression during the 1930s.

Born in Pine Springs, Tennessee, Rodgers was hard at work on the railroad by the time he was fourteen. He worked his way up to brakeman before he was forced to retire at age twenty-seven with the then-incurable disease tuberculosis. He was discovered by a music company scout, and he began recording the songs he wrote in 1927. Before he died at age thirty-five, he had recorded over one hundred hit records, including "Blue Yodel (T for Texas)," "Mule Skinner Blues," "In the Jailhouse Now," and "T.B. Blues."

Though Rodgers was a successful musician, he lost much of his money during the stock market crash of 1929. He died of tuberculosis in New York City, exhausted after a long recording session.

Tina Gianoulis

For More Information

Mazor, Barry. *Meeting Jimmie Rodgers: How America's Original Roots Music Hero Changed the Pop Sounds of a Century.* New York: Oxford University Press, 2009.

Paris, Mike, and Chris Comber. *Jimmie the Kid: The Life of Jimmie Rodgers.* Cambridge, MA: Da Capo Press, 1981.

Porterfield, Nolan. *Jimmie Rodgers: The Life and Times of America's Blue Yodeler.* New ed. Jackson: University Press of Mississippi, 2007.

Rodgers, Carrie. *My Husband, Jimmie Rodgers.* 2nd ed. Nashville: Country Music Foundation, 1995.

"The Singing Brakeman: Jimmie Rodgers." *Boys' Life* (December 1980): pp. 53–55.

1920s

Print Culture

Communication in America was forever changed in the 1920s. With the beginning of radio broadcasting, printed newspapers and magazines were no longer the only sources of common information about happenings in the country or the world. Even though about fifty million Americans listened to the radio by the middle of the decade, newspapers and magazines remained the dominant sources of information during the decade.

Radio news bulletins captured people's interest, but printed sources told the "whole story." Newspapers not only provided serious reporting on news events, they also entertained people with gossip columns, comic strips, or the syndicated *Ripley's Believe It or Not!* cartoons. Pulp magazines, such as *Amazing Stories* and the *Black Mask,* published imaginative tales to entertain readers everywhere. People could buy newspapers and magazines almost anywhere, from boys on the street, at newsstands, and at railroad stations.

Although the advent of radio did cause some newspapers and magazines to merge or cease publication, some new types of magazines started during the decade. Some of the most influential new magazines started in the 1920s were *Time* and *Reader's Digest.* Recognizing that readers were spending less time on long, detailed articles, *Time* and *Reader's Digest* provided condensed summaries of events and topics to provide readers with a lot of information in a small amount of space. The format was a hit and both magazines continue to be two of the most read magazines into the new millennium.

Books remained popular entertainment in the 1920s. During the 1920s, some of the most influential American writers, such as F. Scott Fitzgerald (1896–1940), got their start. Children's books also became popular, with the beginning of the Little Blue Books, Winnie-the-Pooh, Nancy Drew, and the Hardy Boys series. First-run novels cost as much as $1.75, but reprinted hardcover books sold for fifty cents apiece. Drug and other retail stores often had libraries from which people could rent books for a nickel a day.

Better Homes and Gardens

A monthly magazine about home decor and the domestic lifestyle, *Better Homes and Gardens* made its debut in 1922 as *Fruit, Garden, and Home.* It was the brainchild of Edwin T. Meredith (1876–1928), who had first proposed the concept in 1913 as an advertisement in his magazine, *Successful Farming.* The name was changed to *Better Homes and Gardens* in 1924. The magazine came on the scene during the period of rapid social change that followed World War I (1914–18). The census of 1920 revealed that more Americans were then living in cities and towns than in rural areas for the first time in the country's history. From its early days, *Better Homes and Gardens* became an important resource used to define and promote the new urban and suburban lifestyles.

From the beginning, *Better Homes and Gardens* published a combination of articles on design, decor, cooking, and gardening. The magazine also ran contests that solicited home designs and recipes from its readers. *Better Homes and Gardens* was in the forefront of the movement that encouraged Americans to build and own their own homes. In 1932, the magazine introduced its BH&G building-plan service. The service worked with Better Homes in America, Inc., a group with local committees in thousands of communities across the United States. During the decades when new-home construction was practically halted because of the **Great Depression** (1929–41; see entry under 1930s—The Way We Lived in volume 2) and World War II (1939–45), *Better Homes and Gardens* whetted consumer appetites by publishing award-winning designs for attractive, easy-to-build homes. Their home designs helped set the design standards for the postwar American **suburbs** (see entry under 1950s—The Way We Lived in volume 3).

Better Homes and Gardens has lent its logo to a real-estate brokerage service as well as to a series of popular home-improvement books and cookbooks. Since the late 1990s, its Web site has offered similar information online.

Edward Moran

For More Information

Better Homes and Gardens. http://www.bhg.com (accessed June 30, 2011).

Hayden, Dolores. *Redesigning the American Dream: The Future of Housing, Work, and Family Life.* Rev. ed. New York: W. W. Norton, 2002.

"Meredith History." *Meredith Corporation.* http://www.meredith.com/meredith_corporate/company_history.html (accessed June 30, 2011).

Wright, Gwendolyn. *Building the Dream: A Social History of Housing in America.* Cambridge, MA: MIT Press, 1992.

Book-of-the-Month Club

· ·

Founded in 1926, the Book-of-the-Month Club (BOMC) revolutionized the way Americans bought books—and the way they *thought* about books as well. Appreciating fine literature had long been reserved for intellectuals and academics, until BOMC and its respected editorial board brought the works of great writers like William Faulkner (1897–1962), Ernest Hemingway (1899–1961), and John Steinbeck (1902–1968) to the masses.

Others had tried to sell books through mail order before, but only Harry Scherman (1887–1969), a writer and book lover from Montreal, Quebec, Canada, hit upon the idea of organizing his customers into a "club" that would be guided in its selections by a board of literary authorities. Club members committed to purchasing a certain number of books in a certain period of time. This not only proved to be a unique way of marketing books but had a major cultural impact as well. Although some complained that marketing books through the mail "dumbed down" great literature by treating it like just another consumer product, there can be no doubt that millions of Americans were exposed to great books for the first time through BOMC. One famous *New Yorker* cartoon depicted a woman breaking the bad news to her local librarian: "I'm afraid this is goodbye, Miss MacDonald. I'm joining the Book-of-the-Month Club."

So powerful was the BOMC brand name—and the more than one million members it claimed at its peak of popularity—that America's major publishing houses clamored for space in the catalog and for the designation of one of their books as a BOMC "main selection." As time went on, BOMC expanded the concept to numerous "specialty" book clubs devoted to subjects like history, cooking, and crafts. When **Internet** (see entry under 1990s—The Way We Lived in volume 5) booksellers like **Amazon.com** (see entry under 2000s—Commerce in volume 6) and new clubs, especially Oprah's Book Club, threatened to eat away at sales, BOMC responded in 2000 by merging with its leading competitor, Doubleday Direct Inc., to form a new company, Bookspan. With much of its hopes for future growth tied to Internet sales, the newly formed enterprise entered the twenty-first century determined to take Harry Scherman's revolutionary way of selling books into more homes than ever before.

Robert E. Schnakenberg

For More Information

"Book Clubs: Forgotten But Not Dead." *Publishing Trends.* http://www.publishingtrends.com/2000/12/book-clubs-forgotten-but-not-dead/ (accessed June 30, 2011).

Book-of-the-Month Club. http://www.bomc.com (accessed June 30, 2011).

Lee, Charles, *The Hidden Public: The Story of the Book-of-the-Month Club.* Garden City, NY: Doubleday, 1958.

Radway, Janice A. *A Feeling for Books: The Book-of-the-Month Club, Literary Taste, and Middle-Class Desire.* Chapel Hill: University of North Carolina Press, 1997.

Silverman, Al, ed. *The Book of the Month: Sixty Years of Books in American Life.* Boston: Little, Brown, 1986.

Buck Rogers

In January 1929, newspaper readers were introduced to a new type of adventure hero. Anthony "Buck" Rogers was America's first great science-fiction star. The influential *Buck Rogers* strip introduced futuristic exploits set in outer space that featured advanced technologies like laser beams, antigravity devices, atomic warfare, and **television** (see entry under 1940s—The Way We Lived in volume 3). John Dille (1884–1957), one of Buck's creators, quoted in Mike Benton's *The Illustrated History of Science Fiction Comics,* said, "I wanted to produce a

Painting by Anton Brzezinski of images from the Buck Rogers *comic strip.* © FORREST J. ACKERMAN COLLECTION/ CORBIS.

strip which would present imaginary adventures several centuries in the future. I wanted a strip in which the test tubes and laboratories of the scientists could be garnished up with a bit of imagination and treated as realities." The success of *Buck Rogers* sparked a public interest in science fiction that remains strong to this day.

Buck Rogers depicts the adventures of a twentieth-century pilot who is frozen in suspended animation for five hundred years. When he awakens, he discovers Mongol invaders have overrun America. With the aid of Wilma Deering, his companion, he liberates the nation. The pair's exploits continue as they face evil aliens and their most frequent adversaries, Killer Kane and Ardala.

According to scholar Fred Patten in *100 Years of American Newspaper Comics,* the *Buck Rogers* strip became so synonymous with science fiction that, "for the next five decades, science fiction of any sort was popularly known as 'that crazy Buck Rogers stuff.'" The futuristic machines, space flights, and alien creatures that Buck encountered on a daily basis amazed readers. Many later science-fiction writers have said they were inspired by Buck to create their own outer-space tales. Many later science fiction–oriented stories, like ***Flash Gordon*** (see entry under 1930s—Print Culture in volume 2), ***Star Trek*** (see entry under 1960s—TV and Radio in volume 4), and ***Star Wars*** (see entry under 1970s—Film and Theater in volume 4), all display direct influences from Buck Rogers' early adventures. Eventually, other science-fiction heroes would overshadow Buck.

Buck Rogers was one of the first strips to successfully merchandise itself as it inspired a wide variety of toys, games, and books. The character appeared on **radio** (see entry under 1920s—TV and Radio in volume 2) and in popular movie serials starring Buster Crabbe (1908–1983). Although the strip ended in 1967, Buck was revived briefly in the late 1970s in both newspapers and on television. As of 2010, many entertainment Web sites reported rumors that yet another feature film was in the works.

Charles Coletta

For More Information

Benton, Mike. *Science Fiction Comics: The Illustrated History.* Dallas: Taylor, 1992.
The Buck Rogers Home Page. http://www.buck-rogers.com (accessed June 30, 2011).
Caidin, Martin. *Buck Rogers: A Life in the Future.* Lake Geneva, WI: TSR, 1995.
Crawford, Hubert. *Crawford's Encyclopedia of Comic Books.* Middle Village, NY: Jonathan David Publishers, 1978.
Horn, Maurice, ed. *100 Years of American Newspaper Comics.* New York: Gramercy Books, 1996.

Gossip Columns

Gossip columns, and gossip columnists, feed a public craving for information about the rich, the prominent, and the powerful—particularly if that information is secretive and scandalous. Gossip columns are crammed with tidbits, some true and some rumor, about a movie star's love life or a

Gossip columnist Hedda Hopper in one of her many signature hats. © BETTMANN/ CORBIS.

politician's or business leader's behind-closed-doors dealings. To a gossip columnist, privacy is a dirty word. If you are a celebrity, no aspect of your life is beyond the scrutiny of a gossip. Ultimately, gossip serves the purpose of blurring the separation between those in power and the masses. In this regard, a gossip columnist's revelations about a celebrity's private life are the price to be paid for fame, power, or wealth.

Before the 1920s, mainstream journalism reflected an ethic in which respectability ruled, and fact took precedence over rumor. Periodicals such as *Town Topics,* which published tidbits about the wealthy during the late nineteenth century, were not considered reputable. Then came the rise of the movie star, which paralleled the evolution of the motion-picture industry during the early decades of the twentieth century. The public demanded information about their favorite screen idols. The mainstream media began meeting this demand by publishing the accounts of gossip columnists.

Perhaps the most influential newsmonger (someone who spreads gossip) of the first half of the twentieth century was Walter Winchell (1897–1972), a journalist credited with making gossip a media mainstay. The New York–based Winchell started out in 1924 as a columnist for the tabloid *Graphic*. In his column, "Mainly for Mainstreeters," he focused on anything and everything sex-related, from extramarital flings to illegitimate children. Winchell was a journalistic force between the 1920s and 1950s. At the height of his power, two-thirds of adult America read his column, which was syndicated to two thousand newspapers, or listened to his top-rated weekly radio broadcast. Winchell was a maker and breaker of reputations. Given his authority, it is not surprising that he was feared by his potential subjects. He was mindful of the power he wielded. "My column showed you into office," he boasted, "and my column can show you out again."

In the wake of Winchell's popularity emerged Louella Parsons (1893–1972) and Hedda Hopper (1890–1966), Hollywood-centered gossips whose fame eventually exceeded that of Winchell's. Beginning in the 1920s and lasting for several decades, Parsons was the most powerful woman in the film industry, demanding and receiving every movie business scoop. In the 1930s, Hopper began a rival column. Both dissected the lives of movie stars and made and destroyed careers. All too aware of her power, Hopper even cynically nicknamed her home "The House That Fear Built."

Today, gossip columnists are as powerful as ever. In fact, it was one such newsmonger, Matt Drudge (1967–), who first began spreading rumors on his **Internet** (see entry under 1990s—The Way We Lived in volume 5) Web site about the in-office extramarital relationships of President Bill Clinton (1946–). Eventually, Clinton's alleged sexual affairs became mainstream news. With all the subsequent revelations about the private life of a U.S. president, a question emerged: Has the media gone too far in reporting the private affairs of public people? With the popularity of Web sites such as *TMZ.com*, it appears the public is still hungry for even more celebrity gossip.

Rob Edelman

For More Information

Barbas, Samantha. *The First Lady of Hollywood: A Biography of Louella Parsons.* Berkeley: University of California Press, 2005.

Eells, George. *Hedda and Louella: A Dual Biography of Hedda Hopper and Louella Parsons.* New York: Putnam, 1972.

Frost, Jennifer. *Hedda Hopper's Hollywood.* New York: New York University Press, 2011.

Gabler, Neal. *Winchell: Gossip, Power, and the Culture of Celebrity.* New York: Alfred A. Knopf, 1994.

Spacks, Patricia Meyer. *Gossip.* New York: Alfred A. Knopf, 1985.

Walls, Jeannette. *Dish: The Inside Story on the World of Gossip.* New York: Spike, 2000.

Hardy Boys Series

Debuting in 1927, *The Hardy Boys Mystery Stories* were produced in book length by the famous Stratemeyer Syndicate, the company responsible for the **Bobbsey Twins** (see entry under 1940s—Print Culture in volume 3) and **Nancy Drew** (see entry under 1930s—Print Culture in volume 2) series. Readers of the first *Hardy Boys* stories learned that brothers Joe and Frank Hardy were amateur detectives. They tracked down criminals using "up-to-the-minute" technologies like shortwave radio and chased them on motorbikes, planes, and trains. They even had their own laboratory where they examined clues with microscopes and fingerprinting kits. Combining detective mystery with fast-paced adventure, the Hardy boys and their friends were a big hit. They survived the retirement after twenty years of their original writer Leslie McFarlane (1902–1977) and seem likely to remain in print well into the twenty-first century.

The Hardy Boys have long lived up to Stratemeyer's original idea of making them "exciting but clean." The boys never used weapons when fighting crooks and their contact with girls was limited. By the 1950s, they had become ridiculously pure and—as with the *Nancy Drew* series—a process of updating began at the end of the decade. Even so, in the 1960s the straight-arrow Hardy Boys became the target of cruel parodies (humorous imitations).

Over the years, the Hardy Boys have gone from 1920s boys' adventure heroes to television veterans. They appeared on **The Mickey Mouse Club** (see entry under 1950s—TV and Radio in volume 3) and in cartoon form on the ABC television network. The 1969 cartoon actually featured the boys as members of a rock group, and merchandising for the series included two spinoff albums. In 1977, Universal ran *The Hardy Boys/Nancy Drew Mysteries* television series in a prime-time slot that ended with the brothers working for the U.S. Justice Department. In the 1990s, as children's mystery fiction became more violent and graphic, the Hardy Boys began to lose popularity. A strong market for Hardy Boys memorabilia remains, however. The Hardy Boys are both the first and the most successful boy detective series. Their fans say they are the greatest teen detectives ever.

Chris Routledge

For More Information

Finnan, Robert W. *The Hardy Boys Unofficial Home Page.* http://hardyboys.bobfinnan.com/ (accessed June 30, 2011).

Connelly, Mark. *The Hardy Boys Mysteries, 1927–1979: A Cultural and Literary History.* Jefferson, NC: McFarland, 2008.

Greenwald, Marilyn S. *The Secret of the Hardy Boys: Leslie McFarlane and the Stratemeyer Syndicate.* Athens: Ohio University Press, 2004.

Kismaric, Carole, and Marvin Heiferman. *The Mysterious Case of Nancy Drew and the Hardy Boys.* New York: Simon & Schuster, 1998.

Lange, Brenda. *Edward Stratemeyer: Creator of the Hardy Boys and Nancy Drew.* Philadelphia: Chelsea House, 2003.

McFarlane, Leslie. *Ghost of the Hardy Boys: An Autobiography.* Toronto: Methuen/Two Continents, 1976.

Little Blue Books

Little Blue Books were slim, inexpensive reprints of the world's great literature, philosophy, and social thought. They were one of the biggest publishing sensations of the twentieth century. The Little Blue Book Company was founded by Emanuel Haldeman-Julius (1889–1951), who believed that everyone, regardless of income, should be exposed to history's best literature. In 1919, his press in Girard, Kansas, began printing the booklets, which cost as little as a nickel apiece and were small enough to fit in a shirt pocket. The works were wildly popular and eventually sold over five hundred million copies. (As a comparison, by late 2001, the popular **Harry Potter** series [see entry under 1990s—Print Culture in volume 5] had sold over one hundred million copies worldwide.)

Haldeman-Julius and his wife Marcet (1887–1941) were socialists. (Socialists believe that the production and distribution of goods should be owned by the community or the government rather than by individuals, and that all people should share in the work as well as in the goods produced.) Their beliefs had a great deal to do with their desire to bring affordable literature to everyone. They wrote articles on equal rights, befriended progressive authors such as **Jack London** (1876–1916; see entry under 1900s—Print Culture in volume 1) and Clarence Darrow (1857–1938), and edited their own socialist magazine. The Little Blue Books brought all sorts of challenging reading to a huge audience. The titles included such works as *The Theory of Reincarnation Explained, A History of the Modern Christian Church,* and *Kant's Critical Philosophy.* Even the complete works of William Shakespeare (1564–1616) became available through the series.

The Little Blue Books were not all serious literature. The series also included works of fantasy and horror (by authors such as Edgar Allan Poe [1809–1849]) as well as cookbooks, dictionaries, and a book on how to start a business. The series also included some of the first self-help books, and published *What Every Young Girl Should Know* by Margaret Sanger (1879–1966). Her book was one of the first books written for teenage girls on matters of sex and growing up.

Eventually, over two thousand titles were sold. The presses in Kansas ran literally twenty-four hours a day in the 1920s and 1930s. The public gradually lost interest, however, and by the 1970s all that was left was a small mail order business. A fire destroyed the warehouse in 1978, taking with it all the remaining unsold copies of the Little Blue Books. Today, Little Blue Books are still widely available and affordable at bookstores and at **Internet** (see entry under 1990s—The Way We Lived in volume 5) sites like **eBay** (see entry under 2000s—Commerce in volume 6).

Karl Rahder

For More Information

Anderson, Lenore. "Fiftieth Anniversary Celebration of the First Little Blue Book." *Porter Library Bulletin* (Vol. 3, no. 18, May 15, 1969).

Haldeman-Julius, E. *The First Hundred Million.* New York: Simon and Schuster, 1928.

Salmonson, Jessica Amanda. "Hobos & Socialists: Emanuel Haldeman-Julius & the Little Blue Books." *Violet Books.* http://www.violetbooks.com/littleblue.html (accessed June 30, 2011).

Little Orphan Annie

Little Orphan Annie, which has been appearing in newspapers since 1924, is one of the most famous comic strips in history. Created by Harold Gray (1894–1968), it revolves around the adventures of a feisty, red-haired orphan girl who travels across America, meeting every challenge with grit and resourcefulness. In the initial story line, billionaire industrialist Oliver "Daddy" Warbucks adopts Annie. Their relationship became central to the strip as Annie and her father were constantly being separated and reunited.

Gray was a staunch conservative and one of the first artists to inject politics into the comics page. Through *Little Orphan Annie,* he preached a philosophy of rugged individualism and traditional values. Within his melodramatic tales of Annie's exploits, Gray included attacks on the New Deal, income taxes, welfare, and the government's interference with big business. Both Annie and Warbucks continually preached the value of self-reliance. In *100 Years of American Newspaper Comics,* Gray's philosophy is summed up in his description of his little orphan: "Annie is tougher than hell, with a heart of gold and a fast left, who can take care of herself because she has to."

Gray populated his strip with a cast of exaggerated characters who personified aspects of Gray's political beliefs and whose names reflected their personalities. Among the most memorable supporting players were Miss Asthma, director of Annie's orphanage; J. Preston Slime; Phineas Pinchpenny; and Mrs. Bleating-Heart, who embodied all Gray distrusted about liberals. The most frequently seen characters were The Asp and Punjab, Warbucks' mysterious bodyguards, who regularly rescued Annie from danger. One of the strip's most popular figures was Sandy, Annie's faithful dog whose bark—"Arf!"—became a well-known expression. Annie's own favorite exclamation—"Leapin' Lizards!"—also became a catch-phrase. Gray's artistry featured statuesque figures with blank oval eyes.

Little Orphan Annie was one of America's most popular comics for decades. Its characters were soon seen beyond the newspaper pages. Annie has been the subject of several films; a highly rated radio serial of the 1930s and 1940s; and a line of toys, games, and merchandise. In 1977, the musical *Annie* debuted on **Broadway** (see entry under 1900s—Film and Theater in volume 1) to much acclaim. Its rousing song "Tomorrow" has become a classic. The song perfectly captures

Annie's indomitable spirit, as exemplified by the song's first stanza: "The sun'll come out / Tomorrow / Bet your bottom dollar / That tomorrow / There'll be sun!"

Charles Coletta

For More Information

Blackbeard, Bill, and Martin Williams. *The Smithsonian Collection of Newspaper Comics.* Washington, DC: Smithsonian Institution Press, 1977.

Gray, Harold. *Arf! The Life and Times of Little Orphan Annie, 1935–1945.* New Rochelle, NY: Arlington House, 1970.

Horn, Maurice, ed. *100 Years of American Newspaper Comics.* New York: Gramercy Books, 1996.

Markstein, Donald D. "Little Orphan Annie." *Don Markstein's Toonopedia.* http://www.toonopedia.com/annie.htm (accessed June 30, 2011).

Smith, Bruce. *The History of Little Orphan Annie.* New York: Ballantine, 1982.

New Yorker

In February 1925, the inaugural issue of the *New Yorker* magazine was published. Although it struggled in its early years, the weekly magazine would ultimately become a national magazine famous for the quality and breadth of its writing and cartoons.

The cover of the May 24, 2010, issue of the New Yorker, a magazine that has been published since 1925.
© STUDIO 101/ALAMY.

The *New Yorker* was the brainchild of Harold Ross (1892–1951). After World War I (1914–18), Ross began hanging out at New York's Algonquin Hotel with a group of writers and artists that would come to be known as the "Algonquin Round Table." Ross was taken with the wit and sophistication of the group and decided that if he could capture it in a magazine, it would find a readership. Ross, who would edit the magazine for twenty-six years, established the magazine's four basic literary emphases: nonfiction, fiction, poetry, and cartoons. The *New Yorker* went on to excel in all four areas, frequently in the same issue.

The early years of the *New Yorker* featured regular contributions from writers and artists such as Dorothy Parker (1893–1967), E. B. White (1899–1985), and James Thurber (1894–1961).

Their sophisticated work helped to establish the magazine's reputation as a serious literary magazine for intellectual readers, although there were critics who dubbed the magazine "snooty." In 1946, the magazine made journalistic history by devoting an entire issue to *Hiroshima* by John Hersey (1914–1993). The work was a brutal account of America's nuclear bombing of the Japanese city of the same name during World War II (1939–45).

After Ross died in 1951, William Shawn (1907–1992) took over the editorship of the *New Yorker*. Under his guidance, the magazine's reputation as "the best magazine that ever was" continued to grow. Writers such as John Cheever (1912–1982), J. D. Salinger (1919–2010), and John Updike (1932–2009) published some of their best fiction in the *New Yorker*'s pages. The work of cartoonist Charles Addams (1912–1988) continued to present a bizarre world that would become the basis for *The Addams Family* TV show and several *Addams Family* feature films. Continuing the tradition started with the publication of *Hiroshima*, under Shawn's leadership the magazine would devote issues to groundbreaking works such as *In Cold Blood* by Truman Capote (1924–1984), *Silent Spring* by Rachel Carson (1907–1964), and *The Fire Next Time* by James Baldwin (1924–1987). Pauline Kael (1919–2001), among the most famous and controversial American film critics ever, also spent the bulk of her career writing for the *New Yorker*.

Shawn was forced into retirement in the late 1980s, at which time the magazine's reputation took something of a hit. The two editors since 1992, Tina Brown (1953–) and David Remnick (1958–), have modernized the magazine and widened its focus to cover both current events and popular culture. Despite these changes, many agree that in an age of increasing hype and a growing tendency toward the tabloid in the mainstream American press, the *New Yorker* remains a beacon for readers looking for intelligent and sophisticated writing.

Robert C. Sickels

For More Information

Corey, Mary F. *The World Through a Monocle: The New Yorker at Mid-century.* Cambridge, MA: Harvard University Press, 1999.

Gill, Brendan. *Here at the New Yorker.* New ed. New York: Da Capo Press, 1997.

Kunkel, Thomas. *Genius in Disguise: Harold Ross of the New Yorker.* New York: Random House, 1995.

New Yorker. http://www.newyorker.com (accessed June 30, 2011).

Yagoda, Ben. *About Town: The New Yorker and the World It Made.* New York: Scribner, 2000.

Popeye

Popeye, America's most famous sailor man, made his first appearance as an incidental character in the January 17, 1929, installment of the *Thimble Theatre* comic strip. Created by cartoonist Elzie Crisler Segar (1894–1938), the one-eyed, craggy-faced sailor with bulging forearms and ever-present corncob pipe was an unlikely heroic figure. He was un-educated, uncouth, and spoke in a unique dialect peppered with curses and malapropisms (the use of words that sound similar to the intended words but ridiculously wrong). Despite these flaws, Popeye quickly emerged as one of the nation's favorite characters.

Segar created *Thimble Theatre* in 1919 at the urging of publisher William Randolph Hearst (1863–1951), who was looking for a new strip to feature in his many newspapers. The original premise of the strip involved the spoofing of current movies. Segar soon transformed the strip from a gag-a-day feature to an adventure series. His original cast consisted of the slightly seedy Oyl family. Cole and Nana Oyl were the bumbling parents of Castor Oyl, a conniving blowhard, and Olive Oyl, their painfully thin and ungracious daughter. Many of the strip's earliest adventures revolved around the escapades of Castor and Ham Gravy, Olive's first boyfriend. In 1929, Castor and Ham acquired a magical bird known as Bernice the Whiffle Hen. They planned to take the hen to a gambling casino on Dice Island and use the bird's mystical powers to win a fortune. However, neither knew how to operate a boat. They searched the waterfront for someone to sail them to Dice Island and soon encountered Popeye.

Popeye was not designed as a recurring character, but Segar enjoyed him and extended his stay until, eventually, Popeye held the cen-ter stage of *Thimble Theatre*. In *Comics Between the Panels,* Segar's attitude toward the sailor is revealed: "Popeye is much more than a goofy comic character to me. He represents all my emotions, and he is an outlet for them. I'd like

A poster for the 1933 cartoon film Popeye the Sailor Man.
© PICTORIAL PRESS LTD./ ALAMY.

to cut loose and knock the heck out of a lot of people, but my good judgment and size hold me back." Much of Popeye's popularity resulted from his seeming indestructibility. The original source of Popeye's superhuman strength was said to have been from rubbing the head of the Whiffle Hen. Later, spinach was claimed as the source of Popeye's great fighting prowess. In the 1930s, Popeye was so popular that the spinach industry credited Segar with increasing spinach consumption by 33 percent.

Popeye's adventures combined elements of farce (ridiculous situations meant to make people laugh), surrealism (dreamlike representations of the subconscious mind), pathos (situations making the viewer feel pity or compassion), and melodrama (emotional story lines that emphasize the action rather than the characters). The strip also boasted one of the greatest casts in comics. Among those who joined Popeye on his voyages were Poopdeck Pappy, Wimpy, Eugene the Jeep, Swee'Pea, and Alice the Goon. Popeye's most persistent adversaries were the evil Sea Hag, Bluto, and Brutus, his rivals for Olive's affections.

Popeye was a merchandising success and appeared in numerous cartoon shorts. In 1980, Robin Williams (1952–) starred as the sailor in the film musical *Popeye* by Robert Altman (1925–2006). The strip continued for decades after Segar's death, but lacked its creator's unique vision.

Charles Coletta

For More Information

Anobile, Richard. *Popeye: The Movie Novel.* New York: Avon, 1980.

Blackbeard, Bill, and Martin Williams. *The Smithsonian Collection of Newspaper Comics.* Washington, DC: Smithsonian Institution Press, 1977.

Duin, Steve, and Mike Richardson. *Comics Between the Panels.* Milwaukie, OR: Dark Horse Comics, 1998.

Grandinetti, Fred M. *Popeye: An Illustrated Cultural History.* Jefferson, NC: McFarland, 2004.

Marschall, Richard. *America's Great Comic-Strip Artists.* New York: Abbeville Press, 1989.

Sagendorf, Bud. *Popeye: The First Fifty Years.* New York: Workman Publishing, 1979.

Reader's Digest

Published monthly since January 1922, *Reader's Digest* is the most widely read magazine in the world. At its peak in 1984, more than seventeen million readers in the United States subscribed to the publication, which reached another eleven million readers through its nineteen foreign-language editions. Since its debut, *Reader's Digest* has adhered to a simple formula of appealing to time-pressed readers by reprinting condensed versions of articles that have appeared in other publications. The magazine has also applied this format to a spinoff business in book publishing. The *Reader's Digest Condensed Books* series has published hundreds of shortened versions of novels and nonfiction alike.

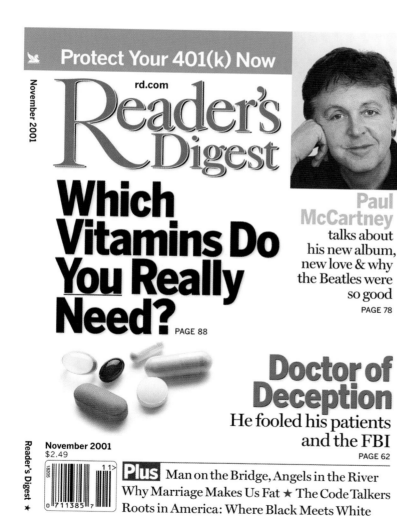

A typical magazine cover for Reader's Digest, *published since 1922.* © AP IMAGES.

The formula for this monthly magazine has remained unchanged for eighty years: approximately thirty condensed articles each issue (one for each day of the month), together with short, humorous stories contributed by readers in such departments as "Life in These United States," "Laughter Is the Best Medicine," and "Humor in Uniform." Articles were traditionally never sensationalistic and rarely controversial, with a tendency toward inspirational, self-help stories. The magazine has been criticized for espousing a generally right-wing, conservative point of view and for evoking nostalgia for a simpler, less diversified America. During the Cold War (1945–89), for example, articles often denounced the evils of communism and criticized groups such as the National Council of Churches for being too liberal, even radical. Over the years, *Reader's Digest* published serious yet simplified articles about important medical and social issues like venereal disease, cancer, and the dangers of **cigarettes** (see entry under 1920s—Commerce in volume 2) and unsafe driving.

Reader's Digest was founded by William Roy DeWitt Wallace (1889–1981), a salesman, and his wife, Lila Acheson (1887–1984), a feminist reformer, who established the Reader's Digest Association in 1921 in the New York City suburb of Pleasantville, where its headquarters is still located. No advertising appeared in the magazine until 1955, when surveys indicated that readers would prefer ads to an increase in subscription fees. The magazine has never accepted tobacco advertising and ran its first liquor advertisement only in 1979. By the late 1990s, the magazine's domestic circulation had fallen to 12.5 million. Its publishers were forced to initiate cost-cutting measures that included layoffs of employees and a redesign of the magazine. The company filed for bankruptcy protection in 2009 and came out of bankruptcy a year later, having shed 75 percent of its debt.

The Reader's Digest Foundation, one of the largest philanthropic institutions in the United States, is known for its support of important institutions such as medical research facilities, art museums, symphony orchestras, and educational projects.

Edward Moran

For More Information

Canning, Peter. *American Dreamers: The Wallaces and Reader's Digest, an Insider's Story.* New York: Simon & Schuster, 1996.

Heidenry, John. *Theirs Was the Kingdom: Lila and DeWitt Wallace and the Story of the Reader's Digest.* New York: W. W. Norton, 1993.

Reader's Digest Version. http://www.rd.com (accessed on June 30, 2011).

Ripley's Believe It or Not!

First seen in 1923 as a daily feature in the *New York Globe,* a cartoon by Robert L. Ripley (1893–1949) brought the phrase "Believe it or not!" into the common language. Ripley's cartoon depictions of amazing oddities, exotic rarities, and outrageous feats rapidly gained popularity as more and more readers, first in New York, then around the country and around the world, eagerly flipped through their papers searching for the latest *Ripley's Believe It or Not!*

Ripley was born in Santa Rosa, California, in 1893 to a working-class family. He was a promising **baseball** (see entry under 1900s—Sports and Games in volume 1) player, who rose through the semiprofessional league and seemed to have a chance to make the big leagues before an arm injury sidelined his career. However, a childhood talent for cartooning came to his aid and he was soon selling his drawings to magazines like ***Life*** (see entry under 1930s—Print Culture in volume 2). In the early 1900s, Ripley moved to New York, where he got a job as a sports cartoonist for the *Globe.* His first *Believe It or Not!* cartoons portrayed amazing sports feats, such as the man who skipped rope 11,810 times straight.

Readers were fascinated by Ripley's pictures. Soon, his look at the bizarre, quirky, and amazing side of life branched out beyond the sports arena. His cartoons began to show such wonders as a will written on an eggshell and a human pincushion who could push hat pins into his skin without pain. Although readers sent him hundreds of letters suggesting topics for his cartoon, Ripley sought even more. He began a series of expeditions around the world to seek out unusual objects and people to showcase in *Believe It or Not!*

In 1933, at the Chicago **World's Fair** (see entry under 1900s—The Way We Lived in volume 1), Ripley unveiled his first "Odditorium," or museum of the exotic and unusual. The fair boasted that hundreds of

The world's smallest male teen, Khagendra Thapa Magar, stands just 22 inches high. He poses in front of a copy of Ripley's Believe It or Not! *in 2010.* © EMMANUEL DUNAND/AFP/GETTY IMAGES.

people fainted at the ghastly sights they saw there. Soon, six more Odditoriums had opened around the country. In 1949, Ripley was given his own weekly television show on NBC, but only a few programs aired before his death of a heart attack. Since Ripley was such an avid recorder of "firsts," it is perhaps fitting that his cartoon, *Ripley's Believe It or Not!* holds the record for the longest continuous cartoon. In 2011, it was still running in almost two hundred newspapers in forty-two countries. There are thirty-two *Believe It or Not!* museums around the world, showcasing thousands of oddities, many of them collected by Robert Ripley himself.

Tina Gianoulis

For More Information

Considine, Bob. *Ripley: The Modern Marco Polo.* New York: Doubleday, 1961.

Corelli, Rae. "Weird? Believe It!" *Maclean's* (Vol. 106, no. 38, September 20, 1993): pp. 50–53.

Jewel, Dan, and Fannie Weinstein. "Rare Bird: Fifty Years After His Death, Robert Ripley's Strange and Wonderful Legacy Lives On—Believe It or Not!" *People Weekly* (Vol. 52, July 12, 1999): pp. 89–92.

Ripley's ... Believe It or Not! http://www.ripleys.com (accessed June 30, 2011).

Time

Time: The Weekly Newsmagazine has been published continuously since March 3, 1923. Founded by Henry R. Luce (1898–1967) and Briton Hadden (1898–1929), *Time* was the first publication in Luce's media empire that would later include *Fortune* (founded in 1930), **Life** (founded in 1936; see entry under 1930s—Print Culture in volume 2), **Sports Illustrated** (founded in 1954; see entry under 1950s—Sports and Games in volume 3), and **People** (founded in 1974; see entry under 1970s—Print Culture in volume 4). Designed for busy readers who wanted a weekly roundup of news and opinion, *Time* pioneered the concept of the widely imitated weekly news magazine. It offered brief, pithy articles organized into departments such as national news, foreign news, the arts, books, religion, education, and finance.

Time soon became known for its unique style, which tried to compress complex ideas and stories into brief digests, often using witty language like puns and new, original words. The magazine's editors often created cute nicknames for the figures being reported on, or they used strings of alliterative (beginning with the same letter) adjectives in describing their subjects. *Time* also helped popularize certain words, such as calling a rich capitalist a "tycoon" or describing someone with an expert's opinion as a "pundit." In its 1939 report of Germany's invasion of Poland, *Time* used the phrase "World War II" (1939–45) for the first time.

Each week, a portrait of an important newsmaker appeared on *Time*'s cover, with "theme" covers becoming more common after the 1980s. Since 1927, when it chose **Charles Lindbergh** (1902–1974; see entry under 1920s—The Way We Lived in volume 2), *Time* selected a "Man of the Year," until 1999, when the award was renamed "Person of the Year." This title is given to people whom *Time* judges to have had an especially important influence on world events. Over the years, the feature has been expanded to include women, groups (such as the under-thirty generation), and even the personal computer.

In 1990, Time-Life, Inc. joined with Warner Communications to form a large media conglomerate known as Time-Warner. In 1998, with its weekly circulation at 4.2 million, *Time* magazine celebrated its seventy-fifth anniversary with a gala at New York's Radio City Music Hall that honored all the living men and women who had appeared on its cover over the years. Since the 1990s, however, subscriptions have fallen sharply, in large part due to the popularity of online news sources.

Edward Moran

For More Information

Clurman, Richard. *To the End of Time: The Selection and Conquest of a Media Empire.* New York: Simon & Schuster, 1992.

Elson, Robert T. *Time, Inc.: The Intimate History of a Publishing Enterprise.* 2 vols. New York: Atheneum, 1968.

Time.com. http://www.time.com/time (accessed July 1, 2011).

Weird Tales

• •

One of the most famous and enduring of the **pulp magazines** (see entry under 1930s—Print Culture in volume 2), *Weird Tales* was founded in 1923 by J. C. Henneberger and J. M. Lassinger to give a voice to writers who might otherwise have no outlet for their dark dreams and wild imaginings. The magazine played a central role in the development of today's literary genres of science fiction, fantasy, and horror.

The magazine struggled to find an audience in its first two years, but then a change in editor signaled an improvement in its fortunes. Its unique editorial goals and the fact that it paid better than any of the other pulps (so called because of the extremely cheap paper that was used to produce them) allowed *Weird Tales* to attract the work of writers who would become giants of the field.

In the 1920s, the "first wave" of important authors included Robert E. Howard (1906–1936; creator of Conan the Barbarian), Seabury Quinn (1889–1969; the most prolific of the magazine's writers), and the legendary H. P. Lovecraft (1890–1937), a Providence, Rhode Island, writer whose atmospheric, moody tales of a race of savage gods formed what is today called the "Cthulhu mythos." The "second wave" arrived in the next decade, bringing such writers as Clark Ashton Smith (1893–1961), C. L. Moore (1911–1987), and Jack Williamson (1908–2006). In the "third wave," which reached the magazine in the 1940s, were Robert Bloch (1917–1994; who would later write *Psycho*), Manly Wade Wellman (1903–1986), Fritz Leiber (1910–1992), and, most important, Ray Bradbury (1920–), perhaps the twentieth century's greatest fantasy writer.

The magazine became known for challenging the traditions and standards of the genre. It could be sexually daring for its day. Some of the gruesome violence in its stories pushed the edges of good taste, even for the pulps. Furthermore, *Weird Tales* was among the first to publish "Sword and Sorcery" (beginning with Robert E. Howard's work) and to blend sub-genres, such as combining science fiction with horror.

As with the other surviving pulps, the magazine went out of business in the 1950s. Such was the loyalty and affection generated by this quirky publication, however, that *Weird Tales* has been revived several times: in 1973, 1978, and 1984. Its most recent resurrection occurred in 1998.

Justin Gustainis

For More Information

Anderson, Douglas A. *H. P. Lovecraft's Favorite Weird Tales.* Cold Spring Harbor, NY: Cold Spring, 2007.

Jaffery, Sheldon, and Fred Cook. *The Collector's Index to Weird Tales.* Bowling Green, OH: Bowling Green State University Popular Press, 1985.

Weinberg, Robert. *The Weird Tales Story.* Gillette, NJ: Wildside Press, 1976.

Weird Tales. http://weirdtalesmagazine.com/ (accessed on July 1, 2011).

Winnie the Pooh

In an entertainment industry dominated by shoot-'em-up computer games and blockbuster action movies, Winnie the Pooh is an unlikely success. The "tubby little cubby" first appeared in 1924 in *When We Were Very Young,* a collection of verse by A. A. Milne (1882–1956). Winnie the Pooh became a household name in 1926 with the publication of the children's story *Winnie-the-Pooh,* illustrated by Ernest H. Shepard (1879–1976). Milne's book became one of the most popular children's books of the twentieth century. Its follow-up volumes, *Now We Are Six* (1926) and *The House at Pooh Corner* (1928) had similar success. At the beginning of the twenty-first century, the popularity of the "bear of very little brain" goes far beyond the preteen audience. Pooh and his friends Rabbit, Piglet, Eeyore (donkey), Owl, Tigger (tiger), Kanga, and Roo remind their adult fans of gentler times. Since the 1990s, Winnie the Pooh has come to rival Mickey Mouse as the face of **Disney** (see entry under 1920s—Film and Theater in volume 2), which purchased the rights to Pooh in 1966. (Disney dropped the hyphens that were originally in Pooh's name.)

Winnie the Pooh and friend Piglet in a scene from the 2003 animated film Piglet's Big Movie. © AF ARCHIVE/ALAMY.

Inspired by his daughters, Walt Disney (1901–1966) made Winnie the Pooh a movie star. The first short feature *Winnie the Pooh and the Honey Tree* was released in 1966. It was the first of three short films that were re-released together a decade later as Disney's twenty-second feature, *The Many Adventures of Winnie the Pooh* (1977). In 1996, the popularity of Pooh and friends was boosted by the thirtieth anniversary release of the original films. This was followed by *Pooh's Grand Adventure* in 1997 and a number of other films, some theatrically released, others going straight to video. In the summer of 2011, Disney released the feature film *Winnie the Pooh*, based on three of the stories in Milne's books.

Durable soft toys based on the Disney Pooh are available for children. In addition, in 2001 Winnie the Pooh products constitute a huge merchandising franchise aimed at two distinct groups of adult customers. Products based on the original pastel Shepard illustrations are marketed directly at older adults and range from high-quality soft toys to table lamps and framed prints. Brightly colored Disney cartoon–inspired products are aimed at younger adults. The rounded, yellow cartoon bear appears on everything from underwear to neckties, clocks, and coffee mugs. The appeal of Winnie the Pooh to adults has been put down to nostalgia. Life in Pooh's Hundred Acre Wood is kinder than in the adult world. Winnie the Pooh and friends offer safety, comfort, and a warm sense of well-being. As the song goes, "He's Winnie the Pooh … willy nilly silly ole bear."

Chris Routledge

For More Information

Harrison, Shirley. *The Life and Times of the Real Winnie-the-Pooh: The Teddy Bear Who Inspired A. A. Milne.* Gretna, LA: Pelican, 2011.

Thwaite, Ann. *The Brilliant Career of Winnie-the-Pooh: The Definitive History of the Best Bear in the World.* London: Methuen, 1992.

Williams, John Tyerman. *Pooh and the Millennium: In Which the Bear of Very Little Brain Explores the Ancient Mysteries at the Turn of the Century.* New York: Dutton, 1997.

1920s

Sports and Games

Along with all the other grand titles of the decade, the 1920s were also known as "The Golden Age of Sports." Players in almost every sport far exceeded fans' expectations and became heroic legends who are still remembered. They included baseball greats Babe Ruth (1895–1948), Ty Cobb (1886–1961), and Lou Gehrig (1903–1941); football heroes Red Grange (1903–1991) and Knute Rockne (1888–1931); tennis aces Helen Wills (1905–1998) and Bill Tilden (1893–1953); and probably the greatest lightweight boxer Benny Leonard (1896–1947) and heavy-weight champion Jack Dempsey (1895–1983). The dominating performance of Americans at the seventh and eighth Olympic games provided Americans with more reasons to follow their favorite sports than ever before. Radio broadcasts of athletic events turned local heroes into national sports icons for the first time.

With so many sports to choose from, Americans became truly sports crazy. Home-run hitter Babe Ruth led the New York Yankees to its first World Series win in 1923. College football rivaled baseball as the most watched American sport. A professional football game between the New York Giants and the Chicago Bears attracted 76,000 paying spectators in 1925. Boxing matches grossed millions of dollars. The Boston Celtics team boosted professional basketball by playing between 125 and 150 games a season for adoring fans. Golf was dominated by the "Three

Musketeers"—Bobby Jones (1902–1971), Walter Hagen (1892–1969), and Gene Sarazen (1902–1999)—who popularized the sport and influenced the drive to construct both public and private golf courses around the country.

The huge sums American sports fans spent watching games funded the construction of giant stadiums for baseball and football. The 62,000-seat Yankee Stadium, or "The House That Ruth Built," opened in the Bronx, New York, in 1923. The 18,000-seat indoor arena at Madison Square Garden in New York City opened in 1925. And university football stadiums that held between 46,000 (University of Washington) and 100,000 people (University of Michigan) opened across the country during the decade. In addition, Americans' interest in playing sports themselves fueled the construction of various recreational swimming and multisport athletic clubs around the country.

Americans' love of sport included many recreational games and activities. Mah-Jongg, an ancient Chinese game, became a craze mostly among women in the 1920s. Introduced in 1922, the game outsold radios within a year and spawned the creation of more than twenty rule books and the sale of silk kimonos (which women donned while playing the game). Simon & Schuster started a nationwide craze with the publication of the first crossword puzzle book in 1924. Soon railroads carried dictionaries for use by their passengers, college teams competed in crossword puzzle tournaments, and the University of Kentucky even offered a course on the puzzle. Children twirled yo-yos and built frontier cabins with Lincoln Logs. For the heartier, dance marathons, the longest of which lasted more than ninety hours, were held across the country.

Charles Atlas

Charles Atlas (1893–1972) became the first nationally recognized American bodybuilder. Born Angelo Siciliano in Italy in 1893, Atlas moved to the United States as a skinny youth. He developed dramatic, shapely muscles using his own system of isometric (non-muscle-contracting) exercises that pitted muscles against each other to build strength. Atlas was dubbed the "World's Most Perfectly Developed Man" in 1921.

Bodybuilder Charles Atlas lifts four boys weighing a total of 500 pounds on October 21, 1945, at New York City's Madison Square Boys Club.
© AP IMAGES.

Atlas became a national celebrity selling his "Dynamic Tension Bodybuilding Course" through the mail. His most famous ad was a cartoon showing a "ninety-seven-pound weakling" who, after being bullied at the beach, uses the Atlas system to become a model of muscular manhood. Atlas died in 1972, but the Charles Atlas Ltd. company still sells his exercise program.

Tom Pendergast

For More Information

Charles Atlas: The World's Most Perfectly Developed Man. http://www.charlesatlas.com (accessed on July 1, 2011).

Hugo, Geraldine, producer. *Charles Atlas: Modern Day Hercules* (video). A&E Biography Series, 1999.

Crossword Puzzles

One of the most enduring fads to emerge from the 1920s—a decade remembered as a time of rebellion, fun, and frivolity—was the crossword puzzle. A crossword puzzle is a grid of numbered squares. Accompanying the grid is a list of clues numbered to correspond to the squares. Puzzlers solve the clues to find words whose letters interlock when they are correctly filled in the blank squares.

Word games have been a feature of many cultures with written languages. Some forms of crossword puzzles have been found on ancient tombs in Egypt, on four-thousand-year-old stone carvings in Crete, and on Chinese antiques. The birth of the modern crossword puzzle, however, is more recent and precise: December 21, 1913. On that Sunday, the *New York World* newspaper published a word puzzle that had been designed by Arthur Wynne (1862–1945), a journalist from Liverpool, England. Wynne's puzzle, which he called a "Word-Cross," was a diamond-shaped grid with no black squares. The new type of puzzle was immediately very popular on both sides of the Atlantic Ocean. Soon dozens of newspapers were offering crosswords in their Sunday editions.

In 1924, the growing crossword fad received a boost when Simon & Schuster published a book of fifty crossword puzzles, complete with pencil and eraser. Within three months, the book had sold forty thousand copies, climbing to five hundred thousand by the end of the year. Though some intellectuals scoffed at the trivial nature of the knowledge required to solve crosswords, puzzlers were happily obsessed. Puzzles appeared everywhere, not only in magazines and newspapers. Puzzles turned up in such unlikely places as the back of menus in the dining cars of Pennsylvania Railroad trains.

Although the intensity of the 1920s fascination with puzzles faded, crossword puzzles have remained a beloved feature of almost every popular newpaper and magazine. Computer programs have been written to help create crosswords. At national competitions, puzzlers show off their skills as they vie for the championship of this otherwise solitary sport.

Tina Gianoulis

For More Information

American Crossword Puzzle Tournament. http://www.crosswordtournament.com (accessed July 1, 2011).

Arnot, Michelle. *What' Gnu? A History of the Crossword Puzzle.* New York: Vintage, 1981.

Augarde, Tony. *The Oxford Guide to Word Games.* Oxford and New York: Oxford University Press, 1984.

Millington, Roger. *Crossword Puzzles: Their History and Their Cult.* New York: Pocket Books, 1977.

Schwarz, Frederic D. "1924: Seventy-Five Years Ago." *American Heritage* (Vol. 50, no. 2, April 1999): pp. 134–36.

Shepard, Richard F. "Bambi Is a Stag and Tubas Don't Go 'Pah-Pah: History of Crossword Puzzles." *New York Times Magazine* (February 16, 1992): pp. 31–33.

Jack Dempsey (1895–1983)

During the 1920s, professional fighter Jack Dempsey—nicknamed the "Manassa Mauler" after his hometown of Manassa, Colorado—was king of the boxing ring. He also was a controversial figure, at once beloved and despised. His participation in one of his sport's most famous and contested matches not only cemented his legend but transformed him into a hero, a mantle he held for the rest of his life.

While still a teenager, Dempsey was boxing as an amateur under the name "Kid Blackie." He eventually turned pro and became the heavyweight champion on July 4, 1919. He knocked out Jess Willard (1881–1968) in the third round, inflicting a broken jaw, two broken ribs, and four missing teeth upon Willard. The day after his victory, however, sportswriter Grantland Rice (1880–1954) accused Dempsey of evading the military draft. Although Dempsey was found innocent in court, much of the public viewed him negatively because of the publicity surrounding the charge.

Dempsey's 1921 bout against Frenchman Georges Carpentier (1894–1975), a decorated World War I (1914–18) combat pilot, was billed as a battle of good versus evil. It was the first boxing match to be

Heavyweight boxing champion Jack Dempsey stops a hard left from opponent Tom Gibbons during a Shelby, Montana, match in 1923. © KEYSTONE PICTURES USA/ALAMY.

broadcast on radio and the first to take in $1 million at the gate. It was fought before ninety thousand fans, the largest audience ever to witness a live sporting event to that date. Dempsey won over the buzz of the crowd with a third-round knockout of his challenger.

Dempsey held the title until September 23, 1926, when he lost it to Gene Tunney (1897–1978) on points in the tenth round. His rematch, held a year later, became one of the most celebrated boxing matches ever. In the seventh round, Dempsey sent Tunney to the floor with a powerful left hook. However, Dempsey did not immediately go to the neutral corner of the ring as the rules required, which led the referee to restart the count. Tunney got up at the count of "nine," which actually would have been "fourteen" had Dempsey immediately retreated. Tunney survived the match and was awarded the win in a ten-round decision. It was Dempsey's final professional match, as he retired immediately afterward.

Dempsey won sixty of his eighty bouts, with six losses, eight draws, and six "no decisions." Fifty of his victories were knockouts, and twenty-five came in the first round. He was truly one of boxing's greats.

Rob Edelman

For More Information

Dempsey, Jack, with Barbara Piatelli Dempsey. *Dempsey.* New York: Harper & Row, 1977.

Evensen, Bruce J. *When Dempsey Fought Tunney: Heroes, Hokum, and Storytelling in the Jazz Age.* Knoxville: University of Tennessee Press, 1996.

The Official Site of Jack Dempsey. http://www.cmgww.com/sports/dempsey/facts.htm (accessed July 1, 2011).

Kahn, Roger. *A Flame of Pure Fire: Jack Dempsey and the Roaring '20s.* New York: Harcourt Brace, 1999.

Roberts, Randy. *Jack Dempsey: The Manassa Mauler.* Baton Rouge: Louisiana State University Press, 1979.

Harlem Globetrotters

The Harlem Globetrotters are a most unusual professional basketball team. They play in no league and have no regular opponents. Instead, they tour the world and take on all comers, blending basic basketball skills, razzle-dazzle athletic prowess, and physical comedy. On one level, the individual Globetrotters, all of whom are African Americans, are multitalented athletes and entertainers. On another level, the flamboyant dribbling, passing, and leaping that are so much a part of their act

Harlem Globetrotter Meadowlark Lemon shows his ball-handling skills to teammate Curly Neal during a 1968 television special. © BETTMANN/CORBIS.

can be seen as outgrowths of the stereotype of African Americans as physically adept jesters who exist only to smile and amuse.

The Globetrotters came into existence in 1927. Their founder, promoter-businessman Abe Saperstein (1901–1966), owned and coached the team and booked its tours. At first, the Globe-trotters were merely a traveling basketball team that usually thoroughly beat the competition. Legend has it that Saperstein injected comedy into the Globetrotters' game to provide additional entertainment for fans who were becoming bored by the team's customary, lopsided victories.

In the 1930s and 1940s, the Globetrotters toured the North American continent. Beginning in 1950, they toured the rest of the world. They were featured in two motion pictures, *The Harlem Globetrotters* (1951) and *Go, Man, Go!* (1954). They began appearing on television in 1954 and eventually starred in their own cartoon series, *The Harlem Globetrotters* (1970–1973); a variety show, *The Harlem Globetrotters Popcorn Machine* (1974); and a television movie, *The Harlem Globetrotters on Gilligan's Island* (1981). While primarily entertainers, the Globetrotters remained top athletes. In the late 1940s—before the ranks of professional basketball were integrated—they beat the champion Minneapolis Lakers. Between 1950 and 1962, they played a yearly series against squads composed of college all-stars, compiling a 162–44 win-loss record.

Star Globetrotters "clown princes" such as Goose Tatum (1921–1967) and Meadowlark Lemon (1932–) savored their fame and never complained that their antics were assaults on their dignity. On the other hand, Connie Hawkins (1942–), a New York City playground legend and future hoop Hall-of-Famer who played with the team in the 1960s, publicly protested that the Globetrotters were compelled to act like Uncle Toms (blacks who eagerly seek the approval of whites). "Grinnin' and smilin' and dancin' around—that's the way they told us to act, and that's the way a lot of white people like to think we really are," he observed. Despite such criticism, the Globetrotters remain highly popular, especially with children. Into the twenty-first century, they continue to tour the world, mixing basketball with comedy. Team members have appeared on television shows, such as *The Amazing Race*. The team has also continued to experiment with the game, adding a "penalty box" and a four-point shot, thirty-five feet from the basket.

Rob Edelman

For More Information

Butler, Robbie. *The Harlem Globetrotters: Crown Princes of Basketball.* Mankato, MN: Capstone Press, 2001.

Green, Ben. *Spinning the Globe: The Rise, Fall, and Return to Greatness of the Harlem Globetrotters.* New York: Amistad, 2009.

Lemon, Meadowlark, with Jerry B. Jenkins. *Meadowlark.* Nashville: Nelson, 1987.

The Original Harlem Globetrotters. http://www.harlemglobetrotters.com/ (accessed July 1, 2011).

Lincoln Logs

Lincoln Logs are a children's building toy invented by John Lloyd Wright (1892–1972) around 1916 and first marketed to the public in 1924. From their introduction, each set contained a number of wooden logs in various lengths that could be fitted together to make log houses and other buildings. This simple toy proved so successful that by the end of the 1990s more than a half-million sets were sold every year.

John Lloyd Wright was the second son of famous architect Frank Lloyd Wright (1867–1959), best known for his Prairie Style architecture and unique houses. John learned design by working with his father on

A sturdy frontier log cabin built with Lincoln Logs.
© COOPERPHOTO/CORBIS.

the Midway Gardens in Chicago, Illinois, and on the Imperial Hotel in Tokyo, Japan. In Japan, Wright saw firsthand how the Japanese used wood construction in a very intricate and beautiful way. Wright also loved children and their toys and games. When he was twenty-five years old, Wright came up with the idea for Lincoln Logs, a simple kit with miniature wooden logs. He chose the name Lincoln Logs after President Abraham Lincoln (1809–1865). Lincoln was famous for his frontier boyhood and for chopping logs to build houses. Wright knew that Lincoln's appeal as a national hero would help make his kits popular. Early packages featured a picture of Lincoln and showed how to make a frontier log cabin.

Lincoln Logs were especially popular in the middle decades of the twentieth century. Parents liked them because they were educational toys. Kids had to think hard about how to use them, and designing log buildings required lots of creative thought. Kids liked them because they could be arranged in so many different ways and they could always have fun playing with them. Along with **LEGO** (see entry under 1950s—Sports and Games in volume 3) building blocks and **Tinkertoys** (see entry under 1910s—Sports and Games in volume 1), Lincoln Logs were one of the most popular and successful toys of the century.

Timothy Berg

For More Information

Brown, Conrad Nagel. "Lincoln Logs." *Inland Architect* (Vol. 115, no. 4, 1998): p. 116.

Walsh, Tim. *Timeless Toys: Classic Toys and the Playmakers Who Created Them.* Kansas City, MO: Andrews McNeel, 2005.

Miniature Golf

For decades, millions of Americans have delighted in games of miniature golf. The game, which combines elements of skill derived from "real" golf with entertainment features aimed at children, has remained popular through the years with players of all ages.

No one is exactly sure who "invented" miniature golf. More than likely, it was developed simultaneously in many different places. Most historians place its origins around the turn of the twentieth century, when wealthy golf enthusiasts began building "golf in miniature" courses on their estates.

This early form of the game was called "garden golf" and featured none of the elaborate obstacles that would mark the game in later years.

Originally a pastime of the leisure classes, miniature golf was soon transformed into a profitable business. In 1928, an entrepreneur named Garnet Carter (1883–1954) began charging people ten cents a round to golf on courses he had built on the rooftops of New York City **skyscrapers** (see entry under 1930s—The Way We Lived in volume 2). This commercial form of mini-golf became popular with movie stars and celebrities. By the 1930s, Americans had taken to the game in droves. During that decade, more than thirty thousand mini-golf courses sprang up across the country. An estimated four million people played the game regularly.

The next boom period for miniature golf came following World War II (1939–45). Businessman Don Clayton (1926–1996) helped spread the game to even more people through his Putt-Putt Golf chain. This chain used the same franchise model as those other 1950s icons, **McDonald's** (see entry under 1940s—Food and Drink in volume 3) and Holiday Inn. The Putt-Putt courses featured simple geometric obstacles and hills. During this period, other course designers began to add many of the colorful obstacles and hazards that people have come to associate with miniature golf. Spinning windmills, revolving statues, and babbling brooks made the golf even more challenging for the players. Later, others would expand on these innovations even further, creating elaborate "theme" courses based on fictional characters or fantasy settings.

With the arrival of young prodigy **Tiger Woods** (1975–; see entry under 1990s—Sports and Games in volume 5), golf became wildly popular in the 1990s. Miniature golf took part in this boom as well. A number of golf and sports celebrities, including Jack Nicklaus (1940–), **Michael Jordan** (1962–; see entry under 1990s—Sports and Games in volume 5), and Hale Irwin (1945–), opened "alternative golf" centers, which combined miniature golf, professional-style driving ranges, and other family entertainment attractions. The popularity of these facilities proves that miniature golf, no matter how it is packaged, remains an integral part of the entertainment landscape in America.

Robert E. Schnakenberg

For More Information

Margolies, John. *Miniature Golf.* New York: Abbeville Press, 1987.
The PMGA: Professional Miniature Golf Association. http://www.thepmga.com/ (accessed July 1, 2011).

National Football League

In the early twentieth century, football was primarily a college sport. After graduation, an all-American college quarterback, end, or lineman had little future in athletics. All this began to change in 1920, when George Halas (1895–1983; legendary player, coach, and owner of the Chicago Bears), and others convened in Canton, Ohio. They were there to organize the American Professional Football Association (APFA). Soon afterward, this fledgling coalition changed its name to the National Football League (NFL).

Harold "Red" Grange (1903–1991) was a University of Illinois star who scored four touchdowns in twelve minutes in a 1924 contest against the University of Michigan. He helped earn the NFL credibility when he signed with Halas's Bears in 1925. Grange, nicknamed "The Galloping Ghost," became the league's first superstar. For the next three decades, different franchises emerged as powerhouses, and other players became NFL heroes. A national championship game was inaugurated in 1933, and the first players' draft was held three years later. One of the earliest classic NFL contests was the "sneaker game," a mid-1930s championship game between the Bears and the New York Giants. At halftime, trailing the powerhouse Bears 10–3, the Giants donned basketball sneakers to improve their traction and gain an edge on the icy Polo Grounds turf. The New York team went on to rout their rivals, 30–13.

As the years passed, the NFL steadily grew. In 1950, it took in three teams from the newly defunct All-America Football Conference (AAFC), a rival league. The following year, the first nationally televised NFL game aired on the DuMont network. However, the main event that reflected the league's maturation occurred in 1958, when the New York Giants and the Baltimore Colts faced off for the NFL championship. A record number of viewers tuned in to watch the game on **television** (see entry under 1940s—TV and Radio in volume 3). They were treated to an electrifying 23-17 sudden-death overtime victory by the Colts. Arguably, this was the greatest game in NFL history.

In 1960, Pete Rozelle (1926–1996) was named NFL commissioner. Rozelle spearheaded an unprecedented growth period for the league. In 1966, he presided over the merger between the NFL and its rival the American Football League (AFL). Initially, both leagues remained separate but met in an annual championship game, which in 1969 became known as the Super Bowl. The Green Bay Packers, long an NFL force, won the first two contests. Before Super Bowl III, **Joe Namath** (1943–; see entry under 1960s—Sports and Games in volume 4), quarterback of the AFL New York Jets, boldly predicted victory over the highly favored Baltimore Colts. Namath sparked the Jets to a shocking 16-7 win. The Jets' win resulted in the legitimization of the NFL-AFL merger, the emergence of the Super Bowl as an important American sporting event, and further NFL popularity and prosperity. Another NFL landmark is the success of the long-running *Monday Night Football* (1970–; see entry under 1970s—Sports and Games in volume 4), which, after thirty-five seasons on ABC-TV, switched to ESPN in 2006.

As of 2011, thirty-two teams, located from Seattle and San Francisco to Tampa Bay and Miami, make up the NFL. Watching them compete on a crisp autumn Sunday is an American ritual.

Rob Edelman

For More Information

Buckley, James, Jr. *America's Greatest Game: The Real Story of Football and NFL.* New York: Hyperion Books for Children, 1998.

Harris, David. *The League: The Rise and Decline of the NFL.* New York: Bantam Books, 1986.

MacCambridge, Michael. *America's Game: The Epic Story of How Pro Football Captured a Nation.* New York: Random House, 2004.

McDonough, Will, ed. *The NFL Century: The Complete Story of the National Football League, 1920–2000.* New York: Smithmark, 1999.

Neft, David S., Richard S. Cohen, and Richard Korch. *The Football Encyclopedia: The Complete History of Professional Football from 1892 to the Present.* 2nd ed. New York: St. Martin's, 1994.

NFL.com. http://www.nfl.com (accessed July 1, 2011).

Peterson, Robert W. *Pigskin: The Early Years of Pro Football.* New York: Oxford University Press, 1997.

Yo-yo

The yo-yo is one of the oldest and most popular toys in the world. The origin of the yo-yo is uncertain. Some stories trace it to such places as China, Greece, Egypt, France, and the Philippines. One thing is certain: In 1928, Filipino Pedro Flores brought the first yo-yo to the United

President Richard Nixon amazes country music star Roy Acuff with his tricky yo-yo at the dedication of the new home of the Grand Ole Opry *in Nashville, Tennessee, on March 16, 1974.* © DAVID HUME KENNERLY/GETTY IMAGES.

States. At a yo-yo demonstration that Flores gave in San Francisco, California, in 1929, Donald F. Duncan (1891–1971) became intrigued by the toy disk on a string. Duncan quickly bought Flores' idea and started the Duncan Company to sell yo-yos. Duncan used catchy advertising campaigns. He sent yo-yo professionals throughout the United States and western Europe to demonstrate yo-yo tricks and develop interest in the product. He set up yo-yo tournaments.

By 1946, the Duncan Company made its headquarters in Luck, Wisconsin, the "Yo-Yo Capital of the World." By 1962, the Duncan Company sold a record forty-five million yo-yos. The yo-yo was given special attention when President Richard Nixon (1913–1994) performed yo-yo tricks on the stage of the **Grand Ole Opry** (see entry under 1920s—Music in volume 2) in 1974 and when the yo-yo was one of the first toys taken into space in 1985. Yo-yos are now made by several companies and continue to be enjoyed by children and adults alike.

Sara Pendergast

For More Information

The National Yo-Yo Museum. http://nationalyoyo.org/ (accessed July 1, 2011).

Malko, George. *The One and Only Yo-Yo Book.* New York: Avon, 1978.

Zeiger, Helane. *World on a String: The How-To Yo-Yo Book.* Chicago: Contemporary Publishers, 1979.

1920s

TV and Radio

The 1920s marked the shift in American culture to electronic media for entertainment and news. The first radios were sold in the United States for home use in 1920. By mid-decade, a decent radio could be purchased for about $35, with higher quality models being sold for up to $350. By the end of the decade, more than five million of the battery-powered radios were sold (although the first television receivers were sold and the first televised programs began in 1928, television became truly popular in later decades).

At first, the broadcasting on radio centered around music, especially the classics and opera. The featured orchestras were often named after sponsors. Listeners could hear the likes of the Ipana (toothpaste) Troubadours, the A&P (grocery chain) Gypsies, the Champion (spark plugs) Sparkers, and the Hoover (vacuum cleaners) Sentinels. Speeches and lectures were also broadcast. Local meetings of civic and professional organizations, such as the Commercial Law League and the Foreign Policy Association, were broadcast in full. Although the programming was uninspired, people would gather around their radios just for the pure novelty of listening to sound coming out of a box. By the end of the decade, radios had become a true craze across the country. The popularity of radios during the 1920s provided a mere glimpse into what would become a national obsession with electronic media gadgets in the following decades.

Radio

For three-plus decades beginning in the early 1920s—before the mass marketing and mass popularity of television—radio was the foremost in-house leisure activity and information-gathering source for millions of Americans. Radio had a profound influence on popular culture. Not only did radio record historical events for posterity, but it forever altered the manner in which information and entertainment were disseminated to the public. **Television** (see entry under 1940s—TV and Radio in volume 3) captures both the eyes and the ears and tends to shut out other senses; it is called a passive medium because viewers tend to become absorbed in watching it and do little else. Radio, however, is an active medium, engaging only the sense of hearing; it allows listeners to use their imagination to conjure up a picture in their minds.

The genesis of radio dates to the 1890s, when Italian inventor-physicist Guglielmo Marconi (1874–1937) pioneered the use of wireless telegraphy. In 1895, Marconi first was able to transmit radio waves short distances; four years later, he succeeded in transmitting a signal across the English Channel. In 1906, American Lee De Forest (1873–1961) furthered the development of the medium by inventing the triode, an electron tube that featured three electrodes (anode, cathode, and grid). His triode made modern radio broadcasts possible. In 1920, KDKA in East Pittsburgh, Pennsylvania, the initial radio station, began broadcasting. At the time, only five thousand Americans had radio receivers. The question of the day—Who would pay for radio?—was answered two years later when New York station WEAF broadcast the initial paid radio commercial. Soon radio stations were sprouting up across the country, with the first major radio networks, NBC and CBS, coming into being in 1926 and 1927. By the beginning of the **Great Depression** (1929–41; see entry under 1930s—The Way We Lived in volume 2) in 1929, the essence of

In the early 1930s, a radio such as this was a familiar sight in 90 percent of homes in the United States. © PETER ARNOLD INC./ALAMY.

popular radio programming was in place. The standard radio format consisted of music, news, and entertainment programs, with paid advertisements liberally sprinkled in between. By the early 1930s, 90 percent of Americans owned at least one radio.

Radio's golden age arrived during the 1930s, with an ever-expanding variety of programming. Some programs featured specific story lines: dramas, comedies, soap operas, Westerns, and romances. Others were variety shows, featuring musical performances and comedy skits. The latest popular songs and rhythms were broadcast live from hotel ballrooms, where the era's top Big Bands were performing. Hollywood stars regularly reenacted their movie roles on radio, with the purpose being to keep them and their films in the public consciousness while promoting their upcoming projects. Indeed, radio—just like movies—proved to be a great escape for the millions of Americans then suffering the ravages of the Depression.

Dozens of the most popular television shows from the 1950s and 1960s started out on radio. These included lawyer series *Perry Mason* (1943–1955 [radio]; 1957–1966 [television]; see entry under 1930s—Print Culture in volume 2); Western dramas *The Lone Ranger* (1933–1955 [radio]; 1949–1957 [television]; see entry under 1930s—TV and Radio in volume 2) and *Gunsmoke* (1952–1961 [radio]; 1955–1975 [television]; see entry under 1950s—TV and Radio in volume 3); and comedy show *The Jack Benny Program* (1932–1955 [radio]; 1950–1965 [television]). Other TV series were derived from radio shows: *I Love Lucy* (1951–1957; see entry under 1950s—TV and Radio in volume 3), the most celebrated of all 1950s situation comedies, evolved from *My Favorite Husband* (1948–1951). Many of the most popular radio stars were comedians and comic actors: Benny (1894–1974); the husband-and-wife team of George Burns (1896–1996) and Gracie Allen (1902–1964); Fred Allen (1894–1956); Bob Hope (1903–2003); and ventriloquist Edgar Bergen (1903–1978). A typical radio situation-comedy was *Fibber McGee and Molly* (1935–1957; see entry under 1930s—TV and Radio in volume 2). Meanwhile, Norman Corwin (1910–) and Arch Oboler (1909–1987) pioneered the development of radio drama. Among the many popular dramatic radio programs: *Gangbusters* (1936–1957); *Suspense* (1942–1962); *Inner Sanctum* (1941–1952); and *The Shadow* (1930–1954; see entry under 1930s—Print Culture in volume 2).

Easily one of the most famous radio broadcasts came on October 30, 1938. Orson Welles (1915–1985), who later became famous as a film director, staged the science-fiction classic ***The War of the Worlds*** (see entry under 1930s—TV and Radio in volume 2) by H. G. Wells (1866–1946). Author Wells's story involves an invasion of Earth by Martians. Director Welles's production was realistically rendered; it was presented in real time, with an announcer declaring, "Ladies and gentlemen, we interrupt our program of dance music to bring you a special bulletin from the Intercontinental Radio News." As a result, untold number of listeners actually believed that New Jersey was being invaded by Martians.

Radio did more than entertain its listeners. On Sunday mornings, preachers sermonized over the airwaves. Most were simply preaching to their flock, but one became infamous. He was Father Charles Coughlin (1891–1979), the "radio priest" of Royal Oak, Michigan, whose audience during the 1930s numbered in the millions and whose radio sermons became increasingly anti-Jewish and pro-Fascist (in favor of direct government suppression of different viewpoints). Meanwhile, beginning in 1933 and lasting until his death, President Franklin D. Roosevelt (1882–1945) wisely used radio to speak directly to U.S. citizens. Some of his speeches were labeled "fireside chats." Utilizing the intimacy that radio creates, he opened each broadcast with the phrase "My dear friends …" and went on to explain his policies and programs in an attempt to elicit public support. Radio also played a critical role in the American public's perception of World War II (1939–45). The legendary reports by CBS broadcast journalist Edward R. Murrow (1908–1965), made during the 1940 German bombing of London, helped solidify public opinion in favor of the Allies. After America's entry into the war, in the wake of the December 7, 1941, surprise attack by the Japanese on Pearl Harbor, radio brought the war directly into every American household. Radio journalists reported directly from the war's hot spots.

In the 1930s, regulation became an important aspect of radio broadcasting. At the beginning of the decade, stations often interfered with the programs of other stations by broadcasting on the same bandwidth. By 1934, the U.S. government created the Federal Communications Commission (FCC), whose charge was to organize stations in such a way that broadcasts could play across the country without overlapping. The FCC also foresaw the danger of having an entity in control of too many stations in one geographic area, thereby having too much control over what information the listeners heard. The FCC then sought to limit the number of radio outlets a company or an individual could own.

With the invention of television and the marketing of television sets in the post–World War II era, radio slowly began to lose its standing within the American home. Radio held onto a listening audience in the 1950s and 1960s as the primary medium for marketing to teenagers the latest **Top 40** (see entry under 1950s—Music in volume 3) **rock and roll** (see entry under 1950s—Music in volume 3) hits. In the late 1960s and 1970s, the rise of FM stations and the free-form experimentation of FM **disc jockeys** (see entry under 1950s—Music in volume 3) helped propel the cultural influence of rock music. In the 1990s, a generation of popular and controversial **"talk radio"** (see entry under 1980s—TV and Radio in volume 5) personalities emerged. Among them were the "tough-love" advocate Dr. Laura Schlessinger (1947–); abrasive arch-conservative Rush Limbaugh (1951–); and **shock radio** (see entry under 1980s—TV and Radio in volume 5) disc jockey Howard Stern (1954–).

Rob Edelman

For More Information

Balk, Alfred. *The Rise of Radio, from Marconi Through the Golden Age.* Jefferson, NC: McFarland, 2006.

Bray, John. *The Communications Miracle: The Telecommunications Pioneers from Morse to the Information Superhighway.* New York: Plenum Press, 1995.

Dunning, John. *On the Air: The Encyclopedia of Old-Time Radio.* New York: Oxford University Press, 1997.

Empire of the Air: The Men Who Made Radio (film). Florentine Films, 1992.

Finkelstein, Norman H. *Sounds in the Air: The Golden Age of Radio.* New York: Maxwell Macmillan International, 1993.

Hilmes, Michelle. *Radio Voices: American Broadcasting, 1922–1952.* Minneapolis: University of Minnesota, 1997.

Ladd, Jim. *Radio Waves: Life and Revolution on the FM Dial.* New York: St. Martin's Press, 1991.

MacDonald, J. Fred. *Don't Touch That Dial: Radio Programming in American Life, 1920–1960.* Chicago: Nelson-Hall, 1979.

Maltin, Leonard. *The Great American Broadcast: A Celebration of Radio's Golden Age.* New York: Dutton, 1997.

Nachman, Gerald. *Raised on Radio.* New York: Pantheon Books, 1998.

Rudel, Anthony J. *Hello, Everybody! The Dawn of American Radio.* Orlando, FL: Harcourt, 2008.

Ryan, Thomas. *American Hit Radio: A History of Popular Singles from 1955 to the Present.* Rocklin, CA: Prima, 1996.

Smulyan, Susan. *Selling Radio: The Commercialization of American Broadcasting, 1920–1934.* Washington, DC: Smithsonian Institution Press, 1994.

1920s

The Way We Lived

The technological advances of the beginning of the century continued to impact lives in the 1920s. Henry Ford (1863–1947) had improved his assembly-line techniques to produce a Model T every ten seconds by 1925. Automobiles were more affordable than ever: Some models sold for as little as $50. By the end of the decade, 23.1 million passenger cars crowded the streets of America. Telephones were in 13 percent of American homes by 1921, and American Telephone and Telegraph (AT&T) had become America's largest corporation by 1925.

New technologies continued to change the way people lived in America. People spent their extra money on luxuries like vacations. Families of almost every income level could enjoy some time away from work. Camping became popular, and cars could take people farther from home and pull recreational vehicles for more luxurious outdoor living. Those with enough money could fly to sunny locations like Florida to enjoy the winter months in warmth. For those who wanted a vacation at home, swimming pools could be installed in their own backyards.

Even though Prohibition officially banned the sale and distribution of alcohol, many people rebelled against the law and snuck into speakeasies (illegal bars) to drink and dance the Charleston to the new music of the time. Dancing was not limited to illegal nightclubs; respectable places like the Savoy Ballroom in Harlem (New York City) became increasingly popular during the decade as people sought out good music and large dance floors. Even teenagers could enjoy the music and dances of the decade at proms, which more and more high schools sponsored across the country.

Air Travel

When the Wright Brothers—Wilbur (1867–1912) and Orville (1871–1948)—made the first powered flight in 1903, they could not have known how important air travel would become. At the time, nobody showed much interest in their machine and the brothers went back to making bicycles. The times would soon change. The first passenger service using winged aircraft began flying the twenty-two miles between St. Petersburg and Tampa, Florida, in 1914. The service could carry only one passenger on each trip, and the service lasted only a few weeks. By 2002, a Boeing 747–400 jetliner could carry 524 passengers up to 8,400 miles. At the beginning of the twenty-first century, air travel is cheaper, faster, and safer than ever before.

Between the years 1910 and 1914, zeppelins were part of the travel scene. The giant airships safely carried a total of about thirty-four thousand passengers. German zeppelins used hydrogen gas to make them lighter than air. Winged "heavier-than-air" machines were less likely to burst into flames than the zeppelins, but they suffered from a lack of engine power. In 1912, American pilot "Colonel" Samuel F. Cody (1861–1913) could fly his four passengers only seven miles. In 1920, pilots still navigated by following roads and railway lines. Passengers often sat in open cockpits wearing goggles and warm clothing. The planes were overtaken by trains when the wind was against them.

After 1920, the early biplanes (planes with two sets of wings) gradually gave way to sleek monoplanes (planes with one set of wings). In 1928, German airlines carried over 100,000 passengers. American companies carried only 60,000 passengers that year, but change came quickly. By 1929, the figure was up to 160,000. To improve passenger comfort, the first flight attendants (called stewardesses back then) were introduced by Boeing Air Transport on its San Francisco-to-Chicago route in 1930. The American air-passenger industry soon became the busiest in the world.

When the first daily international passenger service began between London and Paris in 1919, long-distance travel was changed forever. Within ten years, air travel grew from a dangerous, expensive hobby into big business. With the advent of the jet engine in the 1950s, it became a part of daily life for many people. Every day, thousands of flights operated by dozens of commercial airlines speed millions of Americans across the United States and around the world.

Chris Routledge

For More Information

Corn, Joseph J. *The Winged Gospel: America's Romance with Aviation, 1900–1950.* New York: Oxford University Press, 1983.

Heppenheimer, T. A. *Turbulent Skies: The History of Commercial Aviation.* New York: Wiley, 1995.

Smith, Patrick. *Ask the Pilot: Everything You Need to Know About Air Travel.* New York: Riverhead Books, 2004.

Sternstein, Ed, ed. *From Takeoff to Landing: Everything You Wanted to Know About Airplanes But Had No One to Ask.* New York: Pocket Books, 1991.

Walters, Brian. *The Illustrated History of Air Travel.* London and New York: Marshall Cavendish, 1979.

Baseball Cards

For decades, collecting and trading baseball cards were a ritual of American youth. At first, cards were enjoyed by youngsters and then discarded at the end of the season or when boys became men and were summarily expected to dispose of the remnants of childhood. Today, however, baseball cards are far more than nostalgic remnants of the past or a present-day pastime for the latest generation of youngsters and **baseball** (see entry under 1900s—Sports and Games in volume 1) fans. Cards from decades gone by as well as the newest sets are now highly collectible. Baseball card purchasing has developed into a billion-dollar industry.

The first baseball cards were issued during the 1880s, when the Old Judge Company included them in packs of **cigarettes** (see entry under 1920s—Commerce in volume 2). One of the most famous, and the highest-valued, of all baseball cards originally was a cigarette card. It featured Hall of Famer-to-be Honus Wagner (1874–1955). The Honus Wagner card was found in the T206 baseball card set issued by the American Tobacco Company in 1909. Legend has it that Wagner, a non-smoker, was angered upon learning that his likeness had been included in the series. He demanded that his card be removed from the set. In 2007, a T206 Wagner card was auctioned for $2.8 million.

Trading baseball cards can be fun—and profitable. This rare 1909 Honus Wagner card was sold for $2.8 million in 2007.
© AP IMAGES/KATHY WILLENS.

By the 1930s, tobacco companies had been replaced by gum and candy companies as the primary baseball card distributors. The cards came in packs that most often included strips of chewing gum. The Goudey Gum Company issued a typical, popular set between 1933 and 1941. The paper shortages that resulted when America entered World War II (1939–45) brought a temporary halt to baseball-card production.

The modern era of baseball cards began in 1948, when the Bowman Gum Company issued a set of black-and-white cards. Cards came in packages of one; they were accompanied by a stick of gum, and cost a penny. Also in 1948, the Leaf Company released a set of color cards. Then in 1951, Topps Chewing Gum issued its first cards. Topps quickly became the undisputed king of baseball cards and dominated the market for the next three decades. The company began adding information to their cards, such as players' statistics, personal information, and team logos.

The concept of baseball cards as collectibles was a natural evolution of the hobby. Beginning in the mid-1970s, baby boomers began repurchasing the cards that were links to their youths. Eventually, baseball-card shows were organized across the country to stimulate the purchase of older and newer cards. Older cards that once were bought for pennies now were valued in dollars. Certain "star cards" in mint condition, featuring popular players or Hall of Famers, were valued at hundreds. Soon, cards were worth thousands of dollars. Other companies, including Donruss, Fleer, and Upper Deck, entered the baseball-card business during the 1980s. Then came Studio, Stadium, Pacific, and Pinnacle, among many others. In 1991, Topps ceased including gum with its cards, as a result of complaints that gum stains devalued the cards. In the early twenty-first century, the Major League Baseball Players Association decided to limit the number of companies able to produce baseball cards. By 2010 there were effectively two left, Topps and Upper Deck, which had acquired the rights to the Fleer name.

In the 1990s, baseball-card design became state of the art, with dazzlingly visual graphics. Companies were offering multiple sets during a single season as well as "inserts," or special limited-edition subsets. They began including cards personally autographed by ballplayers as well as cards that included tiny strips of game-used bats and game-worn uniforms. By 2000, a pack of baseball cards cost dollars, rather than nickels and dimes. The following year, Topps celebrated its fiftieth anniversary in the baseball-card business by adding thousands of vintage cards to its packs, including redemption chits (vouchers) for 1952 Mickey Mantle rookie cards, the company's most celebrated card.

Rob Edelman

For More Information

Beckett, James. *The Official Beckett Guide to Baseball Cards, 2010, Edition #30.* New York: House of Collectibles, 2010.

Green, Paul M., and Donn Pearlman. *Making Money with Baseball Cards: A Handbook of Insider Secrets and Strategies.* Chicago: Bonus Books, 1989.

Jamieson, Dave. *Mint Condition: How Baseball Cards Became an American Obsession.* New York: Grove Press, 2010.

Lemke, Bob. *2011 Standard Catalog of Baseball Cards.* 20th edition. Iola, WI: Krause Publications, 2010.

O'Keeffe, Michael, and Teri Thompson. *The Card: Collectors, Con Men, and the True Story of History's Most Desired Baseball Card.* New York: Morrow, 2007.

Pearlman, Donn. *Collecting Baseball Cards: How to Buy Them, Store Them, Trade Them, and Keep Track of Their Value as Investments.* 3rd ed. Chicago: Bonus Books, 1991.

Bungalows

• •

Bungalows were simple houses built across the United States in the first decades of the twentieth century. They were usually small, with sloping roofs and front porches. Their simple style, free of excess ornamentation, made them affordable for many Americans. Because of their availability, more Americans were able to enjoy the benefits of home ownership.

The bungalow style came from a number of influences. Two architects, brothers Charles Sumner Greene (1868–1957) and Henry Mather Greene (1870–1954), began designing what came to be called "Craftsman" bungalows after 1903 in Pasadena, California. They were inspired by the Arts and Crafts movement in England, an art and design style that used forms from nature such as leaf patterns and flower shapes.

An example of a craftsman bungalow in Chico, California. © DOUGLAS KEISTER/CORBIS.

The Greene brothers were also inspired by Asian architecture, which emphasized wood construction. They put these two styles together in the homes they built. The bungalow itself came from the architecture of India. (The term comes from the Indian word *bangla,* meaning "house.") Its simple, functional style proved to be a good fit with the early twentieth-century mood at a time when overly ornate Victorian architecture was falling out of fashion. The bungalow fit the needs of the modern family.

The bungalow might have stayed a regional California style were it not for the efforts of Edward Bok (1863–1930). Bok, the editor of the very popular magazine *Ladies Home Journal,* wanted to promote his image of the ideal American home, one in which women stayed at home with their children. Bok sought to encourage that image by popularizing a simpler home that would be easier to live in. He publicized the bungalow style and even offered architectural plans his readers could buy for five dollars. The houses cost between $1,500 and $5,000 to build. Many of Bok's readers took advantage of the bungalow plans. Bungalows began springing up all across the United States. Although the popularity of the bungalow style faded after 1930, many examples still exist and are highly valued. Even today, numerous companies offer plans for bungalows online and many builders continue to create updated versions of this traditional style of house.

Timothy Berg

For More Information

The Bungalow Company. http://www.thebungalowcompany.com (accessed July 1, 2011).

Clark, Clifford E., Jr. *The American Family Home, 1800–1960.* Chapel Hill: University of North Carolina Press, 1986.

Jackson, Kenneth T. *Crabgrass Frontier: The Suburbanization of the United States.* New York: Oxford University Press, 1985.

King, Anthony D. *The Bungalow: The Production of a Global Culture.* 2nd ed. New York: Oxford University Press, 1995.

Maddex, Diane. *Bungalow Nation.* New York: Abrams, 2003.

McAlester, Virginia, and Lee McAlester. *A Field Guide to American Houses.* New York: Alfred A. Knopf, 1994.

Al Capone (1899–1947)

Chicago mob boss Al Capone, the most notorious gangster in American history, symbolized the breakdown of law and order following the passage of the Volstead Act. The Volstead Act ushered in **Prohibition** (see entry under 1920s—The Way We Lived in volume 2), which made the production and sale of alcohol illegal in 1919.

Born in Brooklyn, New York, Capone came to Chicago, Illinois, as a young man. He took over the gang of Johnny Torrio (1882–1957) in 1925 and became immensely rich through bootlegging, prostitution, and gambling. Ruthless with rival gangs, Capone ordered the Saint Valentine's Day massacre of 1929. His gunmen, disguised as police officers, used submachine guns to wipe out seven of Capone's foes. Capone was finally convicted of income-tax evasion and sent to prison in 1931. After his release in 1939, he lived out the rest of his life in Florida, where he died in 1947.

Capone has been portrayed in films by such actors as Rod Steiger (1925–2002; in *Capone,* 1959), Jason Robards (1922–2000; in *The Saint Valentine's Day Massacre,* 1967), and Robert DeNiro (1943–; in *The Untouchables,* 1987). Capone was played by Neville Brand (1920–1992) in the television series *The Untouchables* (1959–63) and by William Forsythe (1955–) in that show's syndicated revival (1993–94).

Justin Gustainis

For More Information

"Al Capone." *Chicago Historical Society.* http://www.chicagohs.org/history/capone.html (accessed July 1, 2011).

Bergreen, Laurence. *Capone: The Man and the Era.* New York: Simon and Schuster, 1994.

Helmer, William, and Arthur Bilek. *The St. Valentine's Day Massacre: The Untold Story of the Gangland Bloodbath That Brought Down Al Capone.* Nashville: Cumberland House, 2003.

Iorizzo, Luciano J. *Al Capone: A Biography.* Westport, CT: Greenwood Press, 2003.

King, David C. *Al Capone and the Roaring Twenties.* Woodbridge, CT: Blackbirch Press, 1999.

Ness, Eliot, with Oscar Fraley. *The Untouchables.* New York: Messner, 1957.

The Charleston

Perhaps nothing represents the spirit of that decade called the "Roaring Twenties" so much as its biggest dance craze, the Charleston. As the 1920s began, the world was emerging from the horrors of World War I (1914–18), and economic prosperity was spreading among Americans. The solemn, repressive Victorian morals of the previous century seemed to be slipping away. Rebellious youths of the 1920s embraced the wild, the new, and the forbidden, including the hot **jazz** (see entry under 1900s—Music in volume 1) rhythms that were emerging in the cities. The racy dance called the Charleston was created by blacks before becoming wildly popular among whites.

Named for the South Carolina city where it was born, many historians believe that the Charleston had its origins in slavery. African slaves were forbidden such leisurely postures as crossing their legs or raising their feet off the floor. The kicks and crossed knees of the Charleston are thought to represent the slaves' sly rebellion against such rules. By the early 1900s, black Americans were **dancing** (see entry under 1900s—The Way We Lived in volume 1) the Charleston in the South. By 1913, the dance had made its way north to New York City's Harlem, the center of northern black culture. In 1921, the first black musical, *Shuffle Along,* played on **Broadway** (see entry under 1900s—Film and Theater in volume 1). African American dancer Maude Russell Rutherford (c. 1897–2001) danced the Charleston on stage, popularizing the dance for the first time among whites. Soon, the Charleston was the rage across the United States and Europe.

The wild, sexy gyrations of the Charleston made it very popular with 1920s youth. Many of their parents' generation called it "primitive" and "savage" and claimed that the dance would be the downfall of civilization. The Charleston was only one of many popular 1920s dances that had their roots in black culture. Others include the Turkey Trot, the Black Bottom, the Slow Drag, the Jitterbug, and the Cakewalk.

Tina Gianoulis

For More Information

"Charleston." *Dance History Archives.* http://www. streetswing.com/histmain/z3chrlst.htm (accessed July 1, 2011).

Villacorta, Aurora S. *Charleston, Anyone?* Danville, IL: Interstate Printers and Publishers, 1978.

Chrysler Building

Its seventy-seven floors and stainless steel spire made the Chrysler Building for a short time the tallest building in the world at 1,046 feet. It was constructed between 1928 and 1930 by Walter Chrysler (1875–1940) as company headquarters for the Chrysler Corporation. With its steel frame, the Chrysler Building is a "set-back" **skyscraper** (see entry under 1930s—The Way We Lived in volume 2), so called because each "stage" is slightly narrower than the one below, creating ledges at intervals all the way up. Its familiar stainless steel arcs, decorative masonry, and overhanging eagles are an instantly recognizable part of the New York skyline.

Architect William van Alen (1882–1954) finished off the building in dramatic style. He had the entire top section constructed out of sight and lifted into position in under two hours. The building is now

Detroit automotive pioneer Walter Chrysler contructed this iconic New York City skyscraper in the late 1920s. © JOSEPH SOHM/ VISION OF AMERICA/CORBIS.

considered one of the best examples of the "Art Deco" style and an icon of 1920s America.

Chris Routledge

For More Information

Bascomb, Neal. *Higher: A Historic Race to the Sky and the Making of a City.* New York: Doubleday, 2003.

Dupré, Judith. *Skyscrapers.* 2nd ed. New York: Black Dog and Leventhal, 2008.

Great Buildings Collection. http://www.GreatBuildings.com/buildings/Chrysler_Building.html (accessed on July 2, 2011).

Stravitz, David. *The Chrysler Building: Creating a New York Icon, Day by Day.* New York: Princeton Architectural Press, 2002.

Cocktail Hour

The "cocktail hour" was an hour or two of refined, civilized relaxation after work and before dinner when adults had an alcoholic drink—a cocktail—and chatted with friends. The ritual is usually associated with the Jazz Age and **Prohibition** (1920–33; see entry under 1920s—The Way We Lived in volume 2), and with the post–World War II (1939–45) era. The beginnings of cocktail hour are obscure, but cocktail historian Stephen Visakay says that since New York hotels were already serving tea at 5 o'clock in the early twentieth century, "it was a short leap to the 5 o'clock cocktail hour."

Cocktail hour was symbolized by urbane, sophisticated people sipping a martini and enjoying hors d'oeuvres at a club, and was associated with the Hollywood elite such as **Cary Grant** (1904–1986; see entry under 1930s—Film and Theater in volume 2) and Audrey Hepburn (1929–1993). By the 1950s, it had become a common suburban ritual. Cocktail hour—and cocktail culture—made a comeback in the mid-1990s, celebrated in films such as *Swingers* (1996) and in the music of bands like Combustible Edison. Cocktail bars, especially those dedicated to the martini, became popular as well, beginning in the 1990s.

Karl Rahder

For More Information

Lanza, Joseph. *The Cocktail: The Influence of Spirits on the American Psyche.* New York: St. Martin's Press, 1995.

Rothenberg, Randall. "The Swank Life." *Esquire* (April 1997): pp. 70–79.

"Virtual Exhibit." *The Museum of the American Cocktail.* http://www.museumoftheamericancocktail.org/Exhibit/Default.aspx (accessed July 2, 2011).

Visakay, Stephen. *Vintage Bar Ware.* Paducah, KY: Collector Books, 1997.

Charles Lindbergh (1902–1974)

In 1927, aviator Charles Lindbergh accomplished the then-unprecedented feat of flying solo across the Atlantic Ocean. "Lucky Lindy" departed New York's Roosevelt Field at 7:52 AM on May 20. Thirty-three and a half hours later, he landed his plane, the *Spirit of St. Louis,* at Le Bourget Field, on the outskirts of Paris. The nonstop flight, which covered 3,610 miles, instantly transformed the twenty-five-year-old flyer into an international celebrity and media star. He was hailed throughout Europe. He was honored with parades in New York and Washington. President Calvin Coolidge (1872–1933) presented him with the Distinguished Flying Cross.

Lindbergh was destined to make headlines not only for his aviation feats. In what was one of the most notorious and highly publicized crimes of the twentieth century, his twenty-month-old son was kidnapped from

Detroit-born aviator Charles Lindbergh stands in front of his plane, the Spirit of St. Louis, *in May 1927. He crossed the Atlantic Ocean alone from New York to Paris in a then-record-breaking 33½ hours.* © BETTMANN/CORBIS.

the family's New Jersey compound in 1932. The infant's body eventually was discovered in the nearby woods. The crime won Lindbergh much public sympathy and resulted in passage of the "Lindbergh Law," making kidnapping a federal offense.

Then Lindbergh's reputation was tarnished in the wake of the pro-Nazi, anti-Semitic pronouncements he made prior to World War II (1939–45). Such rhetoric made him a national disgrace. He earned further disgrace by attacking President Franklin D. Roosevelt (1882–1945) and embracing an isolationist foreign policy (one that called for the United States not to get involved in European problems). He eventually supported the United States following the Japanese attack on Pearl Harbor in 1941 and worked with the Air Force. Lindbergh went on to author several books which regained him some public respectability. He died in 1974.

Rob Edelman

For More Information

Bak, Richard. *The Big Jump: Lindbergh and the World's Greatest Air Race.* Hoboken, NJ: Wiley, 2011.

Berg, A. Scott. *Lindbergh.* New York: G. P. Putnam's Sons, 1998.

Charles Lindbergh Home Page. http://www.charleslindbergh.com (accessed July 2, 2011).

Demarest, Chris L. *Lindbergh.* New York: Crown, 1993.

Giblin, James Cross. *Charles A. Lindbergh: A Human Hero.* New York: Clarion Books, 1997.

Kessner, Thomas. *The Flight of the Century: Charles Lindbergh and the Rise of American Aviation.* New York: Oxford University Press, 2010.

Lindbergh, Charles A. *The Spirit of St. Louis.* New York: Scribner, 1953.

"Lindbergh History." *The Charles A. and Anne Morrow Lindbergh Foundation.* http://www.lindberghfoundation.org/docs/index.php/lindbergh-history (accessed July 2, 2011).

Miss America Pageant

The Miss America Pageant has been part of American popular culture since 1921. Since its beginning, the pageant has reflected the changing social values of the population, although usually more slowly than the rest of the population. Issues such as racial equality and social conscience have only become a reality in the pageant since the early 1980s. Over the years, contestants have been 1920s **flappers** (see entry under

"There she is, Miss America"—all the 2007 contestants stand onstage in Las Vegas. © EVERETT COLLECTION INC./ALAMY.

1920s—Fashion in volume 2), then glamour girls, then scholars and, by the 1980s, social activists. The pageant is often ridiculed as out of step with the times. Even so, Americans still watch the pageant on **television** (see entry under 1940s—The Way We Lived in volume 3) in very large numbers.

The pageant began as part of a plan by Atlantic City, New Jersey, merchants. They wanted to find a way to extend their tourist season past Labor Day. They agreed to hold a gala festival that would include a beauty pageant. It was first called the National Beauty Tournament, but later the title was changed to Miss America.

Originally a contest of physical beauty only, in 1938 the talent competition became a regular part of the contest. The first college scholarship was given in 1945. Since then, the scholarship fund has grown, and it is now the largest single source of scholarship money for American women.

Just as America's society was experiencing great change in the 1960s, the pageant also faced change. In 1968, over two hundred members of the emerging feminist movement picketed outside Convention Hall during the pageant. Although the **civil rights movement** (see entry under 1960s—The Way We Lived in volume 4) had brought African Americans into many areas of popular culture beginning as early as the 1940s, the first black contestant did not contend for the crown of Miss America until 1970, when Cheryl Brown of Iowa participated. It was not until 1984 that Vanessa Williams (1963–) became the first African American winner.

In the mid-1980s, the pageant decided that social activism should be a part of the pageant. Each contestant was required to choose an issue and to develop a platform on that issue. Since then, platforms have included such topics as **AIDS** (see entry under 1980s—The Way We Lived in volume 5) education, literacy, and veteran's rights. Even as the pageant strives to keep up with changing times, the popularity of the Miss America Pageant continues to wane. Viewership has fallen consistently over the past few decades and the pageant has been dropped by more than one television network.

Jill Gregg Clever

For More Information

Bivans, Ann-Marie. *Miss America: In Pursuit of the Crown.* New York: MasterMedia Limited, 1991.

Goldman, William. *Hype and Glory.* New York: Villard, 1990.

Miss American Organization. *Miss America.* http://www.missamerica.org (accessed July 2, 2011).

Osborne, Angela Saulino. *Miss America: The Dream Lives On.* Dallas: Taylor, 1995.

Watson, Elwood, and Darcy Martin. *"There She Is, Miss America": The Politics of Sex, Beauty, and Race in America's Most Famous Pageant.* New York: Palgrave Macmillan, 2004.

Penicillin

Penicillin—the most famous and one of the most powerful infection fighters of the twentieth century—was discovered by Alexander Fleming (1881–1955) at St. Mary's Hospital in London, England, in 1928. The story goes that Fleming was cleaning out discarded glassware in the laboratory, when he noticed that a green mold seemed to be killing bacteria stored in a petri dish, the special glassware used to grow laboratory specimens. Fleming identified an agent in the green mold that became known as penicillin. It took a further ten years for Fleming's research to be taken seriously. Penicillin was at the forefront of the fight against disease throughout the late twentieth century. It controls many bacterial infections, from minor strep throats to killers such as bacterial meningitis.

Penicillin is not a wonder drug. It is useless against some common infections, including tuberculosis, and it triggers an allergic reaction in many people. Many experts also warn that the overuse of penicillin, and other antibiotics, is leading to a growing risk from resistant strains of bacteria. Nevertheless, penicillin has saved millions of lives, and paved the way for other, more powerful, antibiotics. Without them, even minor injuries and simple surgical procedures would be highly dangerous.

Chris Routledge

For More Information

Bud, Robert. *Penicillin: Triumph and Tragedy.* New York: Oxford University Press, 2007.

Jacobs, Francine. *Breakthrough: The True Story of Penicillin.* New York: Dodd, Mead, 1985.

Tocci, Salvatore. *Alexander Fleming: The Man Who Discovered Penicillin.* Berkeley Heights, NJ: Enslow, 2002.

Wainwright, Milton. *Miracle Cure: The Story of Penicillin and the Golden Age of Antibiotics.* Cambridge, MA: Blackwell, 1990.

Prohibition

Prohibition became law through the Eighteenth Amendment to the U.S. Constitution in January 1919. It was enforced through the Volstead Act of the same year. Prohibition made the sale, transport, and manufacture of alcoholic drinks illegal. It was backed by the Prohibitionist Party and by reformers such as ministers, doctors, and the Women's Christian Temperance Union. The ban lasted from 1919 to 1933 and was an attempt to control moral behavior.

Unfortunately, Prohibition had the opposite effect. Prohibition made drinking fashionable and exciting. Illegal bars known as "speakeasies" sprang up and the bootleggers—makers and suppliers of illegal alcohol—became heroes. Gangsters made fortunes from making and importing alcohol. During Prohibition, the penalty for selling just one drink was five years in jail. Before long, the prisons could not cope with the influx of inmates. Prohibition made the public lose respect for

An illegal still in New York City in the 1920s is examined by two Internal Revenue agents. © BETTMANN/CORBIS.

lawmakers and politicians. The Eighteenth Amendment was repealed in December 1933. It remains the only repealed amendment in the history of the Constitution.

Chris Routledge

For More Information

Behr, Edward. *Prohibition: Thirteen Years That Changed America.* New York: Arcade, 1996.

Okrent, Daniel. *Last Call: The Rise and Fall of Prohibition* New York: Scribner, 2010.

Prom

A rite of passage for generations of American teenagers for nearly a century, the high school prom is usually the first formal event in the lives of young people. For many teenagers, the prom is the most stressful

The senior prom at Anacosta High School in Maryland in 1953 was typical of thousands held across the United States.
© BETTMANN/CORBIS.

event of their lives. It intensifies peer pressure over issues of inclusion and exclusion. Some common stresses include, Will I get a date? Will my choice of a date change my reputation? Who will be excluded from the prom, and why?

The word "prom" was first used in the 1890s as a shortened form of "promenade," a reference to formal dances in which the guests would display their fashions and **dancing** (see entry under 1900s—The Way We Lived in volume 1) skills during the evening's grand march. In the United States, it came to be believed by parents and educators that a prom, or formal dinner-dance, would be an important lesson in social skills, especially in a theoretically classless society that valued behavior over breeding. The prom was seen as a way to instill manners into children, all under the watchful eye of chaperons.

The first proms were held in the 1920s. By the 1930s, proms were common across the country. For many older Americans, the prom was a modest, home-grown affair in the school gymnasium, often decorated with crepe-paper streamers. Prom-goers were well dressed but not lavishly decked out: boys wore jacket and tie and girls their Sunday dress. Couples danced to music provided by a local amateur band or a record player. After the 1960s, especially after the 1980s, the high-school prom in many areas became a serious exercise in conspicuous consumption, with boys renting expensive tuxedos and girls attired in designer gowns. Stretch limousines were hired to drive the prom-goers to expensive restaurants or discos for an all-night extravaganza, with alcohol, drugs, and sex as added ingredients, at least more openly than before.

Whether simple or lavish, proms have always been more or less traumatic events for adolescents who worry about self-image and fitting in with their peers. Prom night can be a devastating experience for socially awkward teens, for those who do not secure dates, or for gay or lesbian teens who cannot relate to the heterosexual bonding of prom night. In 1980, Aaron Fricke (1962–) sued his school's principal in Cumberland, Rhode Island, for the right to bring Paul Guilbert as his prom date, and won. Since the 1990s, alternative proms have been organized in some areas for same-sex couples, as well as "couple-free" proms to which all students are welcome. Susan Shadburne's 1998 video, *Street Talk and Tuxes,* documents a prom organized by and for homeless youth. Other proms are now organized for home-schooled children and even for adults who hope to have more fun at a "do-over" prom for grown-ups.

Edward Moran

For More Information

Best, Amy L. *Prom Night: Youth, Schools, and Popular Culture.* New York: Routledge, 2000.

Medina, Jennifer. "A Second Shot to Have the Best Night of Their Lives." *New York Times.* http://www.nytimes.com/2011/05/12/us/12prom.html?_r=1&scp=2&sq=prom&st=cse (accessed July 2, 2011).

Murphy, Sharon. *Celebrate Life! A Guide for Planning All Night Alcohol/Drug-Free Celebrations for Teens.* 7th ed. Richmond, VA: Operation Prom/Graduation, 2002.

Prom and PromDress Home. http://www.promdress.net (accessed July 2, 2011).

Prom Guide. http://www.promguide.com (accessed July 2, 2011).

Shadburne, Susan. *Street Talk and Tuxes* (video). Ho-Ho-Kus, NJ: Susan Shadburne Productions, 1998.

"Know Your Prom Rights! A Quick Guide of LGBT High School Students." *LGBT Rights: American Civil Liberties Union.* http://www.aclu.org/lgbt-rights/know-your-prom-night-rights-quick-guide-lgbt-high-school-students (accessed July 2, 2011).

Red Scare

During World War I (1914–18), the United States adopted laws designed to discourage dissent and punish any act that might interfere with the war effort. After the war's end, this repressive (domineering) climate continued. The main targets of the repressive efforts were various leftists, Socialists, labor organizers, Communists, and others, all lumped together in the public mind as "Reds."

Fueling the public fears were dramatic social changes after the war. The era saw strikes, race riots, and widespread political agitation, including bombings. One of the bombs, in June 1919, damaged the home of Attorney General A. Mitchell Palmer (1872–1936), who led what were known as the "Red Raids." Ignoring the U.S. Constitution, Palmer's agents arrested and detained many suspected "radicals." Some of these were recent Russian immigrants, and, in December 1919, Palmer ordered 249 of them deported to the Soviet Union. The climax of the Red Scare came in January 1920, when Palmer ordered the arrest of nearly ten thousand people suspected of activities that threatened the well-being of the United States. Many were held without any formal charges against them and held in jail without bail (release from jail after depositing money with the court to ensure the person released will appear for a trial). Almost six hundred foreigners were deported, many of whom faced deportation hearings without the aid of lawyers. Though a public backlash eventually brought an end to the Red Scare, the socialist or radical beliefs that the Red Scare tried to stamp out never did find a strong footing in the United States.

Justin Gustainis

For More Information

Ackerman Kenneth D. *Young J. Edgar: Hoover, the Red Scare, and the Assault on American Civil Liberties.* New York: Carroll & Graf, 2007.

Fariello, Griffin. *Red Scare: Memories of the American Inquisition.* New York: Avon, 1995.

Gengarelly, Anthony W. *Distinguished Dissenters and Opposition to the 1919–1920 Red Scare.* New York: Edward Mellen Press, 1996.

Kovel, Joel. *Red Hunting in the Promised Land: Anticommunism and the Making of America.* New York: Basic Books, 1994.

Murray, Robert K. *Red Scare: A Study in National Hysteria, 1919–1920.* Minneapolis: University of Minnesota Press, 1955.

Walker, William T. *McCarthyism and the Red Scare: A Reference Guide.* Santa Barbara, CA: ABC-CLIO, 2011.

Route 66

Between the 1930s and 1960s, U.S. Route 66—known affectionately as "America's Highway" and the "Mother Road"—defined the culture of the American automobile. The 2,400-mile-long roadway ran through the American Midwest and Southwest, extending from Chicago, Illinois, to Los Angeles, California. Unlike regional roads that began and ended at specific destinations, Route 66 followed a meandering path between the two cities. Leaving Chicago, its course was generally southerly, linking hundreds of cities and small towns in Illinois, Missouri, Kansas, Oklahoma, Texas, New Mexico, Arizona, and California.

The roadway was assigned the numerical designation "66" in 1926. It quickly became the favored thoroughfare for truckers, who relished driving along the flat Southwestern prairie and through its temperate climate. During the **Great Depression** (1929–41; see entry under 1930s—The Way We Lived in volume 2), Route 66 was the major pathway leading Dust Bowl farmers who had been uprooted by soil erosion and the resulting dust storms in the south central states to the promised land of California. As depicted in the great American novel *The Grapes of Wrath* (1939) by John Steinbeck (1902–1968), the road was a symbol of these displaced Americans' quest for stability and prosperity. Stability, however, was not a characteristic of the road itself: Travel on Route 66 often was bothersome and sometimes perilous. Much of it remained unpaved. Riding on it was bumpy and uncomfortable at best. The route could be downright muddy and messy during inclement weather. The paving of the entire route was finally completed in 1938.

After World War II (1939–45), families resettling in the Southwest and in California and vacationers relishing their postwar prosperity frequently traveled on Route 66. Given the length of a trip along the roadway, **diners** (see entry under 1900s—Food and Drink in volume 1), cabins, motor courts (motels), and gas stations were needed to feed and house travelers and to fuel their cars. All became components of America's newly established road culture, the remnants of which exist to this day. The gas stations, **fast-food** (see entry under 1920s—Food and Drink in volume 2) restaurants, and motels that dot almost every major American roadway are linked to the post–World War II roadside architecture established along Route 66 and other, similar roadways.

In the 1950s, the importance of Route 66 began declining with the development of a national **highway system** (see entry under 1950s—The Way We Lived in volume 3), which allowed motorists even faster cross-country access. Eventually, the roadway was taken out of service. By the 1970s, practically all of the original Route 66 had been replaced by modern, four-lane superhighways. Even today, many sections of Route 66, such as Central Avenue, which runs through Albuquerque, New Mexico, bear "Historic Route 66" markers.

The mystique of Route 66 lives on. The roadway was celebrated in popular culture first in a song: "Get Your Kicks on Route 66" (1946), composed by Bobby Troup (1918–1999), a pianist and ex-marine who was driving west after World War II. The lyrics were a musical map of the route, citing its various stops. The song, recorded by Nat King Cole (1919–1965), quickly became a hit. The roadway was further immortalized in the television series *Route 66* (1960–1964), in which two young drifters, Tod Stiles (played by Martin Milner, 1931–) and Buzz Murdock (George Maharis, 1928–), rode cross-country in a Corvette. Tod and Buzz traveled through cities and towns, often encountering fellow outcasts and dreamers. That some of their destinations were not actually located on Route 66 only added to the roadway's romanticism, mythology, and historical significance.

Rob Edelman

For More Information

Crump, Spencer. *Route 66: America's First Main Street.* 2nd ed. Corona del Mar, CA: Zeta, 1998.

National Historic Route 66 Federation. *Explore Route 66!* http://www.national66.org/ (accessed July 2, 2011).

Scott, Quinta, and Susan Croce Kelly. *Route 66: The Highway and Its People.* Norman: University of Oklahoma Press, 1988.

Snyder, Tom. *Route 66 Traveler's Guide and Roadside Companion.* 4th ed. New York: St. Martin's Griffin, 2011.

Scopes Monkey Trial

The Scopes Monkey Trial dramatized the great debate over the teaching of evolution in America's public schools. By the 1920s, many people had accepted the theory of evolution proposed by Charles Darwin (1809–1882), which stated that all life evolved from lower forms. Many Christians, however, continued to believe in the biblical story of creation, in which God created humans in one single act. This belief is known as creationism. This debate was an important divide in the United States between traditional values (which supported creationism) and modern values (which supported evolution).

In 1925, Dayton, Tennessee, teacher John Scopes (1900–1970) was arrested for violating Tennessee's law against the teaching of evolution in schools. He had responded to a challenge by the American Civil Liberties Union (ACLU), a free-speech protection group. The ACLU offered to defend anyone willing to teach evolution in Tennessee in violation of the state's ban on teaching the subject. The ACLU put forth the offer in order to bring attention to what they considered a violation of free-speech rights.

Scopes' trial was the major news event in the summer of 1925. It was the first trial to be broadcast on the radio. Millions of people listened in, gripped by the debate over evolution. Clarence Darrow (1857–1938), a famous lawyer of the time, defended Scopes on behalf of the ACLU. William Jennings Bryan (1860–1925), a three-time presidential candidate and secretary of state for President Woodrow Wilson (1856–1924), led the prosecution. Bryan firmly believed that everything in the Bible was literally true. The biggest moment of the trial came when Darrow called Bryan to the stand as a witness and then proceeded to ask him all kinds of questions about the Bible. Bryan's answers sounded very foolish to many modern people who either heard Bryan on the radio or read about the trial in the newspapers. His testimony at the trial made the traditional-values people, or fundamentalists, look foolish as well. Scopes was found guilty, however, and fined $100. Although Scopes, and the ACLU, lost the trial, the publicity surrounding the trial resulted in a victory for evolution and a defeat for the fundamentalists. The teaching of evolution went unchallenged in the years after Scopes, and controversies about the role of religion and education continue into the present day. The trial reinforced the old American notion that separation between the government and religion was a good and necessary thing, yet Americans still debate the value of teaching religious beliefs and traditions in the schools.

Timothy Berg

For More Information

Conkin, Paul K. *When All the Gods Trembled: Darwinism, Scopes, and American Intellectuals.* Lanham, MD: Rowman & Littlefield, 1998.

Crompton, Samuel Willard. *The Scopes Monkey Trial.* New York: Chelsea House, 2010.

Jordan, Robert J., writer and producer. *Landmark American Trials: Scopes Trial, 1925* (video). Beverly Hills, CA: World Almanac Video, 2000.

Larson, Edward J. *Summer for the Gods: The Scopes Trial and America's Continuing Debate Over Science and Religion.* New York: Basic Books, 1997.

Linder, Douglas. "Tennessee vs. John Scopes; The 'Monkey Trial,' 1925." *Famous Trials in American History.* http://www.law.umkc.edu/faculty/projects/ftrials/scopes/scopes.htm (accessed January 28, 2002).

Standardized Testing

In the century since standardized intelligence and achievement tests were first introduced, they have gained and lost favor many times both among education experts and among the general public. Some experts insist that some form of testing is necessary to evaluate both inborn intelligence and achievement in school; others claim that such tests must always contain prejudice of some sort, and that, at best, they discover who is most skilled at taking the tests.

The idea of testing children and adults to determine their level of intelligence or education grew out of the same scientific spirit that fueled the theory of evolution and inherited characteristics proposed by Charles Darwin (1809–1892) during the late nineteenth century. As scientists began to believe that some qualities were passed from one generation to another, the idea took hold that intelligence was one of those inherited qualities. In the late 1800s, a French scientist named Alfred Binet (1857–1911) designed a test to determine intelligence levels. Binet's test was eventually given the name "Intelligence Quotient," or IQ test.

The first large-scale use of the new IQ test in the United States occurred during World War I (1914–18). Between 1917 and 1919, the U.S. armed services tested over two million soldiers to rate their intelligence. In 1926, scientists and educators who had worked on the army testing program created the Scholastic Aptitude Test (SAT), which was used by colleges to help determine which applicants should be admitted. In 1948, the Educational Testing Service was established to create and score standardized tests.

Since the creation of standardized tests, there has been much debate over their accuracy and fairness. Those who support testing argue that the tests are necessary to show students' level of learning and ability to learn. Many others insist that the tests do not show a student's mental ability, but only her or his degree of comfort with a classroom testing situation. Critics of tests have long claimed that tests favor wealthy white people and are unfairly biased against the poor and people of color. Because of these criticisms, testing decreased somewhat in the politically active 1960s and 1970s.

The 1990s saw a renewed interest in standardized testing as lawmakers began to demand that schools prove that their students were learning. The 1994 Elementary and Secondary Education Act tied federal funding of schools to student scores on national standardized tests. Many teachers, students, and parents have complained that such enforced testing reduces students' love of learning and forces teachers to spend most of their classroom time teaching test subjects.

Tina Gianoulis

For More Information

Bily, Cynthia A. *Standardized Testing.* Detroit: Greenhaven Press, 2011.

"Educational Testing Service." *The Atlantic Monthly* (Vol. 276, no. 3, September 1995): pp. 84–97.

"History of the SAT: A Timeline." *Frontline: PBS Online.* http://www.pbs.org/wgbh/pages/frontline/shows/sats/where/timeline.html (accessed July 2, 2011).

Squires, Sally. "Guiding Your Child Through Testing Mania: The Reason There Are Suddenly So Many Standardized Exams." *Family Life* (November 1, 2001): pp. 60–66.

US Department of Education. "ESEA Reauthorization: A Blueprint for Reform." *ED.gov* http://www2.ed.gov/policy/elsec/leg/blueprint/index.html (accessed July 7, 2011).

1930s
The Great Depression Disrupts America

After the Roaring Twenties, when business was booming and people thought the future looked bright, the stock market crash of October 29, 1929, seemed a minor problem that would quickly remedy itself. America had suffered hard times before; most Americans thought the economy would soon turn around so people could get on with life. The Great Depression (1929–41) thus came as a huge surprise to most people. Of a population of 122 million in 1930, 750,000 people were laid off without pay and another 2.4 million capable workers had no jobs at all. America was definitely not back on track. The economy showed no sign of turning around. The country's largest, most powerful companies had to cut back. The banking system collapsed. Factory workers, miners, and farmers were left unemployed and in many cases penniless. Schools closed. Children could not get enough food. Married women were fired in favor of single women and men. The decade was marred by the suffering of farmers on unworkable "dust bowl" land, hungry children, underpaid workers, and eager, desperate people who could not find work of any kind.

To turn the country around, the federal government decided to step in and help out. The New Deal programs of President Franklin D. Roosevelt (1882–1945) were a set of government programs designed to stimulate the economy. The New Deal offered temporary work, financial support, loans,

1930s At a Glance

WHAT WE SAID:

"All the way": At a soda fountain, an order of chocolate cake with chocolate ice cream.

Brawl: A party or dance. Also called a toddle or pig fight.

Cat: A fan of swing music. Also called an alligator. Someone with a "tin ear" did not like the new music.

Chamber of commerce: Toilet. Also called "crapper" or "honey house."

Coffin nail: Cigarette.

Cramp your style: To bother or interfere with something a person is doing.

"Crap!": "I am upset!"

Dead hoofer: A bad dancer.

"Frankly, my dear, I don't give a damn": These words said by Rhett Butler (played by Clark Gable) at the end of the film *Gone with the Wind* (1939) drew attention because they included a word—"damn"—that was taboo. They have become some of the most famous words ever uttered on screen.

Knuckling down: A term to describe a way of shooting marbles by resting one's knuckles on the ground. A good player could also "clean the ring," or shoot all of an opponent's marbles outside the playing ring.

"Okey dokey": "Okay."

Swing: The most popular music of the decade. The term became popular with Duke Ellington's 1932 hit song "It Don't Mean a Thing, If It Ain't Got That Swing."

Suck up: To try to gain favor through flattery.

Tin Lizzie: A car. Also called "puddle jumper," "Spirit of Detroit," and "Henry's go-cart," the latter in reference to automobile pioneer Henry Ford.

WHAT WE READ:

Cimarron **(1930):** Considered the best novel by Edna Ferber, *Cimarron* illustrates the settlement of Oklahoma during the Land Rush of 1889 and the complex social changes in an emerging American city.

Lone Cowboy **(1930):** Autobiography of Will James, a man who spent many years as a cowboy on the western plains and became a successful writer and illustrator of the Western experience, especially for children.

The Good Earth **(1931):** Drawing on her personal experience growing up in China as the child of missionaries, Pearl S. Buck wrote this novel in about three months, which described the life in China in a way that had never before been published. The book remained on the best-seller lists for nearly two years and won Buck a Pulitzer Prize in 1932.

and bank account insurance to Americans in need. These government projects got people working and kick-started the economy. By the end of the decade, America was getting back on track as new consumer-product manufacturers and service companies expanded their offerings. These new types of companies would take the place of more industry-oriented manufacturers that had dominated the economy in previous decades.

***The Epic of America* (1931):** This history of America and the American vision by Pulitzer Prize–winning historian James Truslow Adams sold five hundred thousand copies.

***Anthony Adverse* (1933):** Known as the best historical novel by Hervey Allen, this book tells a rambling story of life in early America. The royalties from the book sales supported Allen and his family for the rest of his life.

***Good-Bye, Mr. Chips* (1934):** One of the two most popular books by James Hilton, this novel tells the story of a teacher who spends his entire career at an English school and details the changes in the character and his community from 1870 to 1933.

***Gone with the Wind* (1936):** The historical novel by Margaret Mitchell which won her many awards, including the Pulitzer, details life in the South during the Civil War. Although some criticized its depiction of blacks, the novel continues to influence many people's views of life in the South at that time.

***The Yearling* (1938):** Marjorie Kinnan Rawlings's Pulitzer Prize–winning novel about a boy and his pet deer was originally written and marketed to adults, but has since become a favorite of children.

***The Grapes of Wrath* (1939):** John Steinbeck's Pulitzer Prize–winning novel told of the struggles of common people during the Depression. It was the first and most widely read of the "protest" novels published during the era. It had such a strong message of social protest that it was often banned, burned, and debated on the radio.

WHAT WE WATCHED:

***All Quiet on the Western Front* (1930):** A drama about life on the battlefield during World War I, starring Lew Ayres.

***The Big Trail* (1930):** A Western starring John Wayne in his first role.

***City Lights* (1931):** A silent romantic comedy directed by and starring Charlie Chaplin. At a time when "talkies" were all the rage, Chaplin produced what is considered his best film. *City Lights* features Chaplin's famous character "The Little Tramp" in a melodramatic story about friendship and the value of life.

***Public Enemy* (1931):** A gangster film starring James Cagney, Jean Harlow, and Mae Clarke.

***42nd Street* (1933):** A musical starring Warren Baxter, Bebe Daniels, and Dick Powell.

Gold Diggers of 1933: A musical choreographed by Busby Berkley and starring Ginger Rogers, Joan Blondell, and Dick Powell, which featured the popular song "We're in the Money."

***Dracula* (1931):** A horror film starring popular Hungarian actor Bela Lugosi. More than thirty horror films were produced in the 1930s, with sound effects like creaking doors, howling wolves, and crushing bones.

Despite the economic woes of the decade, popular culture made great progress. The 1930s are known as the golden age of both cinema and radio. Technological advances resulted in films of superior quality. The movie studios that had managed to retain their wealth produced films with extravagant settings that let audiences escape their personal problems, if only for a short time. Radio became a more popular

1930s At a Glance (continued)

The New Ziegfeld Follies (1934): A popular variety show starring Fanny Brice, Jane Froman, Vilma and Buddy Edsen, and Eugene and Willie Howard.

It Happened One Night (1934): This screwball comedy, starring Claudette Colbert and Clark Gable, featured witty banter between the two strong leading characters.

Snow White and the Seven Dwarfs (1937): The first feature-length animated film was presented by Walt Disney.

Hellzapoppin' (1938): Ole Olsen and Chic Johnson performed slapstick routines to the delight of New York audiences in this popular musical that ran for 1,404 performances.

Gone with the Wind (1939): Vivien Leigh and Clark Gable star in this epic film about the Civil War. The film was criticized for its portrayal of blacks, but eventually became known as one of the best films in history. It was the first Hollywood blockbuster to include color.

The Wizard of Oz (1939): This musical, starring Judy Garland, whisks audiences into a fantasyland of magic and wonder. The film included such popular songs as "Somewhere Over the Rainbow," "Follow the Yellow Brick Road," and "We're Off to See the Wizard."

WHAT WE LISTENED TO:
Lowell Thomas's news reports: His popular program started in 1930.

The Lone Ranger: This Western radio drama debuted in 1932.

Tom Mix: This radio program started in 1933, though he and his Wonder Horse Tony had an international base of fans from his more than 180 films.

"Fireside chats": President Franklin D. Roosevelt's first radio address occurred in 1933.

"Music Goes Round and Round" (1935): This hit swing song by Edward Farley and Michael Riley captured the feeling of the 1930s and was rarely off the air.

Guiding Light: The first soap opera debuted in 1937. It continued as a radio program until 1956 and then ran as a television show from 1952 to 2009.

The War of the Worlds: In 1938, Orson Welles broadcast a radio adaptation of H. G. Wells's science fiction novel. Listeners thought the presentation was a serious announcement of Martian invasion and panic spread throughout the country.

Amos 'n' Andy: The fifteen-minute broadcast literally stopped other activities each evening as listeners across the nation tuned in to listen to the comedians throughout the 1930s.

medium than in the previous decade. By the end of the 1930s, about 80 percent of American households owned a radio. Radio was so popular that movie theaters would even stop the featured film to broadcast the *Amos 'n' Andy* show (1928–60) to audiences every night.

With the repeal of Prohibition (1920–33), people could legally make and sell alcohol again. Taverns opened across the country. Jukeboxes and

"Flash!": News anchors periodically interrupted scheduled radio programs with this pronouncement, followed by a description of the latest news from Europe.

WHO WE KNEW:

Jack Benny (1894–1974): One of the most popular entertainers in America made audiences laugh for more than fifty years. Benny played an everyday man whose vanity, penny-pinching, and anxiousness gave him ample material to make everyday troubles seem funny. In his most famous skit, a burglar asks Benny, "Your money or your life?" After a long pause, Benny responds, "I'm thinking it over!"

Fanny Brice (1891–1951): One of the most famous vaudeville stars from the *Ziegfeld Follies* of the 1920s. She had her own radio program from 1938 to 1950. She went on to be a movie star and the 1968 play *Funny Girl* was based on her life.

James Cagney (1899–1986): The actor most identified with the high-profile criminals that the American public was so interested in during the 1930s. Because Cagney did not personally enjoy his tough-guy image, he sought out more respectable roles over the years.

Fr. Charles E. Coughlin (1891–1979): A radio priest from Michigan during the Depression. Coughlin's programs were broadcast on sixteen stations and had a huge following. His listeners, mainly Roman Catholics, heard his opinions about the moral consequences of current events and about politics. The conservative priest eventually became most well known for his anti-Semitic views and for his support of German dictator Adolf Hitler.

Joan Crawford (1904?–1977): This glamorous MGM actress, who won fame playing carefree flappers in the 1920s, took on hard-working "shopgirl" roles in the 1930s. Two of her movies were *Paid* and *Possessed*.

John Dillinger (1903–1934): Notorious bank robber and murderer who dodged police between September 1933 and July 1934. During that time, he killed ten people, wounded seven, robbed banks, and escaped from jail three times. His flight was detailed daily in newspapers and on the radio.

Greta Garbo (1905–1990): The delight of sound in movies was perhaps no more evident than when sultry actress Garbo uttered her first lines: "Gimme a viskey. Ginger ale on the side. And don't be stingy, baby." Garbo's silky, accented voice enhanced her stunning beauty in the movie *Anne Christie* (1930).

Martha Graham (1894–1991): The most influential choreographer in America. Her *Primitive Mysteries* of 1931 is a masterpiece of modern dance, and one of the first to incorporate Graham's inventive spiral movements.

recorded music in "juke joints," taverns, or soda fountains offered musical accompaniment to activities that had previously been silent or had relied on live bands. With the financial support and vision of the New Deal, the country heard a larger variety of music than ever before during the decade.

The country's landscape was forever changed by the massive scale and number of building projects that dotted the country. Some of the most

1930s At a Glance (continued)

Herbert Hoover (1874–1964): U.S. president during the nation's most devastating economic crisis. Although some of his programs intended to deal with the Depression were successful, and some were used by his successor, Franklin D. Roosevelt, the public mocked Hoover for his seeming indifference to their plight. "Hooverisms," slang that expressed the common person's difficulties, were coined, including "Hoovervilles," shantytowns found in every large city in America, and "Hoovercarts," cars pulled by horses because the driver could not afford gas.

Howard Hughes (1905–1975): At the beginning of the 1930s, Hughes was the most famous movie producer in the United States and the owner of the Hughes Tool Company that was worth $75 million. In 1935 he broke the air-speed record; in 1937 he was named the best aviator of the year by President Roosevelt, he set a record for flying around the world at record pace in 1938. By the end of his life he was worth $650 million and had become a bizarre recluse and drug addict.

Lindbergh baby: Charles A. Lindbergh Jr., the twenty-month-old baby of famed aviator Charles Lindbergh, was kidnapped on March 1, 1932. The country closely followed the hunt for the perpetrator. Bruno Hauptmann, an illegal immigrant from Germany, was convicted of the crime and executed in 1936, although some say the evidence against him was scanty.

Joe Louis (1914–1981): Heavyweight boxing champion from 1938 to 1949. Louis was the first black man to become known by name across America. He symbolized blacks' ability to conquer racism and discrimination.

Franklin D. Roosevelt (1882–1945): The thirty-second president of the United States led the country out of the Depression with his "New Deal" plan that enlarged the responsibilities of the federal government and into World War II.

Mae West (1892–1980): The most sexual movie star and playwright of the Depression era. After writing Broadway hits, West became a screen star. By 1935, she was the highest-paid woman in the country. One of her most famous lines was "Why don't you come up and see me sometime?"

Walter Winchell (1897–1972): The most popular American gossip columnist. His stories about celebrities won him a broad fan base. His syndicated column ran in more than 170 newspapers and his radio show was heard by 20 million listeners.

impressive skyscrapers and most complicated engineering projects were completed during the 1930s. The Empire State Building (1931) changed the New York skyline. The Boulder Dam (1935; renamed the Hoover Dam in 1947), was an engineering marvel that offered a regular supply of electricity to Los Angeles, California, for the first time when it opened in 1935. The Golden Gate Bridge, which was built between 1933 and 1937, spans a two-mile passage between Oakland and San Francisco, California, standing as a testament to the genius of modern bridge design.

In general, though, life in America during the 1930s was shaped as a result of the Great Depression.

1930s

Commerce

Following the collapse of the stock market in 1929, the American economy went into a period of decline that lasted for an entire decade. This economic collapse, which eventually affected every economy in the world, was known as the Great Depression (1929–41). Across the economy, the market for American goods dried up. America had become the most powerful economy in the world on the strength of its industrial manufacturing, but by the 1930s demand for rail products, steel, and textiles had virtually disappeared. The nation's leading industry, the automobile industry, shrank during the decade as several small, independent carmakers were forced to close. Ford, General Motors, and Chrysler were the largest automobile manufacturers, together supplying nearly 75 percent of the automobiles sold at the beginning of the decade and about 90 percent by the end. In the automobile industry as well as in other manufacturing industries, more and more workers were let go. Unemployment began to climb in the Midwest where most of the manufacturing companies were centered.

Workers during this decade tried to combat job insecurity and poor wages by organizing into unions and striking. Some of the most violent, and deadly, strikes in American history occurred during the 1930s. Unlike the peaceful demonstrations of the late twentieth century, these strikes were vigorously opposed by employers. Companies would hire strong-arm "tough guys" to protect their property and to intimidate workers. In some cases, even the police would physically struggle with strikers. One of the bloodiest conflicts between labor and management was in Harlan County, Kentucky, and lasted the entire decade. Two-thirds of the county's workers were employed by coal companies. The Depression reduced wages and eliminated jobs, making workers worry about their future. More than two hundred children died from 1929 through 1931 in the county. Coal miners unionized and began to battle with coal companies for their livelihoods. Both the miners and the company guards used guns to intimidate one another. The decade-long battle—filled with bombings, shootings, and fistfights—concluded with a strike that the federal government had to end.

In addition to the hardships suffered by workers and the unemployed, farmers also grew desperate during the 1930s. Crop prices fell and banks foreclosed on farms. To try to raise enough money to save their farms, farmers grew more crops, which drove crop prices further down. To make matters worse, there was a long drought, which rendered farmland into unusable "dust bowls" and literally ruined many farms. Many farmers forced off their land in Oklahoma journeyed westward, seeking a better life in California. The plight of these "Okies" was described in the novel *The Grapes of Wrath* (1939) by John Steinbeck (1902–1968).

Though industrial business in America suffered, new companies that made consumer products began to flourish. New products included Alka-Seltzer, ballpoint pens, Clairol hair coloring, and Fisher-Price toys. The economic supports of the New Deal—a set of government programs designed to stimulate the economy—paved the way for more and more of these consumer products to dominate the economy in the coming decades.

Alka-Seltzer

The Bayer company's Alka-Seltzer brand pain-reliever and antacid boasts speedy relief, as well as one of the most notable **advertising** (see entry under 1920s—Commerce in volume 2) campaigns in history. Alka-Seltzer was introduced in 1931 by Miles Laboratories (purchased by Bayer in 1979). The product was originally used by some consumers as a remedy for hangovers. Alka-Seltzer's effervescent (fizzing) tablets release their active ingredients when dissolved in water. Each Alka-Seltzer tablet, which comes in either original, lemon-lime, or cherry flavor, contains 1,916 milligrams of sodium bicarbonate, 1,000 milligrams of citric acid, and 325 milligrams of aspirin. Bayer also manufactures a range of variations on the basic product, including chewable Alka Mints and Alka-Seltzer PM for nighttime relief.

Alka-Seltzer advertisements are considered classics. From 1954 to 1964, its broadcast commercials featured a cheerful animated character named "Speedy Alka-Seltzer," whose voice was supplied by voice-over actor Dick Beals (1927–), and a visual demonstration of two tablets fizzing after being dropped into a glass of water. Speedy, originally known as Sparky, was created by the Wade Advertising Agency in 1951. The brief ditty "Plop, plop, fizz, fizz, oh what a relief it is," composed by Tom Dawes (1943–2007) of Twin Star Music, became one of the most well-known commercial jingles in advertising history. During the 1970s, a familiar Alka-Seltzer commercial depicted a heartburn victim moaning "I can't believe I ate the whole thing!" after giving in to a persistent waiter's demand to order spicy meatballs. The popularity of Alka-Seltzer stems in part from the American consumer's desire for quick solutions to the irritations of daily life.

Edward Moran

Two fizzing tablets have brought relief to millions of consumers for eighty years.
© ROBERT J. HUFFMAN/FIELD MARK PUBLICATIONS.

For More Information

Bayer. *Alka-Seltzer.* http://www.alka-seltzer.com (accessed July 2, 2011).
McGrath, Molly Wade. *Top Sellers U.S.A.: Success Stories behind America's Best-Selling Products from Alka-Seltzer to Zippo.* New York: Morrow, 1983.

Ballpoint Pens

A ballpoint pen is an inexpensive writing instrument whose point is a tiny ball bearing that rotates against a supply of semi-liquid ink sealed in a cartridge. Most ballpoint pens are made of plastic or low-cost metal.

They are typically designed to be discarded after the ink runs dry. Others are designed so that their containers can be unscrewed and their ink cartridge replaced. The first of some 350 U.S. patents for such a device was issued to John Loud in 1888. No practical ballpoint pen was produced until 1938, when journalist Ladislo Biro (1899–1985) patented his own version in his native Hungary. Biro's pen used the same kind of quick-drying, smudge-free ink used to print newspapers. After immigrating to Argentina, Biro applied for a new patent. His patent was licensed by the British government during World War II (1939–45) for use by the Royal Air Force, which sought a pen that would not leak at high altitudes.

After the war, the Eversharp and Eberhard-Faber companies acquired the exclusive rights to Biro Pens of Argentina and began marketing ballpoint pens in the United States under the name "Eversharp CA." The "CA" stood for capillary action, the adhesive force between the molecules of the container and the molecules of a liquid in contact with the container. Meanwhile, a Chicago entrepreneur, Milton Reynolds (1892–1976), ignoring Eversharp's patent rights, started the Reynolds International Pen Company and began selling his own ballpoint, dubbed the "Reynolds Rocket." Reynolds claimed that his pen could write under water, a feature promoted in advertisements by swimming star Esther Williams (1921–). In October 1945, Gimbels' Department Store in New York City began retailing the pens for $12.50 each, selling out its entire stock of ten thousand on the first day. Another early manufacturer, the Frawley Pen Company, began marketing a retractable ballpoint called the Papermate. A successful Papermate promotional campaign featured sales agents writing on their customers' shirts with the company's pens and offering to replace the shirts if the ink did not wash out.

Despite the hype (exaggerated publicity) surrounding ball-point pens, consumers still hesitated to accept them fully because of the product's unreliability. Fountain-pen manufacturers promoted more convenient ink-cartridge models and asked educators to join a campaign arguing that ballpoints impeded good penmanship. In Europe, the Bic pen, manufactured by French entrepreneur Baron Bich (1914–1994) under a royalty agreement with Biro, emerged as the first inexpensive, reliable ballpoint pen in the mass market. After 1960, ballpoint pens finally began to win mass acceptance as the writing instrument of choice around the world.

Edward Moran

For More Information

"Ballpoint Pen History." *The Great Idea Finder.* http://www.ideafinder.com/history/inventions/ballpen.htm (accessed July 2, 2011).

Bellis, Mary. "The Battle of the Ballpoint Pens." *About.com.* http://inventors.about.com/library/weekly/aa101697.htm (accessed July 2, 2011).

Bic World. http://www.bicworld.com (accessed July 2, 2011).

Cobb, Vicki. *The Secret Life of School Supplies.* New York: Lippincott, 1981.

Gostony, Henry and Stuart L. Schneider. *The Incredible Ballpoint Pen: A Comprehensive History and Price Guide.* Atglen, PA: Schiffer Publishing, 1998.

Whalley, Joyce Irene. *Writing Implements and Accessories: From the Roman Stylus to the Typewriter.* Detroit: Gale Research, 1975.

Clairol Hair Coloring

Clairol Hair Coloring revolutionized the way American women treated their hair. Introduced to the United States in 1931 by Lawrence M. Gelb (1898–1980), Clairol promoted hair coloring as an acceptable, appealing beauty treatment for every woman, not a risqué procedure for only the very bold. "Does she or doesn't she?" became the familiar ad campaign for Clairol in the 1950s as more and more women began enhancing their hair colors.

Clairol truly succeeded in making hair coloring like other cosmetics in 1956 with the introduction of "Miss Clairol," the first do-it-yourself hair color. The product was sold with images of homemakers, mothers, and everyday women, not pictures of glamorous beauties. Miss Clairol was a hair color for anyone. From the introduction of Miss Clairol to the 1970s, the number of American women who colored their hair jumped from 7 to 40 percent. And by the early twenty-first century, hair coloring had become such an acceptable cosmetic treatment that women no longer worried if people knew whether or

A year after the introduction of the "Miss Clairol" hair-coloring product, ads such as this were found in many publications. © AP IMAGES/KATHY WILLENS.

not they colored their hair. Some changed their hair color on a whim; others boasted unusual hair colors that could never be mistaken for natural.

Sara Pendergast

For More Information

Clairol. http://clairol.com (accessed July 5, 2011).

"Clairol's Influence on American Beauty and Marketing." *Drug and Cosmetic Industry* (August 1996).

Gladwell, Malcolm. "True Colors." *New Yorker* (March 22, 1999): pp. 70–81.

Fisher-Price Toys

Along with **LEGOs** (see entry under 1950s—Sports and Games in volume 4), **Barbie dolls** (see entry under 1950s—Commerce in volume 3), and **GI Joe** (see entry under 1960s—Commerce in volume 4), Fisher-Price toys have been some of the most popular and successful toys in American history. Most children who grew up after World War II (1939–45) have had at least some experience playing with Fisher-Price toys. The success of the toys came from their ability to give children the tools for imaginative play without confining them to only one activity. Fisher-Price toys were basic, but they allowed children to use their imaginations to create whole worlds with them.

Herman Fisher (1898–1975), Irving Price (1884–1976), and Helen Schelle (1893–1984) began the Fisher-Price company in East Aurora, New York, in 1931. Although the company struggled to survive during

Fisher-Price was one of the first companies to use plastic in toy manufacturing. © FORM ADVERTISING/ALAMY.

the **Great Depression** (1929–41; see entry under 1930s—The Way We Lived in volume 2), when most people had little money for non-essential goods such as toys, it managed to introduce three items—Granny Doodle, Dr. Doodle, and Snoopy Sniffer. These three toys became their early signature toys; that is, toys that were easily identifiable as Fisher-Price toys.

In the two decades following World War II, newly affluent Americans began looking for toys for a new generation of children, a generation known as **baby boomers** (see entry under 1940s—The Way We Lived in volume 3). The toy industry boomed along with the population, and Fisher-Price rode the demographic wave. The company was one of the first to use **plastics** (see entry under 1900s—Commerce in volume 1) in its toys, making the toys feel modern and safer for small children. Over the years, Fisher-Price produced a number of toys that have since become classics. The Bubble Mower sent forth a stream of bubbles as kids pushed it across the carpet. The Corn Popper was a push toy that sent small colored balls flying inside a small clear-plastic dome as it was pushed along. Perhaps Fisher-Price's most enduring toy has been the Little People, simple wooden (and later plastic) people with no arms and legs. Little People inhabited all kinds of structures, from dollhouses to parking garages to airplanes. A barn set came complete with toy animals, tractors, and fences. Other toys had problems, however. In 2007, for example, Fisher-Price recalled almost one million toys featuring characters from **Sesame Street** (see entry under 1970s—TV and Radio in volume 4) and **Dora the Explorer** (see entry under 2000s—TV and Radio in volume 6) due to concerns that they were covered in harmful lead paint.

The company was acquired several times in its history, most recently by rival toy giant Mattel, in 1993. By the early twenty-first century, it was continuing to make its mark as part of the everyday experience of millions of American children, just as it had with their parents in the 1950s and 1960s.

Timothy Berg

For More Information

Cassity, Brad. *Fisher-Price Toys: A Pictorial Guide to the More Popular Toys.* Paducah, KY: Collector Books, 2000.

Cross, Gary. *Kid's Stuff.* Cambridge, MA: Harvard University Press, 1997.

Fisher-Price: Oh, the Possibilities. http://www.fisher-price.com (accessed July 5, 2011).

Fox, Bruce R., and John J. Murray. *Fisher-Price: Historical, Rarity, and Value Guide, 1931–present.* 3rd ed. Iola, WI: Krause, 2002.

1930s

Fashion

American fashions shifted in the 1930s. The 1920s had been a decade of excess during which fashions for both young men and women—the "sheiks" and "flappers"—grew increasingly extravagant. The Great Depression (1929–41) discouraged unnecessary spending on fashion. Americans tried to get by with what clothes they already had, make do with what clothes they could afford, or do without certain garments entirely.

Extravagant fashions for different seasons were no longer affordable to many. Instead, practical clothing that could be worn in many different seasons and for many different occasions filled retail shops. Since most American women could not afford original French fashions, American designers soon created simpler copies of French designs in a variety of price ranges. The most popular dress for women was a simple short-sleeved print dress with a belted waist and a flowing calf-length skirt. Expensive fabrics like silk were replaced with synthetic fabrics or cotton. Instead of buying new outfits for each season, women instead began to accessorize their simple dresses with gloves, hats, jewelry, and the new leg-hugging, sheer nylons. Men wore high-waisted pants and jackets with wide, short lapels during the decade. Instead of tailored vests, many men wore knitted V-neck vests. The zipper, which had been invented nearly two decades before, was now a popular closure for many clothing items.

Nylon

Wallace Carothers (1896–1937) invented nylon while working for the DuPont Company in the 1930s. The name "nylon" was originally a DuPont trademark. Nylon first appeared in the form of toothbrush bristles in 1938. Soon nylon became one of the most widely used man-made materials. It is used in ropes, plastic sheeting, netting, moldings, and woven fabrics. It is also used as an insulating material in electrical goods. Nylon takes the place of steel bearings, gears, and bushings (insulating linings for holes or tubes) in all kinds of machines. It is also widely used in medicine for making splints, sutures, braces and other items. At the start of the twenty-first century, nylon appears in almost all areas of life. Without it, many of the things people take for granted would not exist.

Within two years of the first toothbrush bristles, nylon was being used to make lightweight fabrics for hosiery. Because they were so strong, **nylon stockings** (see entry under 1930s—Fashion in volume 2) were more popular than silk and soon became known as "nylons." Nylon also replaced silk in parachutes, and in military slang a parachute jump was known as a "nylon let-down." By the 1960s, nylon was widely used in objects from furniture to clothing. Occasionally, nylon use has not improved people's lives. In the 1970s, synthetics such as nylon dominated fashion. Like its cousin **polyester** (see entry under 1970s—Fashion in volume 4), nylon tended to encourage sweating. In extreme cases, nylon shirts became charged with static electricity and made the wearer's hair stand on end. Thankfully, nylon is currently most popularly used in sportswear and hosiery.

Nevertheless, nylon is not far from being the wonder material it was once thought to be. Because it is so tough and resistant to wear and tear, it is ideal for floor coverings, tires, inflated balls, pumps, valves, containers, and car body parts. The invention of nylon made possible the cheap mass production of high-quality consumer goods from children's toys to computers and sound systems. Wallace Carothers' invention revolutionized life in the twentieth century and beyond.

Chris Routledge

For More Information

Handley, Susannah. *Nylon: The Story of a Fashion Revolution: From Art Silk to Nylon and Thinking Fibres.* Baltimore: Johns Hopkins University Press, 2000.

Hermes, Matthew E. *Enough for One Lifetime: Wallace Carothers, Inventor of Nylon.* Washington, DC: American Chemical Society, 1996.

Price, Ronnie. *Man Made Magic: When Science Meets Fashion.* London: MX, 2010.

Nylon Stockings

Hosiery made of sheer fabric has been worn by women for centuries. Too light to protect a woman from the cold and uncomfortably hot in the heat of summer, stockings are not a practical garment; they are merely an accessory to make the legs look silky and smooth. **Nylon** (see entry under 1930s—Fashion in volume 2), a material invented by the DuPont Company in 1937, revolutionized stockings for women. Nylon

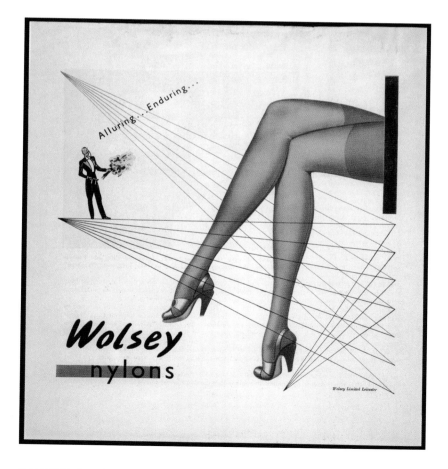

Nylon stockings were big sellers upon their introduction in 1940. © MARY EVANS PICTURE LIBRARY/ALAMY.

stockings shown at New York's 1939 **World's Fair** (see entry under 1900s—The Way We Lived in volume 1) created a stir, making stockings available in a sheer, strong, and affordable fabric. Nylon had the look of expensive silk stockings, which many women could not afford.

When the first nylons hit the shelves in New York City the following year, more than four million pairs were sold within a few hours. In 1940, 672 million pairs of stockings were manufactured. Sales remained strong until the beginning of World War II (1939–45), when all nylon production was converted to military uses. During the war years, women did not forget about nylon stockings. Some young women used eyebrow pencils to make lines down the back of their bare legs to simulate the look of seamed nylon stockings. With the end of the war, nylon stockings were again produced. Soon spandex, a stretchy material, was combined with nylon to make even more appealing stockings that clung to the legs.

British fashion designer Mary Quant (1934–) revolutionized women's fashion in the 1960s with her **miniskirt** (see entry under 1960s—Fashion in volume 4). Miniskirts were so short that they revealed the garters used to hold up stockings. Women needed hosiery to cover up more of their legs. By 1965, the first pair of pantyhose greeted women who were fed up with trying to hide the snaps and clips used to hold up conventional stockings. Although hemlines have since changed many times, women have continued to prefer pantyhose over stockings held by garters or corsets. Women's sheer hosiery sales reached $2.3 billion in 1999, according to the Hosiery Association. The future is not altogether bright for nylons, however. Sales have fallen rapidly in recent years and some sheer hosiery factories have closed. Worse yet, none other than first lady Michelle Obama (1964–) has admitted to giving up on pantyhose because she finds them uncomfortable.

Sara Pendergast

For More Information

Efron, Edith. "Legs Are Bare Because They Can't Be Sheer." *New York Times Magazine* (June 24, 1945): p. 17.

Handley, Susannah. *Nylon: The Story of a Fashion Revolution; A Celebration of Design from Art Silk to Nylon and Thinking Fibres.* Baltimore: Johns Hopkins University Press, 1999.

The Hosiery Association. http://www.hosieryassociation.com/ (accessed July 5, 2011).

Matlin, Jessica. "Make Like Michelle Obama and Ditch the Pantyhose" *Stylist. com.* http://www.stylelist.com/2009/05/16/make-like-michelle-obama-ditch-the-pantyhose/ (accessed July 5, 2011).

1950s

Film and Theater

Although many people and businesses suffered during the Great Depression (1929–41), the movie industry did not. In fact, the 1930s are considered the golden era of Hollywood cinema. Eighty-five million people a week crowded movie theaters across America to escape the emotional strain of their sometimes desperate financial situations. From black-and-white and two-color "B" movies to new three-color Technicolor "A" movies, audiences had huge quantities of movies from which to choose.

The technological advances of color and sound made the best movies truly extravagant. Broadway choreographer Busby Berkeley (1895–1976) created some of the most elaborate musicals. Dancing partners Fred Astaire (1899–1987) and Ginger Rogers (1911–1995) turned dance into an art form on film. Large, powerful movie studios turned actors and actresses, such as Marlene Dietrich (1901–1992), young Shirley Temple (1928–), and Mickey Rooney (1920–), into superstars by featuring them in film after film. Rooney played the popular character Andy Hardy in a series of films that could be enjoyed by the whole family.

Some studios specialized in different types of films. Horror films such as *Frankenstein* (1931) and *Dracula* (1931) terrified audiences. Epic dramas like *Gone with the Wind* (1939) captivated audiences for hours. Western movies captured and enhanced the myth of the American West through sweeping landscape shots and tough cowboys played by the likes of John Wayne (1907–1979). Gangster flicks were especially popular in the 1930s. Actors James Cagney (1899–1986) and Edward G. Robinson (1893–1973) perfected portrayals of nasty movie criminals patterned after real-life gangsters like Al Capone (1899–1947). Capone had become notorious in Chicago, Illinois, during Prohibition (1920–33) when he and his henchmen built a criminal empire by supplying people with illicit alcohol.

For fun, film studios offered screwball comedies, including *It Happened One Night* (1934), featuring the witty banter of stars Cary Grant (1904–1986) and Claudette Colbert (1903–1996), and the Oscar-winning *The Awful Truth* (1937) starring Grant and Irene Dunne (1898–1990). These screwball comedies, combining slapstick comedy and urban sophistication, remained popular from the middle to the end of the decade. Another fun type of film was the animated feature. Walt Disney released its first feature-length animated film, *Snow White and the Seven Dwarfs,* in 1937, to great success. The terrifically successful live-action film *Wizard of Oz* was released in 1939.

The New Deal—a set of government programs designed to stimulate the economy and aid Americans harmed by the Depression—offered support to theaters across the nation. The Federal Theatre Project (FTP) was created by the Works Progress Administration in 1935 to employ actors, directors, and set and costume designers. The FTP made theater affordable to everyday Americans. The FTP was in charge of organizing distinct theater chapters for each state. Until the project lost its funding in 1939, it supported the creation of children's plays, new dramas by American playwrights, and productions of the classic plays of William Shakespeare (1564–1616). The FTP also sponsored theaters for the blind, productions in various languages, and—perhaps most memorably—the "Living Newspaper" dramas that entertained as well as educated audiences about American history. The FTP productions were seen by nearly twenty-five million people. A Negro Theatre Project also paralleled the FTP's development with all-black productions.

Andy Hardy Movies

From the late 1930s to the middle 1940s, the fictional character of Andy Hardy was the most popular teenager in American motion pictures. Andy, an energetic and wholesome teenager, first appeared in a

1928 stage play, *Skidding,* by Aurania Rouverol (c. 1886–1955). This play was purchased by the **MGM** (see entry under 1920s—Film and Theater in volume 2) studio and made into a low-budget film called *A Family Affair* (1937). When that film proved popular with audiences, studio executives planned two additional Hardy family feature films, *You're Only Young Once* (1938) and *Judge Hardy's Children* (1938). By 1939, it was clear that the Hardy family, and Andy in particular, were appealing to large audiences. To make sure that filmgoers recognized the releases of new films about the Hardy family, each title in the series began to include the family's last name. Most of the titles contained the name of *Andy Hardy,* who was the standout character and the focus of each story line.

The films depict a loving family living in an idealized American small town called Carvel. In most of the stories, Andy attends high school, experiences puppy love, and learns practical lessons about friendship, dating, and managing money. The titles suggest the youth-oriented subject matter contained in the scripts: *Andy Hardy Gets Spring Fever* (1939), *Andy Hardy Meets Debutante* (1940), *Life Begins for Andy Hardy* (1941), and *Love Laughs at Andy Hardy* (1946). No matter how complex Andy's problems are, he never fails to benefit from a heart-to-heart chat with his stern but devoted father, Judge Hardy, played in all but the first

A lobby card for the 1940 film Andy Hardy Meets Debutante, *starring Mickey Rooney and Judy Garland.* © PICTORIAL PRESS LTD./ALAMY.

film of the series by veteran film actor Lewis Stone (1879–1953). In the first film, Lionel Barrymore (1888–1954) played Judge Hardy.

Juvenile MGM star Mickey Rooney (1920–) played Andy Hardy in the sixteen feature-length films that compose the series. Rooney's portayal of Andy shows the outward cockiness and inner vulnerability of teenagers of the period, who were pursuing innocent adventures in communities across the country. Because these films were high in entertainment value and featured plot elements to which the majority of American families could relate, they were very popular fare. Only the last film in the series, a belated sequel called *Andy Hardy Comes Home* (1958), was not a success. This story presents a middle-aged Andy who is the head of his own family. Sadly, the beloved character of Judge Hardy had to be written out of the script because Stone had died several years earlier. Moviegoers were disappointed to see a movie about a rather squat, older-looking Andy Hardy weighed down by adult concerns of business and politics. Most fans of the series wanted to freeze their favorite screen teen in time so that he never would get old.

In 1942, at the height of the series' popularity and in a wave of World War II (1939–45) patriotism, a special Academy Award was given to the MGM studio for "its achievement in representing the American Way of Life in the production of the *Andy Hardy* series of films."

Audrey Kupferberg

For More Information

Parish, James Robert, and Ronald L. Bowers. *The MGM Stock Company.* New Rochelle, NY: Arlington House, 1973.
Ray, Robert B. *The Avant-Garde Finds Andy Hardy.* Cambridge, MA: Harvard University Press, 1995.
Rooney, Mickey. *Life Is Too Short.* New York: Villard Books, 1991.

"B" Movies

"B" movies were low-budget productions made during the era of the motion picture–studio system, mainly during the 1930s and 1940s. During this period of time, large movie studios dominated the production and distribution of all movies. There really is no equivalent to the "B" movie today, although low-budget, independent movies such as *Paranormal Activity* (2009) could be considered similar.

During the studio-system era, the motion-picture studios not only made the pictures but also owned the theaters where they were shown. Usually the theaters of the time would show a cartoon, a newsreel of the current headlines, and two feature movies. One was the feature or "A" picture, such as *Gone with the Wind* (see entry under 1930s—Film and Theater in volume 2). The other feature movie was the "B" picture, a shorter, cheaper film that supported the main feature.

The "B" films had less-important directors and stars working on them. Most of these movies were not very good. They were intended to fill out the theater's program for the least possible cost. Many were filmed as a part of a series. Among the more famous film series were those featuring Sherlock Holmes, **Dick Tracy** (see entry under 1930s—Print Culture in volume 2), **Charlie Chan** (see entry under 1920s—Film and Theater in volume 2), and **Tarzan** (see entry under 1910s—Print Culture in volume 1). Many other of the "B" movies were genre films—that is, movies using a conventional and established theme, such as **Westerns** (see entry under 1930s—Film and Theater in volume 2) or **horror movies** (see entry under 1960s—Film and Theater in volume 4). Occasionally an intended "B" movie became a classic, such as *Casablanca* (1942; see entry under 1940s—Film and Theater in volume 3), considered one of the finest movies ever made.

During the 1950s, the meaning of a "B" movie became slightly different. Most horror or monster pictures of the 1950s were considered "B," or lower-class, pictures. Also, most pictures that were shown primarily at **drive-in theaters** (see entry under 1930s—The Way We Lived in volume 2) were considered "B" films. The drive-in theater became extremely popular during this time and kept the "B" film industry working. Roger Corman (1926–) became known as the "King of the 'B's" after producing forty-eight such films between 1955 and 1970.

During the 1960s and early 1970s, the "B" movie was still made, although only a handful of studios were still making money with them. After the 1970s, what was typically called a "B" movie evolved into what is known now as the independent film. The independent film label does not mean these films are all bad, as the label of "B" movie implies. What independent films do have in common with the "B" movie are their low budgets and usual lack of recognition by the film industry. Nowadays, there are film festivals, such as the annual Sundance Film Festival, put on by actor Robert Redford (1936–) in Park City, Utah, strictly for independent films.

Jill Gregg Clever

For More Information

B-Movie Central. http://www.bmoviecentral.com/bmc/ (accessed July 5, 2011).

"B Movies." *CinemaSpot.com.* http://www.CinemaSpot.com/categories/bmovies.htm (accessed July 5, 2011).

Cross, Robin. *Big Book of "B" Movies.* New York: St. Martin's Press, 1987.

Lyons, Arthur. *Death on the Cheap: The Lost B Movies of Film Noir.* Cambridge, MA: Da Capo Press, 2000.

McCarthy, Todd, and Charles Flynn, eds. *Kings of the Bs.* New York: Dutton, 1975.

McClelland, Doug. *The Golden Age of "B" Movies.* New York: Bonanza Books, 1978.

Sterritt, David, and John C. Anderson, eds. *The B List: The National Society of Film Critics on the Low-Budget Beauties, Genre-Bending Mavericks, and Cult Classics We Love.* Cambridge, MA: Da Capo Press, 2008.

Betty Boop

The first important female animated-film character, Betty Boop appeared in more than one hundred cartoons during the 1930s. Originally created by animator Grim Natwick (1890–1990), Betty Boop soon evolved into a sexy, glamorous **flapper** (see entry under 1920s—Fashion in volume 2) who was far more adult-oriented than the innocent cartoon characters created by Walt **Disney** (see entry under 1920s—Film and Theater in volume 2) and other studios of the period. Betty Boop was a short-skirted, leggy figure with an oversize head, tight-curl hairdo, huge eyes surrounded with big lashes, and puckered-up lips. From 1931, Betty Boop's familiar New York–accented voice cooed her trademark "Boop-Oop-a-Doop" greeting. Betty Boop's voice was supplied by actress Mae Questel (1908–1998).

Betty Boop made her debut as a minor character in the 1930 *Talkartoons* short film "Dizzy Dishes." She was portrayed as a liberated and independent woman far ahead of her time, as in the 1932 cartoons *Betty Boop for President* and *Boop-Oop-a-Doop.* In many of the Betty Boop cartoons, popular entertainers of the day (like Cab Calloway, 1907–1994; Ethel Merman, 1908–1984; and Rudy Vallee, 1901–1986) are seen singing and dancing with her. From 1935, Betty Boop began appearing in a Sunday comic strip distributed by King Features Syndicate.

By the end of the 1930s, Hollywood censors declared that the Betty Boop cartoon character was too daring and demanded that her creators stop portraying her in short skirts and low-cut blouses. As a consequence, the Fleischer Studio began portraying a long-skirted Betty Boop in a more domestic setting, with friends that included an inventor named Grampy

During the Great Depression, Betty Boop appeared in more than one hundred animated shorts. © PICTORIAL PRESS LTD./ ALAMY.

and a puppy named Pudgy. Her last cartoon, *Yip, Yip, Yippy!,* appeared in 1939, but there was a revival of interest in her after the 1970s. She made a brief appearance in the 1988 film *Who Framed Roger Rabbit?*

Edward Moran

For More Information

Callan, Kathleen. *Betty Boop: Queen of Cartoons.* New York: A&E Television Networks, 1995.

Lorenz, Brenna, and Megaera Lorenz. "The Heptune Guide to Betty Boop Cartoons." *Heptune.* http://www.heptune.com/betty.html (accessed July 5, 2011).

Morris, Barry. "Betty Boop." *Bright Lights Film Journal.* http://www.brightlightsfilm.com/16/betty.html (accessed July 5, 2011).

Solomon, Charles. *The History of Animation.* New York: Alfred A. Knopf, 1989.

Humphrey Bogart (1899–1957)

Humphrey Bogart was a popular film actor whose career stretched from the early 1930s to the mid-1950s. He is most famous for his cool tough-guy character and his tight-lipped, clipped way of speaking.

After a string of bland roles in the early 1930s, Bogart made his first screen breakthrough in 1936 when he appeared as a convincing hoodlum in *The Petrified Forest.* His performance led to a five-year period during which he was typically cast as a gangster or a villain. In 1941, Bogart's soulful turn as a gangster with a heart of gold in *High Sierra* led to the final era of his career. He became one of Hollywood's most popular leading men, starring in such classics as *The Maltese Falcon* (1941), ***Casablanca*** (1943; see entry under 1940s—Film and Theater in volume 3), *To Have and Have Not* (1944)—during the filming of which he met and fell in love with young Lauren Bacall (1924–), whom he would marry shortly thereafter—*The Big Sleep* (1946), and *The African Queen* (1951). In the 1960s, a young audience that identified with his antiheroic personality rekindled Bogart's popularity. He has remained an icon of cool ever since.

Robert C. Sickels

For More Information

Humphrey Bogart: The Stuff That Dreams Are Made Of. http://bogartfilms.warnerbros.com/ (accessed July 5, 2011).

Kanfer, Stefan, Jeffrey. *Tough Without a Gun: The Life and Extraordinary Afterlife of Humphrey Bogart.* New York: Faber & Faber, 2010.

Meyers, Jeffrey. *Bogart: A Life in Hollywood.* Boston: Houghton Mifflin, 1997.

Sperber, A. M., and Eric Lax. *Bogart.* New York: William Morrow 1997.

James Cagney (1899–1986)

Film actor James Cagney enjoyed his greatest popularity from the early 1930s to the late 1940s. He was a diverse talent who could play in comedies, dramas, and even musicals with confidence, but he remains best known for his roles as a surly gangster.

In 1931, Cagney played his breakthrough role: gangster Tom Powers in *The Public Enemy*. Cagney's trademark cockiness and angry snarl are in full effect in the film, perhaps best exemplified in its most famous scene, in which he unexpectedly grinds a grapefruit in the face of his stunned costar, Mae Clarke (1907–1992). Cagney went on to appear

James Cagney played song-and-dance men or hardened criminals with equal ease.
© CINEMAPHOTO/CORBIS.

as a gangster in a seemingly endless string of films. Although he won an Oscar for Best Actor for his performance as George M. Cohan (1878–1942) in *Yankee Doodle Dandy* (1942), the crowning achievement of his career is arguably his turn as gangster Cody Jarrett in *White Heat* (1949). The film, in which Cagney's character suffers from severe headaches and a strange attachment to his mother, was his farewell to gangster roles. His career was up and down afterwards, but Cagney remains revered for the dangerously explosive personality he brought to his on-screen characters.

Robert C. Sickels

For More Information

Cagney, James. *Cagney by Cagney.* Garden City, NY: Doubleday, 1976.

McCabe, John. *Cagney.* New York: Knopf, 1997.

Thomson, David. *A Biographical Dictionary of Film.* 3rd ed. New York: Alfred A. Knopf, 1998.

Warren, Doug, with James Cagney. *James Cagney: The Authorized Biography.* New York: St. Martin's Press, 1983.

Charlie McCarthy

Charlie McCarthy is perhaps the most famous ventriloquist's dummy in American history. Charlie, the creation of popular actor-ventriloquist Edgar Bergen (1903–1978), was a wise-for-his-years adolescent. Garbed in top hat and monocle (one round lens serving to correct vision, instead of the usual two-lensed glasses), he endlessly flirted with females and spouted wise-cracks to Bergen, his "guardian." Even though he was carved from wood, Bergen made McCarthy seem so authentic that audiences came to view the dummy as a real person.

Bergen imagined McCarthy while still in high school and had him built at a cost of $35. The pair first teamed up in **vaudeville** (see entry under 1900s—Film and Theater in volume 1), then performed on radio and in films. Bergen added two additional dummies to his act: hayseed Mortimer Snerd and spinster Effie Klinker. (A hayseed is an unsophisticated country person; a spinster, an unmarried woman beyond the usual age of marrying.) Although both were popular, neither was as beloved as Charlie McCarthy.

In 1937, Bergen earned a special Academy Award for creating Charlie. The special wooden Oscar presented to Bergen had a movable

Ventriloquist Edgar Bergen and wooden sidekick Charlie McCarthy. © AF ARCHIVE/ ALAMY.

jaw, just like Charlie's. He influenced countless ventriloquists and pup-peteers for generations to come, including Jim Henson (1936–1990), of **Muppets** (see entry under 1970s—TV and Radio in volume 4) and *Sesame Street* (see entry under 1970s—TV and Radio in volume 4) fame, who dedicated his feature film *The Muppet Movie* (1979) to Bergen. Bergen willed Charlie McCarthy to the Smithsonian Institution in Washington, D.C.

Rob Edelman

For More Information

Bergen, Candice. *Knock Wood.* Boston: G. K. Hall, 1984.

Bergen, Edgar. *How to Become a Ventriloquist.* New York: Grosset and Dunlap, 1938. Reprint, New York: Dover, 2000.

"Edgar Bergen, Comedian." *National Radio Hall of Fame.* http://www.radiohof.org/comedy/edgarbergen.html.

Gary Cooper (1901–1961)

Beginning in the late 1920s, lanky, handsome Gary Cooper was one of the top box office stars in **Hollywood** (see entry under 1930s—Film and Theater in volume 2), making ninety-two movies over his thirty-five-year career. Although not a great actor in the classic sense, the Montana-born Cooper had a bashful grin and likable, awkward presence that made him a favorite with audiences.

Mostly associated with **Westerns** (see entry under 1930s—Film and Theater in volume 2), Cooper also appeared in comedies and adventures—and he was at his best playing brave, all-American heroes. He was perfectly cast as a lovable small-town innocent who inherits a fortune in *Mr. Deeds Goes to Town* (1936) and was sweetly personable as the ill-fated New York Yankee Lou Gehrig (1903–1941) in *The Pride of the Yankees* (1942). He won his two Best Actor Academy Awards for his portrayals of characters he was born to play. In *Sergeant York* (1941), a film whose content was designed to prepare audiences for America's inevitable entry into World War II (1939–45), he was Alvin York (1887–1964), the real-life backwoods pacifist-turned-hero of World War I (1914–18). In *High Noon* (1952), he was Will Kane, a solitary sheriff who had cleaned up a western town by standing up to a vengeance-seeking gang. In April 1961, one month before he died, Cooper received a well-earned Special Academy Award "for his many memorable screen performances and the international recognition he, as an individual, had gained for the motion picture industry."

Rob Edelman

For More Information

Dickens, Homer. *The Complete Films of Gary Cooper.* Secaucus, NJ: Citadel Press, 1983.

Janis, Maria Cooper. *Gary Cooper Off-Camera: A Daughter Remembers.* New York: Harry N. Abrams, 1999.

Meyers, Jeffrey. *Gary Cooper: American Hero*. New York: Morrow, 1998.
Thomson, David. *Gary Cooper*. New York: Faber & Faber, 2010.

Dracula

Based on ancient folk tales and myths, the story of Dracula the vampire is the most enduring of all horror stories. The 1897 novel *Dracula* by Bram Stoker (1847–1912) is the first recorded tale of Count Dracula, who rises from the dead to feast on the blood of the living. Adaptations have appeared on film, **television** (see entry under 1940s—TV and Radio in volume 3), and **radio** (see entry under 1920s—TV and Radio in volume 2) and in print many times. From folk tales to TV's *The X-Files* (1993), vampire stories have been used for centuries as a way of explaining strange events. The blood-sucking Count has been most successful in the darkened movie theater, however. With Bela Lugosi (1882–1956) in the title role, *Dracula* (1931), directed by Tod Browning (1882–1962), provided the blueprint for many of the Dracula images that became familiar in American popular culture. The movie also inspired vampire characters, from the Count in **Sesame Street** (see entry under 1970s—TV and Radio in volume 4) to Grandpa Munster (Al Lewis, 1910–) of the TV series *The Munsters* (1964–66). Other TV series such as *Buffy the Vampire Slayer* (1997) take a cool 1990s approach to the vampire myth. Because of the movies, however, Stoker's Count Dracula is still the most famous vampire of them all.

Although Lugosi's Dracula in his tailcoat and cloak has become the best known, it is *Nosferatu, A Symphony of Horrors,* directed by F. W. Murnau (1888–1931), that began the movie industry's fascination with the undead. Murnau's 1922 film stars creepy Max Schreck (1879–1936) in the role of vampire Count Orlock. Even by the higher standards of the twenty-first century, *Nosferatu* has some genuinely frightening moments. The British-made *Dracula* (1958), directed by Terence Fisher, (1904–1980) has also influenced the popular image of the vampire. Starring Christopher Lee (1922–) as Count Dracula and filmed in vivid color, Fisher's film stands alongside Browning's as one of the best adaptations of Stoker's novel. In the late twentieth century, vampire stories became more sympathetic to vampires. *Interview with the Vampire,* the 1994 movie version of the novel (1976) by Anne Rice (1941–), updates the myth by making vampires seem attractive and "normal" as well as frightening. Many other movies and TV series have offered interpretations of the legend of Dracula.

Over a century after Stoker's novel first appeared, the vampire industry shows no sign of weakening. In recent years, the phenomenal popularity of the ***Twilight*** (see entry under 2000s—Print Culture in volume 6) series of books and movies bears this out. Dracula has inspired Halloween costumes, **comic books** (see entry under 1930s—Print Culture in volume 2), cartoons, clothing, and many more consumer goods. Dracula has also helped the tourist industry in Romania, where Vlad III Dracula, a sadistic Romanian prince on whom Stoker's original vampire was loosely based, rests in the crypt of his dark ancestral home. In the twenty-first century, Dracula lies buried deep in the popular imagination.

Chris Routledge

For More Information

Belford, Barbara. *Bram Stoker: A Biography of the Author of Dracula.* New York: Knopf, 1996.

Cohen, Daniel. *Real Vampires.* New York: Cobblehill Books, 1995.

"Dracula Beyond the Legend." *Romania: Travel and Tourism Information.* http://www.romaniatourism.com/dracula-legend.html (accessed July 5, 2002).

McNally, Raymond T., and Radu Florescu. *In Search of Dracula: The History of Dracula and Vampires.* Rev. ed. London: Robson, 1997.

Miller, Elizabeth. *Dracula.* New York: Parkstone Press, 2001.

Miller, Elizabeth. *Dracula's Homepage.* http://www.ucs.mun.ca/~emiller (accessed July 5, 2011).

Pipe, Jim. *Dracula.* Brookfield, CT: Copper Beech Books, 1995.

Skal, David J. *Hollywood Gothic: The Tangled Web of Dracula from Novel to Stage to Screen.* New York: Norton, 1990.

Frankenstein

Frankenstein's monster first hit movie screens in a sixteen-minute silent film by Thomas Edison (1847–1931) in 1910. The 1931 sound feature released by Universal Studios truly made the character's reputation, however. The shambling man-made fiend, based on a creature in *Frankenstein, or the Modern Prometheus* (1818), by British novelist Mary Shelley (1797–1851), so terrified audiences that he became a fixture of the **horror movies** (see entry under 1960s—Film and Theater in volume 4) genre for decades to come. Over the years, *Frankenstein* has been remade, spoofed, and spun off as a televised **sitcom** (see entry under

1950s—TV and Radio in volume 3) and a Halloween costume. But the terrifying original feature has never been equaled.

Boris Karloff (1887–1969) was an obscure British stage actor when he was tapped by director James Whale (1893–1957) to play Frankenstein's monster in 1931. His interpretation of the character differed sharply from the creature as portrayed in Shelley's novel. Where Shelley's monster was intelligent and physically agile, Karloff played the creature as a hulking brute incapable of speech. The film's makeup, applied by Hollywood legend Jack Pierce (1889–1968), also stressed the ghoulish aspects of the character. Enormous bolts protruded from

English actor Boris Karloff as the Monster in the 1931 film Frankenstein. *His physical portrayal in the film differed from that in the nineteenth-century novel and has since been widely copied both on and off the screen.* © PHOTOS 12/ALAMY.

Karloff's neck, while his head was rendered flat and his forehead stitched as if a botched operation had taken place. The frightening image of *this* Frankenstein's monster was so powerful that it has largely replaced Shelley's original conception in the American psyche.

Many scenes in *Frankenstein* have become classic moments in movie horror. In the elaborate laboratory sequence, Dr. Frankenstein brings his creation to life using electricity from lightning. In a touching scene, the monster encounters a little girl playing with flowers by a stream. In the exciting climax of the movie, villagers with torches chase the monster into an abandoned mill and burn it down. These scenes have become so recognizable that they have been spoofed numerous times in films like *Abbott & Costello Meet Frankenstein* (1948) and *Young Frankenstein* (1974), a Mel Brooks (1926–) comedy.

Boris Karloff returned to play the monster two more times, in *The Bride of Frankenstein* (1935) and in *Son of Frankenstein* (1939). He then grew tired of the series. The monster lived on, however, in a string of popular Universal features and later movies from other studios. Television honored Frankenstein's monster with the character Herman Munster (played by Fred Gwynne, 1926–1993), patriarch of the sitcom family *The Munsters* (1964–66). Director Kenneth Branagh (1960–) tried reviving Mary Shelley's original version of the creature in a gruesome 1994 feature. Like the creature itself, it seems the Frankenstein movie cannot be destroyed.

Robert E. Schnakenberg

For More Information

Haining, Peter, ed. *The Frankenstein File.* London: New English Library, 1977.

Hitchcock, Susan Tyler. *Frankenstein: A Cultural History.* New York: W. W. Norton, 2007.

Hoobler, Dorothy, and Thomas Hoobler. *The Monsters: Mary Shelley and the Curse of Frankenstein.* New York: Little, Brown, 2006.

Jameson, Robert. *The Essential Frankenstein.* New York: Crescent Books, 1992.

Kudalis, Eric. *Frankenstein and Other Stories of Man-Made Monsters.* Minneapolis: Capstone Press, 1994.

Clark Gable (1901–1960)

Clark Gable was called the "King of Hollywood" for most of his long career, until his death in 1960. He was one of the first male sex symbols in film. Gable was so popular, he nearly destroyed a clothing industry: After he appeared without an undershirt in his Oscar-winning role in *It Happened One Night* (1934), men everywhere abandoned the garment, paralyzing the industry for a time.

Gable first became a sensation in the film *A Free Soul* (1931), and remained a star until his death. When David O. Selznick (1902–1965) decided to film the Civil War (1861–65) novel, **Gone with the Wind** (1939; see entry under 1930s—Film and Theater in volume 2), the American public demanded that no one but Gable be cast in the role of Rhett Butler. Gable's last role was with **Marilyn Monroe** (1926–1962; see entry under 1950s—Film and Theater in volume 3) in *The Misfits* (1960). He died three weeks after the film finished shooting.

Jill Gregg Clever

For More Information

Harris, Warren G. *Clark Gable: A Biography.* New York: Three Rivers Press, 2005.

Shipman, David. *The Great Movie Stars: The Golden Years.* London: Warner Brothers Books, 1995.

Spicer, Christopher J. *Clark Gable: Biography, Filmography, Bibliography.* Jefferson, NC: McFarland, 2001.

Wayne, Jane Ellen. *Clark Gable: Portrait of a Misfit.* New York: St. Martin's Press, 1993.

Gone with the Wind

Gone with the Wind (1939) is not the most critically acclaimed American film in motion-picture history. That honor goes to **Citizen Kane** (1941; see entry under 1940s—Film and Theater in volume 3), or perhaps **Casablanca** (1943; see entry under 1940s—Film and Theater in volume 3). However, *Gone with the Wind* is arguably the most popular and beloved of all movie epics of its era. Its grand Technicolor imagery, larger-than-life characters, and vivid depiction of a specific place and time in American history combine to make it a legendary Hollywood epic.

Gone with the Wind was based on the best-selling novel by Margaret Mitchell (1900–1949). Her novel, which was published in 1936, won the Pulitzer Prize. The book has since reportedly sold more copies than any other book in publishing history, with the exception of the Bible. *Gone with the Wind* is set before, during, and after the Civil War (1861–65). The plot of the story is melodramatic and sentimental. It

A poster for the 1939 block-buster film of the Old South, Gone with the Wind. *The film grossed millions of dollars and won ten Academy Awards.* © THE KOBAL COLLECTION, ART RESOURCE, NY.

spotlights the fiery relationship between Scarlett O'Hara, a flirtatious, self-centered Southern belle who has come of age at Tara, her family's Georgia plantation, and Rhett Butler, a charming, devilishly handsome rogue. Throughout the story, Scarlett sets her romantic sights on genteel Ashley Wilkes, even though he has chosen to marry his cousin, Melanie Hamilton. Yet clearly, there is only one man who is Scarlett's romantic match: Rhett Butler.

The screen version of Mitchell's story was the brainchild of David O. Selznick (1902–1965), a renowned Hollywood producer who purchased the screen rights to the book against the prevailing wisdom that Civil War stories were box-office poison. The manner in which the film was cast is part of Hollywood lore. Before *Gone with the Wind* went into production, all agreed that only one actor could play Rhett Butler: Clark Gable (1901–1960), the popular **MGM** (see entry under 1920s—Film and Theater in volume 2) star who had been crowned the "King of Hollywood" in a newspaper popularity poll. But who would be cast as Scarlett O'Hara? Dozens of actresses were considered, including the most famous starlets of the day. Additionally, Selznick instigated a highly publicized nationwide search for the perfect woman to play Scarlett. Filming had already begun when the role was awarded to an actress—Vivien Leigh (1913–1967), who was not even American-born. Leigh, who was from Darjeeling, India, and educated in England, supposedly was brought to Selznick's attention by his agent brother Myron Selznick (1898–1944) during the shooting of the "Burning of Atlanta," one of the film's most celebrated sequences.

Gone with the Wind took eleven months to shoot and cost over $4 million—a staggering sum for its time. The 222-minute-long film eventually premiered in Atlanta, Georgia. It went on to win ten Academy Awards, including Best Picture, Best Director, Best Screenplay, Best Actress, and Best Supporting Actress. The Best Supporting Actress award was won by Hattie McDaniel (1895–1952), who played Scarlett's slave, Mammy. McDaniel's Oscar was the first ever won by an African American performer, in spite of what some believed was the film's outdated depiction of blacks and, specifically, slaves.

Rob Edelman

For More Information

Brown, Ellen F., and John Wiley. *Margaret Mitchell's "Gone with the Wind": A Bestseller's Odyssey from Atlanta to Hollywood.* Lanham, MD: Taylor, 2011.

The Filming of "Gone with the Wind." New York: Macmillan, 1975.

Gone with the Wind. http:// http://www.warnervideo.com/gonewiththewind/ (accessed July 5, 2011).

"Gone with the Wind Online Exhibit." *Harry Ransom Humanities Research Center.* http://www.hrc.utexas.edu/exhibitions/web/gwtw/ (accessed July 5, 2011).

Hanson, Elizabeth I. *Margaret Mitchell.* Boston: Twayne Publishers, 1991.

Haver, Ronald. *David O. Selznick's "Gone with the Wind."* New York: Bonanza Books, 1986.

Mitchell, Margaret. *Gone with the Wind.* New York, Macmillan, 1936. Multiple reprints.

Selznick, David O., producer, and Victor Fleming, director. *Gone with the Wind* (film). Selznick International/Metro-Goldwyn-Mayer, 1939.

Cary Grant (1904–1986)

Cary Grant (born Alexander Archibald Leach) was one of the most sophisticated and appealing of male motion-picture stars from the golden age of cinema. In the early 1930s, he first gained fame on-screen playing romantic leading men in light dramas and comedies such as *I'm No Angel* (1933) and *The Awful Truth* (1937). By the close of the 1930s, he had gained success in screwball comedy, a popular kind of escapist humor. Screwball comedies feature attractive, often eccentric characters who act with an unusual sense of abandon. Grant's most notable such film was *Bringing Up Baby* (1938).

Whatever role he played, Grant was adored by female film-goers for his handsome face—dark eyes, tanned complexion, and famous cleft chin. Male audience members admired him for his classy style and off- and on-screen ability to charm his female costars. Many young men emulated Grant's clean-cut, sophisticated look. His manner of speech combined lower-class British Cockney tones, the remnants of a

Cary Grant being chased by a biplane in director Alfred Hitchcock's classic 1959 suspense film, North by Northwest. © THE KOBAL COLLECTION, ART RESOURCE, NY.

poverty-stricken childhood spent in Bristol, England, with an American accent. His unique style of speaking was often imitated by comedians.

The actor's sophistication, combined with uncommon good looks that lasted well into his senior years, made the name of Cary Grant a household word for manly charm and sex appeal. Grant is best remembered for the films *Notorious* (1946), *North by Northwest* (1959), and *An Affair to Remember* (1957), among many others.

Audrey Kupferberg

For More Information

Descher, Donald. *The Films of Cary Grant.* Secaucus, NJ: Citadel Press, 1973.

Eliot, Marc. *Cary Grant: A Biography.* New York: Harmony Books, 2004.

Feldman, Gene, and Suzette Winter, producer and writer. *Cary Grant, the Leading Man* (video). New York: Brighton Video, 1988.

Higham, Charles. *Cary Grant: The Lonely Heart.* San Diego: Harcourt Brace Jovanovich, 1989.

Schickel, Richard. *Cary Grant: A Celebration.* New York: Little, Brown, 2009.

Hollywood

From the early settlers in the 1880s to the aspiring stars of the 1930s, Hollywood, California, has long been the place to start afresh, to build a new life in the sun. In the 2010s, Hollywood remains the dream factory, a place where every waiter and waitress is an aspiring actor, where every bartender, taxi driver, hotel receptionist, and hired helper has a screenplay tucked away in a drawer at home. The reality, of course, is different. Part of the city of Los Angeles, California, since 1910, Hollywood is a town like any other, complete with crime, poverty, and its fair share of sleaze. But Hollywood's real location is in the minds of aspiring film workers.

The sign up ahead, both a destination of place and of mind: Hollywood. © GAVIN HELLIER/ALAMY.

In 1880, Hollywood was just a ranch, named by Mrs. Daeida Wilcox (1861–1914) after a friend's country house. Aiming to attract midwesterners like themselves to the fertile land and the warm climate, the Wilcoxes divided the ranch into lots and laid out streets for a new town. In a few years, Hollywood was thriving. By 1903, a trolley line connected Hollywood (population 500) to Los Angeles. Selig Studios brought the movies to California in 1907 when location shots for *The Count of Monte Cristo* (1908) were filmed at Laguna Beach. At first, most studios were located in nearby Edendale, but in 1910, the Nestor Film Company became the first to set up a studio in Hollywood itself. Ironically, in the very same year, the God-fearing Hollywood Board of Trustees actually banned movie theaters from the town. Even so, by the 1920s most of the studios had moved there. **Silent movie** (see entry under 1900s—Film and Theater in volume 1) stars soon made Beverly Hills and Silver Lake into America's most glamorous postal addresses. The stars themselves were the nearest thing in America to royalty. Temptingly, here was an aristocracy anyone could join.

Hollywood became known as the place in America where anything was possible. Screen stars built strange and elaborate mansions along Sunset Boulevard. They drove around in expensive, imported cars, took drugs, and were openly promiscuous (casual about having many sexual partners). Eventually, public opinion turned against them. In the late 1920s, with the advent of sound in films, many popular actors of the silent era were found to have terrible speaking voices and lost their jobs. Many sank into alcoholism and suicide. To make matters worse, the Hays Commission, a self-regulatory body of the film industry, was set up in the early 1930s to control the moral content of Hollywood movies. Many silent stars found themselves blacklisted (put on a list of people not to be hired) on "moral" grounds.

The 1930s were Hollywood's golden age. Under the so-called "studio system," the major studios controlled every aspect of filmmaking, from preproduction to the operation of small-town theaters. Talented actors, directors, and technicians arrived from Europe to work for the studios. Famous writers like F. Scott Fitzgerald (1896–1940), Dorothy Parker (1893–1967), and William Faulkner (1897–1962) made the journey west to work in pictures. Hollywood became a playground for celebrities eager to get themselves noticed. Private lives became public property, and there was a sense that anything could be bought. As ever, people outdid one another with brash displays of wealth. As crime-writer Raymond Chandler (1888–1959) put it: "In L.A. to be conspicuous you would have to drive a flesh-pink Mercedes-Benz with a sun porch on the roof and three pretty girls sunbathing."

After 1939, things began to change. Antitrust lawsuits broke up the studios' control of film distribution. Many people felt the stars had too much power. In the late 1940s, studio heads blacklisted many prominent writers, directors, and actors, alleging, often without evidence, that they were communists or communist sympathizers. In the 1950s, **television** (see entry under 1940s—TV and Radio in volume 3) began to eat into film-industry profits. **Film noir** ("dark cinema"; see entry under 1940s—Film and Theater in volume 3) matched the suspicion of the times and offered some relief from tumbling profits, but it was not until the 1960s that Hollywood began to recover. Films like **Bonnie and Clyde** (1967; see entry under 1930s—The Way We Lived in volume 2) and **Easy Rider** (1969; see entry under 1960s—Film and Theater in volume 4) shattered the conservative dreams of the old Hollywood but brought audiences back to the theaters.

Since the 1970s, Hollywood has gone through cycles of making big-budget entertainment movies. Films like *Flashdance* (1983), the *Beverly Hills Cop* series, and blockbusters such as **Titanic** (1997; see entry under 1910s—The Way We Lived in volume 1) and *Iron Man 2* (2010) tend to appear during the summer months and are the mainstay of Hollywood's cash flow. In the 1990s, the digital revolution captivated filmmakers, allowing ever more spectacular special effects. In 1999, **Toy Story 2** (see entry under 1990s—Film and Theater in volume 5) became the first film to go from production to presentation in digital form.

In the twenty-first century, real-life Hollywood is a combination of glamour, sleaze, and tourist trap. Most of the studios are part of multinational media corporations. Hollywood has become the world center for all kinds of media productions, from film to the **Internet** (see entry under 1990s—The Way We Lived in volume 5), from television to pornography. The glory days of the studio system are long gone, yet Hollywood remains a potent symbol of the American Dream. Perhaps more than anywhere else, Hollywood exists as both physical place and glittering fantasy.

Chris Routledge

For More Information

Chandler, Raymond. *Playback*. London: Hamish Hamilton, 1958.
Hamilton, Ian. *Writers in Hollywood 1915–1951*. London: Heinemann, 1990.

Silvester, Christopher, ed. *The Penguin Book of Hollywood.* New York: Viking, 1998.

Thomson, David. *The Whole Equation: A History of Hollywood.* New York: Knopf, 2005.

Williams, Gregory Paul. *The Story of Hollywood: An Illustrated History.* Los Angeles: BL Press, 2011.

Zollo, Paul. *Hollywood Remembered: An Oral History of Its Golden Age.* Lanham, MD: Taylor, 2011.

King Kong

King Kong (1933) is one of the most famous of all horror-fantasy-adventure films, combining imaginative technical wizardry with good old-fashioned thrills and an unusual but appealing "Beauty and the Beast" story. Decades before the development of computerized special effects, *King Kong* featured a masterfully conceived and remarkably believable title character—an ape, who during the course of the story is innocently attracted not to a member of his own species but to a pretty young woman.

King Kong is the saga of Carl Denham (played by Robert Armstrong, 1890–1973), a willful filmmaker who heads off to tiny, exotic Skull Island to shoot his latest movie. In his company are Ann Darrow (Fay Wray, 1907–2004), his pretty lead actress, and Jack Driscoll (Bruce Cabot, 1904–1972), the rugged first mate onboard the ship on which the moviemakers are traveling. Upon their arrival, they encounter Kong, the king of the island, a giant ape who takes a liking to Ann. After battling various dinosaurs, Kong eventually is captured and transported to New York City, where he is billed as the "Eighth Wonder of the World" and put on display. Concerned that Ann is in danger when photographers' flashbulbs pop in her face, Kong breaks free and goes on a rampage. In the celebrated final sequence, the ape scales the then-recently-erected **Empire State Building** (see entry under 1930s—The Way We Lived in volume 2). Kong is shot at by machine guns positioned in airplanes. Finally, he falls and plunges to his death.

King Kong was directed by Merian C. Cooper (1893–1973) and Ernest B. Schoedsack (1893–1979), who first worked together as documentary filmmakers before going on to produce and direct fiction features. However, its most significant creative contribution came from

The climatic scene from the much-admired 1933 film, King Kong, *takes place atop the Empire State Building.* © AP IMAGES.

Willis O'Brien (1886–1962), a model-animation and special-effects genius. O'Brien initially experimented with on-screen special effects in 1914. He developed the technique of stop-motion animation, which he first employed in *The Lost World* (1925), an adventure film featuring prehistoric monsters. *King Kong* was his next feature film and his most celebrated work. The ape was actually a small model, whose movements were achieved by manipulating it slightly, photographing it, and moving it again.

King Kong was immediately followed by an inferior sequel, *The Son of Kong* (1933). Decades later, a series of contrived monster movies appeared: *King Kong vs. Godzilla* (1963), *King Kong Escapes* (1968), and *King Kong Lives* (1986). A heavily promoted remake, also titled *King*

Kong (1976), proved disappointing. In 2005, yet another remake appeared, this one with the latest computer animation. Modern-day special effects techniques, such as those used in the latest *King Kong*, or employed by Steven Spielberg (1947–) in **Jurassic Park** (1993; see entry under 1990s—Print Culture in volume 5) and *The Lost World: Jurassic Park* (1997), may have made Willis O'Brien's shot-by-shot stop-motion animation obsolete, but they have not replaced the magic and wonder of the original *King Kong*.

Rob Edelman

For More Information

"King Kong (1933)." *Filmsite.org*. http://www.filmsite.org/kingk.html (accessed July 5,2011).

Goldner, Orville and George E. Turner. *The Making of King Kong: The Story Behind a Film Classic.* New York: Ballantine Books, 1976.

King Kong (film). RKO Radio Pictures, 1933.

Morton, Ray. *King Kong: The History of a Movie Icon from Fay Wray to Peter Jackson.* New York: Applause Theatre & Cinema Books, 2005.

Thorne, Ian. *King Kong.* Mankato, MN: Crestwood House, 1977.

Laurel and Hardy

Stan Laurel (1890–1965) and Oliver Norvell Hardy (1892–1957) formed one of the greatest comedy duos in the history of **Hollywood** (see entry under 1930s—Film and Theater in volume 2). Englishman Laurel (real name: Stan Jefferson) understudied for **Charlie Chaplin** (see entry under 1910s—Film and Theater in volume 1) on tour with Karno's London Comedians. Hardy came from Harlem, Georgia, and began his show business career working in a movie theater. Beginning in the silent era, they became masters of pie-throwing and furniture-breaking. They even won an Oscar for smashing a piano in *The Music Box* (1932).

Like Chaplin, Laurel and Hardy prospered with the arrival of sound in the movies and began to make feature-length films. They play well-meaning fools forever caught up in "another fine mess." Over their careers, they appeared in more than one hundred movies together from the late 1920s through the late 1940s. Laurel's childish squeaky voice and Hardy's useless fatherly advice made them perfect

The famous film comedy team of Stan Laurel (left) and Oliver Hardy appeared together in more than one hundred films. © PICTORIAL PRESS LTD./ ALAMY.

partners. Some sixty years after their prime, the duo's "Cuckoo" theme tune and loveable derby-wearing characters are still instantly recognizable.

Chris Routledge

For More Information

Laurel and Hardy: The Official Website. http://www.laurel-and-hardy.com/ (accessed July 5, 2011).

McCabe, John. *Mr. Laurel and Mr. Hardy: An Affectionate Biography.* London: Robson, 2003.

Mitchell, Glenn. *The Laurel & Hardy Encyclopedia.* Rev. ed. London: Reynolds & Hearn, 2010.

Nollen, Scott Allen. *The Boys: The Cinematic World of Laurel and Hardy.* Jefferson, NC: McFarland, 1989.

Marx Brothers

Although three brothers formed the core of the Marx Brothers comedy team, there were originally five: Leonard (Chico, 1887–1961), Arthur (Harpo, 1888–1964), Julius (Groucho, 1890–1977), Milton (Gummo, 1893–1977), and Herbert (Zeppo, 1901–1979). The five began their comedy career in music hall and **vaudeville** (see entry under 1900s—Film and Theater in volume 1). After Gummo left the act around 1918, the remaining four began to develop the comic routines for which they became famous. The Marx Brothers are best known for the absurd films they made for Paramount in the 1930s. With their combination of slapstick, music, and Groucho's hilarious one-liners, features like *Monkey Business* (1931), *Horse Feathers* (1932), and *Duck Soup* (1933) are among the finest comic films ever made.

The first Marx Brothers film, based on their hit Broadway stage show, *The Cocoanuts,* appeared in 1930. All the films follow a similar pattern. Fast-talking, wisecracking, penniless Groucho pursues rich, older Margaret Dumont (1889–1965), who constantly has to fight off his flirtatious advances. Chico, a cynical Italian immigrant, and Harpo, a mischievous innocent who never speaks, undermine him with their wild antics. Zeppo, the oft-forgotten fourth brother, plays the dull romantic lead. Music is an important part of the films. Groucho first sang his trademark song "Hooray for

The Marx Brothers in their heyday, 1933: (clockwise, from upper left) Zeppo, Chico, Groucho, and Harpo. © AP IMAGES.

Captain Spaulding" in *Animal Crackers* (1930). Later, the tune became the theme for his television quiz show, *You Bet Your Life* (1950–61). Harpo usually gets his chance for an unlikely harp solo at some point in each film.

After *Duck Soup* (1933) failed at the box office, the Marx Brothers were dropped by Paramount. Without Zeppo, they went to **MGM** (see entry under 1920s—Film and Theater in volume 2) where, with the exception of *A Night at the Opera* (1935), their work declined in quality. By 1946, they had broken up for good, but their best comic films remain influential.

Chris Routledge

For More Information

Adamson, Joe. *Groucho, Harpo, Chico, and Sometimes Zeppo: A History of the Marx Brothers and a Satire on the Rest of the World.* New York: Simon & Schuster, 1973.

Kanfer, Stefan. *Groucho: The Life and Times of Julius Henry Marx.* New York: Knopf, 2000.

Louvish, Simon. *Monkey Business: The Lives and Legends of the Marx Brothers.* New York: St. Martin's Press, 2000.

Marx, Arthur. *My Life with Groucho: A Son's Eye View.* London: Robson Books, 1988.

Marx, Groucho. *Groucho and Me.* New York: Da Capo Press, 1995.

Mitchell, Glenn. *The Marx Brothers Encyclopedia.* Rev. ed. London: Reynolds & Hearn, 2008.

Mr. Smith Goes to Washington

The 1939 motion picture *Mr. Smith Goes to Washington* is widely hailed as one of the most insightful films about the American government to come out of **Hollywood** (see entry under 1930s—Film and Theater in volume 2). Directed by Frank Capra (1897–1991), the film depicts the story of Jefferson Smith (James Stewart, 1908–1997). An idealistic young man, Smith is appointed to the Senate and discovers that Washington is populated by lawmakers who lack moral principles. Smith encounters corrupt politicians, gloomy journalists, and citizens who do not care. All view his faith in the system as hopelessly innocent and perilously naive. In the film's most memorable scene, Smith defends himself against false accusations of criminality in a Senate filibuster (A filibuster is an attempt to prevent a vote from being taken; one way is by standing and talking for a very long time. The speechmaking may last for hours or days).

Like many of Capra's films, *Mr. Smith* presents a morality tale in which a common man triumphs over opponents who are more advantageously endowed. Many lawmakers reacted negatively to the film's message that the government needed reform and that average people should be more involved. They thought the film encouraged people to be subversive (more involved in attempts to overthrow or damage the government). Despite this criticism, the film was a huge popular success. In the 1990s, *Mr. Smith Goes to Washington* was named one of the one hundred greatest films ever made in a poll conducted by the American Film Institute.

Charles Coletta

For More Information

Capra, Frank. *The Name Above the Title.* New York: Macmillan, 1971.

Dirks, Tim. "Mr. Smith Goes to Washington." *Greatest Films.* http://www.filmsite.org/mrsm.html (accessed July 5, 2011).

McBride, Joseph. *Frank Capra: The Catastrophe of Success.* New York: Simon & Schuster, 1992.

Rockettes

Since New York's Radio City Music Hall opened in 1932, the name Rockettes has been associated with long chorus lines of high-kicking, long-legged female dancers. Many who have never been to New York or even seen the famous Rockettes have imitated them in talent shows or on-the-spot picture poses. Their widespread fame is a tribute to the public fascination with the controlled excellence of their **dancing** (see entry under 1900s—The Way We Lived in volume 1).

The Rockettes originated in St. Louis, Missouri, in 1925. Their original name was the Missouri Rockets. They were the brainchild of producer Russell Markert (1899–1990), who was inspired by watching the precision dancing of the ***Ziegfeld Follies*** (see entry under 1900s—Film and Theater in volume 1) of 1922. Markert's group was soon discovered

The most famous dance troupe in the United States, the Radio City Musical Hall Rockettes, are known for their signature high kicks, perfomed here outside their home in New York City in 1997. © AP IMAGES/JOHN SIMON.

by New York theater owner Samuel "Roxy" Rothafel (c. 1881–c. 1936), who changed the group's name to the Roxyettes and signed the dancers to perform at his Manhattan theater, the Roxy. In 1932, Rothafel opened a new theater in New York, the lushly decorated Radio City Music Hall. He moved his dance troupe there and changed its name one last time, to the Rockettes.

The Rockettes' performances are marked by tightly coordinated precision **jazz** (see entry under 1900s—Music in volume 1) and tap dance routines, featuring high kicks and controlled arm movements, all moving at the same time. Even the dancers must be about the same size; all Rockettes are between 5 feet 6 inches (181 centimeters) and 5 feet 10 inches (178 centimeters) tall. Though only 36 women perform in the chorus line of each show, there are over 175 dancers in the entire troupe. Most have been white, leading to charges of racism and a responding commitment to the equal opportunity hiring of dancers in the mid-1980s.

Audiences were delighted by the Rockettes' skill, beginning in 1933, when Radio City Music Hall started featuring a movie and a stage show up to four times a day. Regular performances continued until 1971. Since then, Rockettes still perform special shows at Radio City. Their famous Christmas Spectacular is the best-attended live show in the United States. Rockettes have also left New York to travel the world. During World War II (1939–45), Rockettes joined the United Service Organizations (USO), entertaining troops. There is a permanent Rockette show in Las Vegas, Nevada. Since the mid-1990s, troupes of Rockettes have performed the Christmas Spectacular in places as varied as Detroit, Michigan; Mexico City, Mexico; and Myrtle Beach, South Carolina.

Tina Gianoulis

For More Information

Alliotts, John. "Precision Dancing." *Dance Magazine* (Vol. 56, December 1982): pp. 42–45.

Dunning, Jennifer. "Rockettes, Women with a Long Line of History." *New York Times* (Vol. 147, December 27, 1997): p. A11.

Owen, Elizabeth. "50 Years Old and Still Kicking." *Life* (Vol. 5, December 1982): pp. 122–27.

Peterson, Gregory. "What's All White, and Dances in New York?" *The New York Times* (Vol. 134, May 31, 1985): p. 23.

Radio City Entertainment. *The Radio City Rockettes: A Dance Through Time.* New York: Harper Paperbacks, 2006.

"The Radio City Rockettes." *Radio City Music Hall.* http://www.rockettes.com/#/home (accessed July 5, 2011).

Wentink, Andrew Mark. "The Rockettes at Radio City." *Dance Magazine* (Vol. 55, May 1981): pp. 54–59.

Snow White and the Seven Dwarfs

Snow White and the Seven Dwarfs, which premiered in 1937, was the first feature-length animated film by Walt **Disney** (1901–1966; see entry under 1920s—Film and Theater in volume 2). Based on the fairy tale by the Brothers Grimm (Jacob Ludwig Carl, 1785–1863; Wilhelm Carl, 1786–1859), the film depicts the romance and adventure of a beautiful princess. The princess, named Snow White, escapes the murderous intentions of her evil stepmother, the Queen, by finding refuge in the forest with the Seven Dwarfs (Doc, Grumpy, Happy, Sneezy, Sleepy,

A scene from Walt Disney's popular first feature-length animated film, Snow White and the Seven Dwarfs, *in 1937.* © AF ARCHIVE/ALAMY.

Bashful, and Dopey). Learning Snow White is alive, the Queen disguises herself as a peasant and tricks the girl into eating a poisoned apple. Snow White apparently dies, but she is later awakened from her coma-like state upon being kissed by a handsome prince.

Walt Disney began his animation career in the early 1920s. By the mid-1930s, he was operating a large studio that created cartoons with some of animation's greatest characters, notably Mickey Mouse, Donald Duck, and Goofy. In 1934, Disney began work on his dream: a feature-length animated cartoon. Production took three years, as more than six hundred artists toiled on the film. The voice of Snow

White was provided by a young opera singer named Adrianna Caselotti (1916–1997). One of Disney's greatest contributions to the film was his insistence that each of the dwarfs have his own unique personality. Hundreds of names were suggested for the dwarfs before the final seven names were selected.

Though critics predicted the film would fail, *Snow White and the Seven Dwarfs* was an immediate critical and commercial success. One of the film's strongest features was its musical score, which contained several songs ("Whistle While You Work," "Heigh-Ho, Heigh-Ho, It's Off to Work We Go," and "Some Day My Prince Will Come") that have since become classics. The film received a special Academy Award for its advances in animation. Disney re-released the film every few years so that *Snow White* could be enjoyed by succeeding generations of children. The film's popularity remains undiminished into the new millennium.

Charles Coletta

For More Information

Holliss, Richard, and Brian Sibley. *Walt Disney's Snow White and the Seven Dwarfs and the Making of a Classic Film.* New York: Simon & Schuster, 1987.

Maltin, Leonard. *Of Mice and Magic: A History of American Animated Cartoons.* Rev. ed. New York: New American Library, 1987.

Smith, Dave. *Disney A to Z: The Official Encyclopedia.* New York: Hyperion, 1996.

"Snow White and the Seven Dwarfs." *Greatest Films.* http://www.filmsite.org/snow.html (accessed July 5, 2011).

Shirley Temple (1928–)

Born on April 23, 1928, Shirley Temple made her first feature film appearance in 1932. Temple's first starring role was that of an abandoned child in *Little Miss Marker* (1934). In the following few years, Temple was usually cast as an orphaned or abandoned child whose innocence "rescues" the adults around her. Some people found the high moral tone of her films irritating, but Temple had real talent. She could dance, sing, and act even at the age of six. She was Hollywood's biggest attraction between 1935 and 1938, earning $100,000 per picture.

In the 1930s, Shirley Temple dolls and toys and accessories sold well. She also had several hit records. But like many child movie actresses, Temple's cute looks eventually let her down. By the time she was eleven years old, she was past her prime movie-making years. As Shirley Temple Black, she entered politics in the 1960s, eventually becoming U.S. ambassador to Ghana in 1974 and Czechoslovakia in 1989.

Chris Routledge

For More Information

Black, Shirley Temple. *Child Star, USA.* New York: Warner Books, 1989.

David, Lester, and Irene David. *The Shirley Temple Story.* New York: Putnam, 1982.

Fiori, Carlo. *The Story of Shirley Temple Black: Hollywood's Youngest Star.* Milwaukee: Gareth Stevens, 1997.

Haskins, James. *Shirley Temple Black: Actress to Ambassador.* New York: Viking Kestrel, 1988.

ShirleyTempleFans.Com. http://www.shirleytemplefans.com (accessed July 5, 2011).

Child film star Shirley Temple in 1935, whose bright eyes and dimples made audiences throughout the world stand up and cheer during the Great Depression. © HULTON ARCHIVE/GETTY IMAGES.

Three Stooges

Masters of physical comedy, the Three Stooges have been making audiences laugh with their slapstick clowning since the 1920s. The many short and feature-length films they made between 1934 and 1965 gained eternal life through televised reruns. In fact, it could be argued that these bickering halfwits are more popular now than they ever were in their prime **Hollywood** (see entry under 1930s—Film and Theater in volume 2) years.

The founding members of the Three Stooges were Moe Howard (born Moses Horwitz; 1897–1975) and his brother Shemp (born Samuel Horwitz; 1895–1955), who started performing their comedy act on the **vaudeville** (see entry under 1900s—Film and Theater in volume 1) stage in 1923. Two years later, Larry Fine (born Louis Feinberg; 1902–1975) rounded out the trio. In those early days Moe, Larry, and

Larry Fine (left) and Moe Howard try to get to the root of Curly Howard's dental problem in this scene from a Three Stooges short. © HULTON ARCHIVE/GETTY IMAGES.

Shemp supported the straight man Ted Healy (1896–1937). Together they made their first feature film, *Soup to Nuts,* in 1930. Eventually, the Stooges broke with Healy to make short films on their own. Shemp Howard left the group and was replaced by another of Moe's brothers, Curly (born Jerome Horwitz; 1903–1952).

The 1930s and 1940s proved to be the most successful period of the group's career. In a series of two-reel comedies, the trio developed their unforgettable comic characters. Moe was the scheming leader of the group. Larry was his less-intelligent second banana. Curly was the confused, childlike man whose idiocy most often spoiled their plans. Inevitably, the Stooges would turn on each other when things went bad. They slapped each other's faces, poked each other in the eyes, and bonked each other on the head with various blunt objects, all the while trading verbal insults. It was not exactly high-culture comedy, but it took great skill and timing to pull the routine off correctly—and American audiences loved it. Many of their short films are considered classics of slapstick humor.

Age and illness took their toll on the Stooges after World War II (1939–45). First Curly died, then Shemp (who had rejoined the

Stooges after Curly's death). Joe Besser (1907–1988), and later "Curly Joe" DeRita (1909–1993), took turns as the third Stooge, but they were never very popular. The group made a series of children's movies in the 1960s that introduced their comedy to a whole new generation. A new Stooges movie was scheduled to be released in 2012. The directors were the Farrelly brothers, best known for *Dumb and Dumber,* (2004).

Robert E. Schnakenberg

For More Information

Cox, Stephen, and Jim Terry. *One Fine Stooge: A Frizzy Life in Pictures.* Nashville, TN: Cumberland House, 2005.

Fleming, Michael. *The Three Stooges: An Illustrated History.* New York: Doubleday, 1999.

Hogan, David J. *Three Stooges FAQ.* Montclair, NJ: Applause Theatre and Cinema Books, 2011.

Howard, Moe. *Moe Howard and the Three Stooges.* Secaucus, NJ: Citadel Press, 1977.

Kurson, Robert. *The Official Three Stooges Encyclopedia.* Lincolnwood, IL: Contemporary Books, 1998.

Scordato, Mark. *The Three Stooges.* New York: Chelsea House, 1995.

Solomon, Jon. *The Complete Three Stooges.* Glendale, CA: Comedy III Productions, 2001.

The Three Stooges Official Website. http://www.threestooges.com (accessed July 5, 2011).

John Wayne (1907–1979)

John Wayne, whose career spanned from the late 1920s to the mid-1970s, is the most visually recognizable actor in the history of American film. Despite appearing in a great number and wide variety of films, as an actor he is most closely identified with **Westerns** (see entry under 1930s—Film and Theater in volume 2). His roles in a series of Westerns helped make Wayne an American icon who was thought by many to represent the American spirit.

For a ten-year period, Wayne appeared primarily in low-budget Westerns. In 1939, Wayne's long affiliation with director John Ford (1894–1973) began when Wayne played the Ringo Kid in *Stagecoach.* He went on to star in some of Ford's best films, including *Fort Apache*

(1948), *She Wore a Yellow Ribbon* (1949), *The Searchers* (1956), and *The Man Who Shot Liberty Valance* (1962). He also starred in the Westerns directed by Howard Hawks (1896–1977)—*Red River* (1948) and *Rio Bravo* (1959). Both movies are considered among the finest of the genre. Beginning in the 1950s, Wayne became increasingly associated with right-wing, anticommunist politics. By the 1970s, his political stance resulted in an anti-Wayne backlash by a young audience disillusioned with the Vietnam War, of which Wayne was a vocal supporter. Still, his power as a larger-than-life icon of a certain kind of American male—tough minded, hardworking, and determined—remained strong in the early 2000s.

Robert C. Sickels

John Wayne portrayed cowboys in countless films. © PICTORIAL PRESS LTD./ALAMY.

For More Information

Davis, Ronald L. *Duke: The Life and Image of John Wayne.* Norman: Univesity of Oklahoma Press, 1998.

Levy, Emanuel. *John Wayne: Prophet of the American Way of Life.* Lanham, MD: Scarecrow Press, 1988.

Munn, Michael. *John Wayne: The Man Behind the Myth.* New York: New American Library, 2004.

Nardo, Don. *John Wayne.* New York: Chelsea House, 1995.

Roberts, Randy, and James S. Olson. *John Wayne: American.* New York: Free Press, 1995.

Wills, Garry. *John Wayne's America: The Politics of Celebrity.* New York: Simon & Schuster, 1997.

The Western

The American West has long held a powerful appeal to the American imagination. Since the country's beginning, storytellers have fashioned myths about the divine right of Americans to venture into the open frontier and reinvent both themselves and the landscape. The West has been the place where Americans find out who they are and who they are to become. Stories of the mythic West have been told in virtually all forms of American art, including literature, **television** (see entry under 1940s—TV and Radio in volume 3), **radio** (see entry under 1920s—TV and Radio in volume 2), and painting, but nowhere more prominently than in movies. Indeed, the Western is the one true American film genre. Although musicals, comedies, and action films can be set anywhere, the Western can only be set in the American West.

The Western has undergone a slow evolution throughout the twentieth century. The central components of the genre have remained the same—cowboys, Indians, prostitutes, saloons, six-shooters, displaced Easterners, horses, and Western landscapes—but the meanings associated with the Western have changed dramatically.

In 1903, Edwin S. Porter (1869–1941) made ***The Great Train Robbery*** (see entry under 1900s—Film and Theater in volume 1), the first recognizably modern Western. From that time on, Westerns became a staple of the film industry. With a few exceptions, the films from the first period of Westerns, known as the "classical era," were most often **"B" movies** (see entry under 1930s—Film and Theater in volume 2). The movies tended to have the same plot, as if according to a formula. These "B" movies did not challenge people's thinking about the influence of the American frontier in shaping American culture. Perhaps the apex of this era of Westerns is *Stagecoach* (1939), directed by John Ford (1894–1973), a film that has been said to have brought respectability to the genre.

Following World War II (1939–45), Westerns became more respectable, with healthy budgets, notable directors, and star actors. Their content also became much more sophisticated. This new kind of Western became known as the "Adult Western" or "Superwestern." As Andre Bazin writes in "The Evolution of the Western," "The Superwestern is a Western that would be ashamed to be just itself, and looks for some additional interest to justify its existence—an aesthetic, sociological, moral, psychological, political, or erotic interest, in short some quality extrinsic to the genre which is supposed to enrich it." High-points of this period include *High Noon* (1952), *The Searchers* (1956), and *Rio Bravo* (1959).

Finally, out of the wild 1960s came revisionist Westerns, which can be seen as a response to the classical Hollywood and Adult Westerns that preceded them. These films are much more neutral in their treatment of morality and the nature of right and wrong. They still use the standard western characters and images, but they avoid the romantic nostalgia that characterized earlier Westerns. These movies also address the damage caused by Western expansion, especially to Native Americans. Notable films of the revisionist era include *The Wild Bunch* (1969), *Little Big Man* (1970), and *McCabe and Mrs. Miller* (1971).

Beginning in the early 1970s, the production of Westerns began to decline dramatically. By the early twenty-first century, only a few Westerns were being made each year. Despite this, the West maintains its place in the American imagination. Images of the West are used to sell everything from food to pick-up trucks. Americans still believe in an idea represented by Westerns: that Americans have the ability to escape civilization and reinvent themselves in the open spaces of the American West.

Robert C. Sickels

For More Information

Bazin, André. "The Evolution of the Western." In *The Western Reader*. Edited by Jim Kitses and Gregg Rickman. New York: Limelight Editions, 1998.

Cameron, Ian, and Douglas Pye, eds. *The Book of Westerns*. New York: Continuum, 1996.

O'Connor, John E., and Peter C. Rollins, eds. *Hollywood's West: The American Frontier in Film, Television, and History*. Lexington: University Press of Kentucky, 2005.

Simpson, Paul. *The Rough Guide to Westerns*. London: Rough Guides Ltd., 2006.

Slotkin, Richard. *Gunfighter Nation: The Myth of the Frontier in Twentieth-Century America*. New York: Maxwell Macmillan International, 1992.

Tompkins, Jane P. *West of Everything: The Inner Life of Westerns*. New York: Oxford University Press, 1992.

West, Richard. *Television Westerns: Major and Minor Series, 1946–1978*. Jefferson, NC: McFarland, 1987.

Yeck, Joanne Louise. *Movie Westerns*. Minneapolis: Lerner Publications, 1994.

The Wizard of Oz

The 1939 film *The Wizard of Oz,* directed by Victor Fleming (1883–1949), was adapted from the 1900 novel by L. Frank Baum (1856–1919), *The Wonderful Wizard of Oz.* The story is about a young girl named Dorothy, who is knocked unconscious when a tornado hits her Kansas home. She then dreams of waking up in a setting where she meets a scarecrow, a tin man, a lion, munchkins, and a wicked witch. She learns that the only way to return home is to meet a wizard in the

A favorite of all ages, enhanced by appearing on television every year, is the 1939 film The Wizard of Oz, *starring Ray Bolger (left), Jack Haley, Judy Garland, and Bert Lahr.* © PICTORIAL PRESS LTD./ ALAMY.

land called Oz. The wizard informs her that she must secure the broomstick of the wicked witch before she can go home.

Since *The Wizard of Oz* first appeared on CBS in 1956, it has been viewed by well over one billion people, but the movie is far more than a popular means of filling space on TV schedules. References to *The Wizard of Oz* appear in films from **Star Wars** (1977; see entry under 1970s—Film and Theater in volume 4) to *Wild at Heart* (1990). It has inspired Broadway shows, album titles and cover artwork, political cartoons, and even a U.S. postage stamp. Songs from *The Wizard of Oz* have been covered by artists such as Willie Nelson (1933–) and Tori Amos (1963–). With its fabulous characters, catchy tunes, silly humor, and fun-scary plot, *The Wizard of Oz* is a near-perfect fantasy movie.

The role of Dorothy defined the movie career of Judy Garland (1922–1969). With their background in **vaudeville** (see entry under 1900s—Film and Theater in volume 1), Jack Haley (1898–1979) as the Tin Woodman, Ray Bolger (1904–1987) as the Scarecrow, and Bert Lahr (1895–1967) as the Cowardly Lion gave the film a theatrical feel. Even today, the green-skinned and cackling Wicked Witch of the West, played by Margaret Hamilton (1902–1985), is truly terrifying. *The Wizard of Oz* took twenty-three weeks to make. It was the longest shoot in **MGM** (see entry under 1920s—Film and Theater in volume 2) history. There were many problems including injuries to cast and crew. In one incident, Hamilton's green makeup caught fire and she had to complete filming wearing green leather gloves. The "Munchkin" actors were unfairly singled out as causing much of the trouble.

Because the opening and closing "Kansas" scenes are filmed in black and white, the hugely expensive Technicolor "Oz" sequences probably seemed as dazzling to the original audience as they were to the character of Dorothy herself. In 1939, the release of *The Wizard of Oz* was overshadowed by another all-time favorite, **Gone with the Wind** (see entry under 1930s—Film and Theater in volume 2). But it is *The Wizard of Oz* that has spread furthest into American culture. Billed by MGM as "The Greatest Picture in the History of Entertainment," the movie has acquired a mythology all its own. One of the film's many messages is that "dreams that you dare to dream really do come true." As Baum hoped, his story has become an American fairy tale.

Chris Routledge

For More Information

Baum, L. Frank. *The Wonderful Wizard of Oz.* New York: Oxford University Press, 1997.

Fricke, John, Jay Scarfone, and William Stillman. *The Wizard of Oz: The Official 50th Anniversary Pictorial History.* New York: Warner Books, 1989.

Gjovaag, Eric P. *The Wonderful Wizard of Oz Website.* http://thewizardofoz.info/ (accessed July 5, 2011).

Harmetz, Aljean. *The Making of "The Wizard of Oz."* New York: Knopf, 1989.

Rushdie, Salman, Melvyn Bragg and Richard Maltby. *The Wizard of Oz (BFI Film Classics).* London: British Film Institute, 2008.

Warner Brothers. *The Wizard of Oz.* http://thewizardofoz.warnerbros.com/ (accessed July 5, 2011).

1930s

Food and Drink

Many people had enjoyed luxuries during the prosperous 1920s, with its easy credit and installment (regular payment) plans, but the 1930s were a different story. Families across the nation struggled to make ends meet after the stock market crash of 1929 led to the Great Depression (1929–41), a decade-long economic collapse that affected the entire world. Families budgeted their resources and began making goods that they had once purchased ready-made in stores. Food was one item most people could figure out how to make at home. Cookbooks and radio programs offered recipes, including those for "poor man's cake" (a cake made without flour) and green tomato mincemeat, a kind of relish. Instead of buying canned food, women would take the fresh produce from their own gardens and can, pickle, and preserve it. A family of six could be fed on about five dollars of groceries each week, but every penny counted. Sometimes women would shop together to buy items in larger quantities and split the savings, even if the savings were only pennies. Of the processed food that was purchased, Spam and frozen dinners were new favorites.

One dramatic change in the way people drank alcoholic beverages during the 1930s came with the repeal of the Eighteenth Amendment of 1919 and Prohibition (1920–33), the so-called "noble experiment" that had outlawed the manufacture, sale, and transportation of alcohol.

Upon his election to the presidency in 1933, Franklin D. Roosevelt (1882–1945) changed the Volstead Act (the law enforcing the Eighteenth Amendment) to allow the sale of beer. By December 5, 1933, Prohibition ended. The manufacture, sale, and consumption of all alcohol became legal once again. The martini, a cocktail made with gin, became a popular and legal beverage.

Frozen Dinners

From the 1930s to the present, frozen dinners have allowed hungry individuals, who lack the time or cooking skills to whip up nutritious meals, to pop aluminum tins conveniently into the oven (and, later, plastic trays into the microwave) and soon be dining on chicken, roast beef, or macaroni and cheese. If this resulting "instant meal" is no gourmet's delight, and not as healthy as a well-balanced home-cooked meal, at least it is piping hot and filling.

Frozen dinners were first marketed in the late 1930s, but they became wildly popular in the years after World War II (1939–45), when American life became more fast-paced. Women in particular, who traditionally prepared the daily family meals, now were preoccupied with other, outside-the-home pursuits. They were driving their children to and from **Little League** (see entry under 1930s—Sports and Games in volume 2) games or music and **dancing** (see entry under 1900s—The Way We Lived in volume 1) classes. Eventually, they were entering the workforce themselves as a result of a combination of the late-1960s feminist movement and a changing economy that often required women to contribute an additional paycheck to the family bank account. As such, elaborate, home-cooked meals became a luxury—and the invention and evolution of the frozen dinner was first a godsend, and then a cultural phenomenon that revolutionized American home life.

Frozen foods must be quickly frozen; slow freezing causes irreversible damage to the molecular structure of organic material, rendering it inedible when thawed. Clarence Birdseye (1886–1956), whose frozen food empire bears his name, was the first to develop the quick-freezing process. He employed two formulas, one involving the vaporization of ammonia and the other a cold calcium-chlorate solution. Birdseye initially quick-froze vegetables, fish, and fruit in 1924. The first products bearing his company name, Birds Eye, were meats, fish, spinach, peas,

Fried chicken, corn, mashed potatoes, and a dessert: typical TV dinner fare. © JEFFREY COOLIDGE/ICONICA/GETTY IMAGES.

raspberries, and cherries. They were marketed in 1930. Later in the decade, General Foods began selling frozen meals on a limited basis. Many consumers initially viewed such items as inferior to fresh foodstuffs. In addition, fewer than half of all American households at the time were equipped with electric **refrigerators** (see entry under 1910s—The Way We Lived in volume 1) or iceboxes.

During the post–World War II era, the American middle-class was expanding, refrigerators were in abundant supply, and the frozen food industry exploded. Swanson began selling frozen chicken and beef pot pies in 1951. Four years later, the company mass-marketed **"TV dinners"** (see entry under 1950s— Food and Drink in volume 3), so named because they were not necessarily eaten in the dining room but were often placed on "TV trays" and consumed while watching **television** (see entry under 1940s—TV and Radio in volume 3). The first TV dinner, which sold for around $1, was a turkey dinner that included gravy, peas, potatoes, and cornbread. While Birds Eye specialized in individual frozen items, other companies, such as Stouffer's, Banquet, and On-Core, joined the fast-food bandwagon. Dinners were even marketed in packaging that resembled a TV set. In 1972, Swanson launched its "Hungry Man Dinner" line, which included larger helpings of meat and potatoes. In recent decades, a range of frozen items, including **pizza** (see entry under 1940s—Food and Drink in volume 3), cakes, pies, ethnic cuisine, dietary products, and side dishes, also became available.

In 1955, Americans purchased 70 million frozen dinners. In 1960, the number had risen to 214 million. In 1994, it was 2 billion. In 2009, Americans spent approximately $6.1 billion on frozen dinners, and this amount does not include the billions spent on frozen pizzas. No longer a meal for the rare evening when time is short, the frozen dinner is now a mainstay of the American diet.

Rob Edelman

For More Information

"Better than TV Dinners?" *Consumer Reports* (March 1984): pp. 126–27, 170.

Wray, Tom. "Not-So Frozen Market." *The Provisioner.* http://www.provisioneronline.com/articles/packaging-tech-not-so-frozen-market-1 (accessed July 5, 2011).

Stern, Jane, and Michael Stern. *The Encyclopedia of Bad Taste.* New York: HarperCollins, 1990.

The Joy of Cooking

In 1931, with the United States deep in an economic depression, German American housewife Irma Rombauer (1877–1962) faced a bleak future. Her husband had committed suicide, leaving her little money to support a family. Fortunately for herself and a generation of American cooks, Rombauer came up with a clever moneymaking scheme—she would gather recipes from her family and friends and publish a cookbook. That cookbook, called *The Joy of Cooking,* went on to become one of the best-known cookbooks in American kitchens.

Rombauer was not known for her cooking skills, and those who knew her were unsure about the project. She imagined a cookbook designed for inexperienced cooks like herself, middle-class women who had been raised in homes that employed cooks to prepare food for the family. With the financial hardships of the **Great Depression** (1929–41; see entry under 1930s—The Way We Lived in volume 2), few families could afford servants any longer, and housewives needed to learn how to cook. Rombauer hoped to publish an encyclopedia of cookery that would explain every step of cooking in simple, conversational terms, from preparing fresh game (including curiosities such as roast squirrel and stewed porcupine) to setting the table.

In 1931, Rombauer used what little money her husband had left her to publish *The Joy of Cooking: A Compilation of Reliable Recipes with a Casual Culinary Chat.* The first printing sold quickly. By 1935, publisher Bobbs-Merrill bought the rights to Rombauer's book. In 1948, Rombauer's daughter, Marion Rombauer Becker (1903–1976), joined her mother to revise the cookbook. She remained as editor until her death, at which point her son, Ethan Becker (1945–), continued the family tradition as editor.

Over the years, *The Joy of Cooking* has sold some twenty million copies. The book has been revised seven times to update the recipes (the squirrel and porcupine were removed). There are many special editions, such as *The Joy of Cooking: All About Pasta and Noodles,* published in 2000. Although *The Joy of Cooking* is not the best-selling U.S. cookbook (*The Betty Crocker Cookbook* has sold over sixty million copies; see **Betty Crocker** entry under 1920s—Commerce in volume 2), it is without a doubt the "bible" of American cooking, without which no kitchen is complete.

Rombauer's original vision is responsible for her book's place in American culture. Writing in a warm, conversational tone, from one woman to another (and now, with Ethan Becker in the lead, one man to both men and women), Rombauer and the Beckers managed both to demystify and define the arts of cooking and entertaining for generations of women.

Tina Gianoulis

For More Information

Gordon, John Steele. "Out of the Frying Pan: When Irma Rombauer Finally Found a Publisher for Her Famous Cookbook, Her Troubles Began in Earnest." *American Heritage* (Vol. 49, no. 2, April 1998): pp. 20–23.

Gray, Paul. "Ode to Joy: A Classic Cookbook Gets a Total Facelift; Purists Worry; Some Contributors Simmer; Will the Pot Boil Over?" *Time* (November 10, 1997): pp. 92–96.

The Joy of Cooking Home Page. http://www.thejoykitchen.com/default.lasso (accessed July 5, 2011).

Mendelson, Anne. *Stand Facing the Stove: The Story of the Woman Who Gave America the Joy of Cooking.* New York: Henry Holt, 1996.

Spam

Spam is simultaneously one of the most cherished and most hated foods of all time. Around sixty million Americans eat Spam on a regular basis. Millions more have unpleasant childhood memories of the processed meat product and its clinging jelly. Created during the **Great Depression** (1929–41; see entry under 1930s—The Way We Lived in volume 2) by Hormel and Co., Spam is a cheap, convenient food that became popular during the lean years of World War II (1939–45). Although it is often the butt of jokes, some Spam fans take their canned meat very seriously. Soviet leader Nikita Khrushchev (1894–1971) credited Spam with saving the Soviet army from starvation during World War II. In South Korea, Spam is even sold in gift packs.

During the Depression, canned meat was the only form of protein many Americans could afford. Hormel dominated the market, selling tins of beef stew for just a few cents. In 1937, a pork-based luncheon meat joined the product range. Looking around for a name for his spiced meat, Jay C. Hormel (1892–1954) held a competition. Guests

Spam luncheon meat in the recognizable tin with the pull-back lid has been enjoyed—or avoided—by hungry consumers since 1937. © D. HURSY/ ALAMY.

at his New Year's party were forced to "buy" their drinks by suggesting a name. An actor, Kenneth Daigneau, came up with "Spam" (the first two letters of "spiced" and the last two letters of "ham").

In the twenty-first century, Spam has a cult following. Some fans of Spam even write poetry in its honor. Spam's humorous side is partly explained by the name. Early advertising did not help: featuring comedians George Burns (1896–1996) and Gracie Allen (1906–1964), the ads recommended "Spambled eggs" and "Spamwiches."

Though meat is no longer scarce, Spam is trademarked in over 100 countries in 2011. Because the product seems to be everywhere, the word "spam" has come to mean flooding a computer system with unwanted data. To be sure, the tinned meat is more popular than its digital counterpart. The Spam factory at Austin—"Spamtown"—Minnesota, produces 435 cans of Spam every minute. It is estimated that by 2007 over 7 billion cans of Spam had graced breakfast and dinner tables around the world.

Chris Routledge

For More Information

Armstrong, Dan, and Dustin Black. *The Book of Spam.* New York: Atria, 2007.

Cho, John, ed. *Spam-Ku: Tranquil Reflections on Luncheon Loaf.* New York: HarperPerennial, 1998.

Garcia, Dan. *Spam.* http://www.cs.berkeley.edu/~ddgarcia/spam.html (accessed on July 5, 2011).

Hormel Foods Corporation. *It's Spam.* http://www.spam.com (accessed on July 5, 2011).

Wyman, Carolyn. *Spam: A Biography.* New York: Harvest Books, 1999.

1930s

Music

During the 1930s, the country enjoyed the emergence of a range of distinctly American musical sounds. The radio introduced Americans to more types of music than they had ever heard before, and continued to do so when the Great Depression (1929–41) caused declines in phonograph-record sales. Jukeboxes spread music throughout the country in taverns, soda fountains, and "juke joints," especially after the repeal of Prohibition (1920–33).

Though musicians suffered because of the Depression, the New Deal programs of President Franklin D. Roosevelt (1882–1945) supported musicians as never before. The federally sponsored Works Progress Administration Federal Music Project sponsored radio programs, commissioned new work from composers, and sought out unique American musicians to feature in recordings.

Though the Jazz Age had ended, during the 1930s jazz continued to mature as a musical form. Jazz music changed to a sweeter sound. Big bands began transforming it into danceable swing music. Several famous female vocalists got their start as jazz singers in the 1930s, including Ella Fitzgerald (1918–1996) and Billie Holiday (1915–1959).

In America's urban areas, especially Chicago, Illinois, the blues was a dominant musical style in the 1930s. Singers, many from the Mississippi Delta, strummed guitars and sang ruefully about their current situations. Their music was sought out and appreciated by the many Southern blacks who continued to migrate northward during the decade. These "bluesmen," including Charley (Charlie) Patton (1891–1934), Blind Lemon Jefferson (1897–1929), and Robert Johnson (1911–1938), were cheap to record, making blues record sales quite profitable. Boogie-woogie, gospel, and swing music were all influenced by the blues.

Hillbilly music, a folk music from the Appalachian Mountains and the Southeast, became popular through artists such as the Carter family (now known as the Original Carter Family: A. P. Carter, 1891–1960; Sara Carter, 1899–1979; and Maybelle Carter, 1909–1978); Jimmie Rodgers (1897–1933), "the Singing Brakeman"; and Roy Acuff (1903–1992) and the Smoky Mountain Boys. Hillbilly music benefited especially from radio programming like the *National Barn Dance* and the *Grand Ole Opry* broadcasts, as well as from the Mexican radio stations that could be heard in forty–eight states. These folk musicians influenced the later bluegrass music of the decade.

Another style of music that developed during the decade was distinctly western in form. By the 1930s, the American West, with its cowboys and open country plains, had become legendary. This new style of Western music capitalized on the range with its so-called "singing cowboys." Singers such as Gene Autry (1907–1998; nicknamed the "singing cowboy") and Roy Rogers (1911–1998) sang songs like "The Last Roundup" and "The Call of the Canyon" with Texas or Oklahoma accents and dressed in elaborate cowboy costumes. The center of this new western music was Texas, where taverns with new jukeboxes or stages for traveling groups entertained patrons. With the repeal of Prohibition and the resulting increase in the number of taverns occupying the American landscape, western music became more danceable and rowdy by the end of the decade, giving rise to honky-tonk and western swing music.

Big Bands

Big band music emerged in the 1930s as a spirited response to the economic problems of the **Great Depression** (1929–41; see entry under 1930s—The Way We Lived in volume 2). The style of music continued into the 1940s as the soundtrack to World War II (1939–45).

A form of **jazz** (see entry under 1900s—Music in volume 1) music, big band music took jazz and swing styles from the bands of the 1920s and before and put them into arrangements for larger bands. Sometimes these larger bands had as many as twenty or more musicians. These bands usually consisted of saxophones, trumpets, and trombones; a rhythm section of piano, bass, drums; sometimes guitar; and vocalists or other soloists. Big band music could be fast and exciting or slow and mellow. Either way, it was and is great music for listening and dancing to.

The rise of big bands in the 1930s brought jazz music into the mainstream of American life. Jazz was mostly the creation of African Americans. In the 1920s, there were great African American big bands such as the Roseland Ballroom Orchestra, led by Fletcher Henderson (1897–1952), and the Duke Ellington (1899–1974) Orchestra. But in the 1930s, as more white musicians began to discover and play jazz on their own, it crossed over into mainstream America. White band leaders such as Benny Goodman (1909–1986), Tommy (1905–1956) and Jimmy (1904-1957) Dorsey, Glenn Miller (1904–1944), and Harry James (1916–1983) had lots of hits and drew huge crowds. Many of their songs were reinterpretations of songs originally written and recorded by black bands such as Henderson's.

Goodman, nicknamed the "King of Swing," and his band could bring dancers to a frenzy with the wild solos and driving beat of such tunes as "Sing, Sing, Sing." Big band music also launched solo singing stars such as **Frank Sinatra** (1915–1998; see entry under 1940s—Music in volume 3), who first thrilled crowds as a member of the Tommy Dorsey Orchestra. These white bands brought the music to mainstream America, but black big bands extended the music even further. The band of Count Basie (1904-84) was one of the best and hardest-swinging bands of the era. Duke Ellington wrote popular songs such as "In a Sentimental Mood" and "Solitude," but also more complex pieces. Extended orchestral pieces such as "Black, Brown, and Beige" pushed jazz music to new heights. Ellington emerged as one of the great composers of the twentieth century.

During the grim years of the Great Depression, big band music (also called "swing" music) provided an upbeat and uplifting sound. This was dance music, and people could escape their troubles **dancing** (see entry under 1900s—The Way We Lived in volume 1) away the night to the sounds of the big bands. In the 1940s, when World War II took many young men overseas to fight, big band music provided songs of longing and remembrance that matched the sad mood of the war years, songs such as "Long Ago and Far Away" and "I'll Be Seeing You." The popularity of big band music faded when **rock and roll** (see entry under 1950s—Music in volume 3) emerged in the 1950s, but it continues to be played and enjoyed today. A swing revival, in fact, occurred in the 1990s.

Timothy Berg

For More Information

The Big Bands Website. http://www.bigbands.org/ (accessed July 6, 2011).

Berendt, Joachim E. *The Jazz Book: From Ragtime to the 21st Century.* 7th ed. Chicago: Lawrence Hill Books, 2009.

Erenberg, Lewis. *Swingin' the Dream: Big Band Jazz and the Rebirth of American Culture.* Chicago: University of Chicago Press, 1998.

Grudens, Richard. *Star Dust: The Bible of the Big Bands.* Stonybrook, NY: Celebrity Profiles, 2008.

Stowe, David W. *Swing Changes: Big-Band Jazz in New Deal America.* Cambridge: Harvard University Press, 1994.

Walker, Leo. *The Big Band Almanac.* Rev. ed. New York: Da Capo Press, 1989.

Billie Holiday (1915–1959)

Billie Holiday was one of the greatest female jazz vocalists of the twentieth century. Although her life was often rough (including a troubled childhood and problems with drugs as an adult), her music was hauntingly beautiful. Holiday had a distinctive style of singing, phrasing her notes in odd ways unlike any other singer.

Holiday began her career in the 1930s, often singing with bandleader Teddy Wilson (1912–1986). Throughout the 1940s and 1950s, she recorded hundreds of songs with various musicians, with small groups and large orchestras. She gave every song she recorded her distinctive touch, and a number of songs are intimately associated with her, including "My Man," "The Man I Love," and "God Bless the Child." In the late 1950s, her hard living, particularly her trouble with alcohol and drugs, led to the decline of her voice, her career, and ultimately her early death in 1959. However, she remains one of the most influential singers in the history of American popular music.

Timothy Berg

For More Information

Chilton, John. *Billie's Blues: The True Story of the Immortal Billie Holiday.* New York: Stein and Day, 1975.

Davis, Angela. *Blues Legacies and Black Feminism: Gertrude "Ma" Rainey, Bessie Smith, and Billie Holiday.* New York: Pantheon, 1998.

De Veaux, Alexis. *Don't Explain: A Song of Billie Holiday.* New York: Harper and Row, 1980.

Estate of Billie Holiday. *The Official Site of Billie Holiday.* http://www.billieholiday.com/ (accessed July 6, 2011).

Griffin, Farah Jasmine. *If You Can't Be Free, Be a Mystery: In Search of Billie Holiday.* New York: Free Press, 2001.

Hirshey, Gerri. "Mothers of Invention." *Rolling Stone* (November 13, 1997): pp. 44–49.

Holiday, Billie, with William Dufty. *Lady Sings the Blues.* 50th anniversary ed. New York: Broadway Books, 2006.

Robert Johnson (1911–1938)

Robert Johnson is one of the most important figures in the history of **blues** music (see entry under 1920s—Music in volume 2). He played guitar, sang, and wrote songs in the Mississippi Delta blues tradition, which featured singers accompanying themselves on acoustic guitar.

Growing up in Mississippi as the son of poor sharecroppers, Johnson learned early on about the hardships of life, which he later expressed in his music. He was known as a great guitar player, so good, in fact, that legend had it that Johnson received his guitar skills by selling his soul to the devil. Although he only recorded forty-one songs in his short life, including "Crossroads Blues," "Love in Vain," "Terraplane Blues," and "Traveling Riverside Blues," Johnson was a tremendous influence on later blues and **rock and roll** (see entry under 1950s—Music in volume 3) musicians, many of whom recorded his songs. Johnson's musical influence was enhanced by both the mysterious nature of his life and by the suspicious nature of his death—from poisoned whiskey—in 1938. Because of this, and his enormous talent, his music has remained an essential part of blues history.

Timothy Berg

For More Information

Cohn, Lawrence, ed. *Nothing But the Blues.* New York: Abbeville Press, 1993.

Delta Haze Corporation. *Robert Johnson.* http://www.deltahaze.com/Robert%20Johnson.html (accessed July 6. 2011).

Graves, Tom. *Crossroads: The Life and Afterlife of Blues Legend Robert Johnson.* Spokane, WA: Demers Books, 2008.

Guralnick, Peter. *Searching for Robert Johnson.* New York: Dutton, 1989.

Robert Johnson Biography. http://xroads.virginia.edu/~MUSIC/blues/rjbio.html (accessed July 6, 2011).

Wald, Elijah. *Escaping the Delta: Robert Johnson and the Invention of the Blues.* New York: Amistad, 2004.

Jukeboxes

Jukeboxes are a pay-per-use version of **phonographs** (see entry under 1900s—Music in volume 1), record players, and, more recently, **compact disc** (see entry under 1980s—Music in volume 5) players. Often found in bars and nightclubs in the 1930s and after, jukeboxes were invented to provide an inexpensive form of musical entertainment. Customers could put coins in a slot, choose the records they wanted to hear, and then enjoy the music. Jukeboxes could also play records one after the other, providing almost nonstop entertainment. They became popular during the **Great Depression** (1929–41; see entry under 1930s—The Way We Lived in volume 2), when many people could not afford to buy records and many nightclubs could not afford to hire live bands. At a nickel per play, jukeboxes provided an easy way to hear good music.

For just a nickel, the local jukebox would play a popular song of the day. © JOHN JOANNIDES/ALAMY.

Coin-operated music machines existed prior to 1900, but the first jukeboxes date from the 1920s. Some of the major manufacturers were the Automatic Music Company, Wurlitzer, Seeburg, and Rockola. Since the technology was largely the same, jukebox manufacturers distinguished themselves through their boxes' fancy decorative designs, many of which featured colored lights. The term "jukebox" comes from the Southern term for **dancing** (see entry under 1900s—The Way We Lived in volume 1), called "jooking." "Juke joints" were bars where recorded music was played. Thus, jukeboxes referred to the machines themselves. By the mid-1930s, there were more than five hundred thousand jukeboxes in use.

Jukeboxes also helped record companies survive the Great Depression. Jukebox owners had to supply their machines with the new records that listeners wanted to hear. Many machines could keep track of which songs were played most, allowing record companies to learn what kinds of music people most wanted to hear. Jukeboxes played a large role in helping **rhythm and blues** (see entry under 1940s—Music in volume 3) and **rock and roll** (see entry under 1950s—Music in volume 3) music garner popularity with fans and interest from music industry executives. Jukeboxes helped convince record companies that there was a market for this new music. Jukeboxes also allowed people to hear this music when early radio programs refused to play it. Jukeboxes declined in popularity after the 1950s, when more people could afford to buy records, but they played an important role in the development of American popular music and can still be found in many **diners** (see entry under 1900s—Food and Drink in volume 1), bars, and clubs.

Timothy Berg

For More Information

Boehlert, Eric. "Put Another Nickel In." *Billboard* (November 1, 1994).

Chapple, Steve, and Reebee Garofalo. *Rock and Roll Is Here to Pay.* Chicago: Nelson Hall, 1977.

Durham, Ken. "History of Jukeboxes." *GameRoomAntiques.* http://www.gameroomantiques.com/HistoryJuke.htm (accessed July 6, 2011).

The National Jukebox Exchange. http://www.nationaljukebox.com/index.html (accessed July 6, 2011).

Rock & Roll Generation: Teen Life in the 50s. Alexandria, VA: Time-Life Books, 1998.

1930s

Print Culture

Reading remained an important source of news and entertainment in America during the 1930s. Throughout the decade, more than thirty-nine million people read daily newspapers, even though radio had caused the number of different newspapers in publication to decline. By comparison, there were twenty-nine million radios in American homes at the beginning of the decade and thirty-five million by the end of the decade. For the majority of Americans, reading was the most important source of information and entertainment available.

Comic strips and comic books were among the most popular forms of entertainment during the decade. *Blondie,* a comic strip that started in 1930 as a playful story about young people in the Jazz Age, turned into a funny strip about work and family life in America. *Dick Tracy* offered readers an opportunity to plunge into the life of a detective battling vicious gangsters, the criminals that most fascinated people during the decade. Superheroes, including Batman, Doc Savage, Flash Gordon, and Superman, thrilled readers with incredible adventures, secret identities, and unbelievable superpowers.

While many improbable and fantastic stories were sold in book form, some serious fiction was sold as well. *The Grapes of Wrath* (1939) by John Steinbeck (1902–1968), for example, painted a picture of horrible American suffering during the Great Depression (1929–41).

Nevertheless, the most popular kind of book was detective fiction. At a time when every penny counted, cheaper paperback books began to be offered to increase all kinds of book sales.

Magazines such as *Life* and *Family Circle* offered news and stories for the family. *Esquire* courted a male readership and soon became successful featuring some of the best short-story writers of the time, including Ernest Hemingway (1899–1961), F. Scott Fitzgerald (1896–1940), and Sinclair Lewis (1885–1951). *Esquire* also profited by orienting articles exclusively towards male tastes and interests. *Woman's Day* started as a magazine specifically for women. Pulp magazines continued to pump out fantastic stories for the light entertainment of readers throughout the country. In short, American readers had varying tastes, and there was generally something for everybody.

Batman

In 1939, the comic character first known as "The Bat-Man" made his first appearance in a six-page segment featured in the "No. 27" issue of *Detective Comics*. Since that time, the darkly clad and threatening crime fighter created by Bob Kane (1915–1998) has appeared to Americans in **comic books** (see entry under 1930s—Print Culture in volume 2), novels, **television** (see entry under 1940s—TV and Radio in volume 3) shows, and movies. Americans identify with Batman because he is one of them—a self-trained man from the mythical Gotham City with no superpowers and markedly human problems. Batman's humanity has helped make him one of the most universally appealing American comic heroes.

Comic-book readers soon learned that Batman was the alter-ego of millionaire Bruce Wayne. As a child, Wayne had witnessed his wealthy parents' murder in a street holdup. From that moment forward, Wayne dedicated himself to fighting crime. Kane's original Batman was a ruthless, unscrupulous vigilante—a man who would go outside the law to bring evil-doers to justice, sometimes even going so far, in his earliest adventures, as to shoot them himself. Throughout the 1940s, 1950s, and 1960s, a number of different artists and writers worked on various Batman series, resulting in several new characters becoming a regular part of the continuing saga. These characters, nearly as notorious in popular culture as Batman himself, included sidekick Robin (an orphaned circus acrobat whom Wayne adopted), Alfred (Wayne's loyal butler, who, aside from Robin, was the only one who knew of Wayne's double identity), and the villainous Joker, Two-Face, and the Penguin.

In 1966, the dark and mysterious Batman took a different turn when ABC introduced the *Batman* TV series. The show, starring Adam West (1928–) as Batman, was intentionally over-acted. The show made fun of the seriousness of the comic-book series, but was, for a brief time, quite popular. The show was so popular, in fact, that it inspired the creation of Batman paraphernalia—lunch boxes, toys, and clothing were eagerly purchased by and for kids. The series came to an end in 1968, but many people still first think of the show when they think of Batman.

Since the debut of the TV show, the Batman character has appeared in many different mediums. The comic-book line has continued, with new artists and writers pursuing different approaches to the character, especially in the late 1980s and early 1990s. Perhaps the most notable of these efforts was the 1986 graphic novel, *The Dark Knight Returns*, by Frank Miller (1957–). The four-part novel returned Batman to his dark and sinister roots. In addition, six high-profile, feature-length *Batman* films were released from 1989 to 2008, with another one scheduled for release in 2012. (Also, a movie based on the TV show was released in 1966 and an animated film, *Batman: Mask of the Phantasm,* came out in 1993.) *The Dark Knight* (2008), which was released just months after the death of its star, Heath Ledger (1979–2008), is one of the ten top-grossing films of all time.

Because he is symbolic of both America's problems with violence and crime and of American idealism, representing the dark side that lies in each and every person, Batman will likely always retain his place in popular culture.

Robert C. Sickels

Batman and Robin again battle Gotham City's criminal element in another issue of Detective Comics *from DC Comics.* © FLAB/ALAMY.

For More Information

Barrier, Michael, and Martin Williams, eds. *A Smithsonian Book of Comic-Book Comics.* New York: Smithsonian Institution Press and Harry Abrams, 1981.

Burton, Tim, director. *Batman* (video). Warner Brothers/Warner Home Video, 1989.

DC Comics. http://www.dccomics.com (accessed October 14, 2011).

Greenberger, Robert. *The Essential Batman Encyclopedia.* New York: Del Rey, 2008.

Jourdain, William F. *The Golden Age Batman.* http://goldenagebatman. goldenagecomics.org/ (accessed July 6, 2011).

Miller, Frank. *Batman: The Dark Knight Returns.* New York: DC Comics/Warner Books, 1986.

Pearson, Robert E., and William Uricchio, eds. *The Many Lives of the Batman: Critical Approaches to a Superhero and His Media.* New York: Routledge, 1991.

West, Adam, with Jeff Rovin. *Back to the Batcave.* New York: Berkley Books, 1994.

Blondie

Blondie, which has appeared in newspapers since 1930, is one of the most widely read comic strips in history. Created by Murat "Chic" Young (1901–1973), the strip centers on the domestic antics of the Bumstead family. Young developed a simple formula for his strip and seldom varied from four basic themes: raising a family, eating, sleeping, and making a living. In the early twenty-first century, the bumbling husband Dagwood and beautiful wife Blondie appear in more than 2,300 newspapers and boast more than 280 million daily readers reading the strip in 55 countries and in 35 different languages.

Initially, *Blondie* was much different from its familiar suburban setting. It debuted as a "girlie" strip and told the story of Blondie Boopadoop, a flighty **flapper** (an unconventional young woman of the 1920s; see entry under 1920s—Fashion in volume 2). Originally, Blondie was being courted by a wealthy young heir, Dagwood Bumstead, whose parents disapproved of him keeping company with a social inferior. By 1933, Young believed that his Jazz Age characters were becoming irrelevant to readers during the **Great Depression** (1929–41; see entry under 1930s—The Way We Lived in volume 2). He decided to ground the strip in more familiar territory by marrying Blondie and Dagwood and depicting them as struggling newlyweds. Upon their marriage, Dagwood's billionaire father immediately disinherited his son. After this, Young abandoned story continuity and transformed *Blondie* into a gag strip with stories about what goes on in almost every home.

Audiences embraced Young's new emphasis on domesticity. Among the strip's most popular running gags were Dagwood's confrontations with his boss, Mr. Dithers; continuing battles with door-to-door salesmen; and frequent collisions with the neighborhood postman. The strip's most famous creation is the Dagwood sandwich, which contains a mountainous assortment of leftovers precariously arranged between two slices of bread. In 1934, the Bumsteads had a son named Baby Dumpling (later called Alexander). Many strips focused on the couples' attempts to raise a child. The family was completed in 1941 with the arrival of a daughter, Cookie. Overseeing the family was Daisy, the Bumstead dog, and her litter of puppies.

Blondie is one of the most widely circulated comic strip in history, and its characters have appeared in countless books and merchandise. It also served as the basis for a successful series of twenty-eight movies released between 1938 and 1951. The movies starred Arthur Lake (1905–1987) and Penny Singleton (1908–2003) as the Bumsteads. Short-lived sitcom versions of the Bumsteads' exploits appeared on television during the 1950s and 1960s.

The strip features a clean, highly animated style and never veers from its format. In the 1980s, however, modest changes to *Blondie* were introduced to make the strip more contemporary, such as Dagwood joining a carpool and Blondie opening her own catering business. Even in the early twenty-first century, the Bumsteads remain the typical American comic-strip family.

A poster for the 1938 film Blondie, *the first in the series, which ran until 1951.*
© PICTORIAL PRESS LTD./ALAMY.

Charles Coletta

For More Information

Blackbeard, Bill, and Martin Williams. *The Smithsonian Collection of Newspaper Comics.* Washington, DC: Smithsonian Institution Press, 1977.

Blondie. http://www.blondie.com (accessed July 6, 2011).

Horn, Maurice, ed. *100 Years of American Newspaper Comics.* New York: Gramercy Books, 1996.

Robinson, Jerry. *The Comics: An Illustrated History of Comic Strip Art, 1895–2010.* Rev. ed. Milwaukie, OR: Dark Horse, 2010.

Young, Dean, and Rick Marschall. *Blondie.* New York: Harper & Row, 1981.

Young, Dean, and Melena Ryzik. *Blondie: The Bumstead Family History.* Nashville, TN: Thomas Nelson, 2007.

Dale Carnegie (1888–1955)

Dale Carnegie was America's foremost promoter of unwavering optimism and enthusiasm as both a personal philosophy and a manner of approaching the challenges of daily life. Back in 1912, Carnegie began teaching a nonacademic course that, on the surface, was concerned with public speaking. Actually, the issues with which he dealt went beyond typical instructions about speaking before audiences. As his course evolved, Carnegie focused on the manner in which individuals might confront their fears and demons. He saw these fears as barriers that prevented them from reaching their complete potential at their jobs or in their personal relationships.

Carnegie, who previously had worked as a salesman and actor, first taught his course in New York City, at the YMCA on 125th Street in Harlem. His students were businessmen and salesmen who wished to improve their communications skills. He expanded his class' parameters when he began calling on students to express themselves in class, to discuss their life experiences, and to acknowledge publicly their wishes and fears. As the years passed, Carnegie kept fine-tuning the class, which he called "The Dale Carnegie Course in Public Speaking and Human Relations."

Carnegie's critics felt his techniques were too simplistic and even manipulative. In 1936, he published his philosophy in a book titled *How to Win Friends and Influence People,* which became one of the twentieth century's all-time **best-sellers** (see entry under 1940s—Commerce in volume 3). In 1939, he began licensing the course to others to teach across the country. By 2011, more than 8 million people had taken Dale Carnegie courses from Dale Carnegie Training, a corporation that offered the course across the United States and around the world.

Rob Edelman

For More Information

Carnegie, Dale. *How to Stop Worrying and Start Living.* New York: Simon & Schuster, 1948, 1984.

Carnegie, Dale. *How to Win Friends and Influence People.* New York: Simon & Schuster, 1936, 1981.

Dale Carnegie Training. http://www.dale-carnegie.com (accessed July 6, 2011).

Kemp, Giles, and Edward Claflin. *Dale Carnegie: The Man Who Influenced Millions.* New York: St. Martin's Press, 1989.

Longgood, William. *Talking Your Way to Success: The Story of the Dale Carnegie Course.* New York: Association Press, 1962.

Comic Books

Comic books, which first appeared in the 1930s, have entertained children and young adults for decades. They have told stories from a wide variety of genres, including romance, humor, horror, war, and **Westerns** (see entry under 1930s—Film and Theater in volume 2), but are most often associated with tales featuring the exploits of superpower-endowed heroes. The costumed heroes from their pages have been translated into all other forms of popular culture—plastic action-figure playtoys, Halloween costumes, **television** (see entry under 1940s—TV and Radio in volume 3) and **radio** (see entry under 1920s—TV and Radio in volume 2) shows, feature films, and so on—and continue to have a firm grasp on the American imagination.

Comic books first appeared in 1933 with the publication of *Famous Funnies,* which included reprints of popular newspaper strips. In 1935, Major Malcolm Wheeler-Nicholson (1890–1968) launched *New Fun Comics,* which was the first comic book to print all-new material. Early issues featured crime and mystery stories that were popular in the **pulp magazines** (see entry under 1930s—Print Culture in volume 2) of the era. The industry was changed forever in 1939 with the arrival of **Superman** (see entry under 1930s—Print Culture in volume 2). Created by two Cleveland teens, Superman was unlike any other hero ever seen. He possessed immense superpowers, wore a skintight costume, and had a secret identity. Superman was an immediate success. He spawned a vast number of costumed counterparts like **Batman** (see entry under 1930s—Print Culture in volume 2), Captain Marvel, **Wonder Woman** (see entry under 1940s—Print Culture in volume 3), and Plastic Man. The comic-book industry boomed during the 1940s as millions of issues were sold each month. However, by the 1950s, they were criticized by some for emphasizing sex, crime, and violence. Dr. Fredric Wertham (1895–1981) led the anti-comics forces and claimed in his controversial text, *Seduction of the Innocent,* that comics led to juvenile delinquency. The industry responded by creating the Comics Code Authority, a self-censoring body that enforced standards.

The industry rebounded in the 1960s. The characters of **Marvel Comics** (see entry under 1960s—Print Culture in volume 4), like **Spider-Man** (see entry under 1960s—Print Culture in volume 4) and the X-Men, were more "realistic." They often appeared flawed and insecure, and they revitalized the superhero genre of comic books. Superheroes continue to dominate the marketplace, but recent decades have seen the rise of independent and "underground" comics that appeal to an older, more diverse readership. Among the most noteworthy creators of these more "adult" comics are Robert Crumb (1943–), Harvey Pekar (1939–2010), and Art Spiegelman (1948–). By the 1980s, even the superheroes became involved in more mature story lines. Of note, the ***Dark Knight*** (see entry under 2000s—Film and Theater in volume 6), a graphic novel written by Frank Miller (1957–) in 1986, presents an adult view of the Batman legend.

The comic book industry has faced increased competition from TV, VCRs, digital recorders, **video games** (see entry under 1970s—Sports and Games in volume 4), and computers since the 1970s. While DC and Marvel, the leading producers of superhero comics, accounted for just over 70 percent of the market as recently as September 2011, finding a new generation of comic-book readers remains an industry concern. Still, the superheroes remain popular and now regularly appear in films and on television.

Charles Coletta

For More Information

Daniels, Les. *DC Comics: Sixty Years of the World's Favorite Comic Book Heroes.* New York: Little, Brown, 1995.

Daniels, Les. *Marvel: Five Fabulous Decades of the World's Greatest Comics.* New York: Harry N. Abrams, 1991.

Duke University Libraries. *Comic Book Cultures.* http://library.duke.edu/exhibits/comicbookcultures/ (accessed July 6, 2011).

Isabella, Tony. *1000 Comic Books you Must Read.* Iola, WI: Krause, 2009.

Jones, Gerard, and Will Jacobs. *The Comic Book Heroes.* Rocklin, CA: Prima Publishing, 1997.

Kurtzman, Harvey. *From AARGH! to ZAP!: Harvey Kurtzman's Visual History of Comics.* New York: Prentice Hall, 1991.

Melrose, Kevin. "Batman #1 Leads DC Comics Domination of September's Top 20." *Comic Book Resources.* http://robot6.comicbookresources.com/2011/10/batman-1-leads-dc-comics-domination-of-septembers-top-20/ (accessed October 14, 2011).

Pustz, Matthew. *Comic Book Culture: Fanboys and True Believers.* Jackson: University Press of Mississippi, 1999.

Teitelbaum, Michael, et al. *The DC Comics Encyclopedia.* Rev. ed. New York: DK Publishing, 2008.

Detective Fiction

The first true detective story was written by Edgar Allan Poe (1809–1849) in 1841. "The Murders in the Rue Morgue" began the tradition of "classic" detective fiction. Classic detective fiction features a highly perceptive detective, a mysterious crime, and obscure clues. By the 1930s, a second type of detective fiction had appeared. This new detective fiction relied more on action than on working out puzzles. Known as "hard-boiled" detective fiction, it began in America and used American settings, especially the cities of Los Angeles, California, and New York City. The hardboiled (tough-guy) detective with his raincoat and low-brimmed hat is a defining figure of the 1930s and 1940s.

The most famous of the great detectives is Sherlock Holmes, created by British writer Sir Arthur Conan Doyle (1859–1930). Holmes's methods of deduction, his strange lifestyle, and faithful friend Watson are all borrowed from Poe's original story. In "The Murders in the Rue Morgue," the detective uses his powers of deduction to solve the puzzle of how a murderer could commit his crime and escape from a room that is locked from the inside. Many classic detective stories use the "locked room" theme in one form or another. A popular variation is setting the story in a closed community such as an isolated country house or an English village. This became so popular in England that classic detective fiction is often known as the "English" or "Country House" type.

Huge numbers of classic detective stories were published throughout the 1920s and 1930s. In the United States, the most popular writers were Ellery Queen (who was really two people, cousins Frederic Dannay [1905–1982] and Manfred B. Lee [1905–1971]), S. S.

Van Dine (1888–1939, whose real name was Willard Huntington Wright), John Dickson Carr (1906–1977), and Erle Stanley Gardner (1889–1970). Their books are usually written as puzzles; part of the reason people read classic detective stories is to try to solve the mystery before the detective does. Despite having their own styles, these writers all stick to the basic structure laid down by Poe. Whatever the details of particular cases, the mysteries in their stories are solved by an unusually clever detective in a setting that is more or less closed to the outside world.

Writer Carroll John Daly (1889–1958) invented the hardboiled detective with his character Race Williams, who first appeared in 1922. Hard-boiled detective stories appeared in **"pulp" magazines** (see entry under 1930s—Print Culture in volume 2) such as *Dime Detective* and *Black Mask* throughout the 1920s and 1930s. They were written in clipped, everyday language that described action rather than a puzzle to be solved. Hard-boiled detective stories contain graphic descriptions of action, violence, and sex. In the 1920s and 1930s, they seemed very shocking. In the hard-boiled detective story, however, crime was no longer the subject of an interesting and challenging puzzle. Crime had human consequences for the victim, the detective, and society. Hard-boiled detective fiction encourages the reader to identify with the detective. It celebrates "ordinary" people in their efforts to resist crime. By focusing on the detective rather than on the puzzle, hard-boiled detective fiction can also deal with real issues. Since the 1980s, female hardboiled private eye V. I. Warshawski has allowed author Sara Paretsky (1947–) to discuss feminist issues. Walter Mosley (1952–) uses a black detective to explore problems of race.

Hard-boiled detective fiction remains popular at the beginning of the twenty-first century through writers such as James Ellroy (c. 1948–), Elmore Leonard (1925–), and Lawrence Block (1938–). But its heyday was the 1930s and 1940s, when writers such as Dashiell Hammett (1894–1961) and Raymond Chandler (1888–1959) brought high-quality writing to a mass audience. Chandler is the acknowledged master of the hard-boiled detective novel. Through his detective Philip Marlowe, Chandler defined the image of the private eye. A tough but honest man, Marlowe walks the mean streets confronting villains and taking more than his fair share of beatings. Chandler's vivid descriptions and dialogue create novels with a bleak, bitter edge that perfectly captures the mood of their time.

The 1930s were detective fiction's golden age, with vast numbers of detective stories published during the decade published. Since the 1970s, however, the idea that a lone detective of any kind is capable of solving crimes has looked like wishful thinking. Today's detective stories do not rely solely on the deductive powers or the snooping of one detective. Writers now take into account police procedures, forensics (the application of medical knowledge to criminal and legal problems), and genetic testing in their stories. Detectives themselves now come from all racial and ethnic backgrounds. There are gay and lesbian detectives, police detectives, and detectives from all social and professional groups. These changes offer new opportunities for detective fiction and its audience. Detective fiction remains highly popular in all its forms. The growth of the **Internet** (see entry under 1990s—The Way We Lived in volume 5) has led to a revival of publishing short detective stories of all kinds. With its long history of responding to the important issues of the times, detective fiction seems set to remain a central part of America's literary heritage.

Chris Routledge

For More Information

James, P. D. *Talking About Detective Fiction.* New York: Vintage, 2011. Reprint ed.
   Priestman, Martin. *Crime Fiction from Poe to the Present.* Plymouth, UK: Northcote House, 1998.
Symons, Julian. *Bloody Murder: From the Detective Story to the Crime Novel.* 4th ed. London: Pan, 1994.
Thrilling Detective Website. http://www.thrillingdetective.com (accessed on July 6, 2011).
Winn, Dilys. *Murder Ink: The Mystery Reader's Companion.* New York: Workman Publishing, 1977.

Dick and Jane Readers

From 1930 through about 1970, more than sixty-five million U.S. schoolchildren learned to read using the *Dick and Jane* readers published by Scott Foresman and Company. The books took their name from the series' lead characters, a boy named Dick and a girl named Jane, who, with a dog named Spot and a kitten named Puff, lived in a friendly neighborhood of white picket fences. It has been estimated that four out of five of the nation's schools used the *Dick and Jane* readers, ranking them with the nineteenth-century McGuffey Readers as important tools of universal literacy.

The *Dick and Jane* readers used a limited vocabulary and sight-reading method, with frequent repetition of words and phrases so children could remember them easily. The phrase "See Spot run! Run, Spot, run!" is still remembered by millions of adults as the very first sentences they could read on their own. For this reason, some critics thought the stories were boring and lacked the cultural content enjoyed by earlier generations who had learned to read using Shakespeare and the Bible, for example. By the 1960s, the simple sight-reading approach of the *Dick and Jane* readers had fallen out of favor, replaced with readers that emphasize phonics. The readers were also criticized for portraying Dick and Jane in a white, small-town setting that had little relevance to many children of color who were growing up in urban areas. It was not until 1965—in the readers' final editions—that the first African American characters appeared: neighbors to Dick and Jane named Mike, Pam, and Penny.

The first *Dick and Jane* readers appeared in 1930. They were developed by William S. Gray (1885–1960), an authority on teaching, and by Zerna Sharp (1889–1981) and Harry B. Johnson. Working with teachers and school psychologists, the three developed a series using a limited vocabulary technique. The first-grade *Dick and Jane* readers had only three hundred words; the third-grade reader had about one thousand; and the sixth-grade reader had four thousand. Writers were required to limit their stories to a preselected group of words, only a few of which could be introduced on each page. In 1941, the *Cathedral* series of the *Dick and Jane* readers was developed for Roman Catholic schools. In 2003, the books were reissued again, this time as pieces of nostalgia rather than as tools for education. These new versions sold over 2.5 million copies, proving that the public was still enthusiastic about the comforting stories.

Edward Moran

For More Information

Kismaric, Carole, and Marvin Heiferman. *Growing Up with Dick and Jane.* San Francisco: Collins, 1996.

"Reading With and Without Dick and Jane: The Politics of Literacy in Twentieth-Century America." *Rare Book School.* http://www.rarebookschool.org/2005/exhibitions/dickandjane.shtml (accessed July 6, 2011).

Trace, Arther S., Jr. *Reading without Dick and Jane.* Chicago: Regnery, 1965.
Zimet, Sara Goodman, ed. *What Children Read in School: Critical Analysis of Primary Reading Textbooks.* New York: Grune & Stratton, 1972.

Dick Tracy

In 1931, comic strip detective Dick Tracy began his relentless pursuit of bizarre and disfigured criminals. For decades, readers have been thrilled with the strip's mix of highly stylized and almost abstract artwork, realistic police procedural elements, breathless pacing, and brutal violence.

Chester Gould (1900–1985) aspired to be a cartoonist since his boyhood days in Oklahoma. In 1921, he moved to Chicago, Illinois, and worked for several newspapers while attempting to create his own comic strip. He eventually developed an idea for a daily adventure strip that would reflect the gangland violence that was overrunning Chicago during the **Great Depression** (1929–41; see entry under 1930s—The Way We Lived in volume 2) and Prohibition era. Unlike other adventure strips of the period, such as *Tarzan* (see entry under 1910s—Print Culture in volume 1) and *Buck Rogers* (see entry under 1920s—Print Culture in volume 2), Gould's was not set in an exotic locale but rather in a more realistic urban environment.

Gould introduced Dick Tracy to the American public through a dramatic story that set the basic elements of the strip. Tracy was first seen as a helpless witness to the kidnapping of his fiancée, Tess Truehart, and the murder of her father. He immediately joined the police force, saved Tess, and brought the hoodlums to justice. Tracy was soon joined in his battle with the criminal underworld by sidekick Pat Patton and "Junior," an orphan adopted by the policeman.

Gould's main theme was that moral outrage and inescapable punishment must confront ruthless crime. His artistic style was known for its sharp lines and angles, whether drawing people or background. His forbidding use of black complemented his morality tales. The strip was generally structured around Tracy's pursuit of some evil or sadistic villain. Tracy's nasty opponents, who had names like Flattop, B. B. Eyes, Pruneface, and Mumbles, were drawn so that their evil natures were reflected in their appearances. The villains often met grisly fates, such as being riddled with bullets, frozen to death, buried alive, or impaled on flagpoles. Gould balanced these strange, unreal elements with realistic depictions of police procedures and techniques. The strip was also known for its invention of futuristic gadgets, like the two-way wrist radio Tracy employed in his fight for justice.

Dick Tracy helped popularize **detective fiction** (see entry under 1930s—Print Culture in volume 2) not only through his newspaper exploits but also on **radio** (see entry under 1920s—TV and Radio in volume 2), **television** (see entry under 1940s—TV and Radio in volume 3), and film. Although Gould retired in 1977, Dick Tracy continues to fight crime in the nation's newspapers. In 1990, Tracy was introduced to another generation through a stylish film based on the strip, directed by Warren Beatty (1937–) and starring Beatty, Al Pacino (1940–), and Madonna (1958–). A Dick Tracy video game was also released that year.

Charles Coletta

For More Information

Bonifer, Mike. *Dick Tracy: The Making of the Movie*. New York: Bantam Books, 1990.

The Chester Gould-Dick Tracy Museum. http://www.dicktracymuseum.com/ (accessed July 6, 2011).

Crouch, Bill, ed. *Dick Tracy: America's Most Famous Detective*. Rev. ed. New York: Carol Publishing, 1990.

Gould, Chester. *The Celebrated Cases of Dick Tracy, 1931–1951*. New York: Chelsea House, 1970.

Gould, Chester. *Dick Tracy: The Thirties: Tommyguns & Hard Times*. New York: Chelsea House, 1978.

Maeder, Jay. *Dick Tracy: The Official Biography*. New York: Plume, 1990.

Marschall, Richard. *America's Great Comic Strip Artists*. New York: Abbeville Press, 1989.

Doc Savage

Clark "Doc" Savage Jr. was one of the first superheroes to ram, shoot, and punch his way through American popular culture. Beginning in 1933, he appeared in 181 "pulp" novels, several episodes of radio drama, and one movie.

Savage made his debut in the novel, *The Man of Bronze* (a reference to the hero's suntanned skin, acquired while fighting evil in all climates and all forms of weather), which also introduced the first issue of *Doc Savage Magazine.* This publication would feature a Doc Savage novel every month until 1949.

The 1930s saw the beginning of magazines that were known as "hero pulps," built around the adventures of one popular character. The first of the hero pulps featured the exploits of **The Shadow** (see entry under 1930s—Print Culture in volume 2), and it was the runaway success of this publication that inspired Henry W. Ralston of Street and Smith Publishers to envision a new kind of hero. Amidst the gloom and doom of the **Great Depression** (1929–41; see entry under 1930s—The Way We Lived in volume 2), Ralston wanted a character "so strong and so intelligent that nothing can stop him." The job of fleshing out that concept fell to veteran pulp-writer Lester Dent (c. 1904–1959).

Dent created the ultimate mortal man, who would serve as a pattern for the later creation of the even greater heroes such as **Superman** (see entry under 1930s—Print Culture in volume 3)

An exciting 1934 cover from Doc Savage Magazine, *one of the "hero pulp" magazines that were popular during the Great Depression.* © GEOFFREY CLEMENTS/CORBIS.

and **Batman** (see entry under 1930s—Print Culture in volume 3). Doc Savage was a man who made the most of his considerable natural talents. Doc was the richest man alive and one of the best looking. He also had the physique of a superb athlete, which allowed him to run faster, dodge quicker, and hit harder than anyone who was likely to oppose him. Doc Savage was a superb chemist, a brilliant surgeon, and an inventor of unparalleled creativity. He invented a number of gadgets used in his struggle against the forces of evil, including instant-developing cameras, tranquilizing dart guns, and a teleportation device that could break an object down to its essential atoms and reconstitute it somewhere else.

Doc Savage surrounded himself with "the five greatest brains ever assembled in one group." As the books said: "Together with their leader, they would go anywhere, fight anyone, dare everything—seeking excitement and perilous adventure." However, the intellectual power of the "Fabulous Five" often paled in comparison to the brilliance of their leader.

There was a revival of interest in Doc Savage during the late 1960s to early 1970s, when Bantam Publishing reissued most of the original magazine novels as paperbacks whose sensational contents was matched only by its lurid covers. A Doc Savage movie came out in 1970. A radio show aired in the 1930s and again in the 1980s. Bantam began publishing new Doc Savage stories in 1991. Although Doc Savage is no longer a household name, there are numerous fan sites on the **Internet** (see entry under 1990s—The Way We Lived in volume 5).

Justin Gustainis

For More Information

Cannaday, Marilyn. *Bigger Than Life: The Creator of Doc Savage.* Bowling Green, OH: Bowling Green State University Popular Press, 1990.

"Doc Savage." *ThePulp.net.* http://thepulp.net/docsavage.html (accessed July 6, 2011).

Hutchison, Don. *The Great Pulp Heroes.* Buffalo, NY: Mosaic Press, 1996.

Sampson, Robert. *Deadly Excitements: Shadows and Phantoms.* Bowling Green, OH: Bowling Green State University Popular Press, 1989.

Esquire

A monthly men's magazine founded in 1933 by Arnold Gingrich (1903–1976) and David Smart (1892–1952), *Esquire* was originally conceived as a fashion magazine and distributed through men's clothing stores. By the 1960s, it had evolved into one of the United States' most respected monthly magazines. It published hard-hitting articles and high-quality short stories by some of the nation's leading writers, such as Tom Wolfe (1931–), Gore Vidal (1925–), William F. Buckley Jr. (1925–2008), and Garry Wills (1934–). Under fiction editor Gordon Lish (1934–), the magazine helped establish the careers of important short-story writers like Raymond Carver (1938–1988).

Appealing to an audience of sophisticated, style-conscious males, *Esquire* helped define patterns of thinking and standards of behavior for the post–World War II (1939-45) generation of well-off, educated men (and women). The magazine virtually reinvented notions of how American men should act by presenting as role models men who were interested in leisure, who were avid consumers, and who had a keen interest in sex. Such representations of manhood were soon to become commonplace in American culture, but they first appeared regularly in *Esquire.*

From its earliest days, *Esquire* published the work of serious American writers, including Ernest Hemingway (1899–1961), John Dos Passos (1896–1970), F. Scott Fitzgerald (1896–1940), Dashiell Hammett (1894–1961), and Langston Hughes (1902–1967). It featured cartoons by E. Simms Campbell (1906–1971), the only black artist whose work appeared regularly in a mainstream national magazine. Immediately after World War II, the publication veered away from its stylish and literary format in favor of more **Westerns** (see entry under 1930s—Film and Theater in volume 2) and **detective fiction** (see entry under 1930s—Print Culture in volume 2), imitating other **pulp magazines** (see entry under 1930s—Print Culture in volume 3) of the period. In the 1950s, *Esquire* moved to New York and reestablished its sophisticated style under such editors as Ralph Ginzburg (1929–2006) and Clay Felker (1925–2008), who were credited with making *Esquire* one of the country's preeminent periodicals. The magazine published many in-depth articles on important social and cultural issues of the day, like the **civil rights movement** (see entry under 1960s—The Way We Lived in volume 4) and the Vietnam War (1954–75).

By the 1970s, *Esquire*'s circulation peaked at about 1.25 million but soon suffered sharp declines in readership and advertising. After several changes of ownership, *Esquire* was purchased in 1987 by the Hearst Corporation, its present owner, which publishes it under the slogan "Everything a Man Needs to Know." According to its editor-in-chief, David Granger, "*Esquire* is special because it's a magazine for men. Not a fashion magazine for men, not a health magazine for men, not a money magazine for men. It is not any of these things; it is all of them. It is, and has been for nearly seventy years, a magazine about the interests, the curiosity, the passions of men." *Esquire* claimed a circulation of approximately 700,000 in 2011, about half of what it had been at its peak a generation before.

Edward Moran

For More Information

Esquire. http://www.esquire.com (accessed July 6, 2011).

Merrill, Hugh. *Esky: The Early Years at Esquire.* New Brunswick, NJ: Rutgers University Press, 1995.

Pendergast, Tom. *Creating the Modern Man: Masculinity and American Magazines, 1900–1950.* Columbia: University of Missouri Press, 2000.

Polsgrove, Carol. *It Wasn't Pretty, Folks, But Didn't We Have Fun? Esquire in the Sixties.* New York, W. W. Norton, 1995.

Flash Gordon

One of the most popular science-fiction-adventure comic strips, *Flash Gordon* debuted in 1934 and has since continued to thrill readers for generations. The strip focuses on the exploits of Flash Gordon, Yale graduate and "world renowned polo player," as he continually battles the evil Ming the Merciless on the distant planet of Mongo. Originally created by cartoonist Alex Raymond (1907–1956) and writer Don Moore to challenge the popularity of **Buck Rogers** (see entry under

A scene from the 1936 Flash Gordon *serial starring Beatrice Roberts, Buster Crabbe, and Charles Middleton.*
© PICTORIAL PRESS LTD./ALAMY.

1920s—Print Culture in volume 2), *Flash Gordon* quickly established itself as one of the medium's most dynamic and well-drawn series.

Raymond is remembered as the "Rembrandt of the comics page" for his lush, highly detailed artwork. In *America's Great Comic Strip Artists,* Richard Marschall describes Raymond's artistry as a "powerful, lush style of intense portrayals of personality, majestic poses, dramatic compositions, and a totally unique method of realization—romanticism in the comics." Raymond's work combined a unique color sense, formal composition techniques, and pulsating brushwork.

While *Flash Gordon* was distinguished for its artistry, the writing was often poor. The strip was partially based on the novel *When Worlds Collide* by Edwin Balmer (1883–1959) and Philip Wylie (1902–1971). The strip tended to feature one-dimensional characters in unlikely plots. Its first story featured Flash and his companions—the beautiful Dale Arden and brilliant Dr. Hans Zarkov—being transported via spacecraft to the mysterious planet Mongo. There, they encountered futuristic cities, exotic landscapes, and a variety of bizarre creatures. Ming, a cruel dictator, dominated Mongo. Flash battled the tyrant and Aura, his seductive daughter, repeatedly until Mongo was liberated in 1941. Although many of the scripts may have been silly, Raymond's superb artistry took the strip to a higher level. Raymond left *Flash Gordon* in 1944. He later created the popular *Rip Kirby* detective strip, which he handled until his death in a 1956 automobile accident.

Despite Raymond's departure, *Flash Gordon* remained a successful series. In the late 1930s, the strip was translated to film in several popular movie serials starring Buster Crabbe (1907–1983); the final being the classic *Flash Gordon Conquers the Universe* (1940). The characters also appeared on radio throughout the 1930s and 1940s and in a short-lived 1950s television program. In 1980, Sam J. Jones (1954–) starred as the space hero in an unsuccessful film. Into the twenty-first century, Flash Gordon can still be found exploring Mongo in the nation's comics pages. His exploits can also be downloaded on **iPods** (see entry under 2000s—Music in volume 6), a tool that might have once appeared in one of Buster Crabbe's movies.

Charles Coletta

For More Information

Barry, Dan, and Harvey Kurtzman. *Flash Gordon.* New York: Kitchen Sink Press, 1988.

Markstein, Don. "Flash Gordon." *Don Markstein's Toonopedia.* http://www.toonopedia.com/fgordon.htm (accessed July 6, 2011).

Marschall, Richard. *America's Great Comic-Strip Artists.* New York: Abbeville Press, 1989.

Raymond, Alex. *Flash Gordon.* New York: Nostalgia Press, 1967.

The Grapes of Wrath

Published in 1939, *The Grapes of Wrath,* by John Steinbeck (1902–1968), is one of the most celebrated **Great Depression**–era (1929–41; see entry under 1930s—The Way We Lived in volume 2) novels. It tells the story of the fictional Joad family. Following the loss of their crops during the dustbowl, the Joads leave their Oklahoma farm and head west to California. The novel won Steinbeck the prestigious Pulitzer Prize for fiction in 1940. Written in the tradition of the documentary movement of the late 1930s, the novel alternates between narrative chapters and descriptive passages. An Oscar-winning film based on the novel appeared in 1940, starring Henry Fonda (1905–1982) and directed by John Ford (1895–1973). Between them, the novel and film prompted a national debate about migrant workers and farming.

Steinbeck believed in the power of literature to change society for the better. *The Grapes of Wrath* is both a human story and a political statement. It exposes the short-term thinking at the heart of the agricultural economy of the period. It also reveals the terrible working and living conditions of migrant workers in California. Packed into camps with little running water, the Joads struggle to find low-paid work on fruit farms. The documentary sections of the novel are similar to documentary books of the time such as *You Have Seen Their Faces* (1937) by Margaret Bourke-White (1906–1971) and Erskine Caldwell (1903–1987) and *Let Us Now Praise Famous Men* (1941) by Walker Evans (1903–1975) and James Agee (1909–1955). Steinbeck heightened the effect of his documentary by adding a powerful emotional story.

The "Okie" migrants in Steinbeck's novel are presented as uneducated but decent folk, betrayed by big business and an indifferent government. In Kern County, California, agricultural business and community leaders were outraged. The novel's criticism of California growers and other questions of its accuracy soon led to it being banned across America. As a result, Ford's film was produced under tight security. It has a brighter outlook than the novel, but still presents a bleak, unforgiving depiction of the life of an immigrant family during the Great Depression. Despite this wretched situation, and although the Joads suffer terribly, they remain decent people, ready to help others. In the end, Steinbeck's novel is a celebration of the strength and goodness of ordinary people.

Chris Routledge

For More Information

French, Warren G., ed. *A Companion to the Grapes of Wrath.* New York: Penguin, 1963.

The Grapes of Wrath Project. http://theatre.hum.uab.edu/grapesofwrath/students.htm (accessed July 6, 2011).

Steinbeck, John. *Working Days: The Journals of "The Grapes of Wrath," 1938–1941.* New York: Viking, 1989.

Wiener, Gary. *Readings on the Grapes of Wrath.* San Diego: Greenhaven Press, 1999.

Life

Two important U.S. popular magazines have been known as *Life.* The first, a sophisticated humor magazine published from 1883 to 1936, was noted for the **"Gibson Girl"** (see entry under 1900s—Print Culture in volume 1) illustrations made by Charles Dana Gibson (1867–1944). The more famous of the two, part of the *Time-Life* empire of Henry Luce (1898–1967), was published weekly from 1936 to 1972 and at less frequent intervals to this day. With a peak circulation of 8.5 million readers, it was one of the largest of the mass-circulation magazines. By bringing high-quality photojournalism to millions of readers each week, *Life* helped shape public opinion through the **Great Depression** (1929–41; see entry under 1930s—The Way We Lived in volume 2) and World War II (1939–45) years, and into the **Cold War** (1945–91; see entry under 1940s—The Way We Lived in volume 3) period that followed. Some of the most familiar and iconic photographs of the twentieth century appeared in the pages of *Life,* such as the famous shot of a sailor and a nurse embracing during World War II victory celebrations in New York's Times Square.

Henry Luce, who had founded ***Time*** (see entry under 1920s—Print Culture in volume 2) in 1923 and *Fortune* in 1930, bought the rights to use the name from the earlier *Life* magazine, which was in financial trouble. The first issue appeared on November 23, 1936, and cost ten

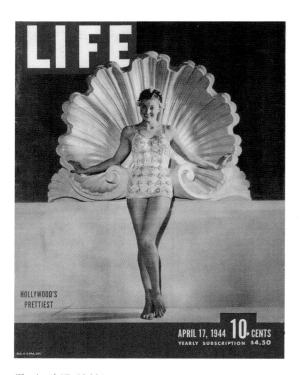

The April 17, 1944 issue of Life, *with the familiar red-rectangle-with-white-letters on the cover, was one of the United States' most popular pictorial magazines.*
© AF ARCHIVE/ALAMY.

cents. The magazine introduced a style and a graphic approach that would remain basically unchanged for the rest of its existence. On its cover appeared a dramatically lit photograph of Fort Peck Dam, one of the era's important public-works projects, taken by Margaret Bourke-White (1906–1971). The magazine's logo, a rectangular red box with the word "Life" in white letters, appeared in the upper left corner, as it would for nearly all of the more than two thousand issues that would follow.

Life adhered to a standard formula over much of the proceeding years. Each issue included a mix of serious photos that illustrated current events, humorous pictures that unveiled the quirky side of life, and comprehensive photo essays on a theme, such as architecture, scientific discoveries, or space travel. Text was kept to a minimum, serving as extended captions for the photographs, which were the real centerpieces of the magazine's appeal. As a mass-circulation commercial magazine, *Life* succeeded in appealing to a large number of Americans who enjoyed seeing the common man (and woman) glorified in its pages each week. Subscriptions fell sharply in the 1960s and *Life* folded as a weekly magazine in 1972. It reemerged as a monthly, however, in 1978, and was published in this form until 2000. More recently, *Life* has entered into a relationship with **Google** (see entry under 2000s—The Way We Lived in volume 6) to host many of its historic photographs and also launched a web site of its own.

Edward Moran

For More Information

Hamblin, Dora Jane. *That Was the Life*. New York: W. W. Norton, 1977.
Life. http://www.life.com (accessed July 6, 2011).
75 Years: The Very Best of Life. New York: Life Books, 2011.
Tebbel, John, and Mary Ellen Zuckerman. *The Magazine in America: 1741–1990*. New York: Oxford University Press, 1991.
Wainwright, Loudon. *The Great American Magazine: An Inside History of Life*. New York: Alfred A. Knopf, 1986.

Li'l Abner

Li'l Abner was one of the most popular comic strips in American history. The strip ran in newspapers from 1934 until 1977. Created by Al Capp (1909–1980), the strip was populated by hillbilly characters that resided in rural Dogpatch. The protagonist was Abner Yokum, a muscle-bound simpleton who lived with his Mammy and Pappy. The strip was an instant critical and commercial success, as readers delighted in Capp's expert mixture of verbal and visual humor. John Steinbeck (1902–1968) considered Capp to be America's greatest satirist, as the strip mocked the nation's social structure, economics, politics, ideals, and contemporary fads.

Capp believed a comic strip could be more than simple entertainment. He used the strip as a soapbox for his beliefs. Both liberals and conservatives denounced the strip over the years as Capp targeted all sides of the political spectrum. The characters of *Li'l Abner* were generally lazy, willing to believe anything, and stupid. They were often repulsively drawn and became embroiled in bizarre adventures. Among the most memorable of Capp's creations are Joe Btfsplk, Fearless Fosdick, Moonbeam McSwine, Sir Cecil Cesspool, the Shmoos, General Bullmoose, and Appasionata von Climax. The strip's most lasting creation was "Sadie Hawkins' Day," during which women could hunt down and legally force a man to marry them. The day became an "unofficial holiday" on college campuses across America. In 1952, the strip gained national headlines when Abner married the gorgeous Daisy Mae Scragg after her years of pursuit. *Li'l Abner*'s characters were featured on radio and in cartoons, films, and a **Broadway** (see entry under 1900s—Film and Theater in volume 1) musical. The strip's popularity declined in the 1970s, leading to Capp's decision to retire *Li'l Abner* in November 1977.

Charles Coletta

For More Information

Caplin, Elliot. *Al Capp Remembered.* Bowling Green, OH: Bowling Green State University Popular Press, 1994.

Capp, Al. *The Best of Li'l Abner.* New York: Holt, Rinehart, and Winston, 1978.

Capp, Al. *My Well-Balanced Life on a Wooden Leg, Memoirs.* Santa Barbara, CA: John Daniel, 1991.

Official Li'l Abner Website. http://www.lil-abner.com/ (accessed July 6, 2011).

Nancy Drew Series

Nancy Drew is the ultimate female private investigator. Her adventures began in 1930, when Mildred A. Wirt Benson (1905–2002) wrote the first *Nancy Drew* mystery novel, *The Secret of the Old Clock,* under the penname "Carolyn Keene." Like the **Hardy Boys** (see entry under 1920s—Print Culture in volume 2) series, the *Nancy Drew* stories were produced by the Stratemeyer Syndicate, a company specializing in mystery series. The *Nancy Drew* mysteries soon became the best-selling juvenile fiction in America. The mysteries remain in print in the twenty-first century. Nancy has adventures every bit as exciting and dangerous as the Hardy Boys', but many of her cases are solved through her "feminine" interest in the arts, crafts, and fashion.

Nancy, whose mother is dead, lives with her father and their housekeeper, Hannah Gruen, in the town of River Heights. She manages the household affairs and even helps her attorney father with his more difficult cases. She is brave, strong, determined, and she never fails to bring crooks to justice. By the 1990s, there were different versions of Nancy Drew to suit different readers. In the *Nancy Drew Notebooks* series, for example, Nancy is in grade school. Older readers can enjoy the *Nancy Drew on Campus* series. Late twentieth-century Nancy deals with issues from drug abuse to premarital sex, although the heroine herself is a model of good behavior.

Over the years, there have been several failed attempts to bring Nancy to cinema and TV audiences, including TV's *The Hardy Boys/Nancy Drew Mysteries* (1977–78) and a series of movies in the late 1930s. The most recent Nancy Drew film, which was released in 2007, also failed to recreate the magic of the books. In the twenty-first century, the *Nancy Drew* books appear in college Humanities courses. Original editions are highly collectable, and several *Nancy Drew* fan sites appear on the **Internet**. There are a number of Nancy Drew video games available as well. Not only was the series a landmark in children's publishing, but Nancy Drew's courage and determination have entertained and inspired generations of young women around the world.

Chris Routledge

For More Information

Billman, Carol. *The Secret of the Stratemeyer Syndicate: Nancy Drew, the Hardy Boys, and the Million Dollar Fiction Factory.* New York: Ungar, 1986.

Lange, Brenda. *Edward Stratemeyer: Creator of the Hardy Boys and Nancy Drew.* Philadelphia: Chelsea House, 2004.

Mason, Bobbie Ann. *The Girl Sleuth.* New ed. Athens: University of Georgia Press, 1997.

Nancy Drew: The Official Home of Nancy Drew Online. http://nancy-drew. mysterynet.com/ (accessed July 6, 2011).

Rehak, Melanie. *Girl Sleuth: Nancy Drew and the Women Who Created Her.* Orlando, FL: Harcourt, 2005.

Paperback Books

The first paperbacks were published in 1841 by a company called Tauchnitz. For the next ninety years, however, other publishers around the world continued to make hardback books, which, for many, were an expensive luxury. In 1934, first Albatross, then Penguin Books, began publishing paperbacks in Britain. Using Albatross's system of color-coding books according to subject matter, Penguin quickly became the biggest paperback publisher. Paperbacks were a great hit. Unlike hardbacks, they could be carried easily, and they were so inexpensive that they could be thrown or given away without regret or hesitation. Paperbacks brought crime fiction, romance, and classic literature to millions of people. Despite a slightly "downmarket" image, in the twenty-first century, paperbacks are by far the most popular kind of book.

In the United States, Robert de Graff (1895–1981) founded Pocket Books in 1939. With its distinctive kangaroo logo (created because kangaroos have pockets), Pocket Books aimed to duplicate the success of Penguin. Their original list of ten titles included Agatha Christie's crime novel, *The Murder of Roger Ackroyd.* Pocket Books sold for twenty-five cents in stores that had never carried books before. Graff realized that at such a low price customers would buy extra books on impulse, so they were stacked according to type. The strategy worked, and Pocket Books sold over 1.5 million copies in the first six months.

Paper shortages damaged the book trade during World War II (1939–45). Overall, though, the war was a good thing for the paperback publishers. By selling shirt-pocket-sized "military editions" to American soldiers, paperback publishers created thousands of readers who might otherwise never have been book buyers. Imprints such as Gold Medal, Ballantine, and Mentor made the 1950s the golden age of paperbacks. From Gold Medal's sensational crime originals to Mentor's list of "respectable" literary authors, paperbacks dominated the book market. Even in the age of **television** (see entry under 1940s—TV and Radio in volume 3) and the **Internet** (see entry under 1990s—The Way We Lived in volume 5), paperbacks sell in huge numbers. Large-format "trade" paperbacks have given them a new respectability. Paperback "novelizations" of popular syndicated television franchises attract thousands of film and TV fans. At first, publishers thought paperbacks would finish off the hardback book. By creating new readers, however, paperbacks have ensured a future for sleek, expensive hardbacks as well.

Chris Routledge

For More Information

CRC Humanities Computing Studio. *The Paperback Revolution.* http://www.crcstudio.org/paperbacks/index.php (accessed July 7, 2011).

Lupoff, Richard A. *The Great American Paperback: An Illustrated Tribute to Legends of the Book.* Portland, OR: Collectors Press, 2001.

O'Brien, Geoffrey. *Hardboiled America: Lurid Paperbacks and the Masters of Noir.* Expanded ed. New York: Da Capo Press, 1997.

Perry Mason

Perry Mason—arguably the most celebrated attorney in all of fiction—personified the ideal criminal lawyer. Mason has been the primary character in dozens of novels (penned by the man who created him, Erle Stanley Gardner, 1889–1970). He was featured in several motion pictures and in a **radio** (see entry under 1920s—TV and Radio in volume 2) series. He appeared in a classic **television** (see entry under 1940s—TV and Radio in volume 3) series; in a second, less-successful series; and lastly, in a succession of made-for-TV movies. Mason, backed by his loyal secretary, Della Street, and a dedicated private eye, Paul Drake, was determined to win his cases. The forces of order and justice were always on his side. He never rested until he successfully nailed the real villain and saved his always-innocent client. In the years before the popularity of the more complex lawyer-based TV series like *L.A. Law* (1986–94), the emergence of Court TV (known since 2008 as truTV), and the broadcast of the murder trial of **O. J. Simpson** (1947–; see entry under 1990s—The Way We Lived in volume 5), Perry Mason's fame was built on his reputation for almost never losing a case.

Canadian actor Raymond Burr stands in a scene from his hit television show Perry Mason *in 1961.* © CBS PHOTO ARCHIVE/GETTY IMAGES.

Perry Mason first appeared on the printed page in *The Case of the Velvet Claws* (1933). Nearly eighty additional novels followed. Then, between 1934 and 1937, Warner Brothers produced six *Perry Mason* feature films. Three actors played the crafty attorney: Warren William (1895–1948), Ricardo Cortez (1899–1977), and Donald Woods (1906–1998). The radio series ran from 1943 to 1955. Four additional performers were heard as Mason on the radio series, which was part soap opera, part detective drama: Bartlett Robinson (1912–1986), Santos Ortega (1900–1976), Donald Briggs (1911–1986), and John Larkin (1912–1965).

By far, the most famous Perry Mason was Raymond Burr (1917–1993), a handsome character actor who played the role on the long-running TV series (1957–1966). Burr was the ideal Mason, lending the character a combination of thoughtful intelligence and steely determination. Appropriately, the last series episode was titled "The Case of the Final Fadeout." Erle Stanley Gardner appeared as the case's judge.

A follow-up series, *The New Perry Mason* (1973–1974), starring Monte Markham (1935–) in the title role, lasted just one season. Then, between 1985 and 1993, an aging Burr replayed Mason in over two dozen highly rated television movies. The first was titled *Perry Mason Returns* (1985).

Rob Edelman

For More Information

Gardner, Erle Stanley. *The Case of the Velvet Claws.* New York: William Morrow, 1933.

Gardner, Erle Stanley. *Seven Complete Novels.* New York: Avenel Books, 1979.

Hughes, Dorothy. *Erle Stanley Gardner: The Case of the Real Perry Mason.* New York: William Morrow, 1978.

Kelleher, Brian, and Diana Merrill. *The Perry Mason TV Show Book.* http://www.perrymasontvshowbook.com/ (accessed July 7, 2011).

Museum of Broadcast Communications. *Encyclopedia of Television.* "Perry Mason." http://www.museum.tv/eotvsection.php?entrycode=perrymason (accessed July 7, 2011).

Pulp Magazines

"Pulp" magazines got their name from the extremely cheap paper that was used to produce them. This inexpensive medium helped keep production costs down. Low production costs meant that the magazines could be sold cheaply—an important consideration during the **Great Depression** (1929–41; see entry under 1930s—The Way We Lived in volume 2), when the pulps were most popular. Many Americans wanted diversions from their troubles, but they could not afford to pay much for them.

The pulp magazines were cheap entertainment, aimed at the widest possible audience. Consequently, they emphasized escapism over literary innovation. Most of them specialized in one of the popular genres, such as detective stories (*Thrilling Mystery, Clues Detective*), Westerns (*Ace-High Western Stories, Texas Rangers*), romance (*Thrilling Love, True Story*), science fiction (*Amazing Stories, Marvel Science Stories, Dynamic Science Fiction*), horror (***Weird Tales** (see entry under 1920s—Print Culture in volume 2), Dime Mystery*), and swashbuckling adventure (*World Wide*

Adventure, **Argosy Weekly** (see entry under 1900s—Print Culture in volume 1), among others. The garish cover illustrations reflected the magazines' contents—they were scary, violent, thrilling, or sexy, and sometimes all of these. During the 1930s and 1940s, over one thousand different pulp magazines were started, although few lasted for the whole period.

A number of these magazines were "hero pulps," dedicated to stories about a single character. The first one focused on the adventures of **The Shadow** (see entry under 1930s—Print Culture in volume 2) beginning in 1931. Others featured protagonists such as **Doc Savage** (see entry under 1930s—Print Culture in volume 2), the Spider, G-8 and His Battle Aces, the Phantom Detective, Secret Agent X, and Captain Future.

Many writers who later earned fame as popular novelists got their start writing for the pulps. John D. MacDonald (1916–1986), Dashiell Hammett (1894–1961), and Erle Stanley Gardner (1889–1970) were known for their mystery and **detective fiction** (see entry under 1930s—Print Culture in volume 2). Max Brand (1892–1944; penname for Frederick Faust) and Louis L'Amour (1908–1988) wrote **Westerns** (see entry under 1930s— Film and Theater in volume 2). Works by such luminaries as Isaac Asimov (1920–1992), Ray Bradbury (1920–), and Robert Heinlein (1907–1988) could be found in the science-fiction pulps. Robert Bloch (1917–1994) and H. P. Lovecraft (1890–1937) penned horror stories.

As the 1940s ended, so did the prime years of the pulps. By the middle of the next decade, they were overtaken by the growing popularity of affordable **paperback books** (see entry under 1930s—Print Culture in volume 2), as well as by a new entertainment medium called **television** (see entry under 1940s—TV and Radio in volume 3).

Justin Gustainis

For More Information

Gorman, Edward, Bill Pronzini, and Martin H. Greenberg, eds. *American Pulp.* New York: Carroll & Graf, 1997.

Goulart, Ron. *Cheap Thrills: An Informal History of the Pulp Magazines.* New Rochelle, NY: Arlington House, 1972.

Haining, Peter. *The Classic Era of American Pulp Magazines.* Chicago: Chicago Review Press, 2001.

Hutchinson, Don. *The Great Pulp Heroes.* New York: Mosaic Press, 1996.

Lampkin, William P. *The Pulp.net: Where Your Next Adventure Was Just a Dime Away!* http://thepulp.net/ (accessed July 7, 2011).

Sampson, Robert. *Deadly Excitements: Shadows and Phantoms.* Bowling Green, OH: Bowling Green State University Popular Press, 1989.

The Shadow

"Who knows what evil lurks in the hearts of men?" went the familiar question that could only be answered by: "The Shadow knows!" The Shadow was the first "hero" of the **pulp magazines** (see entry under 1930s—Print Culture in volume 2) and a later **radio** (see entry under 1920s—TV and Radio in volume 2) program.

The Shadow was first introduced as a daring defender of justice in 1929 on the radio show *Fame and Fortune,* sponsored by pulp publishers Street & Smith. A year later, The Shadow was featured on Street and Smith's *Detective Story Hour.* At first, he was only the narrator, a sardonic, rather sinister presence who introduced the evening's tale of mystery. Then the character caught on, raising a problem for the show's sponsors. Street & Smith sponsored the radio program to boost sales of its *Detective Story Magazine.* Instead, the radio show prompted listeners to demand magazine stories about The Shadow, of which none existed.

Street & Smith quickly announced plans for *The Shadow* magazine (the first of the "hero" pulps) and hired writer Walter Brown Gibson (1897–1985) to pen Shadow novels, which the magazine would feature. Gibson was a fast and surprisingly good writer. He ultimately pounded out 283 Shadow novels (under the pen name Maxwell Grant) and never missed a deadline. He gave The Shadow an alter-ego, Lamont Cranston (and still later another, Kent Allard), a crowd of loyal assistants, and a love interest, Margo Lane. From 1931 to 1949, The Shadow appeared in 325 novel-length adventures in *The Shadow* magazine.

The Shadow starred in his own radio show beginning in 1937, in which he was portrayed by Orson Welles (1915–1985). The show lasted until 1954, although Welles had moved on to greater things long before then.

The first Shadow movie also appeared in 1937. *The Shadow Strikes* starred Rod LaRocque (1898–1969). It was followed by several other low-budget films, all forgettable.

A Shadow comic strip was introduced in 1938, with Gibson as the writer, but it only lasted four years. The Shadow comic books, which debuted the same year, fared better and stayed in print until 1947. An adaptation of The Shadow was published by DC Comics from 1973 to 1975.

In the decades that followed, The Shadow appeared periodically in short stories, novel reprints, and comic books. *The Shadow,* a big-budget 1994 film, starred Alec Baldwin (1958–) in the title role. The film did poorly at the box office, and a planned sequel was never filmed.

Justin Gustainis

For More Information

Eisgruber, Frank. *Gangland's Doom: The Shadow of the Pulps.* Mercer Island, WA: Starmont House, 1985.

Gibson, Walter Brown, and Anthony Tollin. *The Shadow Scrapbook.* New York: Harcourt Brace Jovanovich, 1979.

Sampson, Robert. *The Night Master.* Chicago: Pulp Press, 1982.

The Shadow in Review. http://www.spaceports.com/~deshadow/ (accessed July 7, 2011).

Superman

Superman, the first comic-book superhero, debuted in *Action Comics #1* in 1938. He has continued his never-ending battle for truth, justice, and the "American way" to the delight of his millions of fans ever since. The character established the model of an entire genre of comic-book characters: superheroes, who remain at the core of the comic-book industry. The Superman legend has been retold countless times in **comic books** (see entry under 1930s—Print Culture in volume 2) and reinterpreted in virtually every creative medium, including films, **television** (see entry under 1940s—TV and Radio in volume 3), novels, **radio** (see entry under 1920s—TV and Radio in volume 2), theater, and animation. Superman is a true popular culture icon (symbol) who has persisted throughout the decades and remains the embodiment of all the possibilities of both the comic-book medium and America itself.

Jerry Siegel (1914–1996) and Joe Shuster (1914–1992), two teenagers from Cleveland, Ohio, created Superman over several years during the mid-1930s. Both boys were science-fiction fans and collaborated on

A poster from the 1951 film
Superman and the Mole Men,
featuring actor George Reeves
in his big screen debut as the
Man of Steel. © PICTORIAL
PRESS LTD./ALAMY.

their own stories. In 1933, they produced a mimeographed magazine titled *Science Fiction,* which contained the first version of their most famous creation. Their short story called "The Reign of the Superman" (written by Siegel and illustrated by Shuster) depicted an evil character who terrorized a futuristic city. The pair spent the next several years refining the character. He was transformed into a heroic figure who wore a skin-tight costume. Siegel and Shuster were determined that Superman would see publication. Their goal was achieved when DC Comics purchased the character. The contract signed by the inexperienced young men was one of the most infamous agreements in the comic-book industry's history. They sold all rights to the character for only $130. Although they worked on Superman for a number of years, Siegel and Shuster never shared in the enormous profits generated by their creation.

In developing their hero, Siegel and Shuster combined elements from Biblical stories, ancient mythology, pulp fiction, comic strips, movie serials, and science-fiction tales. The character's origin was first revealed in *Superman #1* (1939). Superman was seen to be the infant son of Jor-El (a noted scientist) and his wife, Lara, citizens of the doomed planet Krypton. Moments before Krypton's explosion, the couple placed their son, Kal-El, into a small rocket and directed it toward Earth. Upon landing on Earth, the child—now the only survivor of Krypton—was discovered by the Kents, a farming couple, who named the boy Clark and raised him as their own son. Superman's fantastic powers were said to come from the effects of the Sun's yellow rays upon his alien physiology. As an adult, Clark became a reporter for *The Daily Planet,* a great Metropolitan newspaper in the city of Metropolis. He protected his heroic identity by portraying the bespectacled Clark Kent as a mild-mannered soul who stood in stark contrast to the courageous Superman. His most significant relationship was with Lois Lane, an aggressive reporter who loved Superman and ignored Clark Kent.

Prior to 1938, most comic books only contained reprinted material from popular newspaper strips. The characters that recurred in comic books tended to be policemen, private investigators, and exotic adventurers. Superman was the first science fiction–based comic-book superhero who boasted fantastic powers. He possessed super-strength, super-speed, and an unerring sense of morality that compelled him to fight for good. Originally, Superman did not have the power of flight. He could, however, leap great distances. As the years progressed, the character was enhanced with other super-abilities. The character's earliest stories were filled with Superman facing modern social ills. Superman was seen confronting lynch mobs, slum lords, war profiteers, and corrupt government officials. In time, a recurring "rogues' gallery" of villains was established. Superman's most constant foes include Lex Luthor, Braniac, Bizarro, Metallo, The Parasite, and Mr. Mxyzptlk.

The success of Superman was immediate as millions of comic-book readers were attracted to this new type of hero. Superman turned comic books into a big business as magazines featuring the character sold nearly a million issues per month. Less than a year after his debut, the Man of Steel was the first character to headline an entire comic on his own. Furthermore, his enormous popularity spawned a horde of other characters in the rapidly expanding superhero genre. These included **Batman** (see entry under 1930s—Print Culture in volume 2), **Wonder Woman** (see entry under 1940s—Print Culture in volume 3), Captain Marvel, Green Lantern, and The Flash.

Superman was not only a comic-book phenomenon, but he also successfully appeared in other media. Superman was voiced by actor Bud Collyer (1908–1969) on the popular 1940s radio program, which began with the dramatic opening lines: "Faster than a speeding bullet! More powerful than a locomotive! Able to leap tall buildings in a single bound! Look! Up in the sky! It's a bird! It's a plane! It's Superman!" That decade also saw the hero appear in movie serials, in comic strips, and on thousands of toys and merchandise. In the 1950s, the character appeared on the classic TV program *The Adventures of Superman,* which starred George Reeves (1914–1959). By 1966, Superman arrived on Broadway in *It's a Bird, It's a Plane, It's Superman,* the first musical based on a comic-book character. In 1978, Christopher Reeve (1952–2004) appeared as Superman in a big-budget, all-star version of the hero's exploits. Its popularity led to several sequels. Superman returned to TV in 1993 in *Lois & Clark: The New Adventures of Superman.* This series emphasized romance over action. The Last Son of Krypton again came to television in 2001 in *Smallville,* which depicts a teenaged Clark Kent's adventures. Superman lives on in the twenty-first century with the arrival of yet another film, *Man of Steel,* in 2012.

In comics, Superman's popularity has waned and surged over the various decades. In 1988, celebrated writer John Byrne (1950–) revamped the character to much acclaim. Sales skyrocketed in 1992 with the infamous "Death of Superman" story line, which showed the hero being killed in action and rising from the grave. DC continues to release several new comics annually. In whatever incarnation, Superman remains a potent force upon the cultural landscape.

Charles Coletta

For More Information

Beatty, Scott. *Superman: The Ultimate Guide to the Man of Steel.* New York: DK Publishing, 2006.

Daniels, Les. *DC Comics: A Celebration of the World's Favorite Comic Book Heroes.* Boston: Billboard, 2003.

Daniels, Les. *Superman: The Complete History.* San Francisco: Chronicle Books, 1998.

De Haven, Tom. *Our Hero: Superman on Earth.* New Haven, CT: Yale University Press, 2010.

Dini, Paul, and Alex Ross. *Superman: Peace on Earth.* New York: DC Comics, 1998.

Dooley, Dennis, and Gary Engle. *Superman at Fifty: The Persistence of a Legend.* Cleveland: Octavia Press, 1987.

The Greatest Superman Stories Ever Told. New York: DC Comics, 1987.

Greenberger, Robert, and Martin Pasko. *The Essential Superman Encyclopedia.* New York: Del Rey/Ballantine Books, 2010.

Siegel, Jerry, and Joe Shuster. *Superman: The Action Comics Archives #1.* New York: DC Comics, 1997.

Siegel, Jerry, and Joe Shuster. *Superman: The Dailies (1939–1940).* Northampton, MA: Kitchen Sink Press, 1999.

"Superman." *DC Comics.* http://www.dccomics.com/sites/superman/ (accessed July 7, 2001).

1930s

Sports and Games

The 1920s were thought to be the "golden age of sports." Throughout the 1930s, however, capable athletes broke previous records in rapid succession. Swimmers swam faster, track stars ran faster, horses raced faster, and race-car and powerboat drivers broke new speed records. The rules of basketball and the design of the football were changed to make the games move faster and to increase scores. In the 1920s, single individuals—such as Babe Ruth 1895–1948) in baseball, Jack Dempsey (1895–1983) in boxing, and Bobby Jones (1902–1971) in golf—were called the best in their sport. In the 1930s, many athletes contributed to their sports. Few, except perhaps Joe Louis (1914–1981) in boxing, Babe Didrikson (1911–1956) in track and golf, and Jesse Owens (1913–1980) in track and field, became shining stars.

Because of the Great Depression (1929–41), many sports teams began attracting audiences in inventive ways. They started to devise methods of earning money without increasing ticket prices. As a result, many sports became more and more commercialized. Radio broadcasts brought sports to more people than ever. Although the broadcasts were free to listeners, the price for broadcast rights and the commercial airtime brought sports teams more money. Bright stadium lights made it possible to draw huge crowds to night baseball games. The organization of all-star games boosted attendance at both baseball and football games.

Heavy betting increased interest in boxing, making it America's second favorite sport (after baseball) during the decade.

Although the majority of sports remained segregated during the decade, in baseball the high-quality play of the teams in the Negro Leagues gained attention from white baseball fans. Track and field athletes like Jesse Owens and Eddie Tolan (1908–1967) gained international acclaim. Women gained recognition as athletes in the 1930s as well. Babe Didrikson entered 634 different sporting events during the decade and won 632 of them. She lost one basketball game and was disqualified from a high-jump competition after having apparently set a world record. Sonja Henie (1912–1969) popularized figure skating. Both Didrikson and Henie became millionaires by demonstrating their sporting abilities. Virnett Beatrice "Jackie" Mitchell (1914–1987) was the first woman to sign with a professional baseball team. Her fame soared when she struck out both Babe Ruth (1895–1948) and Lou Gehrig (1903–1941) in an exhibition game in 1931. Amelia Earhart (1897–1937) set a world record when she flew from New Zealand to Ireland in 1932.

People throughout the United States were fascinated by sports. Children started playing baseball in Little Leagues. Older baseball players could compete in various amateur and semiprofessional leagues, which held local, state, and sometimes national tournaments. Bowling leagues started across the country. The United States Lawn Tennis Association promoted tennis as a sport for everyone—everyone at this time except African Americans, who were invited to play by their own American Tennis Association. At home, board games were popular entertainment. Monopoly, a game that allowed people to buy properties and manage amounts of play money that few had in reality, was introduced.

Babe Didrikson (1911–1956)

At a time when women were still considered the "weaker sex," Babe Didrikson showed that they could be strong and excel in athletics. Didrikson was a sports phenomenon in the 1930s and 1940s who paved the way for Mia Hamm (1972–), Michelle Wie (1989–) and other prominent female athletes of recent decades. She was the first woman to challenge notions of what women could and should do athletically.

Didrikson was born in Port Arthur, Texas, and showed promise in athletics at an early age. Her personal goal was "to be the greatest athlete

Golf phenom Babe Didrikson knocks one down the fairway.
© HARRY WARNECKE/NY DAILY NEWS ARCHIVE/GETTY IMAGES.

who ever lived," as quoted by Susan E. Cayleff in in *Babe Didrikson: The Greatest All-Sport Athlete of All Time.* She was an AAU All-American high school basketball player. In 1932, she single-handedly won the AAU team Track and Field Championships, finishing first in five of the eight events she entered. She then competed in the **Olympics** (see entry under 1900s—Sports and Games in volume 1) of 1932, winning three gold and one silver medals.

In 1934, Didrikson took up a new sport, golf. She won seventeen consecutive tournaments between 1946 and 1947. During her long career, she won eighty-two tournaments and was instrumental in forming the LPGA in 1950. In 1938, she married professional wrestler George Zaharias (1908?–1984). Didrikson died of cancer in 1956 and six years later was named Greatest Female Athlete of the First Half of the Twentieth Century by the Associated Press.

Jill Gregg Clever

For More Information

Cayleff, Susan E. *Babe Didrikson: The Greatest All-Sport Athlete of All Time.* Berkeley, CA: Conari Press, 1995.
Freedman, Russell. *Babe Didrikson Zaharias.* New York: Clarion Books, 1999.
Sutcliffe, Jane. *Babe Didrikson Zaharias: All-Around Athlete.* Minneapolis: Carolrhoda Books, 2000.
Van Natta, Don. *Wonder Girl: The Magnificent Sporting Life of Babe Didrikson Zaharias.* New York: Little, Brown, 2011.

Little League

From its inception in 1939 to the present, Little League has evolved into the primary outlet for youngsters to participate in **baseball** (see entry under 1900s—Sports and Games in volume 1), America's national pastime. Today, well over three million boys and girls from across the globe between the ages of five and eighteen participate in Little League programs.

Little League was founded in Williamsport, Pennsylvania, with the initial league consisting of three teams. In 1947, the first non-Pennsylvania league, located in Hammonton, New Jersey, became an official Little League. By 1950, there were 307 leagues spanning the United States. Little League went international the following year with the establishment of a program in British Columbia, Canada. In 1953 the Little League World Series was first televised on CBS. In 1955 at least one Little League program existed in all forty-eight states.

Throughout the decades, Little League continued to evolve. Separate leagues were created for older boys, for girls' softball, and for children with physical and mental limitations. The 1970s saw the introduction of the aluminum bat.

Many major leaguers began their baseball careers in Little League, including Carl Yastrzemski (1939–), who was the first Little Leaguer to make the Baseball Hall of Fame, Tom Seaver (1944–), Jim

Palmer (1945–), Mike Schmidt (1949–), Nolan Ryan (1947–), Cal Ripken (1960–), and Dale Murphy (1956–). Conversely, countless Little Leaguers who pitched no-hitters and perfect games, had multiple home-run games, or starred in Little League World Series were fated never to play professional baseball, let alone make the majors or earn a spot at the Hall of Fame in Cooperstown, New York.

Those who coach Little League are supposed to teach children baseball fundamentals and then send them out on the field to play with sportsmanship, not to win at all costs. The essence of Little League is clearly stated in its official Pledge: "I trust in God. I love my country and will respect its laws. I will play fair and strive to win. But win or lose, I will always do my best."

Rob Edelman

For More Information

Burroughs, Jeff, and Tom Hennessy. *The Little Team That Could: The Incredible, Often Wacky Story of the Two-Time Little League World Champions.* Chicago: Bonus Books, 1994.

Frommer, Harvey. *Growing Up at Bat: 50 Years of Little League Baseball.* New York: Pharos Books, 1989.

Little League Online. http://www.littleleague.org/Little_League_Online.htm (accessed July 7, 2011).

Newman, Gerald. *Happy Birthday, Little League.* New York: F. Watts, 1989.

Van Auken, Lance, and Robin Van Auken. *Play Ball: The Story of Little League Baseball.* University Park, PA: Pennsylvania State University Press, 2001.

Joe Louis (1914–1981)

In the 1930s, prizefighter Joe Louis emerged as the nation's first African American sports hero. Born Joseph Louis Barrow in Alabama, the "Brown Bomber" held one of boxing's most impressive career records: seventy-one fights, sixty-eight wins, and fifty-four knockouts. However, his greatest achievement was his universal popularity despite America's racial divide.

Louis became a national hero with his 1938 victory over German Max Schmeling (1905–2005). Their fight was one of the most celebrated events in boxing history. The fight came to symbolize the political conflicts between the United States and Nazi Germany (though Schmeling was not a Nazi). Louis was soon the world's most famous

Joe Louis, seen here in 1940, was the world heavyweight champion from 1939 to 1949.
© AP IMAGES.

black man and was a source of pride to millions of African Americans. Whites also responded to the champ's appealing personality and admired him for postponing his career to enlist in the army during World War II (1939–45). Louis held the world heavyweight championship from 1939 until 1949, when he retired. Louis's later years were plagued with drug abuse and financial problems. Still, he is remembered as a boxing legend and an early pioneer in the **civil rights movement** (see entry under 1960s—The Way We Lived in volume 4).

Charles Coletta

For More Information

Gordon, Robert, director. *The Joe Louis Story* (film). United Artists, 1953.

Jakoubek, Robert E. *Joe Louis: Heavyweight Champion.* New York: Chelsea House, 1990.

Joe Louis: The Boxer Who Beat Hitler (video). A & E Network, 2001.

Lipsyte, Robert. *Joe Louis: A Champ for All America.* New York: HarperCollins, 1994.

Margolick, David. *Beyond Glory: Joe Louis vs. Max Schmeling, and a World on the Brink.* New York: Knopf, 2005.

The Official Site of Joe Louis. http://www.cmgww.com/sports/louis/ (accessed July 7, 2011).

Roberts, Randy. *Joe Louis: Hard Times Man.* New Haven, CT: Yale University Press, 2010.

Monopoly

Monopoly is one of the most popular and enduring of all American board games. It is played on a four-sided board. The board is bordered with small squares, most of which are designated as streets in Atlantic City, New Jersey, or as railroads and utility companies. Game pieces include tokens that represent each player, two dice, thirty-two houses, twelve hotels, Chance and Community Chest cards, a title deed for every property, and fake money. The game's objective involves a combination of free enterprise and cutthroat competition. Players purchase,

With over two hundred million games sold, Monopoly has been the world's best-selling board game. © TONYMONO/ALAMY.

build on, and rent out as many properties as possible. The winner is the player who becomes the wealthiest by buying and controlling the most properties; constructing hotels and houses; charging rental fees; handling mortgages, utilities, and interest—and, finally, bankrupting all opponents.

Ironically, Monopoly was devised during the **Great Depression** (1929–41; see entry under 1930s—The Way We Lived in volume 2), when millions of Americans were jobless and many were denouncing the capitalist system. Its inventor was Charles B. Darrow (1889–1967), an unemployed salesman from Germantown, Pennsylvania, who was inspired by The Landlord's Game, which had been copyrighted in 1904. The Landlord's Game was invented not for amusement, but as a teaching tool. The game illustrated the concept that real estate rental fees should be taxed because they resulted in an unearned increase in land values, which profited a few individuals—landlords—rather than the majority—tenants. In 1933, Darrow copyrighted his version of The

Landlord's Game. The following year, he brought it to executives at Parker Brothers, a game manufacturer, who rejected it. Undiscouraged, Darrow and a printer friend hand-produced five thousand games, which Darrow sold to several department stores. The game was an immediate hit, but Darrow found himself ill-equipped to meet the demand for orders. In 1935, Parker Brothers took over production. Monopoly quickly became America's top-selling board game.

Across the decades, over two hundred million games have been sold worldwide, and it has been estimated that five hundred million people have played Monopoly. The National and World Monopoly Game Championships started in 1973. At the championships, expert players from across the globe compete. Countless game variations have been marketed, including everything from a **Disney** (see entry under 1920s—Film and Theater in volume 2) version to a NASCAR edition. The longest Monopoly game on record lasted 1,680 hours, or 70 straight days.

In 2011, Monopoly is sold in 103 countries and marketed in thirty-seven languages, with Monopoly money printed in currency from dollar to deutsche mark to yen. It remains the world's best-selling board game.

Rob Edelman

For More Information

Brady, Maxine. *The Monopoly Book: Strategy and Tactics of the World's Most Popular Game.* New York: D. McKay, 1974.

Darzinskis, Kaz. *Winning Monopoly: A Complete Guide to Property Accumulation, Cash Flow Strategy, and Negotiating Techniques When Playing the Best-Selling Board Game.* New York: Perennial Library, 1987.

"Monopoly: History and Fun Facts" *Hasbro.com.* http://www.hasbro.com/monopoly/en_US/discover/history.cfm (accessed July 7, 2011).

Orbanes, Philip. *Monopoly: The World's Most Famous Game—And How It Got That Way.* Cambridge, MA: Da Capo Press, 2006.

Jesse Owens (1913–1980)

More than any other athlete, track-and-field star Jesse Owens is most closely associated with the 1936 **Olympics** (see entry under 1900s—Sports and Games in volume 1), held in Berlin, Germany. Nazi Party leader Adolf Hitler (1889–1945), who had established a tyrannical grasp

Jesse Owens races down the track during the 1936 Summer Olympics in Berlin, Germany.
© HISTORY/ALAMY.

over Germany in 1933, wanted these Olympic games to act as a widely visible demonstration of Aryan supremacy (Hitler's belief that the white race was superior to all other peoples and races). Owens, not only an American but an African American, won four Gold Medals—for the 100- and 200-meter dashes, the 400-meter relay, and the broad jump— causing Hitler great embarrassment. In an ungentlemanly act, Hitler refused to congratulate Owens, leaving the stadium before the athlete was presented with his medals.

Born to Alabama sharecroppers, Owens had already won international acclaim in 1935 when he set world records in six events as a member of the Ohio State University track team. Upon his return from the 1936 Olympics, he was honored with a ticker-tape parade in New York. From then on, Owens was celebrated as a symbol of democracy and freedom. He served in various capacities as a goodwill ambassador and sports administrator—quite an accomplishment for an African American before the **civil rights movement** (see entry under 1960s— The Way We Lived in volume 4).

Rob Edelman

For More Information

Edmondson, Jacqueline. *Jesse Owens: A Biography.* Westport, CT: Greenwood Press, 2007.

Jesse Owens: The Official Web Site. http://www.jesseowens.com (accessed July 7, 2011).

Owens, Jesse, and Paul Neimark. *Jesse: A Spiritual Autobiography.* Plainfield, NJ: Logos International, 1978.

Schaap, Jeremy. *Triumph: The Untold Story of Jesse Owens and Hitler's Olympics.* Boston: Houghton Mifflin, 2007.

Stock Car Racing

From its origins in the 1930s as a sport for Southern outlaws, stock car racing grew throughout the twentieth century to become one of the nation's most popular sports. Drivers like Jeff Gordon (1971–), Richard Petty (1938–), and Dale Earnhardt (1951–2001) had become household names. Stock car racing's **television** (see entry under 1940s—TV and Radio in volume 3) ratings were topped only by the **National Football League** (see entry under 1920s—Sports and Games in volume 2). Early in the sport's history, the cars were "stock," meaning that they were not modified from the cars that could be bought at a dealer. Stock car racing takes its name from those unaltered cars. True stock cars still race today, but in the bigger races the cars have been modified so that they scarcely resemble their street-legal cousins.

Stock car legend has it that the first racers were moonshiners, men who distilled illegal corn whiskey and raced their cars along dusty dirt roads to get away from the police. Moonshiners who wanted to test their driving skills got together for their first race on a dirt track in the mid-1930s. The races soon drew hundreds of fans. The sport rapidly became more organized. Bill France (1909–1972) staged the first race in Daytona Beach, Florida, in 1936. The race took place on a 4-mile track that was part packed sand, part paved road. Bill Cummings won the race with an average speed of 70.39 miles per hour. With this race, organized stock car racing was born.

Through the late 1930s and 1940s, the popularity of stock car racing grew, with the Daytona race as its biggest event. In 1948, the National Association for Stock Car Racing (NASCAR) was created to provide rules and regulations for the sport. NASCAR began to sponsor races throughout the South, including the annual Southern 500 (the 500 indicates that the race was 500 miles long) race at the famous Darlington International Raceway in South Carolina.

Stock car racing came to the north in 1951 with the first Motor City 250, held in Detroit, Michigan. The major automakers—**General Motors** (see entry under 1900s—The Way We Lived in volume 1), Ford, and Chrysler—saw the sport as a testing ground for their cars. They built car models with stock car racing in mind and used wins on the track to help sell their cars. Soon companies began to offer drivers sponsorship money to carry their company logo on the car. Stock cars became rolling advertisements, but sponsorship money allowed race teams to build ever more powerful cars. Today, NASCAR sponsors some two thousand stock car races throughout the United States. Its premier race series is called the Winston Cup Series. Winners of the series stand to earn several million dollars in prizes and endorsement deals.

Tom Pendergast

For More Information

Beekman, Scott. *NASCAR Nation: A History of Stock Car Racing in the United States.* Santa Barbara, CA: Greenwood, 2010.

Carollo, John, and Bill Holder. *Stock Cars! America's Most Popular Motorsport.* New York: HPBooks, 1999.

Chapin, Kim. *Fast as White Lightning: The Story of Stock Car Racing.* New York: Three Rivers Press, 1998.

Dregni, Michael. *Stock Car Racing.* Minneapolis: Capstone Press, 1994.

NASCAR.com. http://www.nascar.com (accessed July 7, 2011).

Rockets on Wheels. http://www.pbs.org/tal/racecars/index.html (accessed February 13, 2002).

1930s

TV and Radio

Just as the 1930s produced some of the best American movies, they also produced some of the best radio programs, making the decade the golden age of both cinema and radio. More than just a source of news and entertainment, radio provided listeners with a chance to escape their troubles. Popular shows like *Amos 'n' Andy* offered comfort, as did broadcasts like the "fireside chats" of President Franklin D. Roosevelt (1882–1945). Social workers observed that some poor families would give up their iceboxes before giving up their radios. By the end of the decade, nearly 80 percent of American households had a radio.

Comedy shows were among the most popular entertainment on radio, especially *Amos 'n' Andy*. The show was broadcast for fifteen minutes every evening. It was so popular that for those fifteen minutes, telephone use dropped by 50 percent and films were stopped so that movie theaters could play the show for audiences throughout the country. Comedians Gracie Allen (1906–1964), George Burns (1896–1996), Jack Benny (1894–1974), and Fanny Brice (1891–1951), who had had successful vaudeville careers, were guests on various variety programs and made listeners smile. Another successful radio comedy program was *Fibber McGee and Molly*. It starred the husband-and-wife team of Jim Jordan (1896–1988) and Marian Jordan (1897–1961), two vaudeville veterans.

More serious programs also entertained audiences. Serial melodramas called "soap operas" became favorites of both women and men across the country. Shows such as *Guiding Light* offered dramatic stories of family crisis and romantic entanglements. Other dramas offered audiences stories of mystery and crime. Suspenseful programs including *The Shadow, Charlie Chan,* and *Sherlock Holmes* kept audiences on the edge of their seats. Younger listeners and those interested in fantastic adventure could hear stories of superheroes, including *Buck Rogers in the Year 2430, Tarzan, The Lone Ranger, Superman,* and *The Green Hornet.* These stories had spectacular sound effects that mimicked creaking doors, mysterious footsteps, and the galloping hooves of Silver, the Lone Ranger's trusty horse, as well as crunching bones and even the monstrous spilling of blood and guts.

Regulation became the most important aspect of radio broadcasting during the 1930s. At the beginning of the decade, the airwaves were a bit chaotic. Stations interfered with the programs of other stations by broadcasting on the same bandwidth. By 1934, the U.S. government, as a part of its plan for controlling various parts of the economy, created the Federal Communications Commission (FCC). The FCC sought to organize stations so that radio broadcasts could be efficiently played across the country without overlapping. The FCC also foresaw the danger of having a company or an individual in control of too many stations in one area. An individual in control of the radio stations in a certain area, or of a network of stations reaching a large number of people, could have too much control over what information the listeners heard. Fearing that the American public would have access only to one opinion or one point of view, the commission sought to limit the number of media outlets (in this case, radio stations, and later, TV stations) a company or an individual could own.

While radio dominated the airwaves of the 1930s, television received its first dramatic public debut in 1939 at the New York World's Fair. There, President Roosevelt addressed audiences and became the first president to appear on TV. Although those who had enough money to buy the $200 to $600 TV receivers clamored to place their orders, TV did not become a popular medium until after World War II (1939–45). After the war, the economy had rebounded and Americans had more cash for luxuries.

Amos 'n' Andy

In the history of American popular culture, no program was both as popular and controversial as the *Amos 'n' Andy* show. The series, which ran on **radio** (see entry under 1920s—TV and Radio in volume 2) in several formats from 1928 to 1960, is perhaps the most popular radio series of all time. Created by white performers Charles Correll (1890–1972) and Freeman Gosden (1899–1982), the series revolved around the comedic misadventures of two black characters—Amos Jones and Andrew H. Brown. The characters later appeared on their own **television** (see entry under 1940s—TV and Radio in volume 3) program from 1950 to 1953. Although the show was extremely popular, many African American groups, led by the National Association for the Advancement of Colored People (NAACP), charged that the characters were racist caricatures and demeaning to the black community. Complaints about its content eventually led to the cancellation of the radio series and the removal of the TV show from syndication. *Amos 'n' Andy* is now most remembered for perpetuating the stereotypes of black minstrelsy (traveling entertainment). The show also constitutes a prime example of the limited opportunities faced by black entertainers during the first half of the twentieth century.

Gosden and Correll were both white performers with roots in the Confederate South. They met in 1919 while working for an entertainment company that offered its services to amateur and local theatrical groups. By 1925, the two of them had moved to Chicago, Illinois, and were producing a radio show on WGN. The program, titled *Sam 'n' Henry,* centered on Sam Smith and Henry Johnson, two poor blacks who migrated from Birmingham, Alabama, to Chicago to seek their fortunes. Gosden and Correll performed the characters themselves by employing an exaggerated black dialect. Although the series was a popular success, Gosden and Correll left WGN after a contract dispute in 1927. On March 19, 1928, they premiered *Amos 'n' Andy* on Chicago's WMAQ. Like Sam and Henry, Amos and Andy were two poor blacks who had left the South for a better life in the North. Amos was the honest, humble, and intelligent owner of the Fresh-Air Taxicab Company. Andrew "Hog" Brown was a lazy, shiftless, dim-witted schemer.

During its peak, *Amos 'n' Andy* claimed some forty million listeners—one third of the nation. People from all walks of life were enthusiastic fans of the show, including presidents Calvin Coolidge (1872–1933) and Herbert Hoover (1874–1964). Department stores regularly played the program over their loudspeakers. Movie theaters interrupted films so their patrons would not miss the next installment of the series. In *Raised on Radio,* author Gerald Nachman quotes the celebrated playwright George Bernard Shaw (1856–1950), who when asked about his visit to the United States said, "There are three things I shall never forget about America—the Rocky Mountains, Niagara Falls, and *Amos 'n' Andy.*" The series is credited with altering the entertainment habits of the nation. *Amos 'n' Andy* also spurred the sale of radios and provided free entertainment for millions of Americans who were struggling through the **Great Depression** (1929–41; see entry under 1930s—The Way We Lived in volume 2). The show became a national obsession as newspapers printed recaps of the previous night's program. Fans threatened to boycott Pepsodent, the series' sponsor, if Amos's wife was allowed to die. Amos and Andy were not only heard on the radio; they also appeared in films and comic strips, on records, and on a vast array of toys and other merchandise. *Amos 'n' Andy* created several national catchphrases including "Holy mack'el!," "Ah's regusted," and "Buzz me, Miss Blue." The series, which incorporated many elements of ethnic vaudeville humor, was known for its warm, character-driven humor and its large supporting cast. Amos and Andy spent much of their time with a character named George "Kingfish" Stevens, a colorful con man. The Kingfish became so popular that he became more prominent than either Amos or Andy. On the TV series, most episodes centered on the battles between the Kingfish and his nagging wife, Sapphire.

Despite their widespread adulation, Amos and Andy were not loved by all segments of the population. The program was very popular among most black Americans, but a significant minority viewed Correll and Gosden's characterizations as a racial slur. In 1931, the *Pittsburgh Courier,* a black newspaper, received a petition with nearly 750,000 names demanding the program be removed from the local airwaves. Opposition toward the show only increased when it was transplanted to TV, where the cast was entirely composed of black actors. In 1951, the NAACP filed a complaint with CBS stating that the show "strengthened the conclusion among uninformed and prejudiced people that Negroes are inferior, lazy, dumb, and dishonest." Many other blacks rallied to the program, claiming it was one of the few mediums through which black performers could gain recognition and earn a living. They also argued the series presented some admirable black representations, such as doctors, lawyers, and businessmen not seen in other areas of popular culture.

Sociologists and cultural historians have long debated the significance of *Amos 'n' Andy*. Some argue the show was truly funny and simply employed the same kind of characters and malapropisms (misuse of words, often with comic effect) that dominated later black TV **sitcoms** (see entry under 1950s—TV and Radio in volume 3) of the 1970s and 1980s, like *The Jeffersons* (1975—85), *Good Times* (1974–79), and *Sanford and Son* (1972–77). Others counter its characters were degradingly portrayed and validated racist attitudes toward blacks. A 1983 documentary, *Amos 'n' Andy: Anatomy of a Controversy,* explored the series' implications on African American culture. Within recent years, episodes of both the radio and the TV programs have become more widely available. *Amos 'n' Andy* continues to loom large on the cultural landscape and will surely remain a source of controversy and debate.

Charles Coletta

For More Information

Amos 'n' Andy Television Radio Show. http://www.amosandy.com/ (accessed on July 7, 2011).

Andrews, Bart, and Ahrgus Juilliard. *Holy Mackerel!: The Amos 'n' Andy Story.* New York: E. P. Dutton, 1986.

Dunning, John. *On the Air: The Encyclopedia of Old-Time Radio.* New York: Oxford University Press, 1998.

Ely, Melvin. *The Adventures of Amos 'n' Andy: A Social History of an American Phenomenon.* New York: The Free Press, 1991.

Greenberg, Bob, producer and writer. *Amos 'n' Andy: Anatomy of a Controversy* (video). M. R. Avery Productions, 1983.

MacDonald, J. Fred. *Blacks and White TV.* Chicago: Nelson-Hall Publishers, 1992.

Nachman, Gerald. *Raised on Radio.* New York: Pantheon Books, 1998.

Fibber McGee and Molly

One of the most popular **radio** (see entry under 1920s—TV and Radio in volume 2) comedy programs in the 1930s and 1940s, *Fibber McGee and Molly* helped define the situation-comedy (sitcom) format. The two roles were created by Jim (1896–1988) and Marian (1897–1961) Jordan, a couple who had performed in **vaudeville** (see entry under 1900s—Film and Theater in volume 1) before their first radio appearance in

Husband-and-wife radio stars Jim and Marian Jordan lived as Fibber McGee and Molly on the radio dial at 79 Wistful Vista. They occupied that same address for over twenty years.
© NBC/NBCU PHOTO BANK/AP IMAGES.

Chicago, Illinois, in 1924. By the early 1930s, with the collaboration of writer Don Quinn (1900–1973), their act evolved into a comedy show called *Smackout* that was broadcast nationally over NBC. In *Smackout,* the Jordans portrayed the owners of a grocery store that was always "smack out" of everything.

The *Fibber McGee and Molly* show was first broadcast from Chicago on April 16, 1935, to mixed reviews. In the initial show, which alternated swing music with comedy segments, Molly and Fibber both portrayed loud-mouth, talkative characters. Molly spoke in a thick Irish accent. Jim Jordan was nicknamed "Fibber" because of his habit of spinning tall tales on each program. Audiences also enjoyed the show's colorful cast of supporting characters, such as Mayor LaTrivia, played by Gale Gordon (1906–1995), Wally Wimple and "The Old Timer," both played by Bill Thompson (1913–1971), as well as clever plugs for its sponsors by announcer Harlow Wilcox (1900–1960). For eighteen months in the late 1930s, Marian Jordan disappeared from the show for health reasons, now believed to have been alcohol-related, but the show became even more popular after her return.

In the series, sponsored by Johnson's Wax, Fibber McGee and Molly lived at the fictional address of 79 Wistful Vista. Their home contained a junk-filled closet that, beginning in 1940, Fibber would open at the beginning of each episode. The noise—created by sound effects—of the items falling out of the closet became the show's signature. During World War II (1939–45), the McGees began employing a black maid, Beulah, whose character was played by a white man, Marlin Hurt (?–1946).

After losing an audience to the *Texaco Star Theatre* hosted by Milton Berle (1908–2002) on television, the half-hour *Fibber McGee and Molly* show ended its Tuesday-night run on NBC in 1953. The show was replaced by a nightly fifteen-minute version that ran until 1957. The Jordans continued to perform short segments on NBC's "Monitor" series until 1959. A TV version also appeared in the late 1950s.

Edward Moran

For More Information

Dunning, John. *On the Air: The Encyclopedia of Old-Time Radio.* New York: Oxford University Press, 1998.

Fibber McGee and Molly. http://fibbermcgeeandmolly.com/ (accessed July 7, 2011).

Price, Tom. *Fibber McGee's Closet: The Ultimate Log of Performances by Fibber McGee and Molly, 1917–1987.* Monterey, CA: T. A. Price, 1987.

Stumpf, Charles, and Tom Price. *Heavenly Days! The Story of Fibber McGee and Molly.* Waynesville, NC: World of Yesterday, 1987.

Guiding Light

Guiding Light, which premiered on **radio** (see entry under 1920s—TV and Radio in volume 2) in 1937 and later migrated to **television** (see entry under 1940s—TV and Radio in volume 3) in 1952, was the longest running soap opera in broadcast history, running until September 2009. The series was created by Irna Phillips (1901–1972) and

Emmons Carlson and long remained one of the genre's leading and most influential programs. The show's title and logo—a revolving lighthouse beacon—reflected its initial primary character, Reverend John Ruthledge, played by Arthur Peterson (1912–1996). Reverend Ruthledge provided spiritual consul and practical advice to the inhabitants of the fictional town of Five Points. *Guiding Light,* like other **soap operas** (see entry under 1930s—TV and Radio in volume 2), relied heavily upon melodramatic plots, but it was also willing to bring controversial topics to daytime drama.

On radio, *Guiding Light* was a popular drama in which characters encountered the same hardships faced by its 1930s and 1940s listening audience, like economic depression and war. When Peterson left the series, his popular character was killed off and the program's focus shifted to a new cast: the Bauer family. Meta Bauer (played by both Jone Allison and Elling Demming) served as the primary heroine and remained a vital presence on the program for four decades. In the 1960s, Agnes Nixon (1927–) became the series' head writer and guiding force. She was instrumental in introducing taboo (socially unsanctioned) story lines and minority characters to the soap opera world. Although the series' sponsor, Procter & Gamble, was hesitant to incorporate such relevant plots as interracial marriage, rape, and cervical cancer into *Guiding Light,* the audience response was overwhelmingly positive. Soon, other daytime dramas were following Nixon's lead in presenting previously off-limits subject matter. One of the program's most controversial episodes involved a marital rape. The villainous Roger Thorpe's assault on his wife Holly stunned viewers and created effects that would be felt for years on the series.

In the 1980s, Douglas Marland (1935–1993), a veteran soap writer, took charge of the show and began to emphasize the romantic entanglements of the younger characters. One highly charged plot depicted a medical student in bed with a minor (underage person). That decade also saw *Guiding Light's* core family, the Bauers, displaced by the wealthy Spaulding and Lewis families. Reva Shayne (Kim Zimmer, 1955–) emerged as the show's leading nasty character, who married her former father-in-law and attempted to seduce Josh, her former brother-in-law. Later, Reva died and returned as both a ghost and a clone. In the 1990s, the working-class Cooper family gained prominence. Plots increasingly emphasized fantasy and the supernatural to attract younger viewers. Such story lines drew criticism from long-time fans, and because of competition from other media outlets and newer soaps, as well as rising production costs, *Guiding Light* lost half its viewership between 1999 and its conclusion in 2009. Still, its seventy-two years on radio and television demonstrate that its characters and stories struck a deep chord with millions of Americans.

Charles Coletta

For More Information

Carter, Bill. "CBS Turns Out 'Guiding Light.'" *New York Times* (April 1, 2009): p. C1.

Intintoli, Michael. *Taking Soaps Seriously: The World of "Guiding Light."* New York: Praeger, 1984.

Matelski, Marilyn. *The Soap Opera Evolution: America's Enduring Romance with Daytime Drama.* Jefferson, NC: McFarland, 1988.

Poll, Julie, and Caelie Haines. *Guiding Light: The Complete Family Album— Anniversary Edition.* New York: General Publishing Group, 1998.

Schemering, Christoper. *Guiding Light: A 50th Anniversary Celebration.* New York: Ballantine, 1986.

The Lone Ranger

Beginning in the 1930s, millions of children turned to the **radio** (see entry under 1920s—TV and Radio in volume 2) to listen to *The Lone Ranger,* featuring one of popular culture's most enduring **Western** (see entry under 1930s—Film and Theater in volume 2) heroes. Each episode of the radio show began with the stirring phrase "A fiery horse with a speed of light, a cloud of dust, and a hearty Hi-Yo Silver!," which introduced the masked rider of the plains astride Silver, his white stallion. Joined by Tonto, his faithful Indian companion, the Lone Ranger dedicated his life to fighting evildoers and bringing justice to the western United States.

George W. Trendle (1884–1972), an owner of Detroit's WXYZ Radio, created the character. The series quickly spread across the nation and served as the cornerstone of the new Mutual Radio Network. Trendle conceived his character as a Robin Hood of the Old West who upheld the highest ethical and moral standards. In the character's origin story, John Reid, a member of the Texas Rangers, is the lone survivor of an ambush by the dastardly Butch Cavendish Gang. Discovered and nursed to health by Tonto, Reid vows to bring

Actor Clayton Moore as the Lone Ranger, with his white stallion Silver. The popularity of the radio show that started in Detroit in 1933 eventually led to both television and movie treatments of the Masked Man. © PHOTOS 12/ ALAMY.

Cavendish to justice and uphold the honor of his fallen comrades while concealing his identity. Tonto referred to the Lone Ranger as *kemo sabe* (pronounced KEY-moe SA-bee, meaning "trusted friend"). The radio series premiered on January 30, 1933, and aired for more than twenty years.

The cowboy hero, who personified the ideal American man, fascinated America's youth. The Lone Ranger spoke perfectly. He never smoked, drank, or caroused with women. He insisted on only wounding his adversaries; he never shot to kill. Every installment of the radio series began with a dramatic recording of the "William Tell Overture" and ended with a grateful townsperson asking, "Who was that masked man?" as the Lone Ranger rode off to discover new adventures. In a deep voice, he would yell, "Hi-Yo Silver, awaaaay!"

The character's success expanded beyond radio as he later appeared in films and television. The television program, which featured actors Clayton Moore (c. 1908–1999) and Jay Silverheels (1919–1980) as the western duo, aired from 1949 to 1957. They also appeared in several Lone Ranger films. For years after the series ended, Moore made numerous personal appearances as the Lone Ranger while preaching the character's ethical code. A 1981 film, *The Legend of the Lone Ranger,* starring Klinton Spilsbury (1951–), was a financial disaster.

The Lone Ranger continues to appear in comics and cartoons as he brings order to the West. He remains an American icon of courage and integrity.

Charles Coletta

For More Information

"The Beginning of a Legend." *Lone Ranger Fan Club.* http://www.theloneranger. tv/history# (accessed July 7, 2011).

Dunning, John. *Tune in Yesterday: The Ultimate Encyclopedia of Old-Time Radio, 1925–1976.* Englewood Cliffs, NJ: Prentice Hall, 1976.

Lichtman, Jim. *The Lone Ranger's Code of the West.* Palm Desert, CA: Scribbler's Ink, 1996.

Moore, Clayton, with Frank Thompson. *I Was That Masked Man.* Dallas: Taylor, 1996.

Van Hise, James. *Who Was That Masked Man: The Story of the Lone Ranger.* Las Vegas: Pioneer Books, 1990.

Soap Operas

Since the first soap opera aired on Chicago's WGN radio in the early 1930s, serial dramas have attracted hundreds of millions of fans, eager to escape the everyday problems of real life by immersing themselves in the far more dramatic ups and downs of their soap-opera heroes. Although soaps were originally designed to appeal to housewives (the name "soap opera" comes from the household products that were often the main advertisers), modern soap audiences include everyone from business executives to college football players.

The cast from the radio soap opera Beau Brummel in 1930. © BETTMANN/CORBIS.

In the 1800s, well before the invention of **radio** (see entry under 1920s—TV and Radio in volume 2) and **television** (see entry under 1940s—TV and Radio in volume 3), writers like Charles Dickens (1812–1870) created a kind of soap opera, stories full of twists and turns and plenty of melodrama that were published in magazines and newspapers in serial form, that is, divided into parts and published a part at a time. "Cliff-hanger" endings, in which the hero or heroine was left in a dangerous and suspenseful position, were common in these stories. The tense endings served to keep readers eagerly awaiting the next episode to find out what would happen.

After World War I (1914–18), the first radio stations began broadcasting programs that could reach listeners nationwide. By 1930, several networks had formed to create programming for these stations. Programmers filled the evening hours, when families were gathered around the radio, but daytime hours were thought to be largely unprofitable. Then a Dayton, Ohio, schoolteacher named Irna Phillips (1901–1972) approached Chicago radio station WGN with her idea for a fifteen-minute daily serial drama called *Painted Dreams.* The networks seized upon the idea. Soon the airwaves were filled with dozens of the new daytime "soap operas." Shows like *Betty and Bob, Just Plain Bill, The Romance of Helen Trent,* and *Ma Perkins* attracted an audience of forty million listeners, almost double the twenty-first century television soap audience. People living through the economic hardship of the **Great Depression** (1929–41; see entry under 1930s—The Way We Lived in volume 2) could afford few diversions. Listening to the radio was inexpensive. Audiences welcomed the escape that soap operas offered with their tales of overcoming disaster and tragedy.

The arrival of television in the American home in the 1950s was a new opportunity for soap-opera development. Some programs, like **Guiding Light** (see entry under 1930s—TV and Radio in volume 2), simply moved from radio to television, while others, like *Search for Tomorrow, The Edge of Night,* and *As the World Turns,* were created for the new medium. Although many women had held jobs during World War II (1939–45), they had been expected to return home once the men had returned from war. Many of the housewives of the 1950s felt bored and isolated. They welcomed the distraction of the serial dramas on their new television sets.

From the 1930s through the 1950s, soap-opera plots revolved around the problems and complications of family life. Plots twisted and turned around topics like the difficulty of finding and keeping love, affairs outside of marriage, and the troubles involved in raising children. By the 1960s, a changing society was beginning to demand more from its soaps. In the early 1960s, the popularity of prime-time doctor shows led to the creation of soaps like *The Doctors* (1963) and *General Hospital* (1963). In the late 1960s and early 1970s, soaps began to seek out younger audiences. Youth-oriented story lines and a focus on social issues became important. *All My Children* (1970) and *One Life to Live* (1968) were introduced on ABC as soap operas with content that was socially and politically important. In the 1980s, soaps expanded beyond the limits of daytime television with popular prime-time soaps like **Dallas** (1978–91; see entry under 1980s—TV and Radio in volume 5) and *Dynasty* (1981–89). Prime-time soaps have continued to be popular; indeed, most prime-time dramas have begun to lure audiences back with continuing story lines.

Throughout the 1980s and 1990s, social issues, from alcoholism and drug abuse to gay rights, have continued to be a major part of soap-opera story-line development. In an effort to draw in more viewers, soaps have racially integrated their casts. Most formerly all-white shows now have at least a few regular cast members who are African American, Asian, and Latino. Some have even researched ways they can appeal to a broader audience, such as the *General Hospital* spin-off, *Port Charles* (1997). In 2000, *Port Charles* began to use the *telenovela* format, popular in Latino soaps. In the *telenovela* format, stories are completed within a shorter time period. Many critics still insist, however, that soaps still do not really represent people of color and only confront social issues in a shallow and conservative way.

This shallowness of the soaps, along with their melodrama and reliance on such unlikely plot devices as evil twins, faked deaths, and amnesia, have led to a series of soap spoofs, some of which became almost as popular as the programs they satirized. In the late 1970s, two such series, *Mary Hartman, Mary Hartman* (1976–78) and *Soap* (1977–81), poked fun at the unlikely plot twists and emotionalism of the soaps while exploring some social and relationship issues of their own. The 1991 comedy film, *Soapdish,* focuses on the soap opera–like lives of the cast and crew of a popular soap.

Both the popularity of soaps and the number of soaps on network television have fallen drastically since 1990. Once the mainstay of daytime television, only four daytime soaps remain on the networks in the fall of 2011. Even so, soap operas, in all their many forms from Mexico to England to Australia to the United States, remain the most popular form of television drama in the world.

Tina Gianoulis

For More Information

Anger, Dorothy. *Other Worlds: Society Seen Through Soap Opera.* Peter-borough, Ontario: Broadview Press, 1999.

Birnback, Lisa. "The Daze of Our Lives: Soap Watching Is a Real-Life Drama on Campus." *Rolling Stone* (October 1, 1981): pp. 33–36.

Cottle, Michelle. "Color TV: How Soaps Are Integrating America." *The New Republic* (August 27, 2001): pp. 25–29.

Cox, James H. *The Great Radio Soap Operas.* Jefferson, NC: McFarland, 1999.

Ford, Sam, Abigail De Kosnik, and C. Lee Harrington, eds. *The Survival of Soap Opera: Transformations for a New Media Era.* Jackson: University Press of Mississippi, 2011.

Hinsey, Carolyn. *Afternoon Delight: Why Soaps Still Matter.* Santa Monica, CA: 4th Street Media, 2011.

Museum of Broadcast Communications. "Soap Opera." *Encyclopedia of Television.* http://www.museum.tv/eotvsection.php?entrycode=soapopera (accessed July 7, 2011).

Museum of Television and Radio Staff. *Worlds Without End: The Art and History of the Soap Opera.* New York: Harry N. Abrams, 1997.

The War of the Worlds

British author H. G. Wells (1866–1946), the father of science fiction, published his novel *The War of the Worlds* in 1898. The tale concerns an attack on Earth by a force of Martians—a trite idea today, but a fresh concept at the time. However, the story had its greatest impact as a **radio** (see entry under 1920s—TV and Radio in volume 2) drama. Broadcast in 1938, the program fooled many Americans into believing that the Martians had actually landed.

The show was broadcast on the night of October 31, 1938, as part of the regularly scheduled *Mercury Radio Theatre of the Air*. It is perhaps the greatest example of a Halloween "trick or treat" ever devised. The program was the brainchild of Orson Welles (1915-1985), who later gained fame as a movie actor and director.

The broadcast gained its impact from the way the story was presented. Unlike the novel, which is written in typical narrative style, the radio version was structured like a newscast. Listeners heard a program of music interrupted by the bulletin that a giant meteor had struck Grover's Mills, New Jersey. A reporter on the scene then recounted how the "meteor" was apparently a spacecraft. He next described the opening of the hatch, the appearance of bizarre-looking creatures, and their attack on all humans in the vicinity. The invasion from Mars was on.

The program was broadcast nationwide over CBS radio. The resulting panic was also nationwide, as many Americans took the "invasion" story at face value. Some fled their homes; others barricaded their doors and loaded shotguns; still others suffered emotional breakdowns. The number who actually thought an alien invasion was occurring represented a small part of the audience, and a much smaller portion of the population. But thousands believed.

Orson Welles as he performs during his infamous The War of the Worlds *radio broadcast.* © AP IMAGES.

Afterward, Welles protested that there had been no intent to start a panic. He had announced several times, he said, that the program was fiction. But if the listener missed the disclaimer at the show's beginning, the next announcement did not come until forty minutes later, which was too late for many. The hysteria caused by the 1938 broadcast was an early demonstration of the power of the electronic media.

Justin Gustainis

For More Information

Cantril, Hadley. *The Invasion from Mars: A Study in the Psychology of Panic.* Princeton, NJ: Princeton University Press, 1940.

Gosling, John, and Koch, Howard. *Waging the War of the Worlds: A History of the 1938 Radio Broadcast and Resulting Panic.* Jefferson, NC: McFarland, 2009.

Holmsten, Brian, and Alex Lubertozzi, eds. *The Complete War of the Worlds: Mars' Invasion of Earth from H. G. Wells to Orson Welles.* Naperville, IL: Sourcebooks MediaFusion, 2001.

National Portrait Gallery. "Orson Welles and the 70th Anniversary of War of the Worlds." *Face To Face Blog.* http://face2face.si.edu/my_weblog/2008/10/ orson-welles-and-the-seventieth-anniversary-of-war-of-the-worlds.html (accessed July 7, 2010).

1930s

The Way We Lived

The Great Depression (1929–41) that started with the stock market crash of October 29, 1929, affected almost every part of people's lives during the 1930s. The optimism of the 1920s slowly faded as various efforts to "fix" the economic downturn did not work. More and more people lost their jobs and could not find others. Americans suffered as they never had before. Record numbers of people were unemployed. Nearly one million people paraded through towns across the country in "hunger marches" in 1930. For the elderly who lost their life savings in the stock market crash and for those who had purchased on credit and now did not have jobs to support their payments, the 1930s were a disaster. Thousands of sharecroppers in the South—tenant farmers who bought on credit—were unable to pay their landlords and were thrown off their farms. Millions of children lost the chance for an education as thousands of schools closed because of lack of funds to maintain schools and pay teachers. Charities and local governments could not provide enough aid to help the starving. It took several years for business and government to understand and correct the Great Depression.

President Franklin D. Roosevelt (1882–1945), who was elected in 1932, had a plan to help. He reorganized the federal government to offer aid to suffering Americans. His plan, called the "New Deal," offered temporary work, financial support, home and farm loans, and federal protection of bank savings to millions of Americans. The New Deal created the beginning of the modern welfare state, a state that looked out for the physical wellbeing of its population.

Even though many have described the 1930s as a time when life stood still, the way Americans lived did change. Some of the biggest changes came from the massive construction projects during the decade. At the beginning of the decade, some magnificent structures were built, including the Empire State Building (1931) and Rockefeller Center (1934). These privately funded buildings marked a trend among American civil architects toward massive structures, called skyscrapers. They were impressive architecturally and continue to be symbols of the New York City skyline, but they stood mostly empty during most of the Depression. The New Deal created other impressive construction projects. These federally funded projects, including the Fort Peck Dam (1940) on the Missouri River in Montana and the Hoover Dam (1935) on the Colorado River between Nevada and Arizona, were more successful financially. These large federal projects offered electricity to those in need and created revenues (sources of regular income) to repay federal loans on time.

The Depression did not wipe out all the good times. People did find ways to have fun. The automobile continued to be an important part of American life. For some families, it was the one luxury they would not give up. New drive-in theaters offered people a chance to stay in their cars and enjoy films played on huge outdoor screens. The Apollo Theater opened in 1934 in Harlem, New York, as the first entertainment theater for African Americans. Teenagers across America had to postpone marriage because they could not find jobs, but they dated each other to pass the time. Other social activities included such odd fads as goldfish-swallowing contests.

Apollo Theater

From the 1930s to the present, the Apollo Theater, located on West 125th Street in the New York community of Harlem, has been the premier venue in the United States for African American entertainment. The Apollo is no ordinary performing arts hall. It is a cultural institution: a showplace and a meeting place in which black Americans have gathered to celebrate their culture. Countless African American performers have appeared at the Apollo: **jazz** (see entry under 1900s—Music in volume 1) greats; **rhythm and blues** (see entry under 1940s—Music in volume 3), **rock and roll** (see entry under 1950s—Music in volume 3), and soul performers; tap dancers; comedians; and amateurs breaking in their acts.

The Apollo, constructed in 1913, was originally an Irish music hall. Five years later, it became Hartig & Seamon's Burlesque Theater. By the 1920s and 1930s, population shifts and changing demographics resulted in Harlem becoming the largest African American community in the United States. The theater's initial popularity as a talent showcase parallels the period of cultural development among African Americans known as the Harlem Renaissance. In 1932, Duke Ellington (1899–1974) performed his swing-era anthem "It Don't Mean a Thing If You Ain't Got That Swing" at the Apollo. Two years later, a "colored revue" titled "Jazz à la carte" began. Then, in 1935, Ralph Cooper (1908–1982) began hosting the Apollo's legendary Wednesday amateur nights. Cooper's shows were broadcast on the **radio** (see entry under 1920s—TV and Radio in volume 2), which extended an awareness of the Apollo beyond the boundaries of Harlem. A "who's-who" of then-inexperienced African American entertainers boosted their careers by becoming amateur-night winners. Among them were Ella Fitzgerald (1918–1996), James Brown (1933–2006), Billie Holiday (1915–1959), Sarah Vaughn (1924–1990), and Pearl Bailey (1918–1990). Across the years, just about every important African American entertainer played the Apollo, from Count Basie (1904–1984), Nat "King" Cole (1919–1965), and Bill Cosby (1937–) through Luther Vandross (1951–2005), Anita Baker (1957–), and Stevie Wonder (1950–).

In the 1970s, a combination of rising real-estate prices and decreasing live performances by major musicians spelled doom for the Apollo. A 1975 gunfight in the theater's upper balcony during a Smokey

On December 28, 2006, Harlem's historic Apollo Theater was the sight of a memorial service for singer James Brown.
© ELLEN MCKNIGHT/ALAMY.

Robinson (1940–) concert further added to the venue's woes. The theater closed that year and fell into bankruptcy four years later. In the 1980s, it began operation as a nonprofit venue. In 1983, the Apollo became a National Historic Landmark. The Apollo remains in use today as a showcase for the talents of a new generation of African American entertainers.

Rob Edelman

For More Information

The Apollo Theater. *The Apollo Theater-Harlem, USA.* http://www.apollotheater. org/ (accessed July 7, 2011).

Cooper, Ralph, and Steve Dougherty. *Amateur Night at the Apollo: Ralph Cooper Presents Five Decades of Great Entertainment.* New York: HarperCollins, 1990.

Carlin, Richard, and Kinshasha Conwill, eds. *Ain't Nothing Like the Real Thing: How the Apollo Theater Shaped American Entertainment.* Washington, DC: Smithsonian Books, 2010.

Fox, Ted. *Showtime at the Apollo.* Rev. ed. Rhinebeck, NY: Mill Road Enterprises, 2003.

Schiffman, Jack. *Harlem Heyday: A Pictorial History of Modern Black Show Business and the Apollo Theatre.* Buffalo: Prometheus Books, 1984.

Bonnie and Clyde

Bonnie Parker (1910–1934) and Clyde Barrow (1909–1934) are probably the best-known criminal duo of the 1930s. In their brief career of armed robberies, Parker and Barrow traveled around the Southwest and Midwest, murdering a total of between twelve and fifteen people. Newspaper reports of the time exaggerated their crimes, linking them to holdups they could not have committed.

In 1967, Arthur Penn (1922–2010) directed the hit film *Bonnie and Clyde,* remodeling the pair into folk heroes. The bleak violence of the film made sense to Americans coming to terms with student protests, the war in Vietnam (1954–75), and rising crime rates. Although it portrays Parker and Barrow as victims of their desperate times, the film is realistic about the brutality of their crimes. They were shot to death by Texas Rangers near Arcadia, Louisiana, in May 1934. Their bullet-riddled car is on display at a casino in Primm, Nevada.

Chris Routledge

The sedan in which notorious outlaws Bonnie Parker and Clyde Barrow met their deaths in Louisiana on May 23, 1934.
© M. TIMOTHY O'KEEFE/ALAMY.

For More Information

Federal Bureau of Investigation. "Bonnie & Clyde." *Famous Cases and Criminals.* http://www.fbi.gov/about-us/history/famous-cases/bonnie-and-clyde (accessed July 7, 2011).

Friedman, Lester D. *Bonnie and Clyde.* London: BFI Publishing, 2000.

Geringer, Joseph. "Bonnie & Clyde: Romeo and Juliet in a Getaway Car." *Crime Library.* http://www.trutv.com/library/crime/gangsters_outlaws/outlaws/bonnie/1.html (accessed July 7, 2011).

Guinn, Jeff. *Go Down Together: The True, Untold Story of Bonnie and Clyde.* New York: Simon & Schuster, 2009.

Knight, James. *Bonnie and Clyde: A Twenty-First Century Update.* Austin, TX: Eakin Press, 2003.

Penn, Arthur, director. *Bonnie and Clyde* (film). Warner-Seven Arts, 1967.

Schneider, Paul. *Bonnie and Clyde: The Lives Behind the Legend.* New York: Henry Holt, 2009.

Steele, Philip W., and Marie Barrow Scoma. *The Family Story of Bonnie and Clyde.* Gretna, LA: Pelican, 2000.

Drive-in Theater

During the twentieth century, American popular culture placed heightened emphasis on cars in addition to movies. Particularly, before the 1950s, and the mass marketing of **television** (see entry under 1940s—TV and Radio in volume 3) sets, moviegoing was the primary source of out-of-home entertainment. Meanwhile, the accessibility and affordability of automobiles allowed millions a previously unheard-of freedom of movement. These two cultural phenomena became linked with the advent of the drive-in movie theater—a parking lot containing a large, outdoor movie screen. Moviegoers would drive to a gate, pay an admission fee, park on the lot facing the screen, and view the film directly from the car. Large, centrally located speakers initially projected the soundtrack over the entire theater; eventually, cars were equipped with individual speakers.

While the drive-in's popularity peaked around 1960, a few towns around the United States still boast a big screen where audiences can enjoy a film in the open air. © AP IMAGES/RUSTY KENNEDY.

The 1930s through 1950s were the heyday of the drive-in theater. The first drive-in theater, located in New Jersey on the Camden-Pennsauken border, opened on June 6, 1933. The first movie shown was an obscure comedy called *Wife Beware* (1932). Supposedly, the film was chosen because it would not compete with the first-run films then screening in movie houses. The selection of *Wife Beware* was fitting. Drive-in theaters traditionally booked double or even triple bills of **"B" movies** (see entry under 1930s—Film and Theater in volume 2), usually low-budget **horror movies** (see entry under 1960s—Film and Theater in volume 4) or teen-oriented fare, or films that already had completed their first-run engagements. Realistically, the films often were not the primary reason for attending a drive-in. Particularly among teenagers, drive-ins allowed for a privacy that did not exist at home or at school. Thus, drive-ins came to be known among the young as "passion pits."

During the 1930s, drive-in theaters opened across the country, first in Los Angeles, California; Miami, Florida; Boston, Massachusetts; Cleveland, Ohio; Detroit, Michigan; Cape Cod, Massachusetts; and Galveston, Texas. In 1942, 95 drive-ins could be found in 27 states, with the average offering space for 400 cars. The drive-in peaked in popularity after World War II (1939–45). In 1958, 4,063 drive-ins dotted the country. A night at the drive-in was still a popular activity among adolescents, but many drive-ins were family-oriented, offering a household an inexpensive night out. To attract the family trade, drive-ins sometimes offered playgrounds, baby-bottle warmers, fireworks, and laundry services, not to mention concession stands serving such traditional movie-house fare as popcorn, hot dogs, and sodas.

Beginning in the late 1960s and early 1970s, drive-ins went out of fashion for a variety of reasons. Real estate prices were rising; the development of the multiplex theater (which led to an increase in competition with regard to film rental fees) had begun; and the increasing popularity of compact cars made sitting through a double or triple-feature an uncomfortable prospect. In addition, there was an increased level of freedom for teens, allowing them other ways in which to socialize.

Rob Edelman

For More Information

Sanders, Don. *The American Drive-In Movie Theater.* Osceola, WI: Motorbooks International, 1997.

Segrave, Kerry. *Drive-In Theaters: A History from Their Inception in 1933.* Jefferson, NC: McFarland, 1992.

United Drive-In Theater Owners Association. http://uditoa.org/index.html (accessed July 7, 2011).

Empire State Building

After opening on May 1, 1931, the Empire State Building was for forty years the tallest building in the world. Dubbed the "Empty State Building" during the 1930s because most of the 102 floors remained untenanted, the building was constructed in just twelve months. Over a million visitors viewed Manhattan from the open-air observation deck in its first year and it has been popular with the public ever since.

At 1,250 feet, the Empire State Building is less decorative than its smaller 1930s **skyscraper** (see entry under 1930s—The Way We Lived

After eighty years, the Empire State Building still commands the skyline of midtown Manhattan. © PATRICK BATCHELDER/ALAMY.

in volume 2) rival, the **Chrysler Building** (see entry under 1920s—The Way We Lived in volume 2). But its clean lines and elegant "set-backs" are instantly recognized and admired around the world. In 1933, the film ***King Kong*** (see entry under 1930s—Film and Theater in volume 2) made the building a movie star. It has appeared in many films since, including *An Affair to Remember* (1957) and *Sleepless in Seattle* (1993). Forever linked to the **Great Depression** years (1929–41; see entry under 1930s—The Way We Lived in volume 2), and touched by the glamour of **Hollywood** (see entry under 1930s—Film and Theater in volume 2), the Empire State Building has become a symbol for New York itself.

Chris Routledge

For More Information

Bascomb, Neal. *Higher: A Historic Race to the Sky and the Making of a City.* New York: Doubleday, 2003.

"Empire State Building." *Great Buildings Collection.* http://www.GreatBuildings.com/buildings/Empire_State_Building.html (accessed July 7, 2011).

Goldman, Jonathan. *The Empire State Building Book.* New York: St. Martin's Press, 1980.

Tauranac, John. *The Empire State Building: The Making of a Landmark.* New York: Scribner, 1995.

Goldfish Swallowing

Swallowing live goldfish became a wildly popular fad among college students during the spring of 1939. Although the rage only lasted a few months, swallowing goldfish has become synonymous with foolish and short-lived fads.

The craze began in March 1939, when a Harvard University freshman took a bet that he would not swallow a live goldfish. He gathered a crowd to watch, swallowed the fish, and collected $10 from his classmate. Soon the word spread to other colleges. Other students began to take up the challenge, swallowing more and more goldfish each time to top the last record. By the time students were downing dozens of live, wriggling goldfish to uphold their school's honor, the Massachusetts legislature stepped in and passed a law to "preserve the fish from cruel and wanton consumption." The U.S. Public Health Service began to issue warnings that goldfish could pass tapeworms and disease to swallowers. Within a few months of its initiation, the fad died out.

In March 1939, Harvard University, the oldest education institution in the United States, became the newest institution to create the fad of goldfish swallowing when freshman Lothrop Withington Jr., swallowed a live goldfish to win a $10 bet. With the start of World War II later in the year, the fad died out. © BETTMANN/CORBIS.

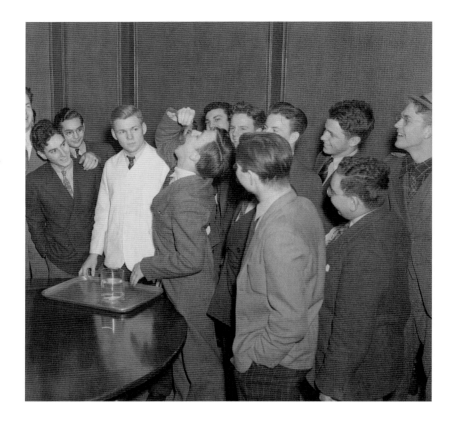

Goldfish swallowing has since been revived from time to time among college students and other young people anxious to prove their daring. One student during the 1970s claimed to have swallowed three hundred of the little fish.

Tina Gianoulis

For More Information

"Goldfish Swallowing." *Bad Fads Museum.* http://www.badfads.com/pages/events/goldfish-swallowing.html (accessed July 7, 2011).

"Swallowing Goldfish." *Olde Time Cooking and Nostalgia.* http://www.oldetimecooking.com/Fads/goldfish.htm (accessed July 7, 2011).

Great Depression

Between 1929 and 1941, America suffered the deepest and longest economic slump of the twentieth century. By 1932, industrial output had

The Dirty Thirties: Eating bread and soup in a breadline was a common sight during the Great Depression.
© BETTMANN/CORBIS.

dropped to the same level it had been at twenty years earlier. Unemployment reached 25 percent. There was widespread homelessness, migration, and even starvation. The causes of the Depression included overproduction, too much private debt, and speculative investments. The glamorous decade of the Roaring Twenties had led to inequalities of many kinds.

Through the need for increased federal aid, the Depression triggered a radical change in the relationship between Americans and their government. After a decade of conservative, isolationist politics, President Franklin D. Roosevelt (1882–1945) introduced New Deal legislation to help get people back to work. It funded building projects, regulated wages, and encouraged cultural programs of a distinctly American flavor. The Depression ended with America's entry into World War II (1939–45). The country rallied to support its troops and soon regained a vigorous economy.

Chris Routledge

For More Information

Agee, James, and Walker Evans. *Let Us Now Praise Famous Men.* Boston: Houghton Mifflin, 1941.

McElvaine, Robert S. *The Great Depression: America, 1929–1941.* New York: Times Books, 1984.

Rauchway, Eric. *The Great Depression & the New Deal: A Very Short Introduction.* New York: Oxford University Press, 2008.

Shlaes, Amity. *The Forgotten Man: A New History of the Great Depression.* New York: HarperCollins, 2007.

Hoover Dam

Proposed in 1910 as a way of fulfilling the dream of a "garden of the West," Hoover Dam was the first of many Colorado River dams proposed to help irrigate the dry land. It remains one of the engineering wonders of the twentieth century. Originally called the Boulder Dam and later rechristened in honor of President Herbert Hoover (1874–1964), an engineer by trade, its four million cubic yards of concrete cost over $165 million to erect. From 1935 onwards, Hoover Dam brought water and electricity to communities in the dry western states.

An engineering feat when finished in 1935, western states have water and electricity because of the Hoover Dam on the Colorado River in Nevada. © RON NIEBRUGGE/ALAMY.

BOWLING, BEATNIKS, AND BELL-BOTTOMS, 2nd edition

Amidst the **Great Depression** (1929–41; see entry under 1930s—The Way We Lived in volume 2), the dam became a symbol of revival. It has appeared in films, in **advertising** (see entry under 1920s—Commerce in volume 2), and on collectibles of all kinds. The elegant curve of Hoover Dam is an enduring image of the American West. Unfortunately, this great monument to progress also helped kill one of the continent's natural wonders. By the 1980s, the Colorado River's many dams and developments had prevented the river itself from reaching the sea.

Chris Routledge

For More Information

U.S. Bureau of Reclamation. *Hoover Dam.* http://www.usbr.gov/lc/hooverdam/ (accessed July 8, 2011).

Dunar, Andrew J., and Dennis McBride. *Building Hoover Dam: An Oral History of the Great Depression.* Reno: University of Nevada Press, 1993.

Hiltzik, Michael A. *Colossus: Hoover Dam and the Making of the American Century.* New York: Free Press, 2010.

Stevens, Joseph E. *Hoover Dam: An American Adventure.* Norman: University of Oklahoma, 1988.

Ranch House

The ranch house style of housing emerged in the 1930s and came to dominate the **suburbs** (see entry under 1950s—The Way We Lived in volume 3) by the 1950s. The style comes from Southwestern house styles, one-story pueblos, and Spanish colonial houses that expressed freedom and space. The ranch house normally stands one story tall, with asymmetrical roof lines, and a garage that faces the street and often dominates the entry of the house.

The ranch house became common in the suburbs; its rambling design made possible by the abundance of space outside cities and the popularity of cars for commuting to work. The ranch house reflected what many Americans seemed to want in their lives: their own plot of land; an open, spacious house with close connections to the outdoors; and lots of leisure amenities: swimming pools, barbecue grills, swing sets for the kids, and perhaps a bit of space for a garden. Ranch houses were most popular between 1935 and 1975, although the style is still built on occasion.

Timothy Berg

For More Information

Hess, Alan, and Noah Sheldon. *The Ranch House.* New York: Harry N. Abrams, 2004.

McAlester, Virginia, and Lee McAlester. *A Field Guide to American Houses.* New York: Knopf, 1984.

Samon, Katherine Ann. *Ranch House Style.* New York: Clarkson Potter, 2003.

Wright, Gwendolyn. *Building the Dream: A Social History of Housing in America.* New York: Pantheon Books, 1981.

Skyscrapers

The high cost of real estate led to multistory buildings being created in American cities beginning in the 1850s. By the 1880s, very tall buildings had become status symbols, not only for the cities in which they appeared but for the cash-rich corporations that built them. In the twenty-first century, almost every American city has at least one skyscraper. When the rest of the world thinks about American cities, it thinks of skyscrapers. The skyscrapers of Manhattan are as recognizable a symbol of New York City as the Eiffel Tower is to Paris, France, or Tower Bridge to London, England. Following America's lead, the skyscraper has become a symbol of influence and economic power in Asia, the Middle East, and Europe.

Two technological developments made skyscrapers possible. The invention of the elevator by Elisha Graves Otis (1811–1861) in the 1850s meant that people could be carried to the upper floors. One of the problems with early skyscrapers was that the extra-long elevator cables stretched, making it impossible to line up the elevator car with every floor. The other development is known as "steel framing." As masonry buildings go higher, the walls need to become thicker at the bottom. William LeBaron Jenney (1832–1907) began to work on steel framing in Chicago in the 1880s. Using this technique, the weight of the building hangs

The Petronas Towers in Kuala Lumpur, Malaysia, was the tallest building in the world from 1998 to 2004. © JOSÉ FUSTE RAGA/CORBIS.

on a steel frame that takes up very little space and allows uniformity in a structure's supportive dimensions.

Many of the most famous buildings in the world are skyscrapers. The **Empire State Building** (see entry under 1930s—The Way We Lived in volume 2), built in 1931, was the tallest in the world for forty years. (In 2011, that title was held by Burj Khalifa in Dubai, United Arab Emirates.) Others, such as the Art Deco **Chrysler Building** (see entry under 1920s—The Way We Lived in volume 2), completed in 1930, are admired as much for their stunning looks as for their dramatic height.

Skyscrapers are used to solve problems of space in overcrowded cities around the world. By concentrating many thousands of people in a very small space, however, they also cause congestion and overcrowding on the streets below. History suggests that the most important role of the skyscraper is a cultural one. Tall buildings are the best way for countries and corporations to display their wealth, power, and technological strength.

Perhaps the most famous skyscraper will always be one that no longer exists. The World Trade Center, which began being built in 1966, was located in the heart of the financial district in New York City until September 11, 2001 (**9/11;** see entry under 2000s—The Way We Lived in volume 6), when a commercial airliner commandeered by terrorists slammed into the north tower; eighteen minutes later, another hijacked airplane crashed into the south tower. Within two hours, each damaged tower fell to the ground. Thousands were killed in the subsequent destruction.

Chris Routledge

For More Information

Ascher, Kate. *The Heights: Anatomy of a Skyscraper.* New York: Penguin Press, 2011.

Dupré, Judith. *Skyscrapers.* 2nd ed. New York: Black Dog and Leventhal, 2008.

Skyscrapers (video). Boston: WGBH and PBS, 2000.

SkyscraperPage.com. http://skyscraperpage.com/ (accessed July 7, 2011).

Willis, Carol. *Form Follows Finance: Skyscrapers and Skylines in New York and Chicago.* New York: Princeton Architectural Press, 1995.

"World Trade Center." *The Great Building Collection.* http://www.GreatBuildings.com/buildings/World_Trade_Center.html (accessed on July 11, 2011).

Twelve-step Programs

Alcoholics Anonymous (AA), with its twelve basic principles for changing behavior, was founded in 1936. Twelve-step programs have since become the most popular addiction treatment method in the United States. With groups to combat everything from gambling to the use of narcotics to overeating, the formula that was developed to help alcoholics fight their addiction has become the model for changing all sorts of behavior. Some critics claim that twelve-step programs themselves become a sort of addiction and that members feel helpless to live their lives without the help of their twelve-step group. Many others, however, insist that their attendance at twelve-step groups has saved their lives and given them back their self-respect.

The twelve-step idea was created by a Vermont man named William Griffith Wilson (1895–1971). Wilson was a successful businessman who lost everything because he could not control his drinking. Inspired by the teachings of a British spiritual movement called the Oxford Group and a long, searching conversation with another alcoholic, Wilson decided that only alcoholics could help other alcoholics quit drinking. In 1936, he formed a group he called Alcoholics Anonymous based on twelve basic principles. The basic ideas underlying the twelve steps are that alcoholics must admit that they are powerless over alcohol and need to look to a higher power, such as God, for help. They must also continually examine their own behavior, admit when they have done wrong, and make amends to those they have hurt.

In 1941, the **Saturday Evening Post** (see entry under 1900s—Print Culture in volume 1) published an article about AA, and thousands of alcoholics were drawn to the organization for help. By 1951, an offshoot organization was formed, Al-Anon, which offered support for families and friends of alcoholics. In the 1970s and 1980s, with the rise of the self-help movement and increasing awareness of addictive behaviors, the number of twelve-step groups increased dramatically. Dozens of groups were formed. Adult Children of Alcoholics (ACOA), Artists Recover Through Twelve Step (ARTS), Sex and Love Addicts Anonymous (SLAA), and Narcotics Anonymous (NA) are only a few of the modern twelve-step groups. Modern twelve-step groups attract more than two million members in 150 countries. Members attend free meetings to talk with others who wish to stop engaging in the same addictive behavior.

They read and discuss Wilson's writings. Dramatic films about addiction and recovery like *The Days of Wine and Roses* (1962) and *28 Days* (2000) have further helped to popularize twelve-step programs.

Tina Gianoulis

For More Information

Alcoholics Anonymous Homepage. http://www.aa.org (accessed July 7, 2011).

Banfield, Susan. *Inside Recovery: How the Twelve Step Program Can Work for You.* New York: Rosen, 1998.

Cheever, Susan. "The Healer: Bill W." *Time* (June 14, 1999): pp. 201–4.

Edmeades, Baz. "Alcoholics Anonymous Celebrates Its 50th Year." *Saturday Evening Post* (July-August 1985): pp. 70–75.

Lemanski, Michael J. "Addiction Alternatives for Recovery." *The Humanist* (January 2000): pp. 14–18.

Minnick, Ann Marie. *Twelve Step Programs: A Contemporary American Quest for Meaning and Spiritual Renewal.* Westport, CT: Praeger, 1997.

"Unforgettable Bill W." *Reader's Digest* (April 1986): pp. 65–72.

Wall Drug

The Wall Drug Store, located in Wall, South Dakota, is probably the most unusual drug store in the world. Since 1936, it has been a popular tourist attraction in the American heartland. Wall Drug is known for many unlikely things, including signs stationed all over the world in places like Moscow, Russia, and Paris, France, proclaiming the distance to Wall Drug in South Dakota. There is even a sign pounded into the ice at the South Pole reading "Wall Drug, Free Ice Water, 9,333 Miles." Why all the fuss about a drug store in the middle of nowhere? Because Wall Drug has become one of the world's biggest "in-jokes."

Wall Drug is certainly the only reason most people ever visit the dusty town of Wall, South Dakota (population 875), lying between the Badlands and the Great Plains. During the summer season, some 20,000 people visit on a typical day, passing through on nearby I-90. They come to experience a place that feels like it invented kitsch (cheap and sometimes tasteless objects and souvenirs), a tourist trap that is so tacky and unhip that it has become paradoxically cool.

On Main Street in Wall, Wall Drug takes up an entire block in the tiny downtown, filling a fifty-thousand-square-foot building. Inside,

Known for offering free ice water to thirsty travelers since the 1930s, Wall Drug is a big store in a small South Dakota town, a destination for filling prescriptions or buying souvenirs. © NATIONAL GEOGRAPHIC IMAGE COLLECTION/ALAMY.

visitors are confronted with a dazzling assortment of souvenirs for sale: rubber tomahawks, cowboy-themed ash trays, refrigerator magnets depicting nearby Mt. Rushmore, hokey postcards that say "Blind Date in Montana," a "jackalope" hunting license. Restaurant-goers can still get a cup of coffee for a nickel and order a buffalo burger. There is an art gallery at Wall Drug, a western-wear shop featuring Stetson cowboy hats and expensive boots, and exhibits on American Indian culture and history. And, yes, prescriptions can be filled at Wall Drug.

Since it opened during the **Great Depression** (1929–41; see entry under 1930s—The Way We Lived in volume 2) with its offer of "free ice water," Wall Drug has grown to be a famous location as well as a place stuck in time. That is why people keep coming back.

Karl Rahder

For More Information

Jennings, Dana Close. *Free Ice Water: The Story of Wall Drug.* Aberdeen, SD: North Plains Press, 1969.

Kaplan, Steve. "The Drug Store That Ate South Dakota." *Travel-Holiday* (June 1989): p. 90.

" Wall Drug Store." *RoadsideAmercia.com.* http://www.roadsideamerica.com/story/2216 (accessed July 7, 2011).

"Wall Drug." *WallDrug.com.* http://www.walldrug.com/t-history.aspx (accessed July 7, 2011).

Where to Learn More

The following list of resources focuses on material appropriate for middle school or high school students. Please note that the Web site addresses were verified prior to publication, but are subject to change.

Books

America A to Z: People, Places, Customs and Culture. Pleasantville, NY: Reader's Digest Association, 1997.

Beetz, Kirk H., ed. *Beacham's Encyclopedia of Popular Fiction.* Osprey, FL: Beacham, 1996.

Berke, Sally. *When TV Began: The First TV Shows.* New York: CPI, 1978.

Blum, Daniel; enlarged by John Willis. *A Pictorial History of the American Theatre, 1860–1985.* 6th ed. New York: Crown, 1986.

Brinkley, Douglas. *The Great Deluge: Hurricane Katrina, New Orleans, and the Mississippi Gulf Coast.* New York: Morrow, 2006.

Brooks, Tim, and Earle Marsh. *The Complete Directory to Prime Time Network and Cable TV Shows, 1946–present.* 9th ed. New York: Ballantine, 2007.

Cashmore, Ellis. *Sports Culture: An A to Z Guide.* New York: Routledge, 2000.

Condon, Judith. *The Nineties (Look at Life In).* Austin, TX: Raintree Steck-Vaughn, 2000.

Craddock, Jim. *VideoHound's Golden Movie Retriever.* Rev. ed. Detroit: Gale, 2011.

Daniel, Clifton, ed. *Chronicle of the Twentieth Century.* Liberty, MO: JL International Pub., 1994.

Dunning, John. *On the Air: The Encyclopedia of Old-Time Radio.* New York: Oxford University Press, 1998.

Dunning, John. *Tune in Yesterday: The Ultimate Encyclopedia of Old-Time Radio 1925–1976.* New York: Oxford University Press, 1998.

Ehrenreich, Barbara. *Nickel and Dimed: On (Not) Getting By in America.* New York: Metropolitan Books, 2001.

Epstein, Dan. *20th Century Pop Culture.* Philadelphia: Chelsea House, 2000.

Finkelstein, Norman H. *Sounds of the Air: The Golden Age of Radio.* New York: Charles Scribner's, 1993.

Flowers, Sarah. *Sports in America.* San Diego: Lucent, 1996.

Friedman, Thomas L. *Hot, Flat, and Crowded: Why We Need a Green Revolution—and How It Can Renew America.* New York: Picador, 2009.

Gilbert, Adrian. *The Eighties (Look at Life In).* Austin, TX: Raintree Steck-Vaughn, 2000.

Godin, Seth. *The Encyclopedia of Fictional People: The Most Important Characters of the 20th Century.* New York: Boulevard Books, 1996.

Gore, Al. *An Inconvenient Truth.* Emmaus, PA: Rodale Press, 2006.

Grant, R. G. *The Seventies (Look at Life In).* Austin, TX: Raintree Steck-Vaughn, 2000.

Grant, R. G. *The Sixties (Look at Life In).* Austin, TX: Raintree Steck-Vaughn, 2000.

Green, Joey. *Joey Green's Encyclopedia of Offbeat Uses for Brand-Name Products.* New York: Hyperion, 1998.

Green, Stanley. *Encyclopedia of the Musical Theatre.* New York: Da Capo Press, 1976.

Hischak, Thomas S. *Film It with Music: An Encyclopedic Guide to the American Movie Musical.* Westport, CT: Greenwood Press, 2001.

Katz, Ephraim. *The Film Encyclopedia.* 6th ed. New York: Collins, 2008.

Kirkpatrick, David. *The Facebook Effect: The Inside Story of the Company That Is Connecting the World.* New York: Simon & Schuster, 2011.

Lackmann, Ron. *The Encyclopedia of American Radio: An A–Z Guide to Radio from Jack Benny to Howard Stern.* New York: Facts on File, 2000.

Lebrecht, Norman. *The Companion to 20th-Century Music.* New York: Simon & Schuster, 1992.

Levitt, Steven D., and Stephen Dubner. *Freakonomics: A Rogue Economist Explores the Hidden Side of Everything.* Rev. ed. New York: Harper, 2009.

Lissauer, Robert. *Lissauer's Encyclopedia of Popular Music in America: 1888 to the Present.* New York: Facts on File, 1996.

Lowe, Denise. *Women and American Television: An Encyclopedia.* ABC-CLIO: Santa Barbara, CA, 1999.

Maltin, Leonard, ed. *Leonard Maltin's Movie Encyclopedia.* New York: Dutton, 1994.

Martin, Frank K. *A Decade of Delusions: From Speculative Contagion to the Great Recession.* Hoboken, NJ: Wiley, 2011.

McNeil, Alex. *Total Television: The Comprehensive Guide to Programming from 1948 to the Present.* 4th ed. New York: Penguin, 1996.

National Commission on Terrorist Attacks. *The 9/11 Commission Report: Final Report of the National Commission on Terrorist Attacks Upon the United States.* New York: Norton, 2004.

Newcomb, Horace, ed. *Encyclopedia of Television.* 2nd ed. Chicago: Fitzroy Dearborn, 2004.

Packer, George. *The Assassins' Gate: America in Iraq.* New York: Farrar, Straus, and Giroux, 2005.

Rosen, Roger, and Patra McSharry Sevastiades, eds. *Coca-Cola Culture: Icons of Pop.* New York: Rosen, 1993.

Schlosser, Eric. *Fast Food Nation.* New York: Houghton Mifflin, 2001.

Schwartz, Herman M. *Subprime Nation: American Power, Global Capital, and the Housing Bubble.* Ithaca, NY: Cornell University Press, 2009.

Schwartz, Richard A. *Cold War Culture: Media and the Arts, 1945–1990.* New York: Facts on File, 1997.

Sennett, Richard. *The Culture of the New Capitalism.* New Haven, CT: Yale University Press, 2007.

Sies, Luther F. *Encyclopedia of American Radio, 1920–1960.* 2nd ed. Jefferson, NC: McFarland, 2008.

Slide, Anthony. *Early American Cinema.* Rev. ed. Metuchen, NJ: Scarecrow Press, 1994.

Tibbetts, John C., and James M. Welsh. *The Encyclopedia of Novels into Film.* 2nd ed. New York: Facts on File, 2005.

Tibbetts, John C., and James M. Welsh. *The Encyclopedia of Stage Plays into Film.* New York: Facts on File, 2001.

Vise, David A. *The Google Story.* Updated ed. New York: Delacorte Press, 2008.

Weisman, Alan. *The World Without Us.* New York: St. Martin's Press, 2007.

Wilson, Charles Reagan, James G. Thomas Jr., and Ann J. Abadie, eds. *The New Encyclopedia of Southern Culture.* Chapel Hill: University of North Carolina Press, 2006.

Woodward, Bob. *Bush at War.* New York: Simon & Schuster, 2002.

Web Sites

Bumpus, Jessica. "The Noughties' Fashion Highlights." *Vogue* (December 22, 2010). http://www.vogue.co.uk/spy/celebrity-photos/2010/12/22/the-noughties (accessed September 23, 2011.)

Markowitz, Robin. *Cultural Studies Central.* http://www.culturalstudies.net/ (accessed August 7, 2011).

"The Noughties: Year by Year." *The Sunday Times,* October 20, 2009. http://women.timesonline.co.uk/tol/life_and_style/women/the_way_we_live/article6881549.ece (accessed September 23, 2011).

"100 Songs That Defined the Noughties." The *Telegraph,* September 18, 2009. http://www.telegraph.co.uk/culture/music/rockandpopfeatures/6198897/100-songs-that-defined-the-Noughties.html (accessed September 23, 2011).

"Pictures of the Decade." *Reuters.* http://www.reuters.com/news/pictures/slideshow?articleId=USRTXRYG2#a=1 (accessed September 23, 2011.)

"A Portrait of the Decade." *BBC News,* December 14, 2009. http://news.bbc.co.uk/2/hi/8409040.stm (accessed September 23, 2011).

Washington State University, American Studies. *Popular Culture: Resources for Critical Analysis.* http://www.wsu.edu/%7Eamerstu/pop/tvrguide.html (accessed August 7, 2011).

Yesterdayland. http://www.yesterdayland.com/ (accessed August 7, 2011).

Zupko, Sarah. *Popcultures.com: Sarah Zupko's Cultural Studies Center.* http://www.popcultures.com/ (accessed August 7, 2011).

Index

Italic type indicates volume number; **boldface** indicates main entries; (ill.) indicates illustrations.

A

A&P Grocery Company, *1:* 56
The A-Team, *5:* **1284–85,** 1285 (ill.)
AA. *See* Alcohol
Aaron, Hank, *1:* 102; *3:* 785
ABBA, *4:* 1073; *6:* 1503
Abbey Road, *4:* 929
Abbott, Bud, *3:* 575, 575 (ill.)
Abbott, Scott, *5:* 1278
Abbott and Costello, *3:* **575,** 575 (ill.)
Abbott and Costello Meet Frankenstein, *2:* 422; *3:* 575
Abbott and Costello Meet the Keystone Kops, *1:* 190
ABC (American Broadcasting Company), *3:* 668; *5:* 1399
   1990s shows, *5:* 1399, 1400
   cable TV, *4:* 1121
   news anchors, *3:* 663
   radio network, *3:* 752
   TV network, *3:* 797; *4:* 962
Abdul, Paula, *6:* 1589 (ill.), 1590
Abdul-Jabbar, Kareem (Lew Alcindor), *4:* 962
Abercrombie & Fitch, *1:* 176; *5:* 1350 (ill.), **1350–51**
Abortion, *4:* 1186–88, 1187 (ill.)
Abrams, J. J., *4:* 1009; *6:* 1606
The Abyss, *4:* 1056
Accessory, mood rings, *4:* 1050–51
Accounting practices, Enron scandal, *6:* 1474–76
Acheson, Lila, *2:* 336

Acid rock, *4:* 924
ACLU (American Civil Liberties Union), *2:* 386
Acoustic guitars, *3:* 754
Acquired Immunodeficiency Syndrome (AIDS). *See* AIDS
"Act Naturally," *3:* 606
Action
   The A-Team, *5:* 1284–85, 1285 (ill.)
   The Dukes of Hazzard, *4:* 1127–28
   Flipper, *4:* 989 (ill.), 989–90
   Ghostbusters, *5:* 1230–32, 1231 (ill.)
   Indiana Jones movies, *5:* 1200, 1232–34, 1233 (ill.)
   Rambo movies, *5:* 1234–36, 1235 (ill.)
Action figure, G.I. Joe, *4:* 877–78, 878 (ill.)
Action TV series
   CSI: Crime Scene Investigation, *6:* 1463, 1467, 1590–91
   The Fugitive, *4:* 990–91
   Lost, *6:* 1606–7, 1607 (ill.)
   Miami Vice, *5:* 1296 (ill.), 1296–97
   24 (TV show), *6:* 1617–18
Activism, environmental. *See* Environmentalism
Activism, social. *See under* Social activism; Social movements
Actors and actresses, *2:* 407–8
   Andrews, Julie, *4:* 913 (ill.), 914
   Baker, Josephine, *2:* 286 (ill.), 286–87
   Ball, Lucille, *3:* 820–22, 821 (ill.)
   Bergman, Ingrid, *3:* 552, 554, 576, 577 (ill.)
   Blair, Linda, *4:* 1057 (ill.), 1058

D

E

Gelatin dessert (Jell-O), *1:* 66–68, 67 (ill.)

Gelb, Lawrence M., *2:* 398

Gelbwaks, Jeremy, *4:* 1150

Geldof, Bob, *5:* 1248

Gemayel, Bashir, *5:* 1265

"Gene, Gene, the Dancing Machine," *4:* 1132

General Foods, *2:* 451

General Lee (car), *4:* 1128

General Mills, *2:* 262–63

General Motors (GM), *1:* 140 (ill.), **140–41,** 158

General reference books, *1:* 212–13

Generation X (X-ers), *5:* **1318–20,** 1336, 1349, 1416

    extreme sports, *5:* 1392

    Friends, 5: 1338, 1415–16, 1416 (ill.)

Genital herpes and warts, *4:* 1191

"Genius Bar," *6:* 1472

Gentlemen Prefer Blondes (Loos), *2:* 251

George, Peter, *4:* 899

The George Burns and Gracie Allen Show, 3: 832

George Olsen and His Music, *2:* 282

Georgia Jazz Band (Ma Rainey's), *1:* 158

"Georgia Peach," *1:* 104

Gerber, Daniel Frank and Dorothy, *2:* 304

Gerber baby food, *2:* **304–5,** 305 (ill.)

Geritol, *3:* 823

German measles epidemic, *4:* 1189

Germanotta, Stefani Joanne Angelina, *6:* 1542

Germany, Volkswagen Beetle, *3:* 718 (ill.), 718–20

Gershwin, George and Ira, *2:* 255, 311; *3:* 610

Gertie the Dinosaur, *1:* 157, **185–87,** 186 (ill.)

"Get a clue!," *4:* 1040

Get Crunk: Who U Wit: Da Album, 6: 1529–30

Get Rich or Die Tryin', 6: 1464

Get Smart, 3: 682, 835

"Get Your Kicks on Route 66," *2:* 385

Getz, Stan, *1:* 74

Ghettos, *4:* **1017–19**

Ghostbusters, 5: **1230–32,** 1231 (ill.)

G.I. Bill, *3:* 556

G.I. Joe, *3:* 553; *4:* **877–78,** 878 (ill.)

G.I. Joe: Rise of Cobra, 4: 878

Giant (film), *3:* 728

Gibb, Andy, *3:* 612

Gibbons, Tom, *2:* 348 (ill.)

Gibson, Althea, *3:* 785–86

Gibson, Charles Dana, *1:* 84, 85 (ill.); *2:* 485

Gibson, Debbie, *3:* 612

Gibson, Dorothy, *1:* 246

Gibson, Henry, *4:* 1001

Gibson, Josh, *1:* 115

Gibson, Mel, *6:* 1507–9

Gibson, Walter Brown, *2:* 494

Gibson Girl, *1:* **84–85,** 85 (ill.)

Gibson Guitar Company, *3:* 755

Gibson Man, *1:* 85

Gifford, Chris, *6:* 1598

Gifford, Frank, *4:* 1108 (ill.), 1109

Gifford, Kathie Lee, *4:* 987, 1136

Gift-giving, on Mother's Day and Father's Day, *1:* 232, 237–38

Giggle water, *2:* 250

Gilbert, A. C., *1:* 217

Gilbert, Melissa, *4:* 1137

Gilbert, Sara, *5:* 1298 (ill.)

Gillespie, Darlene, *3:* 827

Gillespie, Dizzy, *1:* 73

Gillespie, Leonard, *4:* 988

Gilliam, Terry, *4:* 1146, 1146 (ill.), 1147

Gilligan's Island, 3: 833; *4:* 992 (ill.), **992–93**

Gillis, Dobie, *3:* 810 (ill.), **810–11**

Gilpin, Peri, *5:* 1414

Gilroy, Zelda, *3:* 810

Gimble's department store, *2:* 270; *3:* 648

Gingrich, Arnold, *2:* 480

Ginsberg, Allen, *3:* 765, 766, 776

Ginzburg, Ralph, *2:* 481

Girdles, Spanx, *6:* 1490–91

Girl Guides (Britain), *1:* 244

Girl Scouts, *1:* **243–45**

The Girl with the Dragon Tattoo, *6:* **1554–55**

"The Girl without Fear," *1:* 157

Girls. *See also* Children's life and culture; Teenagers; Young women; Youth culture

    Barbie, *3:* 708–10, 709 (ill.)

    Cassidy, David, *4:* 1149 (ill.), 1150

    Sassy, 5: 1263–64

    teen idols, *3:* 693 (ill.), 693–95

"Girls Just Want to Have Fun," *5:* 1200

Gish, Dorothy, *1:* 181; *2:* 251

M

N

U

(W)

X

Y